Y0-ELN-748

O 910.09
McD   H4017

                    H

McDonald
Treasure beneath the sea

the sea.   Cranbury,
          1974, c1972.

(7/21/77 Hotho 12.00)

Great Britain. 2.
    Great Britain
ogy. 3. Great Britain
   I. Title.

Lee County Library
73-3931

4017

Lee County Library System
"BOOKS CAN BE RETURNED TO ANY
LIBRARY IN THE SYSTEM"

CAPTIVA MEMORIAL LIBRARY

Treasure Beneath the Sea

ALSO BY KENDALL McDONALD:

THE WHITE BATON
RED SKY AT NIGHT
SPEARFISHING IN BRITAIN (WITH P. SMITH)
THE WRECK HUNTERS (WITH R. JEFFERIES)
THE UNDERWATER BOOK (Ed.)
HOW TO GET MORE FUN FROM YOUR BOAT
THE SECOND UNDERWATER BOOK (Ed.)
MORE THAN SKIN DEEP
FISH WATCHING AND PHOTOGRAPHY

Treasure Beneath the Sea

KENDALL McDONALD

SOUTH BRUNSWICK AND NEW YORK: A. S. BARNES AND COMPANY

© Kendall McDonald 1972

First American Edition published 1974.

Library of Congress Catalogue Card Number: 73-3931

A. S. Barnes & Co., Inc.
Cranbury, New Jersey 08512

ISBN 0-498-01401-0
Printed in the United States of America

910.09
mc

HL 4017

Preface

In the misty grey, brown, green, or sometimes even blue, of the seas around Britain, divers are at work on ancient wrecks. Their work is little known, and even more rarely applauded.

This book is for them—and for all who like to read of daring and adventure. For the divers in this book have fought the unsettled waters, the usually poor visibility and the strong tides of the seas around us. Not for them the easier, clearer, calmer, warmer waters of the Mediterranean, where many people still mistakenly believe the only serious underwater archaeological work can be done.

This book is their answer. It is also a plea to those who give much time and money to the cause of research to pause before they unload their bounty on some expedition bound for sunnier lands—and consider the rewards of similar interest in the history of our own islands.

That fact that the men named here have achieved so much for so little makes their triumphs even greater. I am delighted to have dived with them—and, even more, to call them my friends.

1972   KENDALL MCDONALD

5

Lee County Library System

"BOOKS CAN BE RETURNED TO ANY LIBRARY IN THE SYSTEM"

Contents

Introduction

NO-ONE has ever been completely safe on any stretch of water, and today's scientific safety devices can no more guarantee that accidents will not happen, than could primitive man in his dugout canoe be entirely sure of arriving safely at journey's end.

Sinkings, large and small, have taken place since man first ventured on the water. In fact, there is little that has to do with the history of Britain which is not connected with the seas around our coasts, or the rivers which feed them.

Man has used the sea as source of food from time immemorial. He has also used it as a highway for travel. As a result the seas and rivers of the world are one great museum—into them has sunk every kind of container which man has used to carry himself and his belongings on the water.

No-one could describe the seas around Britain as anything but inhospitable. More ships have sunk around the coasts of this country than around the shores of any other country in the world. Many of these wreckings have been recorded; many more have not.

Fragments of the earliest writings give us some idea of what toll must have been taken of earlier less seaworthy ships. Britain has always been a centre for trade. But a great number of the ships that we have sent out—and the ships that have come to us—have ended their days, not in some friendly port, but broken on the bottom of the sea, the victims of war, piracy, treachery, bad seamanship, bad construction or, more simply, bad weather.

In this book I have used the term 'skin-diving' to cover the art of diving with the compressed-air Aqualung, simply because it is the description of modern diving that the general public have adopted. It is an odd thought that 'skin-divers' rarely dive in just their skin, but, almost without exception, wear a close-fitting neoprene suit to protect them from the cold of the depths. Yet who can argue that the word 'skin-diver' is not a much more exciting description of the game than the more accurate 'Aqualung diver'?

Be that as it may, it would be very wrong not to mention here the way that the British Sub-Aqua Club has helped and encouraged the work of the wreck detectives, in addition to its major role in guiding the activities of all Britain's amateur divers.

From the 60,000 trained divers that the Club has produced since its formation in 1953—and from the ranks of the thousands undergoing training in branches of the Club all over Britain—have come, and are coming, skilled underwater photographers, skilled underwater geologists, skilled underwater marine biologists, together with those whose skill is only in the safe use of the Aqualung and a desire to explore a world that most people never see. From the ranks of all those divers have come too the men who seek, find and record our sunken history—the Wreck Detectives.

It is important here to stress that you cannot become a wreck detective overnight. To join their ranks you need to become first of all a trained diver. And that means joining the British Sub-Aqua Club and undergoing a proper course of instruction in the use of compressed-air breathing apparatus. So if you feel that you would like to explore the sunken wrecks around Britain, you should write to the Director of the Club at 160 Great Portland Street, London W1N 5TB for details of the nearest branch to your home.

This book, then, is about wreck detectives and the discoveries they have made around the coasts of Britain. They all possess one basic skill in common. The use of the Aqualung—made up of a demand valve to supply air at the correct pressure for depth and one or two bottles of compressed air—is second nature to them. In fact it is probably true that the only time they notice they are using it is when something goes wrong!

This means that the use of this equipment—it puts the searching ability of the modern skin-diver as far in advance of the 'hard-hat' or helmet diver as the helicopter is of the balloon—enables them to concentrate all their other underwater skills on the sunken ship before them.

But even such skilled men and women needed guidance when they found their wrecks. And as the sport of skin-diving grew and grew—in Britain at the moment it is undergoing what can only be described as a growth explosion—so that guidance emerged with the formation of the Committee for Nautical Archaeology in 1964.

The aim of the Committee was simple—to develop and to guide underwater archaeology. To their aid came the British Sub-Aqua Club, the Institute of Archaeology, the National Maritime Museum, the British Museum, the Science Museum, the Society for Nautical Research, the Council for British Archaeology, and the Services.

Together they hoped that the wealth of knowledge left on the sea-bed in the sunken ships could be brought to the surface and documented—for no book or shipwright's plan now known can replace the underwater history books that lie untouched around the coasts of Britain.

They have had their triumphs and their disasters. But their influence on British diving has been immense. In the chapters of this book you will see that influence time and time again. . . .

CHAPTER 1

The Case of the Wreck Full of Pins

including the discovery of the Seaford amphora,
the stone anchors of Lulworth, Dartmouth and
Ilfracombe, the Roman wreck on Pudding Pans,
the Selsey catapults, and the lost land of Pende.

THE small boat nosed into the place they call the Green Pool and the engine puttered into silence. The first splash was the anchor going over, the second and third the entry of two black-suited Aqualung divers.

For a long, long while the calm surface was broken only by the mushrooms of expired air from the divers down below. Above the spot towered the Angrouse Cliffs, a one-mile-long stretch of sheer rocks on the western coast of the Lizard peninsula, in Cornwall. These cliffs have become well known over the centuries for the number of sailing-ships that have crashed to silence on them. But that roll of unhappiness is not their only claim to fame—it was from the heights of Angrouse that Marconi transmitted his first trans-atlantic radio message in December, 1901.

But this was May 1969 and the divers surfaced and dived again until they had spent nearly two hours under water in that particular spot under the cliffs. Finally, they got back into the boat, and what happened then is best told in the words of one of those divers, Richard Larn:

Whether it was the cold or suppressed excitement that made my numbed hands shake, I cannot truthfully say. After two hours underwater that evening in May, a deep marrow-chilling cold had set in and an awful involuntary shuddering began.

Once back aboard the boat I hardly had the strength to shed my gear, let alone ease the wrist of my suit open to extract the silver disc I had put there for safe keeping. Apart from ten minutes spent taking a number of under-water photographs of some extraordinary cannon, that one coin—for I felt sure that is what it was—had occupied almost my complete attention for both dives. I remember thinking that my left wrist, already encumbered by a watch and steel bracelet, was an uncomfortable, if not damned stupid, place to stick coins. But it was a trick I had learnt while diving in the Scillies on the wreck of Sir Cloudesley Shovell's *Association* [see Chapter 6]—a trick which eventually leads to a painful, but satisfying, patch of raw flesh, which divers nicknamed 'Gilstone wrist' after the rocks on which the *Association* sank.

Peter McBride watched closely as my shaking fingers rubbed at the surface of the disc. Obscure shapes changed to letters, then letters to words, and our excitement mounted, but still neither of us spoke. Finally the inscription was clearly legible: 'Ferdinand IV. Xyng et. Boh. Rex. Coron. in. Regem. Romanorvm. XYIII.IV.NY. MDCLIII', which roughly translated reads: 'Ferdinand IV, crowned King of Bohemia and the Romans, 1653'. Only then was the silence broken. I couldn't help but state the obvious, 'Christ, that's old'. It certainly was old, three hundred and sixteen years old to be exact, and, assuming that the date of this coronation medallion bore some relation to the date the vessel sank, then apart from the Armada wrecks, this could be one of the oldest authenticated wreck sites in the country.

That particular day, 2nd May 1969, started off pretty much as any other; little was I to know that by nightfall I would be deeply involved in a wreck project that was to last two years. A phone call from Peter McBride about mid-morning started it all off—for me at least—a casual invitation to call in his office and discuss 'something' of interest. At that time we were both serving in the Royal Navy, at the air station at Culdrose, in Cornwall, and therefore working in close proximity.

Peter didn't say much, just sketched a rather odd-shaped object and asked what I made of it? After some thought, and turning the sketch upside down a couple of times, I decided that it could only be an iron cannon, but the like of which I had never seen before. Only then did I learn that this object, and possibly others, existed on the sea-bed near Mullion, having been located by Peter the previous evening whilst snorkelling. There and then we agreed that a joint dive on the site was necessary, to clear up the mystery.

Whilst it might sound blasé, cannon sites in Cornwall are literally ten-a-penny, and having jointly found three new sites on the Lizard and one at Kynance Cove in as many months, neither of us were exactly ecstatic as we left the shelter of Mullion harbour and headed north-west. A watery sun was already low, throwing Angrouse cliffs into deep shadow, so that as we nosed into a small rock gully known as Polyglas, the 'Green Pool', the sheer forbidding rock face made the sea appear inky black. Without delay I dressed—a quick check on camera settings, watch-winder screwed hard down, bezel set, open and close the right hand valve of my inverted Aqualung to equalize pressure in the bottles—and over the side.

Although exceptionally cold, the water was crystal clear and perfect for photography, although a little dark to rely on natural light. After one quick swim around the site, I methodically photographed all twenty-three cannon which were visible.

It was not until our next visit, two days later, that we realized how fortunate we had been. Only then did we learn that a sewer outfall discharged directly over the site. By some freak combination of wind, sea, tide and the 'inactivity' of the inhabitants of Mullion, we had chosen the one day when conditions were perfect. Over the next two years, by which time we had an accumulative total of more than 400 dives on the site, we never once encountered such visibility again—or got such clear photographs.

The cannon were odd in that the majority had been worn down by the scouring action of shingle, so that only half of the barrels remained. The bore of each gun appeared as an open trough, in the breech end of which sat a cannon-ball, apparently made of brass, which oddly enough appeared to have suffered no erosion whatsoever. These were of course iron, but had every outward appearance of being non-ferrous; a phenomenon still not explained, but due, no doubt, to some form of electrolysis, or the concentrated effluent present.

Another interesting feature of the cannon was the bed of solid 'concretion', ten or twelve inches thick, on which each gun was perched, and from which brass and copper artifacts protruded in abundance. In general, the sea-bed was shingle. It was obvious that this was very deep in places, and constantly on the move. As far as I could tell from that first brief period on the site, it appeared that the vessel had hit the cliffs beam-on, had sunk intact into this one steep-sided gully, and that a great deal of material probably lay covered by the shingle.

I selected an area of the wreck at random, choosing the seaward end of the site—not only because this was most likely to be the stern section, but because there was less surge there, and started to uncover the sea-bed. It took all of half an hour to uncover completely a reasonable area, during which time I recalled that someone once recorded in an archaeological report I had read, 'fine shingle and sand will not remain underwater on a gradient greater than 17° to the horizontal'—the reader has my assurance that this is a profound and correct observation.

It was almost as if fate had meant that silver medallion to be found, for there, in the centre of the small area uncovered, chosen quite at random, on edge and almost buried in concretion, was the thin silvery outline of my 'coin'. Only one quarter of an inch of its blackened face showed, but the edge shone like new, and instinctively I knew what it was, and its importance in establishing the identity of this wreck.

Perhaps the purists will condemn me for moving it, but I knew that we might never locate that one small area again. That item represented some immediate evidence of age, possibly nationality, and it must be recovered at all costs.

The rock-hard substance known as 'concretion', the chemistry or formation of which is still not understood, is a feature of all wrecks, and the older the vessel, the greater its concentration and hardness. It will commence to form on wreckage within months of its submergence, and then progressively thicken, until it presents the under-water archaeologist with a formidable barrier. There is one bonus, however, in that the substance excludes oxygen from whatever it is covering, and hence will preserve artifacts that would otherwise corrode and waste away to nothing.

It took almost two hours hard chipping before I lifted out the lump of sea-bed that had held my 'coin' and brought it to the surface—along with a great handful of the second peculiar feature of this wreck, brass pins.

The leading question now was, what should we do for the best? So many possibilities existed, and it was important that we choose the correct one. Competition in the south-west can be fierce.

To advertise openly the site or its location would at once bring down every local diver for miles, and half the diving population of the country soon afterwards. If we kept the wreck to ourselves, the chance of intruders was greatly reduced, but we had no hopes of keeping it secret for long, since our continued presence in one spot on the coast would attract local attention. We took the best possible action that night, by going home and sleeping on it, and in the cold, hard light of day agreed that we would form a working group of three divers, all of whom must be capable of making a positive contribution.

For want of a better name we called ourselves, 'The Ferdinand Research Group', taking the name from the medallion, and the wreck automatically became known as 'Ferdi'. As a group we agreed that all costs would be shared, and that we would apply for a Crown Estate Commission lease of the relevant piece of sea-bed, in the meantime leaving the wreck completely alone. The project offered a considerable challenge, since we knew nothing about the wreck, and it was doubtful if anyone else did—so we embarked on what I now consider to have been a worth-while and fascinating piece of detective work.

Our initial application for a lease was refused, basically on the grounds that we did not have the support of the Committee for Nautical Archaeology. We therefore made our case to the committee, received their support and approval, and within two months were the proud holders of a parchment which stated—'This lease made between The Queen's Most Excellent Majesty of the first part, The Crown Estate Commissioners of the second part,' and ourselves as third, 'witnesseth that in this lease the word landlord means the Queen's Majesty and Her Successors—hereby demise unto the tenants all that piece of land covered by water, being part of the bed of the sea near Polurrian Cove, Mullion, in the County of Cornwall, which said piece of land is hereafter called the demised premises' . . . . A nominal fee of £5 per annum was charged for the lease, in return for which we had a measure of legal protection; strong enough to frighten off the majority of divers, although this or any similar lease has yet to be upheld in a court of law.

In addition we had the advantage that Peter McBride

lived in a bungalow overlooking the site, whilst his charming wife Bridget worked in the Polurrian Hotel, even closer. The third member co-opted into the team was Roy Davis of Bodmin, a highly qualified electrical engineer, and one of the most dedicated and practical divers one could wish to know. Between the three of us we had a considerable cross-section of skills, and now felt confident to undertake a full archaeological survey and excavation.

We commenced serious work at the height of the summer, having already formulated our plans, obtained the largest ordnance survey maps possible of the area, and started in on the research to identify the wreck. As July changed into August, so the volume of holiday traffic increased, and with it the volume of discharge from the sewer! We even seriously considered blocking off the pipe the day before each dive, but had visions of overflowing bathrooms and irate health inspectors with no soul for archaeology—and decided against it. Eventually, conditions became too bad even for our seasoned stomachs, as well as a serious health hazard, so we were forced to abandon the survey, just when we should have been under-water every minute we could spare. Fortunately, we were able to complete our triangulation survey both above and below water, measured every cannon in great detail, and uncovered enough artifacts to keep us busy for the remainder of the year.

The variety and quantity of the items found under the shingle was quite remarkable, considering the age of the wreck. For example, Peter located a bronze breech-block from a cannon, two huge ingots of lead, each weighing some 300 lb, copper cakes and hundreds of pins. These were followed by Roy's uncovering of several brass candlesticks, iron knife and carpenter's chisel and gouge blades, a variety of shot and musket balls. Other items included musket and pistol barrels, all bearing the indentation of a proof mark, but too far gone to identify. These did, however, serve to confirm the vintage of the wreck, since the sling breech tang and style of breech plug were consistent with the mid-seventeenth century.

At the first opportunity, we were back on the site again, measuring, shifting shingle, using our air-lift,[1] and carefully plotting everything that might have a significance. A trial excavation was made in the vicinity of the medallion 'hole', but all this took a great deal of time, and coupled with other diving activities on the Lizard and the north coast of Cornwall, it was winter before we were aware of it, and the gales set in.

Now was the time to really concentrate on research, and

[1] An air-lift is a device for moving mud, sand or shingle away from a wreck site. In its simplest form all that is needed is a cylinder of compressed air and a length of tube. The air is fed into the open end of the tube and will suck up sand and small stones as it rushes up the pipe. More sophisticated versions have air from a compressor on the surface fed into the lower end of the pipe through an aperture in the side. Large bore pipe and a powerful compressor make such a suction that vases and pottery will be smashed and whisked into the pipe in seconds!

we methodically covered every possible source of information, not only in Cornwall, but the whole country and several places in France and Germany. We covered manor rolls, court rolls, fine rolls, port books, letters in the Duchy of Cornwall office, papers in the Public Records Office relating to Admiralty rights of wreck, correspondence relating to Lord Admirals of Devon and Cornwall, patents concerning the manufacture of pins and a hundred and one other things. None of this brought us a single step nearer finding out what the ship was or when it sank, but slowly a picture of what we had found emerged. We had located the wreck of a large, armed merchantman, one that had carried at least 26 guns, of which 23 were 9 ft long, 22 pounders.

The bronze breech-block confirmed that at one time the vessel was armed with bronze cannon. It was possible she only carried them as cargo, but the former is more probable. Much later we found a reference in some local papers relating to the manor of Predannack, in which 'William John the younger of Penzance in 1744 paid the Lord of the manor for the privelage of carrying timber, anchors, guns and other things of great value from and through the tenement called Methes, alias Merres, at Mullion'. This may or may not be connected with 'our' wreck, but confirmed our suspicion that the locals had worked the wreck at the time of sinking.

Vast quantities of shot were uncovered, most of which had retained its original weight, so that we could identify each size with ease. There was far too much for a normal ship's armament, so we must assume that some of it was cargo, as were the lead ingots, copper cakes, iron nails and brass pins. The nails were in perfect condition, falling neatly into thirteen distinct sizes, the largest being a massive 24 cm long, down to 4 cm. Since the preservation of vintage iron which has been under water is difficult to say the least, we experimented with various techniques, finally 'potting' a full set of nails in epoxy resin, where they are preserved for all time.

We then got around to the pins, and these too fell into neat categories of four distinct sizes. Their number suggested that many thousands of them were packed into kegs or barrels, and that perhaps hundreds of these barrels were carried on board. There is a wealth of history and interest in the domestic pin [see Appendix 1 and 2], but I must confess that it had passed me by until now. We encountered them in every corner of the site; they penetrated our gloved fingers as we cleared away shingle, they pricked our fingers as we picked them up—but gradually a sort of affection developed towards them. After an hour or more of sheer manual labour under water, humping rocks, shifting shingle or holding the end of a tape—you could always have a change of scenery by picking up a couple of hundred pins! If nothing else, it broke the monotony, and as a result, we amassed literally thousands of them—and learnt a great deal concerning their manufacture and importance.

By the Spring of 1970 we had collected a great mass of information, but it was now quite obvious that unless we had a major break-through in our work, we would never identify this wreck. For the period in question there just is no recorded information available, and with vessels being wrecked in Mounts Bay at regular intervals, no one bothered to make any special mention of this or any other particular loss.

Over the Easter holiday we grubbed in the sea-bed, took more measurements, found more and more interesting arti-facts, mostly brass this time—and a number of the most obscure items imaginable (see Fig. 1). These consisted of two small spheres of lead, not unlike musket shot in size and weight, yet joined together by a piece of very heavy brass wire, some five inches long, wound into a tight coil. They had the appearance of shot, or something meant to be fired from a musket, but the best authorities in the country have never seen their like. We then made two finds which we felt sure would assist in the wreck's identification, but again we were to be disappointed. The first was a beautiful brass miniature saint with clasped hands, perfect in every detail, standing only two and a half inches tall; whilst the second was an intact pewter plate.

rewarded by the sight of a perfect miniature crest on the rim. It depicted a Tudor rose, surmounted by a crown, within which were the initials HB. Strangely, the maker's mark on the under-side of the plate, an angel with outstretched wings, also included the letters HB, and we felt sure that here was the vital clue we so badly needed.

There are probably as many pewterers' marks recorded as there are hall marks of silversmiths, if not more, yet amongst the thousands we consulted, none of them were identical with ours. The explanation for this is either that it was an English pewterer whose mark was lost when the Great Fire of London destroyed the 'touch plate', or, it is a Continental pewterer whose mark has been lost as a result of war or sheer age. The nearest we have come to this crest to date is that of Henri Berckenn, who worked between 1671 and 1700, or Henri Bourvelier of 1653, since the angel motif appears to have been connected with Montbéliard. If either of these gentle-men was the maker of this plate, then the vessel was probably

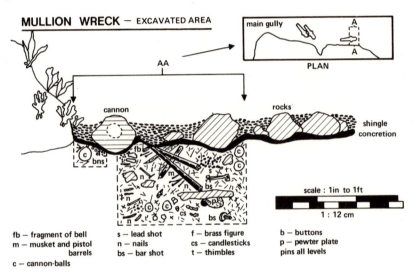

FIG. 1. A cross-section of part of the Mullion Pin Wreck
Based on a drawing by Richard Larn

The plate was found beneath a large rock, buried deep in the only hole we had fully excavated until then. It was completely black with age, and folded in half, and the pros-pects of bending it out flat without causing it to crack were remote. There was a faint mark on the under-side of the plate, but nothing visible on the upper surface—at least, not on the part we could inspect.

I retained the plate in that condition for over a week, wanting to open it out, but afraid of the damage I might cause. Several silversmiths and antique-dealers were con-sulted, but none of them were prepared to attempt the task. In desperation, I read up the details of pewter and decided that if this was as old as we suspected, then it was good-quality stuff, and would withstand some rough treatment. It took two days of gentle heating and bending, a fraction at a time, until I got it opened out, and then beaten flat so that the crease hardly showed. Not a crack appeared, and I was

French or Flemish—but we think we shall never know for certain.

A number of small brass buttons were found too, all bearing the same Tudor rose as the crest, whilst the bowls of clay pipes marked EB were the work of one Edward Battle of Bristol, 1660, which suggests that the ship called either at Bristol to load, or at least in one of the west country ports—perhaps Penzance or Fowey.

It is quite remarkable that we had so many seemingly useful clues, yet were quite unable to establish the name, date or nationality of this vessel. So far after two years' continued work on the site, we had at first two possibilities regarding her identity. Both came from the 'Bibloteca Cornubiensis' by Boase and Courtney which mentions, 'Penrose, John of Manaccan. Papers relating to the loss of the French ship *San Salvador* near the Lizard, and John Penrose's right to a fifteenth part of the wreck. 1669'; also, 'the loss of a Genoese ship of 800 tons. 48 guns, with a reputed value of £100,000 lost on the Lizard in 1667'. Letters in the Calendar of State Papers refer to this same vessel as a 'Dane', a 'Hamburger' and a 'Dutch ship of 500 tons, laden with masts, deals and provisions for the French Kings fleet'.

But Dick Larn and his fellow-detectives are now almost sure that the Mullion wreck is the *Santa Christo de Castello*, wrecked on or about 5th October 1667, with her cargo valued at £100,000. Almost sure—for a process of elimination, after searches in the Duchy of Cornwall's records, and examination of the Domestic and State papers at the Public Record Office in London, leaves only this ship as a proper candidate for the long-lost wreck.

That is how Richard Larn reported on his sensible and responsible approach to the excavation and identification of the wreck of a mid-seventeenth century merchantman. An old ship, but not the oldest shipwreck of which British divers have found traces.

For many years after the amateur divers of Britain started exploring the sea-bed around our coasts it was realized that sooner or later they would find traces of the early civilizations which had come to conquer us or to trade with us, but no-one was really optimistic about the form those discoveries would take. It was felt likely that what traces there were would be likely to be smashed beyond all hope of reconstruction—just chips of pottery protected from final destruction in some sheltered gully on the sea-bed.

The truth proved to be different beyond a marine archaeologist's wildest dreams.

We knew that the history of the British Isles was one with the history of shipping. Ships, probably flat-bottomed, with skin sails were travelling from Southern Spain to the West of England, Scotland and even Sweden, at the end of the British Neolithic period nearly four-thousand years ago (around 2000 B.C.). We know they were seafarers, for their elaborate tombs are on the western sea-routes. Other tomb-builders sailed the seas too, but they came from the Pyrenees and Southern France to settle in south-west Scotland, Ulster and the Isle of Man.

And those ancient ships did not pass without trace. In the Gwavas Lake area, off Newlyn, in Mounts Bay, the divers of the Penzance Branch of the British Sub-Aqua Club found pieces of a fifteenth-century pottery vase, but in the same area they soon discovered artifacts of an even earlier date. Three querns (millstones) were found by Dennis James, Alan Griffiths, chairman of the Penzance branch, and Ray Dennis during separate dives. Two of these, say the archaeologists, are certainly Roman or early Iron Age. The other is of a later date.

Then Ray Dennis found a seven-inch-long stone with a hole drilled in it. This looks remarkably like part of an early stone-and-wood anchor.

Altogether the sea-bed in the area sounds remarkably like an archaeological treasure-house. On later dives the Penzance men have seen cannon-balls, iron cannon, copper sheathing, and a great number of ancient anchors. It is an area that will undergo serious archaeological inspection during the coming years.

A fine example of a stone anchor recovered by divers is already on display at the National Maritime Museum, Green-

wich. It weighs about a hundredweight and a half, and it came from the sea-bed just outside Lulworth Cove, Dorset.

The discovery of the anchor followed the recovery by Albert Greenland, of Bromley Branch of the British Sub-Aqua Club, of a pottery 'cone' in the same area. When this 'cone' was shown to Joan du Plat Taylor, of the Committee for Nautical Archaeology, it was identified as the base of an unguent bottle from the Roman occupation period. Greenland was asked if he would dive again in the area to see if his find was an isolated one. Was the bottle flung overboard from some passing ship because the neck was broken—or was there an ancient wreck in the area? Certainly the bottle was Mediterranean-made, but experts said that they had never seen one like it in this country —the nearest place that such a type of bottle had been found was near Cologne, Germany.

Greenland dived again, and was just as surprised as anyone else when he found a large stone, buried under small rocks and shale, but with enough of it standing clear for him to see that a hole was bored right through it. He says that he recognized it at once as a stone anchor, as he had recently seen photographs of some found in the Mediterranean.

After a great deal of under-water effort Albert Greenland, together with two other Bromley Branch divers, John Humphreys and Mike Greenhough, raised the anchor with the help of a forty-gallon oil drum, which they filled with compressed air from their Aqualungs.

More stone anchors in various parts of the country were to follow that one to the surface. From Ilfracombe, from Dartmouth and from Seaford.

These are on display at Fort Bovisand, the home of the School for Nautical Archaeology at Plymouth. If you wish to see these relics of our long-forgotten seafaring past, you will be made most welcome if you call at the Fort.

The importance of these anchors is great. From the anchors the size of the ship that carried them can be deduced. Diving-archaeologist Honor Frost says that the size of most Mediterranean Bronze Age anchors would sink the modern fishing-boat from the same area. Half a ton is not uncommon, and from this one can estimate that the Bronze Age ships that carried them were about sixty feet long, and were in the region of two-hundred tons.

So, suddenly, the belief that we were going to have to look exclusively to the warm, clear waters of the Mediterranean for evidence of early shipping—which we would then have to apply to our own history—was challenged. Of course, we still know little about the ships that plied around our coasts in the really early days. But, thanks to divers, we are learning fast.

Probably the first form of water transport was the dugout. Then Britain's first inshore fishing-boat possibly appeared, in about 1500–1200 B.C. This is what some archaeologists have called the North Ferriby boat, but they do not want to be taken too seriously. The boat is named after the place it was discovered, and, in fact, only a section was unearthed.

The Ferriby boat appears to have been designed for estuary work on the Tyne. It was carvel-built with the planks lashed together with withies.

Then comes a big gap in our knowledge and a jump in time

A clue to a very ancient wreck?
John White with the neck of the amphora,
which he found under the sea at Seaford

to A.D. 1190–1430. This is the period given by radio-carbon tests to an oak-pinned frame, which had in turn been wooden-pegged on to a dugout canoe shell. It was found at Kentmere, near Kendal in the Lake District, and was clinker-built. In October 1970 Mr Roy Botting, of Gillingham, an excavator-operator employed by the Kent River Authority to widen and deepen ancient channels in the Graveney Marshes, a remote spot on Kent's north-east coast, sank his excavator bucket into the side walls of Hammond's Drain. As the bucket came up he saw a piece of ancient timber sticking out. He stopped work immediately and reported his find.

Mr Botting had certainly done the right thing. Experts from Canterbury Royal Museum probed around and found that they were exploring a forty-foot-long ship buried under eight feet of silt. The boat, designed for rowing, has been dated as late ninth century A.D. Miss Louise Millard, curator of Canterbury Royal Museum, found pottery and tile fragments in the bottom of the boat, as well as the original mooring hawser of plaited osiers. At first sight the ship looked like a merchant coastal vessel, but the detective work is still going on at the time of writing. Each timber, as it is taken from the marsh, was wrapped in plastic to prevent it crumbling completely on exposure to the air, and was then taken to the National Maritime Museum to be reimmersed in water in a special tank.

Similar preservation treatment was carried out at the Guild-hall Museum on timbers that were found in September 1962 during excavations for the Blackfriars Bridge Underpass. The timbers turned out to be part of a river or estuary barge of Roman times and careful archaeological survey by Mr Peter R. V. Marsden found out some fascinating things about her.

In a layer of fine grey clay on the bottom of the boat they found a piece of leather, decorated with a dolphin (a typical Roman design), broken barrel staves and a wooden mallet. On top of the clay, and still on the inside of the barge, was a thick layer of coarse river gravel, which was deposited after the boat sank. In this gravel they found fragments of about sixty different Roman pots, several dozen Roman shoe-soles, the 'bungs' from Roman amphorae (wine jars), broken Roman bricks and tiles and a millstone. The pottery showed that the barge had been in use in the second century A.D.

Mr Marsden, one of this country's leading archaeologists, found too that part of the starboard side of the barge had collapsed inward—sealing in the dating evidence. This collapsed timber had also covered a rectangular socket, cut in a floor timber, which, thought this wreck detective, had been the stepping-place of the mast.

This collapse over the mast-step was of vital importance and interest. For it had protected something lying in the bottom of the mast-step—a worn Roman bronze coin of the Emperor Domitian, minted in A.D. 88 or 89.

Writing of his excavation, Mr Marsden stressed why the discovery of this ship—she was about fifty-five feet long and with a beam of some twenty-two feet—was so important:

The shape and construction of the ship are like no other ship of the Roman period which has so far been found. The

reason for this seems to be that the vessel is of native British construction. The species of oak from which all the timbers had been cut, is native to Central and Northern Europe and is not found in the Mediterranean.

The coin found in the mast-step was not the least remarkable feature of the ship, and it is interesting to note that, nowadays, it is a custom to place a coin in the construction of a wooden ship, to bring luck to the vessel, and those who sail in her. It is surely more than a coincidence that the coin lay reverse uppermost, showing the figure of Fortuna, the Roman goddess of luck, holding a ship's steering oar. It seems that the coin was chosen specially because of its appropriate reverse type.

Later Peter Marsden was able to return to the subject again after more research:

The origin of the custom is not known, but the apparent luck motive would suggest a pagan origin.

It is possible that in ancient times a sacrifice was made to the gods to bring good fortune to a new ship, but when coinage became common, a money payment was substituted.

It is interesting to note here that many fishing-boats in the Mediterranean have a splash of red paintwork at the bows. This, it is said, is a modern 'hangover' from the ancient custom of sacrificing some animal and splashing the blood on the bow of the boat to ensure a good voyage. This may or may not be true, but Peter Marsden certainly found evidence to support his money theory.

In the wreck of a Roman merchant ship, called Cretienne A by diving archaeologists, discovered off the Mediterranean coast of France, a coin was found in the mast-step in June 1962. In November 1963 in the mast-step of a wreck at Port Vendres in the Mediterranean, off the coast of France again, another coin was found. The coin in this case was of the Emperor Constantine, and had been minted in London during the early fourth century A.D.

The existence of this custom [says Marsden] certainly means that in all future excavations of ancient ships, especially of those vessels which had sunk accidentally, the archaeologist should hunt for a possible coin, which would not only give additional evidence of this custom, but also some good dating evidence for the wreck.

There is evidence of this practice being in existence in modern days, and in fact the racing yacht Sovereign—one of our unsuccessful challengers for the America's Cup—had a sovereign placed underneath her new mast in 1963.

But so far as the open sea is concerned, the problem at the moment is not so much in dating any Roman wreck as in finding it.

There can be little doubt that a Roman wreck took place on Pudding Pan shoal, off Whitstable, Kent. We can even date it to about A.D. 160.

First wreck detective in this case is Edward G. Goldring, Borough Engineer and Surveyor of Chelsea, who is a first-class diver of the British Sub-Aqua Club. He used to live at Whit-

Evidence of our seafaring past. This is the boat, believed to date back to the ninth century, discovered recently during drainage operations on the Graveney Marshes

stable, in a house which looked out to sea at a group of shoals, two of which are oddly called Pan Sand and Pudding Pan. His research into the history of the area uncovered some fascinating facts.

In about 1780 Thomas Pownall (a former Governor of Massachusetts) wrote an article for *Archaeologia* about red earthenware Roman pottery which was used by the wives of the fishermen who had dragged up the pots in their nets, from a shoal some four miles off Herne Bay. A special search produced more pots. And there the matter rested for about twenty years, until Reginald A. Smith presented a paper to the Society of Antiquaries of London on 'The Wreck on Pudding Pan Rock' (Proc. Soc. Ant., Vol. XXI, No. II). His paper included a list of 238 specimens, together with a record of more than thirty potters' names. Finds of moulds and debris at Lezoux, in the Allier district of France, led to the identification of Lezoux as the site of the factory which produced the pots that ended up

on Pudding Pan. Now it was possible to add a date to the pots—about A.D. 160.

Smith said—and on the evidence who can disagree?—that the pots must have been in transport from France to England when lost in the Pudding Pan area. To say that the Society of Antiquaries were interested in Smith's paper is probably an understatement, for several of the Fellows immediately got together and hired a diver to search the sea-bed in the area. Hugh Pollard, the diver, worked for a week diving and dredging. In this week he worked over a wide area from Swalecliffe to the Pan Sands, and recovered three pieces of pottery.

Since Pollard's diving some pottery has been brought up by dredge from the area around the Pudding Pan, but Goldring, who has spoken to some of the few surviving dredgermen of Whitstable and retired sailors, says that now the finds are few and far between. Two skippers of the Seasalter and Ham Oyster Fishery Company told him that in forty years of

Major Hume Wallace with a catapult ball from under the sea – or rather half of one, matched with another half from a ballista missille found on the land. On the left is half of the 153-lb ball raised from the sea south of the Mixon off Selsey Bill, Sussex, compared with half of one found under the car park outside the walls of Pevensey

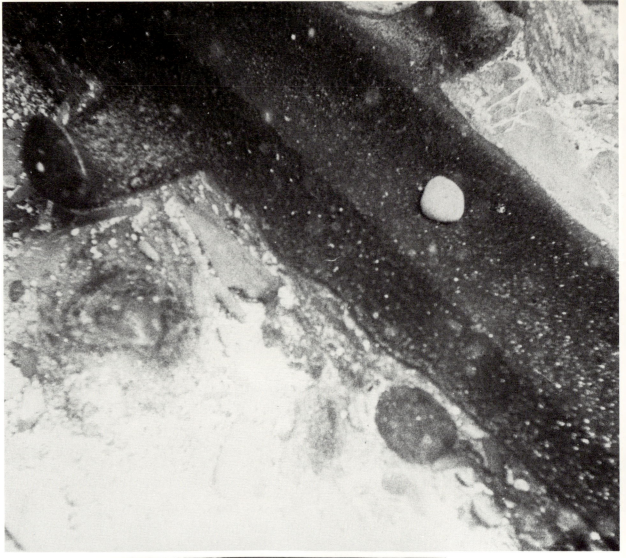

The effect of the centuries of immersion on the cannon on the Mullion Pin Wreck

This 22-pounder iron cannon has become part of the rock and the trunnions and bore have been worn flat.

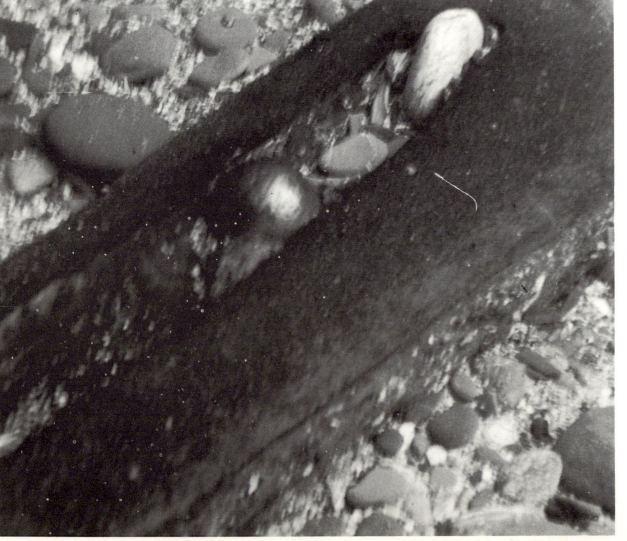

In the worn-away bore of this cannon, the ball still sits in place.

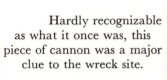
Hardly recognizable as what it once was, this piece of cannon was a major clue to the wreck site.

Photographs underwater by Richard Larn. *Copyright :* The Ferdinand Research Group

dredging they had between them picked up about six pieces of pottery.

One skipper gave the area where finds have mostly been made as 'immediately East of the intersection of a line through Herne Bay Clock Tower to Herne Mill and a line through West Pan Sand Buoy and the Pan Sand Beacon'.

The list of pottery recovered by 1909 showed 282 pieces, but that number must have grown. The original collection has been split up and added to, and Pudding Pan pottery can be seen at museums in Whitstable, Herne Bay, Maidstone, Rochester, Canterbury, Leicester, Kingston, Liverpool, Bristol and London.

Was there in fact a wreck? The amount of pottery recovered could have formed only part of a ship's cargo—a small part, at that—so the idea that part of the deck cargo was jettisoned to enable the ship to ride a storm cannot be rejected. On the other hand, the whole ship—or a large part of her—could be down there, perhaps sunk into the sea-bed near Pudding Pan.

Goldring, who has dived many times on the site, believes that a diver might have a chance of finding one of the heavier pieces. What he has in mind are the large and heavy shallow dishes with spouts. He thinks that if these were partially buried upside down on the sea-bed it is possible that dredges will have passed over them without dragging them up.

Another experienced diver in the area is Hugh Singer, a Whitstable dentist and former treasurer of the British Sub-Aqua Club. Pudding Pan interests him so much that he has written

a leaflet about it for divers.

He tried a different method of detection in his attempts to pin-point the site of a possible wreck. He searched out early charts and sailing documents and compared them with modern charts.

Of his research he says:

If we consider that the Pans were washed out of Pan Sand by tidal action they would travel in a south-westerly direction on the flood tide, which is considerably stronger than the ebb in the opposite direction. Thus the progress by tidal drift would be in this south-west direction along the hard sea-bed until arrested by one of the boulders or until the Pans ended up against the rough Shoal to the S.W. of Pan Sand, called Pudding Pan. Any missing this 'net' would then continue to travel on down towards Whitstable.

But before divers rush off to check this research underwater they should note that Hugh Singer stresses the area is not one for beginners, even though on one rare occasion he did find visibility of up to twenty feet. 'The tides are tricky,' he says, 'and a calm sea can suddenly turn into a nasty chop.'

The chances of finding the wreck of a Roman ship around the coasts of Britain seemed very slim indeed. But suddenly, in May 1970, a London diver found the neck of an amphora off the coast of Sussex. (See Fig. 2.)

The diver, John White, a 28-year-old married man with two

21

The way the artifacts were raised from the Mullion Pin Wreck –
in lumps of concretion covered in pins. Sackfuls of this sort of material
were brought ashore, then broken up to reveal (*see below*) iron shot,
pistol musket, grape, 9-pounder and 22-pounder, plus bar shot,
the largest of which would not fit any cannon found on the wreck.
Notice the odd 'Musket shot' joined by wire (no one has yet explained
how or why this was used)

children, lives in Arundel Square, Islington, and earns his living as a dispatch rider. He started diving in August 1968, and is a member of Holborn Branch of the British Sub-Aqua Club.

That day in May was warm and sunny, and the sea was flat calm. John White, his brother George and Bob Barrett were finning over a sea-bed of soft muddy sand with rocky gullies in it of depths varying from two to six feet. They were diving off Seaford Head, between Hawks Brow and Yellow Falls. They were between thirty and thirty-five feet down, and the visibility varied from four to five feet.

As he breasted the top of one of the gullies, John White noticed a round hole. He looked closer, and could see the top of some sort of handle. He cleared the sand away from it, and then, to use his own words:

I could see that it was the top of a pot of some sort and the hole I had seen was looking straight down the neck. I gave it a tug, but at first it would not move at all. It was not until

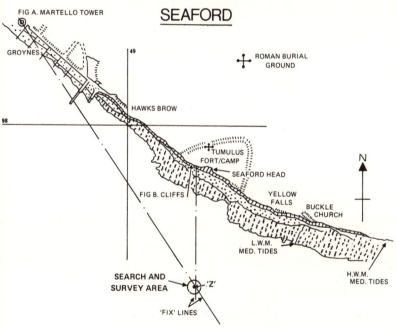

FIG. 2. Where the Nautical Archaeological Group of Holborn Branch, BSAC, made their finds

two of us gave it a good yank that it came free. I now realize, of course, that it was a mistake to handle it in this way, but at the time it seemed the most sensible thing to do.

Back on the beach there was a lot of speculation about what it could be. For all I knew one of the ribald suggestions could have been right. Then it was suggested that it could be part of an amphora.

If he had done wrong in jerking at the amphora neck, John White now redeemed himself completely—he took the pottery along to the Institute of Archaeology and showed it to Joan du Plat Taylor. Miss Taylor asked him to leave it for a more detailed examination by experts.

A few days later Joan Taylor told him that his find was the neck of an amphora from the first or second century A.D., and that it was possibly made in Spain. It was at that moment that John White realized the importance of what he had found. 'While I was explaining to Miss Taylor how I made the find', he says, 'she gasped when I told her how I had yanked at it and said that you should never pull anything free like that or even raise it, but mark the spot until something could be properly organized'.

Holborn Branch were quick to realize that they needed to know how to handle this sort of archaeological work and Lieutenant-Commander Alan Bax, RN, a prominent member of the Committee for Nautical Archaeology, came along to one of their meetings. He urged them to survey the area properly. And so the Holborn Nautical Archaeological Group was formed.

The Holborn group did exactly as they were asked. And on 7th June 1970 they dived on the site and laid lines in a square pattern with each corner being tagged—as was the original find point. And the Holborn divers made another discovery—a holed stone which was nearly twenty inches long and fourteen inches wide at the widest part. The holes through it—or rather one of them—carry the distinctive cupping effect given by a stone-headed bow drill. Was this the anchor from the same wreck as the amphora?

It could be. But there is an added complication. On the cliffs above the point where the discovery was made are the remains of an ancient camp, and cemetery. Was this the anchor of a ship, or was it one used—as we know they were—in a religious connotation on some land-site? Holborn Branch will go on diving to find out.

One of the men most concerned with the past shipping history of Britain is Major Hume Wallace, chairman of Kingston Branch of the British Sub-Aqua Club, underwater geologist and archaeologist. It is probably inaccurate to call him a 'wreck detective', for he is concerned with a wider field than any one particular wreck.

He has in fact discovered, off Selsey, what was once a great harbour and river estuary. There is some evidence that Hume Wallace has located the now submerged entrance to a considerable estuary of ancient times, which could be the mouth of a river which Ptolemy considered important enough to name and list with its latitude and longitude in his *Geography* of about A.D. 150. This was the Thrice-blessed River—one of five river mouths that Ptolemy listed on the south coast of Britain, and which included the Fall, Tamar and the Exe.

But if I can't say that Hume Wallace is a 'wreck detective', what I can say is that there is one wreck that he would dearly like to find—the wreck of a Saxon longship, or even a small crushed piece of one, provided that it had a great stone ball resting on top of it.

This wish comes from his discovery of the remains of a Roman fortress (at the Mixon beacon of today) guarding the entrance to the lost estuary.

This fortress was not placed by chance—it guards the entrance to the estuary, and where the deep navigable channel would have passed under the fortress walls, Hume Wallace and Kingston divers have found underwater a large number of round

From the Mullion Pin Wreck too came this much-battered, folded pewter plate. *Below*, after the plate has been carefully 'unfolded' the crest is perfectly clear. But whose crest is it?

Photos : The Ferdinand Research Group

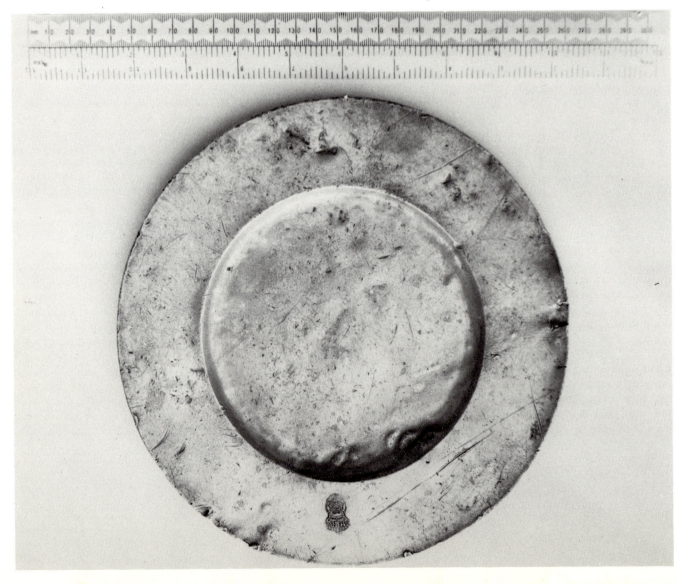

stone catapult or 'ballista' balls. The manner that these are scattered on the sea-bed suggests that they have been fired, rather than having rolled down to the depths of the Mixon Hole when the fortress walls collapsed.

In fact I found two such round stone balls—some two feet in diameter—within 250 and 300 yards of the probable catapult site in 80 feet of water. (And some stones farther out still which must have been cut by man.)

It is, of course, possible, as Hume Wallace points out, that all the missiles were fired in practice, since the Roman Army, like all efficient military forces, was insistent upon regular target practice. But it is, of course, also possible that some missiles were fired in anger, and found a target, since Saxon and other German raiders were active in the English Channel from the beginning of the third century. And when the end of Roman Britain came, soon after A.D. 450, Selsey was the place where the South Saxons won their first bridgehead and established their kings. It is unlikely that they would have bothered to do so in the unsheltered open area that is Selsey today.

Selsey, or, somewhere very close to it, is renowned in their legends as the 'Cymenesora' or coming-ashore place from which they began the conquest of Sussex. The conquest was a long-drawn-out affair which only finally came to an end with the taking of a great fortress at the other end of the county in the year A.D. 491, when 'King Aella took Pevensey from the Welsh and slew all therein'.

Says Hume Wallace:

There is a remarkable connection between the two fortresses where the conquest of Sussex began and ended—Pevensey is the only other place in Britain where such large catapult balls are found. But then Pevensey is the only other British fortress, Roman or medieval, controlling the entrance to a harbour, in the case of Pevensey the now silted-up Pevensey Lagoon.

In his researches Hume Wallace found an interesting section in J. Dallaway's *History of the Western Division of Sussex*, published in 1815, which suggests that in those days similar balls were lying about at Church Norton, at the north end of the Isle of Selsey. Dallaway writes: 'The weapons of a ruder age, large stone balls some of considerable diameter lie scattered abroad'. But none are to be found there today. Probably the 'Gentlemen of Sussex', who paid for the publication of Dallaway's book, descended on the place and took them all for their gateposts.

This was frustrating for Hume Wallace, but Heron Allen and Saltzman, who did a trial dig in the mound at Church Norton in 1910, found evidence of Roman military occupation and a puzzling platform of Mixon stone some 18 inches thick, 21 feet long and 9 feet wide—with a sloping ramp at the end. This sounds very much like a ballista (or catapult) platform. If Hume Wallace's geographical reconstruction of the Isle of Selsey is correct for Roman times, it would lie only two to three hundred yards off the centre of the channel giving access to Selsey's eastern harbour from the north-west.

To Major Hume Wallace, who was a 'Gunner' for twenty-five years, the whole subject is one of absorbing interest, and one to which he is able to bring his own wartime expertise.

He studied the ancient literature on artillery and found that the largest machines could fire the sort of missiles found at the Mixon either in static siege operations or in a naval or anti-naval role. This use applies also with gunpowder artillery—the largest pieces were so heavy that the only convenient way to use them is to mount them in a ship or in a static location (where the target moves towards the gun or is at a fixed distance from the gun).

His next step was to raise some of the sunken ballista balls from eighty feet of water at the bottom of the Mixon Hole. This was done by means of lifting bags filled with compressed air until they were buoyant enough to float the balls to the surface.

The two missiles raised were from a point south of the fortress site. They weighed 45 lb and 157 lb respectively. Hume Wallace's calculations, allowing for the loss of weight on both balls due to worm burrowings (more serious in the case of the smaller one) showed that these would approximate to the ancient weights of one talent and three talents. Both these weights are frequently mentioned in classical descriptions of the balls and the machines which fired them. Two Roman talents equalled approximately one English hundredweight.

Catapults capable of throwing a three-talent ball were the largest used by the Roman legion's artillery, but much larger ones are known to have been used in static installations. In fact, the largest known from records is a ten-talent machine constructed by Archimedes. This huge machine could, it seems, throw a large projectile between three and four hundred yards. For longer-range work the same machines were loaded with smaller missiles or metal darts.

During the siege of Jerusalem (A.D. 70), for example, the Romans and the Jews were slinging one-talent balls at one another at a range of about 1000 yards. Josephus records that one removed the head of a friend while they stood chatting on the battlements!

Sadly, it seems that not one authentic drawing of the larger machines survives, but one Greek writer, Philo of Byzantium (*circa* 100 B.C.), does give very detailed descriptions and dimensions of a three-talent machine. Like all unique ancient manuscripts, his description must be treated with care—there is no other source against which to check it, or even to check that it was copied correctly—but a three-talent machine, based on his report, would be about 57 feet high and 78 feet long. Philo adds that Archimedes constructed ten similar machines for the navy of King Hiero of Syracuse.

Hume Wallace points out that such monster catapults could not have just been 'placed on the deck', from the point of view of stability, and he believes that the whole ship must have been constructed round the catapult, in the same way that a dreadnought was constructed round its guns.

It is interesting to note too that Philo in his treatise also traces the development of all the types of throwing machines in use in his time, starting with the simple bow or crossbow.

He explains that they all work on the same principle—the sudden release of stored energy—and explains that energy can be stored in many ways for throwing purposes. He lists the deflection of a bar of wood, metal or horn as in the cross-bow, goes on to the torsion of a rope or bundle of fibres, and writes of metal springs and the use of compressed air!

Even though Philo goes on to say that compressed-air machines were not very popular owing to their unreliability and the difficulty of maintenance, it is a shattering thought for those brought up to believe that the Principle of the Conservation of Energy and Boyle's Law were not thought of until the seventeenth century.

Though the chance of finding the wreckage of an ancient ship sunk by one of Selsey's catapult batteries is extremely remote, anyone who has worked as hard as has Hume Wallace at the past history of the Selsey area is entitled to a dream, and Hume Wallace has his—he dreams of finding an ancient ballista battleship with the ballista driven by compressed air!

Farther down the coast to the east, more diving into history is going on.

Divers concerned in this search for the past are from the Brighton and Worthing Branch of the British Sub-Aqua Club under the guidance of their former president, Arthur Ridout. They are trying to find a 'lost land' called Pende.

Pende occurs as a place-name in the Lancing-Shoreham area in documents between 1250 and 1420. The references are mostly to the shipment of cargo. There was a commission to inspect the sea-wall at 'La Pende' in 1358, and the final date, 1420, saw a ship sail from 'Pende juxta Shoreham' for Rouen. The 1587 map only shows an area of water between beach and land, and a map of 1622 refers to four pieces of masonry in the sea, one mile from shore.

Diving has continued over the past few years, but so far with no marked success. But this does not mean that the Brighton divers have given up. The discovery of Pende is just going to take them a little longer, that's all.

The diving for Pende is aimed at filling one of the gaps in our knowledge of our past shipping history. When it comes to ships themselves we need every scrap of information that the divers can find.

CHAPTER 2

The Case of the Ship which
Leaned Too Far

including the story of the Mary Rose, lost in 1545, the Grace Dieu, burnt in 1439, and the Royal George, capsized in 1782.

IN crime stories—and in real life—there is always the dogged detective, the one who refuses to give up until the case is solved. It is no different in the undersea world of wreck-detection, but one man is probably the most dogged of them all. If ever anyone qualified for the title of wreck-detective it is that same man, Alexander McKee.

In his search for one particular ship McKee has met with so many setbacks and disappointments that anyone less determined would have abandoned the quest long ago. Mention the name of the ship, the *Mary Rose*, in diving circles and you are talking about Alexander McKee.

The *Mary Rose* was one of over one hundred ships which had gathered together in Portsmouth Harbour in July 1545 for review by King Henry VIII before they put to sea to fight the French.

In fact, by the time that Henry VIII arrived at Portsmouth, beacons were burning to warn that the French fleet, commanded by Admiral d'Anneboult, had assembled and sailed out into the Channel, and orders had gone out to all the King's ships within range to join the Fleet at Portsmouth.

The *Mary Rose* was a big Tudor wooden battleship of 700 tons, and was, perhaps, 150 feet long and of 50 feet beam. Shortly after his arrival at Portsmouth, Henry appointed Sir George Carewe, one of his particular favourites, to be his Vice-Admiral aboard *Mary Rose* (in some documents of the time Mary Rose is spelt 'Marye Rose', but even the experts seem to disagree over which was the correct spelling). And then Henry went to dine with the Lord Admiral, John Dudley, Viscount Lisle—later Duke of Northumberland—and his officers on board the flagship, *Greate Henry*. During this meal the French fleet was sighted, and the King gave orders for his fleet to sail. Contemporary manuscripts then give this description of what happened next:

And first he hath secret talks with the Lord Admiral, and then he hath the like with Sir George Carewe, and at his departure from him, took his chain from his neck, with a great wistle of gold pendant to the same, and did put it about the neck of the said Sir George Carewe, giving him also therewith many good and comfortable words.

The King than took his boat, and rowed to the land, and every other captain went to his ship appointed unto him. Sir George Carewe being entered into his ship commanded every man to take his place, and the sails to be hoysted; but the same was no sooner done, but that the Mary Rose began to heel, that is, to lean on the one side.

Sir Gawen Carewe being then in his own ship, and seeing the same called for the master of his ship and told him thereof, and asked him what it meant, who answered, that if she did heel, she was like to be cast away. Then the said Sir Gawen, passing by the Mary Rose, called out to Sir George Carewe, asking him how he did? who answered, that he had a sort of knaves, whom he could not rule.

And it was not long after, but that the said Mary Rose, thus heeling more and more, was drowned, with 700 men which were in her; whereof very few escaped. It chanced unto this gentleman, as the common proverb is 'the more cooks, the worst potage'. He had in his ship a hundred mariners, the worst of them being able to be a master in the best ship within the realm, and these so maligned and disdained one the other, that refusing to do that which they should do, were careless to that that they ought to do; and so contending in envy, perished in frowardness.

The King this meanwhile stood on the land, and saw this tragedy, as also the lady the wife to Sir George Carewe, who with that sight fell into a swooning.

The King being oppressed with sorrow of every side, comforted her, and thanked God for the other, hoping that of a hard beginning there would follow a better ending. And notwithstanding this loss, the service appointed went forward, as soon as wind and weather would serve; and the residue of the fleet, being about the number of one hundred and five sails, took the seas. The Frenchmen perceiving the same, like as a sort of sheep running into the fold, they shifted away, and got them into their harbours; thinking it better to lie there in a safe skin, than to encounter with them of whom they should little win.

Though the *Mary Rose* had scarce left harbour when she sank, the French were to claim later that it was their cannon-fire which sank her. In fact there is no record of any engagement at all and a contemporary painting shows the *Mary Rose* sinking before the fleets had met, if indeed they did. A copy of the painting can be seen in the offices of the Corporation of Portsmouth.

The loss of the *Mary Rose* was obviously a heavy one. She had been laid down in 1509, and was a reliable as well as a large ship. In addition to the great loss to the Navy of the skilled men on board, the sinking of the ship herself could not be just forgotten. So within days of her sinking there were great plans to raise her. On 1st August 1545 the Duke of Suffolk wrote to Sir William Paget a letter which was, to say the least, optimistic. 'I trust', he wrote, 'by Monday or Tuesday at the farthest the Marye Rose shall be weighed up and saved'. What gave rise to this statement we shall never know. *Mary Rose* was on the bottom about 50 feet down and getting her up would be a major salvage operation using two ships—one on either side. Perhaps they had miscalculated the amount of mud that had seeped into her, but *Mary Rose* was not raised, and in 1552, Viscount Lisle wrote a letter to Sir William making it clear that there was great doubt about how much of worth could be stripped from her by divers in the position in which she now lay.

There appears to be no extant record of what those divers of Tudor times were able to recover from the sunken ship. but it would be wrong to think that they could not work at all at such depths. For all their primitive arrangements—perhaps a diving bell with air supplied to them from weighted barrels lowered down, or, worse, the divers using only the air trapped inside the bell—divers of those days whether using a diving bell or not could reach a wreck at such a depth, and carry out limited work.

The *Mary Rose* was then forgotten—until the 1840s. Then, so the story goes, divers of the Royal Engineers who were working on the wreck of the *Royal George* misread their bearings and got themselves dropped by accident on the near-by wreck of the *Mary Rose*. That is the story, but what is now certain is that the Engineer divers under the command of Colonel Pasley did not light on the *Mary Rose*. But some other divers did—and they brought up five brass or bronze cannon, all dated to the 1530s, and twenty others of iron, from the area. The iron cannon were breech-loaders. This is of particular interest, as breech-loading was not generally adopted again until Victorian times.

The *Mary Rose* was, however, not only important because of her armament.

Alexander McKee first became actively interested in sunken ships in the Solent in 1965. He quickly realized the importance of the *Mary Rose*. There is an enormous gap in our knowledge of the history of shipbuilding. The only significant evidence we have of the striking developments that took place between 1066 and 1628 lies in the wreck of the *Mary Rose*.

This last statement is not exactly true, but it is as near as makes no difference, for though the wreck of Henry V's *Grace Dieu* lies in the Hamble river, three-quarters of a mile above Bursledon Bridge, so far little has been learnt from her timbers. She was built in 1418, and was laid up in the Hamble, but was accidentally burnt in 1439. Timbers that remain give her length as something over 135 feet, and her beam at about 37 feet.

You can see the *Grace Dieu*, or rather what is left of her, at low water in the spring and autumn. She was surveyed in 1933, and again in 1967. Maurice Young, of the Southampton branch of the BSAC, with his archaeological group carried out a diving search of the stern (which is out in the river) in appalling muddy conditions in 1967. On 8th October 1967, they reported to the Committee for Nautical Archaeology:

A search was carried out in 12 feet of water with a visibility of six inches (which is usual for this area), working from a search line 12 feet long, thus giving us coverage of a 24-feet-diameter circle centred on what I took to be the sternmost extremity of the wreck. Nothing of real interest was found, however, except several large pieces of rock (not local) which I believe to be ballast from the ship. No large timberwork was observed, other than that identified as frames, which is by no means conclusive, as there may well be large amounts of it buried under the mud. More diving and probing might prove this to be the case.

And there for the moment rests the investigation of this ship which was huge for her time—she was bigger than *Greate Henry*, which sailed from Portsmouth at the time of the loss of the *Mary Rose*—and only a little smaller than Nelson's *Victory*. A clinker-built ship, she was listed as 1400 tons.

So there was little to be learned from the *Grace Dieu*. Everything, it seemed to Alexander McKee, depended on the *Mary Rose*. If the hull and more of the armament was preserved under the sea, the *Mary Rose* would be the answer to a marine archaeologist's prayer.

And he had yet another thought. If the ship itself was so important, surely the gear and equipment of the many hundreds of officers and crew, from Vice-Admiral to cabin boy, would be important too. In other words, a cross-section of Tudor military and naval society had gone down with the *Mary Rose*. Now, if they were to be preserved . . . .

The thought that the *Mary Rose* could be there, perhaps lying under protective mud (as the *Wasa* of Sweden had been since her sinking in 1628) spurred McKee on.

The *Wasa* had been one of the ships built for the King of Sweden to beat off the threat from the Hapsburg Empire. In the summer of 1628 she was to make her maiden voyage—and on 10th August 1628 she set sail from Stockholm Harbour, heeled to the wind and as her open gun-ports took in water, capsized and sank to the bottom, with all flags flying and all sails set. The comparison with the sinking of the *Mary Rose* is obvious.

Protected by the mud, the *Wasa* remained in her watery grave until diver-archaeologist Anders Franzen found her and she was finally raised on 4th May 1961. She was towed to dry-dock, and can be seen today in a special museum.

Could the *Mary Rose* be Britain's *Wasa*? That was McKee's thought. A thought only, for he had yet to find the sunken ship.

But instead of McKee going all out to discover the grave of the *Mary Rose*, it was at this point that he realized that he did not know enough about underwater archaeology to be sure that he would know what to do with the *Mary Rose* if indeed he were fortunate enough to find her. The case of the *Mary Rose*, McKee decided, was going to be a long one.

28

So, in 1965, he launched 'Project Solent Ships'. His plan, with the help and support of Southsea Branch of the British Sub-Aqua Club, was to investigate some of the dozen or so historic wrecks which lie off Portsmouth.

'Project Solent Ships' got under way with the wreck of the *Royal George*. The *Royal George* was important for two reasons. First there was the story that Colonel Pasley's Royal Engineer divers had dived on the wreck of the *Mary Rose* by accident, and that it was near to the wreck of the *Royal George*. And secondly, McKee felt that as the Royal Engineer divers had blown up the wreck of the *Royal George*, at least 'Project Solent Ships' divers could do no more damage.

The *Royal George* was the flagship of Rear-Admiral Kempenfelt. She capsized at Spithead on 29th August 1782, and nearly 900 lives were lost. That ghastly death-toll included women and children. The reason for this was that the *Royal George*, a battleship of 108 guns, was about to sail from Portsmouth with the the rest of a British fleet to relieve Gibraltar, which was being besieged by the French. It was a time for fond farewells, and she sank as the last stores were being loaded and many wives, children, relatives and friends were on board to say goodbye.

McKee worked out where the *Royal George* was by transferring old positions on to modern charts—and landed right on it—or at least on a mound of shingle that could well be the *Royal George*. He found a 32-pounder cannon-ball and a small pottery jar which was almost buried. This was subsequently dated to the late eighteenth century, the time of the sinking of the *Royal George*.

In the meantime McKee carried on his land detection work, and came across accounts by the divers who had actually found the *Mary Rose* and the cannon—not Pasley's men, but the inventors of the first really usable diving helmet. These were the Deane brothers. McKee found a report that one of the brothers, John Deane, had been working on the wreck of the *Royal George* in 1836, when he had been asked by some Gosport fishermen for help in clearing their nets from some obstruction. Deane dived and found the *Mary Rose*—a ship that was by then almost completely covered by sand, mud and clay. Bits of timber still showed, and so did one gun, according to the old report. But McKee suspected that the Deanes, out of consideration for the fishermen, would have cleared any surface obstruction left.

As a result of these clues and of his diving McKee concluded that not only would there be nothing left of the *Mary Rose* above the surface, but also that the wreck must lie much nearer to Spit Sand to the north-east of the *Royal George*. And there at the end of 1965 the diving had to finish.

But McKee worked on throughout the winter. Then came his first break-through. Together with another well-known local diver, John Towse, Alex McKee visited the Hydrographic Department of the Admiralty. There they found a large-scale Admiralty Chart which showed the positions not only of H.M.S. *Edgar* (a ship of 70 guns which blew up at Spithead on 15th October 1711, killing all on board) and the *Royal George*, but also that of the *Mary Rose*. And the *Mary Rose* was marked as half a mile north-east of the *Royal George*, near Spit Sand!

So far so good. Alex McKee now went to the Public Record Office in Chancery Lane, where he found a bulky file containing the correspondence between John Deane and the Board of Ordnance about the guns he had raised from the *Mary Rose* in 1836 and 1840, together with a report of a committee set up by the Board in 1836 to identify the wreck as that of the *Mary Rose*.

And in addition to all that, just to prove McKee's theory completely right, there was Deane's request for 13-inch bombshells with which to remove the surface traces of the wreck in 1840!

In the summer of 1966 Alexander McKee dived with Margot Varese, a diver-archaeologist from London University, on the site that they suspected was the grave of the *Mary Rose*. They made two underwater sweeps of the area and found a distinct mound-and-depression appearance of the sea-bed. The mound pointed south-east, which McKee noted joyfully was the last-known heading of the *Mary Rose* at the time that she sank. But they could find no timbers on the surface of the mound, nor could they feel anything solid when they probed under the soft surface.

By the year's end McKee was a frustrated underwater detective. He was sure that he knew the exact spot where the *Mary Rose* lay, but could he prove it? More important, how was he going to prove it?

As this moment what might be called the equivalent of Scotland Yard's forensic department came to his aid. Just when McKee needed something that would penetrate the mud above what he was sure was the *Mary Rose*, Joan du Plat Taylor introduced him to John Mills of E.G. and G. International, who were planning a four-day period of trials and demonstrations to potential customers of their latest sonar instruments.

The demonstration was of two instruments operated together. One is side-scan sonar, which shows the patterns and contours of the surface of the sea-bed; the other is a pinger probe, which penetrates the sediments of the sea-bed to show their composition.

This means that as you move over the surface you have a 500-foot view of the sea-bed either side of the ship on one instrument and a deep penetration of the sea-bed, perhaps to hundreds of feet, directly below your keel on the other. McKee, because of weather and of demonstration demands, was not to get his chance until the last few moments after the demonstrations were over. Then he was allowed 'one or two quick runs' over the site of the *Mary Rose*.

Says McKee:

On board were the Home Office, Police, oil companies, and representatives of a Dutch geological institute. With such an audience I felt a trace of 'first night nerves'. Being used only to conning motor boats over the area, I did not allow sufficiently for the larger turning circle of the steamer.

So on the first run we passed in front of the bows of the *Mary Rose* instead of directly over her. This proved to be fortunate, because at a range of 200 feet the sidescanner picked up the wound in the sea-bed of the wreck's entry, to the astonishment of all concerned, not least myself. Another run, and this time both sidescanner and pinger picked up the wreck—showing that it was twenty feet under the sea-bed.

So McKee had found the *Mary Rose*—or had he? Such scientific evidence only showed that there was something unusual there under the sea-bed, and though McKee was sure that this was the *Mary Rose*, he would have to have some more positive proof than some disturbance of the sea-bed.

Security of the site was worrying him too. What, he said to the Committee for Nautical Archaeology, was to stop someone coming along and blowing great holes in the sea-bed at the site in the hope of finding a bronze gun worth several thousand pounds today?

In early 1968 McKee formed the Mary Rose Committee and they found the answer. They applied to the Crown Estate Commissioners for the lease, for the purposes of archaeological prospection, of some 1200 square feet of sea-bed around the wreck. The application was made in the name of The Mary Rose (1967) Committee, which had been newly formed expressly for this purpose, and to obtain in this way legal protection for the wreck site. The lease was granted—at an annual rent of £1!

At this time the Mary Rose Committee consisted of Alexander McKee; archaeologist Mrs M. H. Rule; a trustee of the Society for Nautical Research, Mr W. O. B. Majer; and a member of the Committee for Nautical Archaeology, Lieutenant-Commander Alan Bax, RN. The fact that the lease had been granted was vastly important for the protection of any wrecks discovered in the future. In fact renting the sea-bed may well become as commonplace for underwater wreck-protection in the future as 'Trespassers will be prosecuted' notices are on land.

With the problem of looters at least partially erased from his mind, Alex McKee worked on. Two more days' work at sea with the instruments gave more undersea readings.

Now McKee began to be able to build a three-dimensional site map. A sort of 'W' began to become clear under the sea-bed. It was roughly ship-shaped, pointing to the south-east and with an 'under-mud' length of about 170 feet. The depth of the buried 'W' varied between 5 and 15 feet *under the mud* (see Fig. 3). It was not clear whether the W was a cross-section through the hull or merely the upper surface of the wreckage. As the work was all entirely experimental, McKee had nothing to turn to for comparison. The only answer was to find out what lay under the mud by excavation. And that had to wait for 1969.

At the start of the year McKee wrote down what he hoped to do: (*a*) establish that the 'W' feature was in fact a wreck; (*b*) establish that wreck as that of the *Mary Rose*; (*c*) investigate the condition of her timbers; and (*d*) find out just how much of the hull remained.

And the way of doing it was to:

Excavate a trial trench from the port side to the starboard side of the wreck to make sure that it was a wreck and not a geological feature; to take a sample of the structure for measurement and dating; and by going down to the deeply buried port side at the waist, finding either the ends of frames, or, alternatively, intact bulwarks.

The fact that this last intention would need a trench fifteen feet deep at that point—and of a width that would avoid all danger of a cave-in on the diver digging—doesn't seem to have worried McKee one little bit.

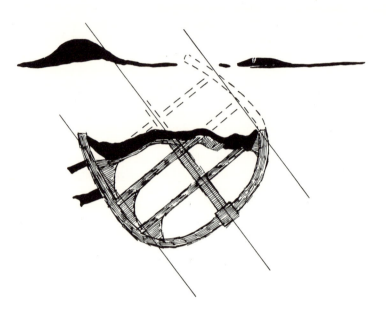

FIG. 3. Alexander McKee's own sketch of the *Mary Rose* under the sea-bed

McKee's earlier ideas of bringing up some artifact from the wreck that would give a firm dating were abandoned, because Maurice Young, the leader of the Southampton Branch of the British Sub-Aqua Club (which had now taken over the main load of the diving work), had done research that showed that the scour pits produced by wrecks in mud could collect any old artifact from anywhere washed across the sea-bed. Rather than risk picking up an artifact or object from any Solent wreck which had been washed into the site, McKee determined to go for actual woodwork.

But at first there were many setbacks. When the good weather came there was no finance. Boats were inadequate, and moorings non-existent. And early excavation proved not exactly impressive. At the end of the year the 'big trench' visualized was exactly forty feet long, only three to six feet deep and four to five feet wide. Below five feet—and remember, all this was taking place some fifty feet below the surface—digging became very difficult.

It was difficult despite the help of the Portsmouth City Fire Brigade, who laid hoses down to the sea-bed and 'water-jetted' away the sediments of hundreds of years. Then the Royal Engineers Diving School (the 17th Port Regiment) rigged up a nine-inch air-lift which sucked away enough overburden from one particular spot to enable a nine-foot-deep contact to be probed. The contact covered a wide area. In went the corer, and the shock vibrated through to the diver's hands. It was wood—but wood so hard that it bent the metal lips of the corer! At this moment of discovery the *Mary Rose* had to be left under the sea-bed for another year.

Finance was finished. The year's diving was finished, and

An 8ft-long gun, which had been underwater since 1545, when the *Mary Rose* sank
(in full view of Henry VIII) is swung
ashore. Note the timber splints

Photo by Alexander McKee

McKee, still determined not to give up, was, to say the least, gloomy about his chances in 1970. In 1969 he had struck wood. That was something, but if he was to advance his identification of the wreck in 1970 he needed more money, more equipment and more expert assistance. Somewhat to his surprise, he got all three.

The finance problem was solved in three stages. The first and most important help at that point came from the divers themselves. Divers from Southampton Branch of the British Sub-Aqua Club, Southsea Branch, BP Meadhurst Sub-Aqua Club (a special branch of the BSAC) and Plessey Radar Sub-Aqua Club formed themselves into a Mary Rose Association, and, because they were determined to start work early in the season, pooled their resources. Then they hired a motor fishing vessel belonging to Anthony Glover, who halved his charges because of his own personal interest in the project.

The divers' support was quickly followed by that of Portsmouth Corporation, who, through their arts sub-committee, came up with a grant of £100. The third stage of financial support came from a new enthusiast to the project, Stanley Googe, who rapidly raised £130 in cash from various commercial concerns.

Googe's activities did not stop with fund-raising. He then persuaded other firms to contribute equipment on loan to the project, while Peter Aitcheson, of the plant-hire firm of William Selwood, designed and built within twenty-four hours a most efficient six-inch air-lift. The firm also backed the *Mary Rose* project with more plant and expert personnel. More expert advice and assistance came from the Captain of the Port (of Portsmouth) and the Diving Officer of H.M.S. *Reclaim*, the Royal Navy's own diving ship.

These two naval gentlemen solved the problems of moorings directly over the site of the wreck. The object of the 1970 work was still to be the same—to identify the wreck as that of the *Mary Rose*. This meant lengthening the trial trench to ninety feet long, and digging a number of deep shafts at selected points to a depth of seven to eight feet and into the wreck.

With his finance and equipment problems at least temporarily solved, Alexander McKee was able to resume work. Under fifty feet of water the top five feet of the sea-bed seemed to be of a light nature. The divers started finding objects in the course of their digging, but where they were found seemed to depend on the density of the object. For example, part of a ship's lantern dated around 1700 was found wedged under a plank seven feet down—and the plank was almost certainly from the *Mary Rose*. On the other hand, a wooden lavatory seat of much more recent vintage was hardly buried at all. And in the trench they had dug the year before the divers found various new items—plastics, polythene bags, dead weed and empty shells, one length of 35 mm film and a tarpaulin.

These items and the top sediments were easily removed, but at about five to six feet down they hit a layer the divers called 'the blue clay'. And the airlifts and water-jets could not break it up. The divers cursed the blue clay, for it meant hard labour—digging by hand with shovels and hand tools, breaking it up so that the air-lift could then suck the debris away.

That the wreck was much more deeply buried than when John Deane found it in 1836 was obvious to McKee and all the divers. Though when Deane found it, it 'was so deeply buried in the sand that the diver could find nothing to which he could affix a rope', the wreck seemed now to have sunk another five feet. In other words, the extra depth seemed to be the deposits since 1836. This seemed excessive to McKee until he observed the effect of the Isle of Wight ferries, which crossed the site for three hours either side of low water on every tide for more than twelve hours out of the twenty-four. They have probably been doing so for one hundred years.

The divers would hear a high-pitched whine, which came closer and closer, passed overhead and then receded into the distance. At the same time the visibility would be reduced to about six inches! And that was the Isle of Wight ferry, that was! McKee had suffered this stirring of the sediment in his diving since 1965.

But it took the 1969 Powerboat Race to claim the really dramatic prize for sea-bed disturbance—the mass start left the entire trench area 'smoking' for hours as though the whole sea-bed were on fire!

Though the divers hardly thought that there could be anything worse than the blue clay, they found a layer of lighter material under it, which appeared to be even stiffer.

But they worked on. Within a few weeks of the trench being first started in 1969, shoals of bib or pouting took up residence. Blennies and small conger eels also moved in, excavating for themselves holes in the sides of the trench. Then came some crabs, and a lobster in the process of shedding its shell.

By probing the divers had found a solid resistance about twelve feet below the original sea-bed level, and they had hammered a metal probe rod firmly into this resistance. This was to be the site of a shaft that they called 'the Deep Contact'. And there they started to dig. They thought they were on the starboard side of the wreck in the area of the waist, just forward of amidships. Five feet down they struck a thick band of decomposing weed holdfasts—the tough stalks that hold the long fronds of laminaria weed to something firm on the sea-bed.

The reason for this layer soon became apparent. Dead weed began to fill the shaft. Drifting weed wrapped itself round the divers' masks. All the dead weed of the Solent seemed to be making a beeline for the excavations.

McKee argued that weed would collect anywhere there was something that broke the current. The layer of long-dead weed that they were now digging through could well have taken shelter long ago behind the wreck of the *Mary Rose* when it was proud of the sea-bed.

More important, it now looked as though the mysterious 'W' trace of the echo sounders and pingers was this layer of dead weed—a layer of weed two to four feet thick, that was once inside the upper part of the wreck at a time when this was falling to pieces on the sea-bed, but still formed enough of an obstruction to trap the weed being washed along by the tides.

And this also meant bad news—it meant adding another two to four feet to the depth at which the wreck was lying under the seaweed layer. Even so, McKee felt they should continue to dig along the line of the trial trench. It was a temptation to move back to the stern of the ship where the sterncastle would have been—its height would mean that it would be that much nearer to the surface. They could have exposed timber much earlier by digging there, but the wreck site lies in No. 3

Berth of the Spithead Anchorage, an area which is disturbed by both heavy anchors and fishing trawls.

McKee shuddered to think of the damage that one sweep of a trawl could cause to the fragile wood of the sterncastle once it was exposed. A local Notice to Mariners was issued by the Harbour Master, forbidding anchoring and trawling in the area, and this reduced the risk, but it still remained.

This danger also influenced the diving team's method of marking the wreck site. At the start of the 1970 season a hundred-foot tape was laid down and held taut by divers, while twelve-foot metal rods were driven into the trench bottom to hold it down. (The tape worked well, but by the end of the season was cut into seven pieces, probably by trawls. The rods all survived except for one. But a hundredweight mooring block was swept into the Deep Contact shaft.)

At the start of the 1970 season the only equipment the divers possessed were their bare hands and a number of spades. Even so, they set to work to try to expose some of the contacts they had already probed. The two they chose were some ten feet from the south-western end of the trench and seven to eight feet below sea-bed level. As this only meant digging down another three to four feet below the trench-bottom they concentrated their efforts on these contacts.

Only three to four feet to go! However, that mere three feet took three operations with shovel power and one more with the Fire Brigade's water-jet before the objects could be exposed, while in the middle of it all part of the clay of the trench collapsed inward—fortunately without injuring or trapping any of the divers.

The main contact turned out to be a plank ten feet in length and riddled with the borings of teredo worm. It was about a foot wide and about four inches thick. It had been fastened with wooden treenails, and had been broken at one end. In the mass of concretions on it was a large metal hook. It was tempting to link the hook and the break in the plank with Deane's removal of timber in 1840, but they would never be able to prove it. Maurice Young, who is a shipwright as well as a very experienced diver on the site, thought the plank probably came from the main hull, fairly high up near the bulwarks. Mr W. O. B. Majer, who is a student of ancient shipbuilding, thought it came from even higher, just possibly from the castling. Both agreed that the plank came from above the waterline. McKee was happy anyway as it fitted perfectly with the deductions he had made on his site map of where they were digging.

More woodwork emerged from other shafts. One was identified as a 'fashion piece'—a kind of curved capping to smarten up the sides of either the stern or forecastle.

The other was a 'staghorn', or large wooden cleat associated with the ropes controlling the yards on the foremast.

More equipment was now available, and with it more ambitious ideas. They decided to try to go down the full distance to the port side. A shaft was therefore dug directly over the mound that marked the estimated position of the port side of the ship. This westward shaft went down much faster than the one from the east, and it was soon twelve feet below sea-bed level.

Working conditions in these shafts were appalling. The walls of this westward shaft, for example, were higher than the walls of the rooms in an average house. Once the divers had finned down to the sea-bed fifty feet below their boats, they were then confronted with a black hole. Had anyone been working in it with air-jet, air-lift or even just bare hands, the visibility would have been almost nil. The diver had now to sink down into the darkness of the shaft, pass through a layer of weed that was collecting deeper and deeper in the shaft day by day, and finally grope for the bottom of it all in order to start work.

In such conditions it is not surprising that when a gun was found in the westward shaft neither Maurice Young, nor Percy Ackland, nor Alex McKee could at first be sure that it was a gun at all.

But [says McKee] I felt it was—the first and only time that I have had a hunch—and even this was based on the bumps made by the reinforcing rings and prior knowledge of the kind of guns raised from the Mary Rose by the Deanes.

The discovery raised another problem—how to handle such a large, heavy object without risk. Theoretically, a built-up gun is much weaker than a cast piece. But the Ministry of Public Building and Works provided a ship with a crane, then a dockyard crane to lift the gun (suitably splinted) over another ship and on to a lorry. The time elapsed between the gun breaking surface at Spithead and its arrival in the Conservation Laboratory at Southsea Castle Museum was just over three hours.

When the gun was first lowered on to the deck of the lifting ship, we saw that a few inches of one of the rings was clear of concretion, and for about ten minutes before it rusted over, this was ordinary grey metal—just as it must have appeared in July, 1545, before the ship sank.

Though it was nearly eight feet long, the 'gun' turned out to be just the barrel of a wrought-iron breech-loader. It looked like the kind which was made from bars of metal held into barrel shape by hoops or rings of iron. The bore was about $3\frac{3}{4}$ inches, and the barrel was slightly bent. The muzzle end was blocked with 18 inches of blue clay, which had to be removed with a chisel, it was so hard. The other end was blocked by a $3\frac{1}{2}$-inch shot still in the breech.

McKee had expected that the shot would have been of stone, as this is what Deane had reportedly found, but this was pig-iron and in mint condition. It was as it had been loaded some 425 years ago. The oakum wadding was still in place, and that too was in good condition. The black powder charge had played some part in the excellent state of the shot. The gun appeared to be a companion piece to the one raised by Deane in 1840, which has been in Southsea Castle for several years, and is badly damaged. (It will be interesting to see how much more can be saved of this new gun, which will have been treated immediately by modern methods of conservation.)

The importance of the armament of the *Mary Rose* lies in both the guns themselves and the way they were used. The loss of the ship was certainly due to water pouring in through her open gun-ports as she heeled. Another contemporary document makes this point very clearly:

A goodly ship of England called the Mary Rose was by to much foly drowned in the midst of the haven, for she was laden with muche ordinaunce and the portes left open, which they were ferie low and the great ordinaunce unbreeched. So that when the ship should turne the water entered and sodainly she sank.

The use of gun-ports was then in its infancy. We know that the *Greate Henry*, the same ship on which Henry VIII entertained his captains before the loss of the *Mary Rose*, had two rows of opening ports after her rebuilding between 1536 and 1539, but we do not know if she had those ports when first built. Really heavy guns could not be used by ships to fire broadsides until the invention of opening gunports, as great guns had to be fitted low down in the ship for the sake of stability.

We are talking about really heavy guns when we are looking at the armament of the *Mary Rose*. Some of the brass muzzle-loaders recovered by Deane from the *Mary Rose* in 1836 were bigger than almost identically shaped and designed guns used at the battle of Trafalgar, almost 360 years later. Both the structure of the ship and her armament, which set the style for naval guns right up to Nelson's time and beyond, are therefore vitally important to our knowledge of history.

Alexander McKee has, of course, in the course of his wreck detection on the *Mary Rose*, gone into her armament very thoroughly. In his preliminary report on the excavations he wrote:

The Anthony Roll [a contemporary record of ships and their armament] lists the heavier iron guns of the Mary Rose in the following order: Port pieces, slings, demi-slings, quarter slings, fowlers. My own view is that the port pieces were on the lower gun deck, which alone had ports, and are probably represented by the heavy 8-inch calibre gun raised by Deane on 15th August 1836, and which is now No. 10 in Class 1 in the display at the Rotunda at Woolwich. The length of the barrel, plus chamber is 9 ft 8 in; the barrel alone measuring 7 ft 10 in, or about the same as our gun. Total length including stock is 13 ft 1 in. Our piece is therefore of small bore in relation to barrel length and may be regarded as a comparatively high-velocity gun of its kind, which presumably explains why it fired shot instead of stone shot. It may well be a sling and I would expect it to be sited on the upper gun-deck, port side, in the waist.

But the main difficulty [McKee adds], is that we do not know with certainty what Tudor gun-names really meant.

Upon examining the gun raised by McKee, Mr K. Barton, the Curator of the Portsmouth City Museum, was immediately convinced that the gun came from the crater made by Deane in the course of his work on the wreck. He thought this because of the corrosion. This indicated that the gun had been subjected to a slight deterioration over a long period, followed by a much more rapid deterioration over a shorter period.

The slight bending of the barrel was, the experts thought, consistent with a gunpowder explosion and this would fit in with Deane's request for 'bomb shells' to remove surface traces of the wreck in 1840.

But McKee and his fellow-detectives were to have one more surprise that season. Portsmouth Dockyard X-rayed the gun from outside the barrel. The Tudor gunsmiths had rolled a wrought-iron sheet into a cylinder and welded it, then added reinforcing rings. It revealed to the world a previously unsuspected method of construction of those great guns of long ago.

At the start of the 1971 season McKee and his team made another discovery. They found sections of the forecastle intact and in good condition under the mud. 'The only marks are those made by the tools of Tudor shipwrights', said McKee, adding that this discovery had accomplished in one day something he had thought would take the entire season.

More diving and more digging into the sea-bed will bring to light more of the *Mary Rose*'s guns. That work is going on now, for McKee is not going to give up until the full state of the ship below the mud can be accurately determined.

Then and only then will he know if the *Mary Rose* can be raised to the surface and become Britain's *Wasa*—a great ship of the past preserved for the future to see. If she can be raised, then one thing is certain—McKee will not give up until his dream comes true.

NOTE: Archaeologist Mrs Margaret Rule, curator of the excavated Roman palace at Fishbourne, near Chichester, Sussex, and a member of the *Mary Rose* exploration team since 1967, decided at the age of forty to start taking diving lessons with the Aqualung, and thereby set a good example to other archaeologists. Before Mrs Rule took diving lessons she had only been able to examine objects brought up from the *Mary Rose* by other divers. 'I want to go down and see for myself where each item is found on the seabed', she says.

CHAPTER 3

The Case of the Mountaineer Who Started at the Top

including the Spanish Armada ships, the Santa Maria de la Rosa and the Gran Grifon, both lost in 1588.

THE Armada, you might think, is historically an open and shut case. Well documented, well written about, and well, what more is there to say?

The truth is that the saga of the Armada has been so coloured and distorted over the centuries that it seems that we must go back to the actual ships themselves to find out the whole truth about it. There is, of course, only one place to find those ships today and that is the sea-bed.

Mention the Armada to any marine archaeologist, or any diver for that matter, and one name springs immediately to mind. This man has devoted years of his life to the search for knowledge of those Armada ships, missed a fortune from a sunken Spanish ship by a hairsbreadth—and dismissed it as the luck of the game—and now continues his research into the history of Elizabethan times by diving in search of one of the most famous ships in all British maritime history.

So if ever there was a man who qualified for the title of wreck detective it is Sydney Wignall of Old Colwyn, Denbighshire.

Syd Wignall's interest in the possibility of finding Armada wrecks off the coast of Ireland began in 1961, but before that he was a mountaineer of international standing, had led an expedition into the Himalayas, and had even been captured by the Red Chinese on a charge of trespass and spying. Mountaineering and diving attract the same kind of people. The risk factor — though any diver will tell you that it is greater for mountaineers — seems to be the common link, but the two sports do have the affinity of adventure.

Certainly Syd Wignall felt the pull of Aqualung diving, and soon he was acting as cameraman for a RAF diving-club expedition to a sunken Roman wreck off Filicudi, one of the Lipari Islands near Sicily. This gave him the taste for diving—but, more important, it gave him the thrill of delving into the past history of man. Soon he was reading avidly—and researching deeply—into the history of lost ships. The Armada and its shipwrecks quickly became an obsession . . . .

The primary object of the Armada has never been in doubt, and at least that is one thing upon which historians do agree.

Philip of Spain's problem was exactly the same as that, many years later, of Adolf Hitler. Philip wanted to rule England—therefore he had to cross the Channel and attack London. Like Hitler, he had a vast army on the Continent, in the Low Countries, and needed to invade across the Channel. To do this he employed Alexander Farnese, the Duke of Parma. Parma's task was to assemble the army and the invasion barges. The only drawback was that the Royal Navy—or the Elizabethan equivalent—commanded the Channel. And that is where the Armada came in. This vast fleet was to cover the operation and prevent the English attacking the soft underbelly of the invasion, the barges containing troops.

The plan, of course, went wrong. Though no fully-decisive battle was fought in the Channel, the weather played up and the Armada was driven, harried by the English ships, away from any likely crossing point. The Armada ships were loaded with everything that an invasion of England would require—cash, cannons, water and wine—but this was really a disadvantage when the gales started. Already badly hurt by English attacks off Gravelines, where Drake, Hawkins, Howard, Frobisher, all the great names, gave a good account of themselves—the Armada ran before a south-west wind. Then the storms came, and the wind drove the ships away to the north.

The voyage of the Armada became a painful mockery of the comparatively easy victory the crews had been led to expect. North and still farther north they went, until they had gone so far that the Duke of Medina Sidonia, on board his flagship *San Martin de Portugal* and in command of what was left of the Armada, could take his ships westward avoiding the Orkneys and the Shetlands and out into the North Atlantic to begin the long last leg home. The Duke led his ships—those that were still with him—westward towards Rockall before he turned south. He was convinced that no quarter would be given to the crew of any ship unfortunate enough to be forced to land in Ireland.

It was a ghastly wallow of ships that travelled down the west coast of Ireland, and nothing like the proud Armada that had sailed so confidently on 28th May 1588. It was now August, and the shot holes in the Spanish ships, added to the storm damage, meant that even the Duke of Medina Sidonia's flagship the *San Martin* was leaking like a sieve. Stores had gone mouldy or drained away from badly made casks, and there was no water to spare for the horses and mules, which were flung overboard on the Duke's orders. His further orders about the daily rations give some idea of the state that the Armada ships were in. Each man was entitled to eight ounces of biscuit, a pint of water and half a pint of wine—and no more.

One of the ships in convoy with the Duke of Medina Sidonia was the *Santa Maria de la Rosa*, officially described as the vice-flagship of the squadron of Guipuzcao. She had been badly mauled in the running fight with the British ships, and had at least four cannon-balls still lodged in her wooden hull. Her rigging and sails were in tatters. She was taking water.

To add to the misery, her crew were down to half-strength, due to disease and a food and water shortage. What water they had was green and scummy, and had to be strained through their teeth to prevent them swallowing foreign objects that had found their way into or grown in the water butts. What food there was was stinking. And then came the gales from the south-west.[1]

The *Santa Maria* decided to take the line of least resistance and head for the land to seek shelter there.

On or about 29th September 1588 the ship was close to the western tip of Kerry. If those on board realized they were too close to the land for safety, there was really nothing much they could do about it, but hope that some sheltered bay would suddenly open up before them. Abreast of Dunquin the land seemed to be closing in all round them. Ahead and to port there was Dunmore Head, and to starboard the little island of Beginish merged into the background of Great Blasket Island. But the bay hardly provided the sort of anchorage that the eyes of those on board ached to see. The water in the bay could hardly have been called calm, and driven by the on-shore wind parts of it almost boiled.

A shout from the forepeak and a pointing finger dragged all eyes to starboard, and there was what to those tired sailors must have seemed a miracle. Tucked in the shelter between the Great Blasket and Beginish were two great Spanish vessels—other survivors of the rout of the Armada.

Here it must have seemed to the captain of the *Santa Maria de la Rosa*, Martin de Villafranca, was the aid he desperately needed. He ordered a gun to be fired to signal to his comrades in their safely anchored ships that he needed their help. But there was no sign of any assistance from the anchored ships as he moved towards them, so another gun was fired.

Still nothing happened, and so Villafranca gave the order to cut away their last anchor from its ready position, catted at the bow. Where the *Santa Maria* had lost her other anchors we shall never know, but when two sailors with axes cut away the restraining ropes the anchor plunged to the bottom and

[1] It is not surprising that the Armada had such a hard time in its voyage down the west coast of Ireland. Recent research has shown that the north-west section of the Irish coastline gets an average of 40.5 gales per year, with 12 of those rated as severe. And the south-west is not far behind, with 36.1 as the average annual number of gales—and 7 of those are rated as severe.

held. Within moments the ship swung head to wind, and some easing of the movement of the ship was immediately noticeable.

This, even though the ship still pitched and tossed in the waves racing in before the wind, was a great relief, and the men on the *Santa Maria* began to have more hope of survival. Surely when the weather eased the men from the other galleons would come across to them in boats and help them out with food and water? Some even thought that all their troubles were now over. The date was 21st September 1588. The time: 12 noon.

The *Santa Maria* was now only 'two cables lengths' from the other ships, but they were not to know that the two Spanish ships already anchored there—the *San Juan de Portugal*, under the command of the Armada's vice-admiral Juan Martinez de Recalde, and the *San Juan* of the Castille squadron, commanded by Marcos de Aramburu, one of the fleet's paymasters—were in no better state than their own. The two galleons had between them only one good boat that could have reached the *Santa Maria*, and in the condition of the sea at that time between the ships it would have been madness to try to get that boat across.

The commanders had heard Villafranca's signals, but they could do nothing but watch and hope the weather eased. Aramburu's account of what happened that day still survives, and, probably because he was a paymaster, he made a careful note of everything that occurred, even before he and Recalde saw the *Santa Maria* come in:

The 18th, 19th and 20th [of September] we remained in the same port without being able to get out. Juan Martinez went on taking water; and I, having no long-boat or other boat, could do nothing; and he but little, and that with much labour.

On the morning of the 21st the wind began to blow from the west with terrible violence. Clear, with but little rain. The ship of Juan Martinez drifted down on ours.

In fact this accident nearly sank both ships. Martinez's ship smashed into the stern of that of Aramburu, broke the grip of both their anchors and nearly took them out into the storm-whipped waters of the Sound. But, writes Aramburu: 'He dropped anchor with another cable and, having smashed our lantern and the tackle on our mizzen-mast, brought the ship to'.

This incident was obviously nearly a disaster, but nothing, it seems, would put off Aramburu from his records. He goes on:

At midday the ship Santa Maria de la Rosa, of Martin de Villafranca, came in by another entrance nearer the land, towards the north-west, and on coming in fired a gun, as if seeking help, and another when further in. She had all her sails torn to ribbons, except the foresail. She anchored with a single anchor, as she had no more. And as the tide, which was coming in from the south-east, beat against her, she held on till two o'clock, when it began to ebb, and at the turn she commenced drifting, about two splices of cable from us, and we with her; and in an instant we saw she was going to the bottom while trying to hoist the foresail, and immediately she went down with the whole crew, not a soul escaping —a most extraordinary and terrible occurrence.

The man who found the Armada wreck of the
Santa Maria de la Rosa is Syd Wignall (*centre*).
With him here are Karl Bialowas (*left*) and
Chief Petty Officer 'Mick' Roberts of the Royal
Navy. They are looking at a device for under-
water triangulation and the correct plotting
of objects found on the wreck site

In fact Aramburu's ship had a lucky escape, for the stricken *Santa Maria* could so easily have dragged them to the bottom, as their anchor cables were obviously entangled.

The disappearance of the *Santa Maria*—almost before Villafranca's crew had time to move to obey his screamed command to hoist the foresail—could only mean that she had struck some submerged rock.

But Aramburu was wrong about not a soul escaping. One sailor 'naked upon a board' did reach shore alive. He was the son of the pilot on board the *Santa Maria*—Giovanni de Monana, a Genoese who had been taken into service with his father at Lisbon. Now he was taken to Dingle to be examined by James Trant, the local agent of Sir Edward Denny. Trant had already examined a boatload of Spaniards who had been captured by English soldiers when they came ashore from Recalde's galleon in search of fresh water and food several days earlier. From this interrogation Trant already had a good idea of conditions out there near 'The Ferriters Great Island', as Blasket was called. He had reported: 'In the flagship there is left but twenty five pipes of wine and but very little bread, and no water but what they brought out of Spain, which stinketh marvellously, and the flesh meat they cannot eat, the drouth is so great . . . .'

Trant, it is fair to comment, was, like most Englishmen of the time, gloating happily over the Spaniards' plight. Now another stood before him. Poor Giovanni, described as 'marryner' did his best to answer all the questions, but, as he spoke Italian and a little Spanish and his answers were written in English by an Irish clerk, some of the written report of the examination must be regarded as suspect.

He is quoted as saying that the Prince of Ascoli, bastard son of the King of Spain, had been among those lost. In fact he even described the man, and the colour of his clothes. But we know that the Prince had been put ashore in France and was unable to join the ship again when it sailed. This sort of error is probably due to the language difficulty, with the interrogator not understanding that the prisoner was using the past tense about the Prince having been on board. The local Irish had no doubts at all about the story, however, and one of the places where bodies from the wreck were buried—Dunquin—is still known to this day as the Grave of the Son of the King of Spain.

What was of much greater interest to the interrogator of Giovanni was his tale of how much gold and silver had been left in the ship when it sank, and also his reports of how much armament the ship carried. He said, or is noted as saying, that she carried: '50 great pieces, all cannons of the field: 25 pieces of brass and cast iron belonging to the ship; there were also in her 50 tuns of sack'. His estimate of the cash on board amounted to some 50,000 golden ducats and 50,000 silver ducats and the plate of gold and silver owned by the rich persons on board at the time.

The answers sounded grand and interesting. The *Santa Maria* was a ship of some 950 tons, and had started the campaign with about 300 soldiers and sailors on board. It is important to stress here that if the interrogator and the clerk got the presence of the Prince of Ascoli wrong, they were obviously quite capable of getting their tenses mixed up over the cannon. The reason for emphasizing this will become clear later on.

The information was duly passed on to London, but there was nothing that the salvors of those days could do about the wreck of the *Santa Maria de la Rosa*. She was, to all intents and purposes, outside their reach—largely because of her position, and not because of the depth.

So there the *Santa Maria* lay. Aramburu and Recalde both got back to Spain, but Recalde died soon afterwards. And soon the actual resting-place of the *Santa Maria* was forgotten. The legend of a great treasure ship sunk somewhere in Blasket Sound lived on, but the weather and the tides put off any serious search for her remains. The nearest we know that anyone actually did get to her was the case of a fisherman in the 1830s who found a small brass cannon in his nets. It is said that it had a coat-of-arms on it bearing a device of an uprooted tree and that it was taken to Clonskeagh Castle, Dublin. Don't look for it there. It disappeared in the 'Troubles', and, of course, some blame the Black and Tans for melting it down for scrap.

One of the great authorities on Armada wrecks was William Spotswood Green, and in May 1906 the *Geographical Journal* printed a very complete account by him of the Spanish losses around the coasts of Ireland. He was also responsible for 'Armada Ships on the Kerry Coast' (Proceedings of the Irish Academy of February 1909, Volume XXVII, Section C, N12),

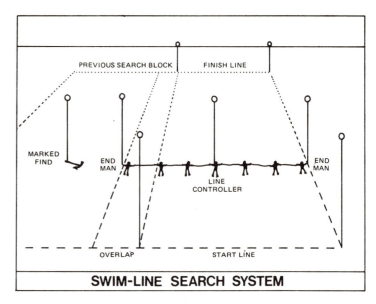

FIG. 4. The swim-line search system which finally located the wreck of the *Santa Maria de la Rosa*

but his work should be treated with caution. Green placed the site of the wreck of the *Santa Maria* as Stromboli Rock.

Stromboli Rock is submerged on the mainland side of the Sound opposite to An Gob, the easterly headland of the Great Blasket. It is shown on Admiralty charts as having two and a half fathoms (fifteen feet) over the rock at low water, but Green considered that the rock may well have been awash in 1588, and says that the rock seems to have been smashed when HMS *Stromboli* ran into it in about 1850.

There were few serious expeditions to the site until July 1963, when Syd Wignall arrived on the scene with Joe Casey and other members of St Helens Underwater Club. They spent two weeks searching Blasket Sound for the Armada ship, and though Syd Wignall now likes to describe the expedition as 'a light recce' the divers did get a very good idea of conditions and developed a healthy respect for the underwater conditions in the area.

Other expeditions were launched with other divers, but the poor conditions and strong tides beat them too. And in June 1963, James Hewitt, a diver on holiday from Newcastle-upon-Tyne, failed to surface while diving in Blasket Sound, and was later found dead in ninety feet of water.

Syd Wignall had learnt from his previous expedition what sort of conditions he could expect to find in the area where the *Santa Maria* had sunk. He knew, too, that unless some reliable and comprehensive search method could be evolved the chances of finding the Armada ship would really depend on luck.

But he had not given up. More time went into research, and he started negotiations with the Spanish Government, whom he believed still to be the rightful owners of the wreck. In 1965 he was awarded an exclusive five-year salvage licence from the Ministry of Marine in Madrid. (This licence was extended for a further seven years from 1969.) Now he planned a bigger and better expedition, but the problem of finding the wreck still loomed large in his thoughts.

Then, in October 1965, Syd Wignall met the man who had the answer. The meeting took place in Malta, and the man was Lieutenant-Commander John Grattan, OBE, RN. Grattan had just assumed command of the Mediterranean Fleet Clearance Diving Team. He has since then has been promoted to Commander.

Wignall and Grattan found out almost immediately that they had similar interests in the field of marine archaeology. And Syd Wignall conveyed to Grattan his fears about the prospects of being able to locate the *Santa Maria*.

Grattan had the answer—the swim line underwater search system. It was used by some of the Royal Navy's Clearance Diving teams, but was not in general use in the Navy. John Grattan offered to adapt the technique to suit Syd Wignall's needs in Blasket Sound. What is more, he agreed to lead the diving operations there for two and a half months upon completion of his tour of service in Malta. Since the tour lasted two and a half years, this would not be until 1968, but Syd was prepared to wait.

They talked for hours about the problem. Commander Grattan had been able to rely on teams of well-trained and disciplined Royal Navy Clearance divers—would he be able to do the same sort of search using volunteer amateurs? They were to find out.

In the February 1968 issue of *Triton*, the magazine of the British Sub-Aqua Club, an article by Syd Wignall appeared telling of his research and the forthcoming expedition and then went on:

Participants are offered the unique opportunity to work (note the word 'work') on a wreck of great historical importance at a minimum cost to themselves.

It sounds too easy and too soft, doesn't it? Well, it isn't, and here comes the crunch. Blasket Sound is not a place for the inexperienced. Participants must be in sound health, and have no history of heart or respiratory complaints. Discipline for obvious reasons will be tough. Every one will have a job to do and will be told to do it, or pack up and go. . . .

There are not, nor will there ever be, any committees involved in this expedition and it will be run almost entirely on Royal Navy lines and discipline. For the above reasons, then, there is no room for friends or passengers. Every volunteer must be a diver. If you want to have a 'jolly time' by the seaside at our expense, do not apply. If you like hard work, don't mind being soaked to the skin and frozen, cut and bloodied, fed up to the teeth with the word 'Armada' and tired, but still determined to soldier on with a smile, then you are probably just the chap we are looking for. And you will probably have one hell of a ball. . . .

You might think that such tough talk might put off a lot of amateur divers. Well, perhaps it did, but the fact remains that over one hundred divers applied to join the expedition. This was whittled down to forty-two, who represented twenty branches of the British Sub-Aqua Club and the Navy, Army, Marines and RAF.

Joking affectionately about those divers to the audience for his fine film of the expedition at the British Sub-Aqua Club Brighton Conference in 1970, Syd Wignall said: 'Between them I would say they contained the most remarkable cross-section of mentally unbalanced people ever gathered together in one spot . . . .' When the laughter died down Syd added: 'We have this on good authority because one of them was a graduate in psychology and he said we were all mad!'

John Grattan was in charge of the diving and Colin Martin took over the wreck survey. First of all, of course, came the searches by the swim-line method. This had worked before so well that in 33 minutes' diving 35 Royal Navy divers had searched 1,400,000 square yards of Mediterranean harbour floor to locate some lost equipment—that is an area of some 290 acres. It sounds impossible. But basically all the method involves is a number of divers strung along a line on the bottom, all moving forward together and all responding to control and guidance from the surface. All! In fact it needs highly skilled diving and, more important, highly skilled control from the surface. John Grattan provided the skill and the divers did the rest.

In fact the area searched by this method in Blasket Sound exceeded 15,000,000 square yards, or over 3000 acres. The credit for this, says Syd Wignall, must go entirely to the efforts of John Grattan, who had trained the divers in the use of this search technique.

Syd Wignall describes the swim line as an underwater visual vacuum-cleaner: 'it beats as it sweeps as it sees. We even picked up chicken bones. Believe me, we missed nothing in Blasket Sound'. They did in fact find seven Armada anchors, which had come from the ships of Recalde and Aramburu and one which must have come from the *Santa Maria*. All were broken in some way, which gives point to the sixteenth-century saying that something was 'as rotten as a Spanish anchor'.

The swim line found something else of vital importance. One of the searchers suddenly found a rock that was not on the charts—a rock that came so close to the surface that when he stood on it his hands were out of the water.

This explained a great deal. It explained how it was that the *Santa Maria*, which drew only fifteen feet could have struck Stromboli Rock at high tide when there is twenty-six feet of water over it. The simple answer—she didn't. She struck this uncharted rock. If you look on an up-to-date Admiralty chart of the area today you will see John Grattan's correction putting that rock into the charts.

Then the searchers found a pile of stones on the bottom. Diver Mike Edmonds sat on them and idly chipped away at one with his diving knife. Almost at once a great cloud of black drifted from the 'stone'. It was in fact an iron cannon-ball.

So on 4th July 1968, after they had searched over 3200 acres of Irish sea-bed, Sydney Wignall and his team got their reward —they found her.

Perhaps, to be more accurate, they had found a great heap of ballast stones and cannon-balls, but strangely enough there was no sign of the twenty-five cannon mentioned by the one survivor. In fact there was no sign of any cannon at all. They had without doubt found a wreck site that seemed to fit in with all the other details, but they could not yet say that this was without doubt the *Santa Maria de la Rosa*. There were iron and stone shot there as well as lead ingots with Spanish markings, but this was not enough.

So in 1969 Syd Wignall returned with twenty divers to explore the site more fully, and though they didn't need it got confirmation that Blasket Sound was no place for novice divers or novice boat-handlers. Three times inflatable boats were capsized by the seas, and on one occasion Wignall and six others were thrown right out of their sixteen-foot boat by a thirty-foot wave! However, they went on with their survey of the wreck site, and hit the jackpot when Jeremy Green of Oxford University's Laboratory for Archaeology carried out a search with a metal detector. He located a large pewter plate under the ballast mound.

The plate was unearthed, and near it was found a human skeleton to which was still attached the remains of cloth purse with a silver and gold coin. Then another pewter plate was found.

Positive identification of the wreck was made when both those pewter plates were found to have inscriptions on the rim. Not much; just one word—'Matute'. Several days later the research was completed, and there could no longer be any doubt that the *Santa Maria* was found.

To understand why we have to go back to our sole survivor. Among all the things he said, and which were noted down at his interrogation, was one vital sentence. Giovanni de Manona had said 'Matute was the Captain of the Infantry of that ship'. Syd Wignall spotted it, and went back to his research papers and there in the muster of Spanish officers taken at Corunna before the Armada sailed was the same name—Captain Francisco Ruiz Matute of the Regiment of Sicily.

The whole of the rest of the 1969 season was spent on surveying the site, air-lifting shingle surrounding the wreck, and removing ballast stones to uncover the ship's timbers.

The divers were working at between 100 and 115 feet, and they found that below the turn of the bilge, the entire structure of the ship seemed to be in a fine state of preservation. They

The final proof that the Armada wreck was that of the *Santa Maria de la Rosa*. The name 'Matute' found on this pewter plate in the wreck was that of the captain of the infantry on board – Francisco Ruiz Matute, of the Regiment of the Camp of Naples

41

At work on an
Armada wreck over
100 feet down in a
bay in Ireland. A
surveyor measures
timbers of the *Santa
Maria* protruding
through the ballast
mound. Notice the
grid laid over the
site to help with
accurate plotting
of the finds.

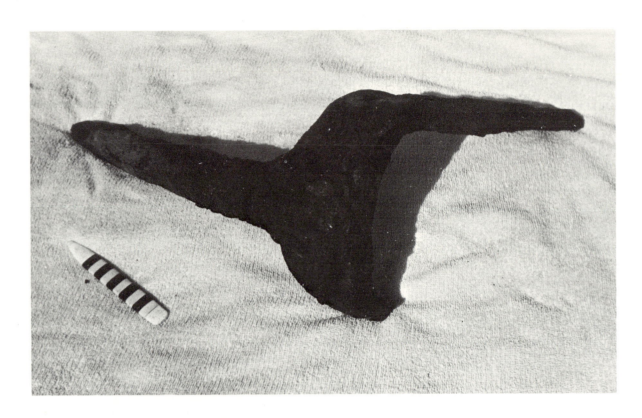

Two finds from the wreck of
the Armada ship, *El Gran
Grifon*. Top, part of the rudder
pintle and below, the breech
block of a small swivel cannon

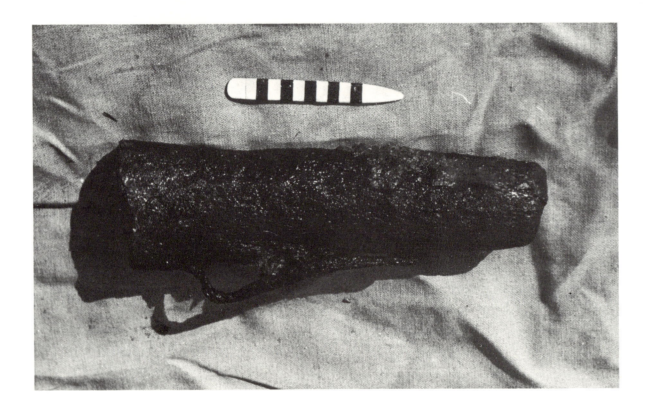

found lead ingots, then a study of the mast stepping-box seemed to provide confirmation also that the *Santa Maria* had broken her back and lost her mainmast as she sank. In the galley area at the foot of the mainmast the divers found broken pottery, a flint for lighting fires, brushwood, a broken pewter goblet, a brass balance pan and even a whole Brazil nut!

Of the guns there was still no sign. Syd Wignall subscribes to the theory that the *Santa Maria*'s crew jettisoned the guns in bad weather farther north up the coast of Ireland and kept only a small bronze swivel gun for signalling.

This theory, if correct, also tells us a great deal about the condition of the Armada ships by this time, for it means that the crew had abandoned any idea of defence or attack and were only concerned with running for home as quickly as they could.

We know that the *Santa Maria* did fire two shots on entering Blasket Sound to indicate her distress, and it does look as though that gun—if that was all she had left—was the one hauled up by that fisherman in 1839.

During the 1969 season Wignall heard that a rival expedition was planning to descend on the *Santa Maria* site. 'This sort of thing is a current problem to anyone doing a serious scientific excavation on a shipwreck that might contain treasure', says Wignall. However, the rivals were defeated without any face-to-face battles or underwater skulduggery so beloved by film-makers. In a now famous action in the High Court of Admiralty in Dublin, Wignall successfully resisted the 'boarders' and was granted a permanent injunction. The action on the *Santa Maria* is now 'case history', and is recognized as such in both the English and Irish courts. Syd Wignall considers this a major legal breakthrough for the protection of wrecks of archaeological importance in the future. He says that it provided not only the means to prevent intruders from interfering with wrecks, it also prevents them from even visiting the site.

As for treasure, so far the divers have located one silver and one gold coin. Of course, one doesn't yet know what might be found under the stones and encrusted cannon-balls in the area, but Syd Wignall does not think that a great deal of treasure will be found there. For the record, the two coins found were a gold double escudo of Philip II and a silver four-real piece.

Sydney Wignall received recognition of his work on the *Santa Maria*. As a tribute to the team-work of the forty-three divers who took part in the expedition, the Duke of Edinburgh's Prize of the British Sub-Aqua Club was awarded to him.

The Duke of Edinburgh was President of the Club from 1961 to 1964. When he resigned from the presidency in 1964 Prince Philip proposed that he should mark his association with the club by awarding an annual prize. The Duke of Edinburgh's Prize is awarded annually to the member or group of members of the British Sub-Aqua Club, who are adjudged to have undertaken, published or completed an important project in the underwater field during the year under review. Prince Philip himself makes the final selection from the top three entries.

In 1970 Wignall was off again. Together with Colin Martin, who has written the full story of the *Santa Maria de la Rosa* he went on another of his 'light recce' trips to Fair Isle, off the north coast of Scotland. Here he hoped to find the wreck of yet another Armada flagship, the *Gran Grifon*.

The *Gran Grifon* was the *capitana* (flagship) of the hulks, or *urcas*, the armed supply ships of the Armada. She was commanded by Juan Gomez de Medina, and ran into squalls when she was travelling westward with the rest of Medina Sidonia's survivors. This was on 17th August 1588, and when daylight came the next day the *Gran Grifon* could not be seen by the Armada lookouts. She did in fact reach some sort of shelter in Fair Isle. Local legend said that the ship had reached Stroms Hellier cove, and that most of the crew had escaped to safety on the island when she foundered by climbing from masts and rigging on to the cliffs. They had been repatriated to Spain, via Scotland after some six weeks' stay on the island.

Salvage attempts had been reported in 1728 and 1740, when bronze cannon were raised. Since that time the wreck had not been touched.

Local legend seemed to be right. She took only three dives to find. Colin Martin actually landed on top of a fine bronze gun on the very beginning of his third dive. In fact it was only when he was clearing some water from his mask that he found he was sitting on a cannon.

The site of the *Gran Grifon* had also on it the lead ingots that Syd Wignall and his Armada divers were coming to recognize as a standard sight at the scene of any Armada sinking. But there were also a great number of wrought- and cast-iron guns.

Later on the Fleet Air Arm Sub-Aqua Club arrived to help with the survey of the site. They found a rudder pintle from the ship, a rigging knife and many cannon-balls. The Fleet Air Arm divers felt that the ship drove bow first into Stroms Hellier, wedging herself between the rocks in the middle of the inlet and the cliffs to the east.

Colin Martin has gone back to Fair Isle to survey the site for Lerwick Museum, who in turn have leased the sea-bed area from the Crown Estate Commissioners to ensure its safety from plunder. This has been done with many shipwreck sites around Fair Isle and the Shetlands generally to protect them. It is not surprising to find that on Fair Isle there is the wreck of an outward-bound Dutch East Indiaman, the *Noodvreek*, which sank in 1728 (see Chapter 7).

CHAPTER 4

The Case of the Spanish Treasure

including the loss in 1588 of three more Spanish Armada ships, the Girona, La Trinidad Valencera and the San Pedro El Mayor. And not forgetting the yacht the Dutch gave to Charles II.

EVERY series of detective stories must have its Maigret. The wrecks around the coasts of Britain have their Maigret too, though if George Simenon's 'Maigret' solved his mysteries as quickly as did Robert Stenuit, the whole detective story would be over in the first chapter. There the similarity with Maigret, that superb fictional French detective, must end—for Robert Stenuit is a Belgian, and a diver of international repute.

He is also an author, and his book *The Deepest Days* (see Bibliography) tells in detail the story of his collaboration with Edwin Link (inventor of the famous Link Trainer, on which thousands of Second World War pilots were trained to fly, on the safety of the ground) during which Stenuit set up a world record by living under the sea at a depth of 432 feet.

Stenuit was also interested in Armada wrecks—he had kept a file on them for years . . . .

The storms from the south-west had taken their toll of the Armada. What was left battled down the coast of Ireland, but by the beginning of September, the Duke of Medina Sidonia was no longer able to see many of the great ships that had set out so hopefully with him from Corunna. One by one they had peeled off from the ragged formation as the going got even worse.

One of those great ships, now turning in towards the land for shelter, was the carrack *La Rata Santa Maria Encoronada*. Carracks were really armed merchant ships, but *La Rata* was more than that. She had towering overhanging bows and a great sterncastle, and all the guns crammed into her made her much more than an armed merchantman. She was a ship of war. But you wouldn't have it known it now.

The *Rata*, under the command of Don Alonso Martinez de Leiva, Captain-General of the Milan Cavalry, had been the first Spanish ship to fire on the English off the Lizard many weeks before. But the various encounters—in which she had always been in the van—and the storms had left her wallowing, shot-battered, and with her sails in tatters.

It was not the way the Spanish nobility had visualized the ship of De Leiva. He was a national hero, one of the greatest knights in Spain, and the favourite of Philip II. The nobility had competed to serve under him in the Armada—and if they were too old themselves had sent their sons to join him. For

they were certain that De Leiva would be at the head of the victorious parade through London when the Armada had done its job.

De Leiva had earned his reputation in other battles, and the fact that he headed for land—he needed fresh water and shelter for repairs—showed just how badly he was in trouble. De Leiva was not the sort of man to give up easily. If he was forced into land—against orders—then his ship was about to sink.

High waves drove *La Rata* on towards the coast of Ireland and she entered Blacksod Bay, in County Mayo. But even there the winds were so strong that there was nothing the crew could do to prevent her stranding off Ballycroy.

But De Leiva was not beaten yet. He landed all his men and all their possessions and then fired what was left of his ship. He knew that there could be no escape by sea, and at first he prepared for a land battle against whoever came. Whether he thought the enemy would be the English or the Irish we shall never know. His first move was to take over the castle at Ballycroy, but after a short while he seemed unhappy about the castle as a defensive spot and moved everything to the Mullet Peninsula.

There he was joined by another ship's company that had come ashore at Inver, in Broadhaven. They waited for an attack that never came. But from out of the driving winds behind them came another ship into Blacksod Bay. This was the *Duquesa Santa Aña*—and as far as De Leiva was concerned she was the answer to his prayers.

The *Santa Aña* looked like a ticket home to Spain. So he embarked all the men into the *Santa Aña* and set sail once again. This time his plan was to sail north to the Scottish islands, where he was sure he would find sympathizers. Once there he would reorganize his men and the ship for the final voyage back to Spain.

But by now his presence in Ireland was known, and a letter from the Lord Deputy to the Privy Council tells how a search for him got under way. The search could hardly have started before De Leiva was off in the *Santa Aña*. De Leiva, however, again found himself on board a ship that was in desperate need of repairs, and should really not have sailed without them. Soon they were bucking hard against storm winds, and De Leiva knew that they would not get much farther. In fact

before she had sailed seventy miles they were forced on shore again. This time the stranding was more serious and the *Santa Aña* was completely wrecked in Loughros Bay, in County Donegal.

Some idea of De Leiva's situation can be obtained from studying the examination of James Machary—at least, that was how they spelled it when he was examined in Tipperary before Lord Deputy Fitzwilliam later in the campaign.

Machary was a Spanish sailor (which in itself makes the spelling of his name suspect) who had been pressed into service in Lisbon and had served on board the *Santa Aña*. He told his examiners how De Leiva had saved everything from the first ship, *La Rata*, and how he had taken these on board the *Santa Aña*—'all the goods they had in the ship of any value as plate, apparel, money, jewels, weapons and armour'.

The moment when a diver's dream comes true. Robert Stenuit (*right*), on the spot where the Armada ship *Girona* sank, examines some 4-escudo coins. The gold chain was almost three yards long. The coins and the chain were only a few of the treasures found by Stenuit and his team of divers

45

He told, too, how De Leiva once again organized the salving of everything possible from the *Santa Aña*, and how he had been injured in doing so.

Said Machary: 'There fell a great storm which broke in sunder all their cables and struck them upon the ground', and De Leiva 'was hurt in the leg by the capestele of the ship in such sort as he was able neither to go nor ride'. Although he had once again saved his men and their belongings, De Leiva was now badly hurt by the capstan accident.

In fact he was so badly hurt—it sounds as though the cables were under strain from the capstan and whipped free when they snapped, smashing into De Leiva—that he had to be carried on a litter. In fact four men carried him nineteen miles across country to Killybegs, south of Loughros Bay, where they had been told some more Spanish ships had run ashore.

The number of Armada ships that smashed on the rocks of Ireland, were beached, foundered or otherwise came to grief there, has never been settled. Most reliable estimates and research puts the number between seventeen and twenty, dependent on whether you accept that ships which just disappeared can be counted as 'scored' to the Emerald Isle.

The incredible sights which met the eyes of the City of Derry divers when they located the wreck of the Armada ship, *La Trinidad Valencera*

guns 'ready to fire' poking out from rocks and others lying in bronze splendour on the sea-bed.

Certainly we have no reason to doubt the fact that a large number of ships found the part of Ireland where De Leiva now found himself to be journey's end. In fact we have an eye-witness. In his letter to the Privy Council about the landings and wreckings on the west coast of Ireland, he says:

As I passed from Sligo, having then gone 120 miles, I held on towards Bundrowes (in the county of Leitrim) and so to Ballyshannon, the uttermost part of Connaught that way, as some say, but denied so to be by O'Donnell and his followers, and riding still along the sea coast, I went to see the bay where some of those ships wrecked, and where, as I heard, lay not long before 1200 or 1300 of the dead bodies.

I rode along upon that strand near two miles (but left behind me a long mile and more), and then turned off from that shore leaving before me a mile and better's riding, in both which places they said that have seen it, there lay as great store of the timber of wrecked ships as was in that place which myself had viewed, being in mine opinion (having small skill or judgement therein) more than would have built five of the greatest ships that I ever saw, besides mighty great boats, cables and other cordage answerable thereunto, and some such masts for bigness and length, as in mine own judgement I never saw any two could make the like.

So ships were coming in all over the place. De Leiva's information was that the ships he was seeking were not victims of the sea. In this his information was a little wrong. Three Spanish ships had indeed headed for the harbour of Killybegs. One of them did not quite make it and was wrecked outside the harbour. The second, it seems, got in, but was smashed to pieces on the shore. The third, a galley called the *Girona*, though badly damaged, was safely at anchor.

De Leiva must have been quite a man, for on arrival in Killybegs on his litter he set the survivors from the two Killybegs wrecks, the crew of the *Girona*, and the crews of the ships he had brought with him, to work to repair the ship. They used timber from the ship which had been wrecked inside Killybegs to do this, and then De Leiva loaded all the men—about five crews in all, probably over one thousand men—all the plate, the money, the jewels and all the weapons to hand into yet another ship. He was carried aboard and the *Girona* sailed again on 16th October 1588. De Leiva was still sticking to his plan to sail north for the Isles of Scotland. But he didn't get very far.

A letter from Mr Henry Dulse dated 26th October 1588 tells the Privy Council the news he had recieved from a man he sent to spy on the Spaniards at Killybegs:

The 16th of this instant October the said gally departed from the said harbour with as many Spaniards as she could carry, and sailing along the coast towards the Out Isles of Scotland, wither they were then bound, struck against the rock of Bunboyes [near Dunluce], where both ship and men perished, save only five who hardly got to shore; three of which five men came the next day, being the 17th, in company with Sorley Boy M'Donnell unto O'Neill's house at Strabane, where they certified of their late shipwreck.

Sorley Boy's coming to Strabane at this time was to get O'Neill's daughter to wife. This rock of Bunboyes is hard by Sorley Boy's house (of Dunluce).

One of those five survivors was James Machary, who was mentioned earlier in this chapter quoting his examination at Tipperary.

De Leiva had gone down with the ship. So had all the plate, jewels and treasure that he had struggled so hard to save. But it was not so much the treasure that worried the English authorities as the armament of the ship. The brass cannon said to be on the ship were complete working weapons. These—together, of course, with the money—were a tempting thought for local rebels. The Irish needed cash and, above all, cannon to resist the English, and suddenly it seemed that both these commodities were delivered almost to their doorstep (even if they were underwater).

The English authorities in Ireland took a very serious view of it—so did those at home. In fact instructions were sent at once to Sir George Carew, Master of the Ordnance, to make haste to Northern Ireland to retrieve all he could from the sea before it fell into enemy hands.

Sir George was pretty busy at the time—he was picking up cannon from another wreck in Southern Ireland. He wrote then, though his diver was working in only thirty feet of water, 'our diver was nearly drowned, but Irish aqua vitae [whiskey] hath such virtue as I hope of his recovery'. Whether it was the whiskey or the work, Sir George and H.M.S. *Popingay* took nearly a year to get around to translating haste into action. When he arrived to raise the guns he was too late. The Mac-Donnels, helped by two of the Spanish survivors, had already raised the guns and helped themselves to two chests of treasure. The guns were later used to defend Dunluce Castle against the English.

At this point it is interesting to turn to the *Geographical Journal* of May 1906 and the Rev. William Spotswood Green once again (see Chapter 3). Green was considered until recently to be a highly reliable source. About the wreck of the *Girona*, he wrote:

She was driven at midnight on to the Rock of Bunbois near the Giants Causeway. . . . Tradition connects the wreck of the Girona with a little bay called Port Na Spagna to the eastward of the Giants Causeway, but those who reported from personal knowledge said she was wrecked on the Rock of Bunbois, that is, in English, the Rock of Bushfoot, which is a little to the westward of the Causeway . . . .'

Mr Green then quotes the Lord Deputy of reporting on 31st December 1588 as follows: 'That three fair pieces of brass lie among the rock of Bunboyes where Don Alonso was drowned, and can be recovered . . . .'

And Green adds: 'Taking all things into account, I incline to the conclusion that the remains of the Girona lie off Bush River near Port Ballintrae'.

There the matter rested until Sydney Wignall came on the scene in 1963. His visit could hardly be called an expedition. He did some diving under Dunluce Castle to eliminate the area, and then in his diving report wrote:

Local legend says that the wreck of the Girona is connected with the little bay or Port (or Point) na-Spagna. This was worth investigating. We were surprised to find a steep-sided cove with cliffs about 300 feet high, vertical and in places overhanging. The only foot access is via a frighteningly narrow sheep track. No place to carry up cannon by hand.

One important factor, however, was that the little cove, although almost inaccessible, was covered with a multitude of flotsam and jetsam, everything from spars, buoys, cans, rope, deadwood, all piled up on the shingle. No other beach within an area of miles had such a collection. As we looked we could even see new debris being carried in shore by the current.

Is the origin of the name Point-na-Spagna due to the fact that the Girona sank elsewhere, but that most of the bodies were carried in here by the freak currents? It looked to me as though anything floating in the sea in the Bushmills area might end up in Point-na-Spagna.

Syd Wignall was closer at that moment to the wreck than he knew, but he turned his attention away to the *Santa Maria de la Rosa*, with the results that I have detailed in the preceding chapter.

In *The Wreck Hunters*[1] I wrote the story of Syd Wignall's short visit to the area. What I didn't know then was that Robert Stenuit in Belgium was keeping a file of wrecks. In 1958 he became interested in the wreck of the *Girona* and gave it a three-star marking for its archaeological interest and its treasure. He read my account and added it to his file. In June of 1967 he went to North Antrim, after spending what he now calculates were six or seven hundred hours in the libraries of five countries researching into the loss of the *Girona*.

Stenuit weighed all the evidence he had collected, and dismissed the official reports on the grounds that the English spies had been told lies to conceal the recovery of some of the treasure. He found there was a Spaniard Rock, a Spaniard Cave and, of course, Port-na-Spagna. So Stenuit preferred to rely on local tradition, dived near Port-na-Spagna, and within an hour had found the *Girona*.

Telling the British Sub-Aqua Club conference at Brighton in 1970 about this, Stenuit said:

The bottom when we dived first was extremely difficult to see because we arrived there in late April—visibility was very poor—kelp was covering everything and made it very difficult to see even such large objects as cannons or anchors. Large piles of boulders covered everything that might have been seen.

The first object I saw, was a large whitish 'pig' of lead. I turned it over and I saw stamped on it five crosses of Jerusalem. I knew then that I had found the Girona. Then I found a few grey pebbles which on closer inspection turned out to be pieces of eight. Right there—just lying there among the rocks—waiting for someone to pick them up.

Then Stenuit and his team of divers started really to find

[1] *The Wreck Hunters* (Harrap, 1966).

things on that tumbled bottom. They found an anchor, then in a cave, in which objects seem to have been piled up by storm surge, came the first of the real treasures, a gold chain and jewellery.

During that first expedition in 1967—it only lasted two weeks —Stenuit discovered enough to show that he had made one of the major archaeological finds around the coasts of Britain. Enough to show, too, that the site of the sinking of the *Girona* had all the signs of becoming one of the great treasure finds around our coasts.

After two weeks of diving Stenuit returned to Belgium and kept his secret well. In April 1968 he returned with another expedition, this time fully equipped to cope with the conditions that existed on the site.

Now the expedition was working from two large inflatable boats, had four highly competent divers, and support equipment including compressors. They started diving at the end of April, and conditions were very bad. Stenuit remembers the hailstones, being frozen before diving, and being so cold in the water that they could only work for three-quarters of an hour each day.

The first task was to make an accurate map of the bottom. This they did, and then each artifact they found was carefully plotted on to it. They found and raised the anchor by means of inflatable bags, and towed it to shore.

Some parts of the rocky bottom contained large pockets of sand. These had to be sifted through. Slowly as the season progressed the water grew warmer, until towards the end of that season's expedition they were working five or six hours a day. The water was shallow, which helped—some twenty to thirty feet only.

Much of the *Girona*'s treasures were encrusted in a sort of black concretion. This was chipped away in lumps and raised, to be broken apart very carefully.

From this black concretion came cannon-balls, gold coins, jewels, lead shot and copper rods. Where there was no concretion the divers used a water pump powered by an engine in one of the boats to wash away the sediments.

They started finding silver and more gold coins. Then up came a gold salamander with rubies down its back. Ducats, pieces of eight . . . and then the pace hotted up. From finding gold coins one at a time, they discovered twenty or so together in one pocket of sand.

Pestles, mortars, religious medals, forks (forty-eight of them —though previous to Stenuit's discovery they were not thought to have been in such general use). Dolphins in the shape of supports for a silver clock, or in the form of a tooth-and-ear pick.

Many objects were badly damaged, and Stenuit knew this was because gale after gale over the centuries had moved the items around over the sea-bed. Silver candlesticks, seals and twelve gold rings, most of them in excellent shape. One of the rings had two diamonds left in the setting. There was a touching inscription on another ring which displayed a heart held by a hand, and the words: *No tengo más que darte* (I have nothing more to give you). A silver crucifix . . . the divers worked on, but at the end of September the weather broke.

Stenuit and his divers returned to Belgium, but Stenuit was still too full of his ship to rest. He spent the winter deep in research on the arms on some of the jewellery he had recovered, matching them to the coats of arms of the knights who were known to have sailed with the Armada. He researched, too, on something they had recovered which they suspected was part of a navigational instrument, but even the National Maritime Museum could not positively identify it.

Stenuit studied the background to the two small bronze guns they had raised in the summer. When the breech blocks were carefully opened at the Ulster Museum in Belfast, both guns were found to be loaded! He also thought that one of the other guns, a medio sacre, was one of three taken by the Duke of Medina Sidonia from his own land artillery to equip the galleasses of the Armada. This was because the gun had a levelling device only used in land artillery. Stenuit believes that the fact they found so few cannon is accounted for by the fact that a great deal of the armament was jettisoned to make way for all those extra people.

Two astrolabes were also discovered—there are only about twenty left in the world.

Stenuit had also found a number of gold Spanish waistcoat buttons and compared them with those worn by Sir Francis Drake in a contemporary engraving. They were identical! 'So', he said, 'guess where Sir Francis got them from!'

Research kept Stenuit busy all winter, but he and his divers returned to the site in the spring of 1969. With bigger lifting bags, they were now able to move boulders weighing as much as nine tons. And it was worth it. Day by day they began to build up a gold chain—at the rate of two links a day. The links were scattered far and wide, and some indication of the care that Stenuit's divers took to recover the tiniest objects can be judged by the fact that at the end of that expedition they had a chain a yard and a half long. And then they found another, complete this time—three yards long. Then another. In the end they had eight of them. These chains were worn as a display of wealth, and also as a sort of instant cheque book. To pay a bill you merely twisted off the right number of links and handed them over.

They found pewter plate, more rings, gold jewellery in the shape of a book (perhaps a religious relic), 115 copper coins, silver coins, 756 of them in denominations of two reales, four reales, and eight reales (or pieces of eight).

Ducats . . . and then 405 gold coins, all of which were in excellent condition. Some of the silver coins had suffered badly —escudos, and one coin from Naples so rare that Stenuit could not find it in any of the special publications he studied.

Some further indication of the way the divers were cleaning the sea-bed of even the tiniest artifacts comes when you know that in the first year of Stenuit's work on the *Girona* they found six gold frames, some complete with their lapis lazuli cameos, and then went on in the second year to find another five. Stenuit suspects the cameos were a set of twelve, and sounds vaguely surprised that his intense search of the sea-bed failed to find the twelfth! The cameos are of Byzantine Emperors.

I have only given an indication here of the importance of Stenuit's discoveries—and the hundreds of items they found. After all his hard work Stenuit was naturally anxious that the items from the *Girona* should not be split up and sold with some artifacts ending up, isolated, in various collections all over the world.

To his audience at the Brighton Conference of the British Sub-Aqua Club in 1970 he said: 'I am trying very hard to see that the Ulster Museum will be able to purchase and keep the whole collection in a special room which is waiting for them. I think it would be a fitting place for the collection to stay for ever'.

Fortunately, in 1971 Ulster did just that. The Ulster Museum has now been able to buy the Girona Collection, and to keep all the items together for display to the general public.

As you will read further on in this book, objects recovered in quantity from historic wrecks are liable to be auctioned and broken up into lots as small as a single coin, and the impact of the whole array of recovered objects is completely lost. Stenuit is right. The Girona collection should be kept together. And one can only be thankful that it is.

* * * * *

But Stenuit's discovery was not the most recent discovery of an Armada wreck by divers. Nor was the ship they found the last to leave the Duke of Medina Sidonia's battered procession down the west coast of Ireland . . . .

The Duke had done his best. Some sort of myth seems to have grown up around the story of the Armada that it was the sea that beat them, not the English ships. In fact, the Duke of Medina Sidonia had lost seven of his best ships before he even escaped into the North Sea. All the great ships of Spain had been battered by the English ships—some have even been described as having blood running out of their scuppers, so great were the casualties on board. The Duke himself had a wound in the thigh, and men had been killed all around him.

Some idea of conditions on board the Armada ships can be gained by reading that on the morning of 9th August more than half the fleet had ignored the signal to face the enemy once again. And the Duke had held a court-martial on board and sentenced twenty captains to be hanged. Only one was in fact hanged and paraded through the fleet at the yard-arm of a pinnace *pour encourager les autres*; the others were removed from their ships and given into the custody of the Judge Advocate General.

Such tactics, of course, did nothing to raise morale, and when the final tests came for many of the ships as they turned down the west coast of Ireland and ran straight into gales, it is not surprising that some ignored orders to give Ireland a wide berth and headed for what shelter they could find.

So it was with *La Trinidad Valencera*, an armed merchantman of 1100 tons. She was in a bad way. She was leaking badly, her store-rooms were already flooded, and as there seemed no likelihood of stopping the flow of water into her, her commander, Don Alonso de Luzon, ordered her master, Don Beltran de Salto, to find what shelter he could in Irish waters.

On 14th September 1588 *La Trinidad Valencera* sailed into Inishtrahull Sound and ran up along the coast of Inishowen still driven on by a westerly gale. Her search for shelter finally ended in the haven of Glenagivney Bay where, with much thanks, her anchors were dropped. But even at anchor her pumps were needed to keep her afloat.

The ship was originally a Venetian merchantman and had

belonged to the Grand Duke of Tuscany. Her name then was the *Balanzara*. She was in Lisbon with a full cargo of merchandise when she was commandeered by the Duke of Medina Sidonia's orders, renamed *La Trinidad Valencera*, and made part of the Armada.

As a warship she carried 360 men, and was heavily armed with 42 cannon. But by the time she dropped anchor in Glenagivney Bay she had far more than 360 men abroad. Off the north coast of Donegal she had picked up most of the crew of another Armada ship, which was foundering, the transport *La Barca de Amburgo*. In fact, on board her by the time she reached shelter were nearly 600 men.

It is understandable that the first action after reaching the anchorage was to start ferrying some of the men ashore. At first all they had with which to ferry themselves ashore were two small boats, but as time passed local boats joined in and the shuttle service went back and forth for almost two whole days. As the number of people on board got smaller, so did the efforts on the pumps. Finally pumping stopped altogether. When it did so, the water gurgled steadily into the holds and then, with a sudden lurch—which probably caught the rest on board by surprise—the *Trinidad* settled down to the sea-bed. Despite this gentle end to the ship, some reports say that forty men were drowned when she sank.

The same reports put the number of those brought to shore safely at 540. These men under the command of Don Alonso were directed by the local people to the house of the Catholic Bishop of Derry, Dr Reamonn O'Gallagher, who was known to be active in helping Armada survivors. But they never got there. On their march they came up against some of the Queen's forces, about six hundred men under the command of Richard and Henry Hovenden, who were the Earl of Tyrone's foster-brothers.

After a small skirmish and a great deal of parleying, the Spaniards, under promise of fair treatment, laid down their arms and were then robbed of anything they had of value.

The next day the Spanish officers, including Don Alonso, were taken aside and the rest of the Spaniards lined up in a field. At a signal the troops set upon the defenceless men and massacred them—one description says that the infantry were on one side of the field and the calvalry on the other; between them the slaughter took place. Three hundred were killed on the spot, but about 150 escaped by running through a bog where the troops dared not follow. The survivors were brought by local people to the Bishop, who sent some on to Mac Sweeney at Doe Castle and the others to Sorley Boy (who figured in the *Girona* story).

About forty-five officers were taken to Drogheda. Some died on the way or in prison. The rest, Don Alonso still among them, were taken to England and were later ransomed.

And the wreck of *La Trinidad Valencera* settled deeper into the sandy sea-bed to which she had sunk . . . .

On 11th January 1971 there was nothing unusual about the training night of the City of Derry Sub-Aqua Club (now a branch of the British Sub-Aqua Club) at the local baths which they used for getting beginners accustomed to the Aqualung. These baths nights are the usual thing with any sub-aqua club.

Though they are used, most importantly, for training beginners, they are also a meeting-place for all the club's trained divers. If they are not training others, they gossip among themselves. And in this gossip details of dives, wrecks and other underwater information are passed back and forth among the members. Now, the Londonderry divers have always been interested in wrecks in their area, just like any other group of divers all over Britain and, for that matter, the world.

They had always known about the *Valencera*. They knew, too, that her wreckage should be in Glenagivney Bay. All their research showed this—as did many hours of discussion (and many pints of Guinness) with the local fishermen of the area. The Londonderry divers found it difficult to decide whether the stories the locals told were indeed folklore handed down from generation to generation or whether they were based on information sown in the locals' minds by other researchers who had visited the Bay over the years in search of the wreck.

However, two years ago the Club decided to start serious search-work in the Bay to try to find the *Valencera*. All their searches failed. Many a dive came to nothing, and they began to wonder if there really was anything left to find.

But that January night at the baths was different. (Not that the divers knew it at the time.) Their diving officer 'Charlie' Perkinson pinned up, as he had many times before, a list of dives for those training to qualify for 'club diver' standard.

The notice is shown overleaf.

On 20th February 1971 thirteen divers turned up for the training dive. Paddy Stewart was one; Archie Jack was another. They were swimming along quite normally, when suddenly they came face to face with the muzzle of a cannon sticking out of a rock crevice. 'Ready for firing' was their description when they surfaced. Both men saw it at the same time, and almost swallowed their mouthpieces with surprise. Though this dive had been scheduled as a search for the *Valencera*, no one seriously believed they would find it—after all, there had been many dives before in the same area which had produced nothing.

Jack and Stewart called the other divers over to witness the cannon. Careful bearings were taken from the surface. The moment the team was ashore, 'Charlie' Perkinson held an impromptu meeting, at which it was decided that the find should be kept a secret between the thirteen of them until the legal aspects of the wreck could be sorted out.

It says much for these thirteen men that the secret was kept for two weeks until the legal problems were sorted out, though each one was bursting to tell his diving friends the news. Finally on 2nd March all the club's members were told, and a Press release was issued on 4th March.

From that moment on their find was public knowledge. But the Londonderry divers had organized themselves well. Their sixty members included many men with professional qualifications ideally suited to task of doing a proper archaeological survey of the remains of the Armada ship.

Right from the start the club had realized the historical importance of their find and established their claim to be 'salvor in possession' by buoying the wreck. Negotiations had begun with the Spanish Government to acquire the rights to the wreck. They stressed to the Press, who descended on them, that their work was not a treasure hunt—pointing out the fact

CLUB DIVES — LEADING TO 'CLUB DIVER' TEST

Place	Date	Dive Leader	Remarks
Malin Head	January 16	C. Perkinson	20 Metre Dive
Glengad	January 23	J. Whellan	Wreck
Lough Swilly	January 31	C. Perkinson	Deep Dive—Wreck
Malin	February 6	J. Davidson	
Glenagivney	February 20	J. Whellan	Search for Armada Wreck
Rathlin Isl.	March 6	C. Perkinson	H.M.S. Drake
Malin	March 14	J. Whellan	20 Metre
Lough Swilly	March 27	J. Davidson	Wreck
Lough Swilly	April 10	C. Perkinson	Wreck
Arranmore	April 17	J. Davidson	Deep Dive + Wreck
Arranmore	April 24	J. Whellan	
Arranmore	May 2	C. Perkinson	Complete Deep Dives
Portnablagh	May 8	J. Davidson	Wreck
Open	May 15	C. Perkinson	
Testing	May 22/23	CHP/JD/JW Belfast Examiners	Club Diver Candidates

that the survivors had two days to get off the wreck, and it was hardly likely that they would have left any portable treasure such as coins or jewels aboard.

The thirteen divers who had been on the initial dive—C. H. Perkinson, Dr J. Whellan, G. Heatley, D. O'Donnell, J. Sculltock, C. Villa, J. Kydd, Father Michael Keavney, P. Stewart, A. Jack, B. Mooney, A. Ashworth, E. Green (and seven-year-old Ross Perkinson, who had also gone on the trip)—had played their part by keeping the secret, but now they took an active role in the work of surveying the site.

The site is sheltered, facing due east with a slight diagonal current due to the tides. The depth is thirty feet to the sandy bed. The area is extremely well sheltered from the frequent west and north-west gales by cliffs. The east wind is a hazard in the bay, but it is less frequent and less severe. The divers had two ways of getting to the site. A sandy strand, served by a steep cliff road, was only 400 yards from the site. The other route is by boat, and the nearest harbour is the fishing harbour six miles away at Glengad.

From the moment that the cannon were found, it was clear to the Londonderry divers that there were many other artifacts present in the sand. Most seemed confined to an area of about two hundred square feet. Along the east side of the site are two ridges of rock with a gully some ten to twelve feet deep between them. Many objects were concentrated in this gully. Visibility is normally at least twenty feet.

The sand seemed to be the preservative on this site. In fact, articles appeared and reappeared as the sand patterns shifted over the next few weeks. Even so objects were heavily covered with concretion, and one of the first finds was so thickly covered that the divers were convinced that they had found a swivel gun. They humped this piece of concretion from TV studio to TV studio, telling all of Ireland that this was, so they thought, an Armada swivel gun.

Later, when the concretion was gently tapped to remove the covering of the centuries, they had a swivel gun all right, but part of the shape was a very well-preserved pair of navigational dividers. These were in such good condition that the original toolmaker's markings could be clearly seen.

Apart from the cannon, the first finds were iron and stone cannon-balls, a pewter vase, a small piece of a pottery jar and various lumps of concretion, which remained to be broken open to find out the contents.

But it was the cannon that were the real glory of the site. Though the *Valencera* was reported to be carrying forty-two cannon, other reports that came to light in the club's research suggested that a more correct figure would be thirty-two. And of these a good proportion were likely to be made of bronze.

The largest cannon made at that time would be the 'whole cannon', which fired a 50-lb iron shot from a bore of $7\frac{1}{4}$ inches, was 12 feet long, and weighed 4 tons. The *Valencera* was said to have carried four of these.

The Londonderry divers in those first few weeks of exploring the site found one beauty—a whole cannon of bronze with a coat-of-arms—and what looked extremely like the breech of a second poking out of the sand. Several other bronze cannon were also just visible in the sand swells.

It is not surprising that the Derry divers lived, talked and dreamed nothing but Armada cannon. They hoped that their discovery would contribute to research on the actual firepower of the Armada, but it is not given to many divers to make such a discovery in their diving lifetime, and naturally enough the divers revelled in it.

But more was to come.

Though the City of Derry divers knew by now that they had made a major discovery of great archaeological importance, they really did not know how great until the arrival on the scene of one of the leading experts in the world of nautical archaeology to give them his opinion of their find.

The two men who know most about Armada wrecks in this country are Syd Wignall and Colin Martin. Both wrote to the committee set up by the Derry divers to handle their discovery. Both stressed the importance of raising the surface items—after they had been plotted in position on the initial survey—before the arrival of any 'pirates'. Two weeks before Easter 1971 the Derry divers had completed their survey work, locating, buoying and plotting all visible items. Then they had a major problem—how were they to raise cannon weighing three and a half tons and get them ashore where they could be properly handled?

Finally this was solved when the chairman of the Salvage Committee, Andy Robinson, found a trawler skipper who could make the lift. Len Forbes, the skipper, was not the sort of man to be beaten by any Spanish cannon. At his home port of Portstewart, in Northern Ireland, about twenty miles from Glenagivney Bay, he got a derrick from a scrap-yard. With this and a hand-winch he rigged up a lifting system, which proved very successful. So successful, in fact, that on the Tuesday before Easter a bronze culverin weighing one and a half tons was raised with no trouble.

The trawler then sailed into the little port of Moville, and the first cannon to see the light of day since the sinking of *La Trinidad Valencera* was hoisted ashore by the local coal crane. The next day the first whole cannon was swung ashore. On the third day of the big lift the third cannon—another whole cannon—came ashore under the watchful camera eye of Colin Martin, who had now dropped all his earlier work to help with the survey of the site. On the Saturday the fourth cannon

Recovering the guns of *La Trinidad Valencera*

The moment of recovery. A whole bronze cannon from the Armada breaks surface. The cannon came up gleaming as though it had been lost only yesterday.

PHILIPPVS
REX

The elaborate decoration on the cannon including the coats-of-arms of both England and Spain.

was brought safely in. This one was a beautiful culverin of Venetian origin.

Colin Martin's appreciation of the historical significance of the find to the Committee for Nautical Archaeology after his visit to the site is of great importance. Here is an expert reporting on the value of what the Derry divers found:

Four bronze guns have now been raised. Two are a matching pair of 7¾ in bore whole-cannons, with lifting and breech dolphins, both dated 1556 and bearing the full arms of Philip II encircled with the insignia of the Order of the Golden Fleece. The escutcheon is of particular interest in that it quarters the lions of England—an honour to which Philip was entitled for, at that date, he was married to Mary Tudor. The breech inscription, identical on each gun, reads:

IOANES MANRICVS A LARA FIERI CVRAVIT
OPVS REGIMY DE HALVT
ANNO 1556

(Freely translated, this means: Juan Manrique de Lara [who was Captain General of the Spanish Artillery] had the cannon made by Remigy de Halut [a famous cannon-founder with workshops at Malines near Antwerp].)

One of these guns is in near perfect condition, having been totally buried in sand; the other, which had been exposed directly to seawater, is somewhat defaced by surface corrosion.

It is premature to attempt to identify the other two guns with any certainty, but both are long small-bore 'culverin' types, and appear to be Italian in character. It may not be over fanciful to suggest that these might be guns from the ship's own armament, while the whole-cannons are more likely to be part of the ship's increment of ten added at Lisbon. Don Alonso de Luzon, in his interrogation, states that the ship carried 32 pieces of brass and iron (evidently he is here recalling the figure of her *original* armament, if the patently more reliable figure of the Lisbon muster is accepted) '*whereof 4 were cannons of brass*'; but what kinds the rest were, how many of brass, or how many of iron, he knoweth not, neither whether the same will be saved or not'.

Don Alonso seems remarkably ignorant of the technicalities of his ship's armament on this reckoning, but then he was a soldier, and may have held things nautical in some contempt; then again, he may have wished to impart to the English no more information of this kind than he had to. Whatever type and number of guns the ship actually carried, it is extremely probable that most or all of them lie today in the vicinity of the wreck.

The City of Derry Sub-Aqua Club does not intend to begin a systematic programme of excavation and recovery until a full survey has been carried out and adequate conservation facilities arranged. None the less, recoveries already made in the course of this survey indicate the character and condition of what is to be found on the site. Roundshot—stone and iron—is numerous, and traces have been noted of musket and arquebus barrels. Pottery has survived well, and it is probable that whole vessels will lie buried in the sand. The greater part of a copper kettle has been found,

crushed but restorable to its original shape. An almost complete pewter vessel has been recovered. Most startling of all is a pair of brass navigational dividers, found within the matrix of an iron concretion, which has survived in quite perfect working order for almost four centuries. It seems certain that all manner of artifacts—domestic, personal, military and maritime—lie in the sand, in an often remarkable state of preservation. It is, moreover, the more deeply buried and hence at present invisible objects which will have survived in the best condition of all.

In addition, traces have been noted of the ship and its fittings, and it will be surprising if sections of the lower hull do not remain, buried under sand and ballast. Already some large baulks of timber have been found, apparently jointed in some kind of structural sequence. At least one anchor has been discovered, together with iron components evidently from a capstan.

Without question this find is one of quite outstanding interest to maritime historians, archaeologists, and the public generally. The site can be expected to throw much light on the armament of the Spanish Armada, particularly with regard to the heavier battery pieces. A study of the structural remains will probably add technical detail to the knowledge of large sailing-ships at this critical period of their development. The fact that the ship is a Venetian one is particularly opportune, since much knowledge of contemporary Venetian shipwrightry has already been gleaned from documentary sources. The discovery of machinery—evidenced by the postulated capstan parts—may illuminate or even add to the knowledge of 16th century nautical technology.

From the social and military viewpoint, the site seems certain to contain a great quantity of well-preserved objects which can be expected to form a collection on a par, for example, with recoveries from the Roman frontier fort at Newstead in Scotland or the sunken 17th century city of Port Royal in Jamaica—a collection, that is, representing an entire community and its way of life. The museum possibilities of this are too obvious to stress. The story of this wreck, moreover, is so well documented in contemporary sources, and so many named individuals can be associated with her, that some of the discoveries are likely to bear direct links with events and people. . . .

Colin Martin was obviously impressed. But they still needed to know how much the sand concealed. The man who could answer this was the next to arrive on the scene. Jeremy Green is the expert in the use of complicated instruments that will tell you what is concealed by just such a site as the Derry divers had found. He is the expert in this country on metal detection on marine archaeological sites. He spent six days on the *Trinidad* site and his survey revealed that in a 200 foot by 200 foot square area were the biggest collection of Armada objects ever discovered.

Such richness is perhaps best illustrated by the fact that after the divers had raised one of the whole cannon, they found in the sand where she had been lying a brass latch cover which was designed to keep the touchhole dry—and it fitted back perfectly!

Work now goes on. The British Sub-Aqua Club have given the Derry divers their support. Other concerns are joining in too. And the ship which sank over 380 years ago is slowly being brought back to life—or if not life, at least to the notice of the world of today.

*   *   *   *   *

What more hopes are there of Armada wrecks for British divers? For perhaps the best chance of success we should turn to Devon. I say this because we know without any doubt that an Armada ship did strike on the coast of Devon, but with the present boom in skin-diving I would be silly to forecast with any certainty where the next find of an Armada ship will be made.

The *San Pedro el Mayor* was a hospital ship of medium size, about 550 tons burden. She had left Spain with the rest of the Armada with thirty sailors and one hundred soldiers on board— and some fifty others whose task was to tend the sick and organize the hospital. She was an *urca*, or hulk, a cargo-carrier which had been pressed into service, and was one of a squadron which had fourteen ships in it. They were slow compared to the galleons and galleasses, but were needed for the supplies they carried.

We know that the *San Pedro* was off Plymouth on 21st July 1588 during the first skirmishes—and three months later she was back again. But she was no longer the ship she had been. It is thought that in that dreadful journey round the British Isles she called into the Blasket Sound, but one thing is certain, that at some time in her attempt to get back to Spain, with the

wounded and dying who had been transferred to her during the battles and afterwards, her captain and crew abandoned all hope.

This despair is the only thing that can account for the fact that after leaving Ireland she turned east in search of any port, English or French—anywhere, in fact, where she could seek shelter and help for her wounded and dying. With the south-westerlies still behind her, she was blown into the Channel. There were fewer and fewer left on board with the strength to control her. Finally there were not enough even to cope with the sails and tackle. Hither and thither she was blown, until she was heading straight for the nest of her enemies, Plymouth. Then the wind shifted a little and she came into Bigbury Bay and then, with no control at all, into Hope Cove. And there on the Shippen Rock her voyage ended. Soon she was a complete wreck, and the dead and dying went down with her.

Out of the original 180 men, only 40 survived. What about all the sick and wounded who were taken aboard her during

Diving around our coasts can be cold and tiring work. Here, Archie Jack and Pat Stewart, the two divers who first discovered the wreck of the Armada ship, *La Trinidad Valencera*, together with diver Stan Donaghey, after coming ashore with more finds.

the battles? That alone gives you some idea of the state the *San Pedro* was in before she hit in Hope Cove.

The 'search' of the survivors on first landing would account for the coins that have been found on the beach at Hope from time to time—they may have been trampled into the ground in the struggle for loot.

Alternatively, of course, they could have come from the wreckage of the ship. There seems to be no positive evidence that parts of the ship did not sink intact to the bottom. In fact we have some evidence that large parts did find their way to the sea-bed. A diver, George Tessyman of Dartmouth, once found the frames or ribs of some ancient vessel there buried in the sand, but when he returned to the spot two weeks later to make a proper investigation a storm had shifted the sea-bed, and search as he might he could not find the shipwreck again.

Much more recently, John Humphreys, who runs the diving service 'Nautech' from premises at Green Street Green, in Kent, and is a former Diving Officer of Bromley Branch of the British Sub-Aqua Club, had a strange tale to tell of a dive in Hope Cove.

He dived in the Cove without knowing the story of the *San Pedro*. He swam from Outer Hope towards the bay and around the Shippen Rock. He found that the rock and shale bottom finished in a line with the seaward end of the harbour wall and there the sand began.

At this spot [says Humphreys], which was only about ten feet deep, there was a shelf—I thought it was rock at first—covered with kelp, and to the best of my memory about twenty yards long.

I particularly remember the scour on the beach side, which was filled with dead spider crabs which the local fishermen had rejected from their catch. Later that year I read an account of the wreck in *The Wreck Hunters* [see Bibliography] and like many another diver I decided that the next time I returned to Hope I would have a closer look. The next opportunity to do this was in 1969 and I found the same shale and rock bottom around the Shippen, but the ledge near the end of the wall had disappeared! Obviously the sand had shifted and covered it. As the only place a wreck can hide there is under the sand—and the sand in Hope Cove does shift about—it seems logical to me that she is down there almost within wading distance of the quay.

In fact John Humphreys told me that he thinks that the *San Pedro* could be uncovered by divers wading about with air-lifts at low tide!

*　　*　　*　　*　　*

When Charles II returned to this country after eleven years in exile he arrived back in England aboard a Dutch-built yacht of less than 100 tons. For reasons best known to himself, Charles was so impressed by this particular vessel that he remarked that he would have an identical one built for his own personal use. As a diplomatic gesture, the magnificent yacht, built for the Prince of Orange, was presented to the

King in 1660 as a gift. Along with the yacht went two ornamental bronze cannon, specially cast in Amsterdam that year, but since a King's ship justified more than two guns, a matching set of eight smaller cannon were commanded of Sir William Compton, Master General of the Tower of London. In due course these were cast and finished, then placed aboard in late 1661.

Charles II chose the name *Mary* after his sister, the Princess Royal, widow of William II of Orange, as a compliment to the Dutch, and took possession, ensuring that every taste and luxury was catered for aboard. The yacht, a 'smak', of 92 tons, measured 67 feet overall, with an 18½ foot beam, initially carried only the ten bronze cannon, the Dutch guns measuring 5 ft 11 in long with a 3½ in bore, and the English guns 5 ft 0½ in with a 3 in bore, but in later years the vessel carried up to twenty guns. She served the King for only about a year, after which she passed into the hands of the Navy, who used her as a yacht on ceremonial occasions and a stores or passenger carrier between times, mostly between Ireland and Holyhead. It is therefore doubtful if either Nell Gwynne or Louise de Kéroualle, Duchess of Portsmouth, ever had the pleasure of being entertained aboard!

In 1674, when she was still only fourteen years old, it was proposed that she be scrapped, but she was still in service on 25th March 1675 when she struck a rock and sank off the south side of the Anglesey Skerries, close to Holyhead, while returning from Ireland, drowning the Earl of Meath and thirty-four passengers and crew; the captain, twenty-three marines, and two sailors were saved.

The site of the wreck was well known at the time, and in the Domestic State Papers at the Public Record Office there are many references, including one that states, 'a Welsh vessel saw the *Mary* underwater', but it would now appear certain that no salvage whatsoever was carried out until the present day. Bronze cannon have always been valuable, and would have been the first items recovered.

For the next 296 years the wreck lay undisturbed. Then, in mid-July 1971, it was accidentally discovered by divers. Who found it first is in question, but certainly the Merseyside Branch of the British Sub-Aqua Club consulted Dr Peter Davies of the Liverpool University, the area representative for the Committee for Nautical Archaeology, and asked his advice. Dr Davies was able to get hold of eight cannon, and commence preservative treatment. Some of the guns are badly eroded or corroded, and may well be beyond treatment.

A point worth noting at this stage is the fact that no one locally knew the name of the wreck. Newspaper accounts suggested she was a seventeenth-century privateer, but others shrewdly suggested a royal ship, and were not far wrong. Syd Wignall, who had been intimately connected with work on two Armada shipwrecks (see Chapter 3), assisted in raising four of the cannon, and then, in conjunction with Dr Davies, set about identifying the ship. Both Peter McBride and Dick Larn, who have worked together for several years on old wrecks (see Chapter 1) were approached, and within a few minutes simultaneously turned up the same name from their wreck files. This information, with details of the vessel's armament, con-

Recovered from the sea: *Above*, one of the two ornamental
bronze cannon, cast in Amsterdam, and presented to Charles II
in 1660 with the yacht *Mary*.
Photo Peter McBride

Below, one of the eight matching bronze cannon, cast in the
Tower of London in 1661 for the Royal yacht *Mary*.
Photo Peter McBride

struction, copies of her drawings and paintings of her at sea under sail, were all made available to Dr Davies, who decided to form a research group and pool everyone's knowledge.

Since then a great deal of work has been done on the site, which lies in thirty feet of water, and silver coins of Elizabeth and Charles I, bar and round shot, musket-balls, lead ingots and pewter utensils have been recovered, as well as a diamond and emerald brooch.

A great mound of ballast is still under investigation, composed not only of lead blocks but of old iron shot, of a much larger calibre than the guns she carried. This was presumably because the necessary weight could not be achieved by using conventional shingle or stone. As already mentioned, a reference exists to the *Mary* carrying twenty guns, and this theory may be supported by the fact that the muzzle of at least one iron cannon protruded from the ballast heap.

There can be no argument that the *Mary*—since it was the first royal yacht—is of great historical interest. However, in this particular case the need for any sort of triangulation survey with meticulous plotting of finds seems unnecessary, as there are few modern wrecks so well documented, and every conceivable detail can be unearthed quite readily.

Found again after 296 years below the sea: The royal yacht of
Charles II, the *Mary*, from a painting by Van de Velde
in Amsterdam.

CHAPTER 5

The Case of the Capsized Captain

*including a dreadful month for the Admiralty in
1691 and the loss of H.M.S. Coronation,
H.M.S. Harwich and H.M.S. Exeter.*

CAPTAIN Charles Skelton knew that his ship was doomed from the moment he gave the carpenters the order to cut the great masts away—and that desperate act did nothing much to right her. It was a race between the sea flooding in below decks, where a great leak could not be plugged, and the rocks of Penlee Point, Cornwall, marked by the white froth and spume driven on the south-east gale.

Skelton's luck—and he had a great deal of it in the twenty years of his Royal Navy career—had finally run out. Within minutes he was to die, with over three hundred of his men, as his ship, H.M.S. *Coronation*, capsized on 3rd September 1691.

Skelton's luck had started in January 1672. He had then every reason to think he was lucky—for he was appointed Second Lieutenant of His Majesty's Ship *Gloucester*.

To a large extent Skelton's fortune would be either made or lost by the ship to which he was appointed. If the *Gloucester* took rich prizes he would, he knew, be entitled by his rank to a good share of the booty. The number of prizes taken by any ship depended not only on the ship but on the skill and daring of her captain.

The man who was captain of the *Gloucester* gave Skelton great confidence in his good fortune, too—for John Holmes certainly was not lacking in daring. And as for skill—well despite the fact that in 1672 Holmes was only just in his thirties, he had seen more than his share of sea battles already, and had not only survived, but also had been promoted time and time again.

John Holmes, Skelton knew, was a man they were already talking of as destined for high office—and not just because his brother was Admiral Sir Robert Holmes.

It was therefore no wonder that in 1672 young Charles Skelton was delighted to be serving under John Holmes. His satisfaction was complete when he found that the *Gloucester* was one of a squadron commanded by his own captain's brother, the famous Sir Robert.

Only one thing may have marred his total happiness. To take prizes it is almost necessary to have a war on your hands. And at the moment—January 1672—there was no war. True, there was a feeling in the air. And Samuel Pepys, that determined Clerk of the Acts of the Navy, was appealing desperately

for money for the Navy, but that in itself could hardly be taken as a sign of a coming war for Pepys seemed to do little else.

But there were people who knew for sure that a war was coming. England must have a great fleet by the spring, for the King and his Ministers were now committed to a secret alliance with the French. Their aim was to destroy the Dutch Republic. England was to sink her fleet and seize her colonies. The French army would attack her on land.

In February the hustle started. The first-, second- and third-rate ships were made ready. But years of neglect did not make the preparation of a great fleet all that easy. Though Charles Skelton joined his ship at Portsmouth, the *Gloucester* was, like other men-of-war, scarcely ready for sea. And by no means all the ships were even there, let alone prepared for action.

Sir Robert Holmes flew his flag in the *St Michael*, and of them all she was probably the best prepared. From the deck of the *Gloucester* Skelton could see other great ships. Close at hand was the *Resolution*, commanded by Thomas Butler, Earl of Ossory. There too was the *Cambridge* of Captain Hollis, Captain Legg's *Fairfax* and the *York*, commanded by Captain Elliott. The lighters went back and forth between the men-of-war, loading shot and powder, provisions and stores of all kinds.

Though there could be little doubt that action was planned very soon, Skelton knew that his captain, John Holmes, was far from satisfied with the stores that the *Gloucester* had so far managed to get on board. And all the time as the stores came aboard the rumours came with them. But the shape that those rumours took upon land was nothing compared to the form those same rumours acquired by the time they got below decks on the *Gloucester*.

Skelton had a vast admiration for his captain, and this esteem never faltered, despite the endless drills that Holmes put his crews through during this waiting time. Daring Holmes was, but daring without a well-trained and disciplined ship's company was not enough. Between drills young John Holmes—and Skelton with him—fumed over the slowness with which his ship was being made ready for war.

On board the *St Michael*, Sir Robert fumed even more. He must have known of the King's design, and that war would be soon forced upon the Dutch. In the first few days of March he could stand the waiting no longer. He sent a rider with a letter from Portsmouth to London, requesting permission to attack homecoming Dutch ships in the Channel. And by a relay of horses his reply came galloping back. It was the answer he wanted. Despite the fact that no declaration of war had been made, he was given permission to attack any Dutch ships he found.

The reason for Sir Robert's impatience to get to grips with the Dutch may well have been patriotism. It may, on the other hand, also have had something to do with the fact that the Dutch Smyrna Fleet was on its way up-Channel, laden with silks and precious goods from the East.

A hurried conference with his captains followed his receipt of permission to attack Dutch shipping. Sir Robert was going to sail regardless of how many ships he could take with him—his whole fleet should have numbered thirty-six men-of-war. He had in fact five, including the *St Michael*.

And with those he sailed to meet nearly sixty Dutch merchant ships guarded by a dozen men-of-war. True, surprise was on his side, but even such a dirty trick was hardly likely to weigh much in his favour when the shooting started.

Young John Holmes was furious when he found that he and the *Gloucester*, plus two other ships, would be delayed several hours behind his brother's little squadron. The reason for this we do not know. It may have been a shortage of stores; it was certainly not planned—for Sir Robert could do with every ship available.

On 12th March 1672 Sir Robert made contact with the Dutch Smyrna Fleet off the Isle of Wight. The Dutch were, it seems, not expecting trouble, and so were surprised by Sir Robert's demand to their Admiral that he should strike his colours.

It was about noon when the meeting took place. With the *St Michael* were *Resolution*, *Cambridge*, *Fairfax* and *York*.

Lest we think too hardly of Sir Robert, it is only fair to say that an eye-witness (from the *Resolution*) of this encounter does say in the State Papers of Charles II (at the Public Record Office) that Sir Robert did fire a warning gun, announced his identity, and called upon the Dutch Admiral to strike. The Dutch Admiral appears to have been puzzled by this request—as well he might, as war had not been declared—and sent his lieutenant aboard *St Michael* to obtain clarification.

The Dutch lieutenant did not, apparently, take too kindly to Sir Robert's ultimatum. 'Having given some saucy language to Sir Robert', he was promptly clapped into the hold, and the fight started with a burst of small shot and full broadside from the *St Michael*. The Dutch seem to have tumbled very quickly to what was happening, because the eye-witness on *Resolution* notes that they formed a line and put their merchantmen on the other side of it.

Sir Robert was, it seems, caught out by this manœuvre, for the whole Dutch line passed him, pouring in shot after shot. By six o'clock that night Sir Robert's *St Michael* was pretty badly shot up, and, in fact, he found the ship so disabled that he moved his flag from the *St Michael* to the *Cambridge*. The fight was now moving down Channel, and Charles Skelton in *Gloucester*, no less than his captain, could hear the sound of guns from far away.

The truth was that the Dutch were putting up such a stout defence that Sir Robert's impetuosity looked very likely to bring about an English defeat. He obviously had not reckoned on the eleven men-of-war, which carried from forty to fifty guns each, nor on the fact that the fifty-six merchantmen were not all sitting ducks. (In fact, some sixteen to twenty of them carried between twenty and thirty guns apiece.) As a result of their fire, the *St Michael* was badly disabled, and the *Resolution* did not look in much better shape. The balance of power when the next day would dawn looked very much in favour of the Dutch.

This balance was tipped slightly by the arrival at the scene of battle very early in the morning of young John Holmes and his *Gloucester*, together with the *Sussex* and another ship. It was hardly a pleasant first glimpse of the face of war for young Charles Skelton. He saw the *St Michael*'s rigging in tatters, she was badly shattered in all decks, and the wounded lay in rows on what remained of her fore-deck.

But at first light the battle was joined again. The opposing ships were now off Rye, and it looked very much as though the Dutch would soon be in home waters with little loss, despite the English treachery.

But Skelton had little time to lick the wounds of war. At first light Captain John Holmes ordered all hands to action stations. The sails filled, and the 50-gun *Gloucester* bore straight down on the 54-gun *Hollandia*, the flagship of the Dutch Rear-Admiral Van Nes.

Closer and closer went the *Gloucester*, and Skelton's nerves must have been strained to breaking-point—for despite the storm of small shot and ball that the *Hollandia* and her sister ships poured upon them, John Holmes held his fire. Closer and closer, and now the *Hollandia*'s sides loomed above the *Gloucester*, but still there came no order to fire.

What Skelton's feelings were at that moment of time we cannot know, but finally, with a crunch of wood on wood, the *Gloucester* and *Hollandia* were locked 'arme and arme'. At that moment, and not before, came the order to the *Gloucester*'s gunners to fire. And the broadside that they fired could not miss. Now the order was to fire at will, and Skelton was far too busy organizing his boarding parties with the *Gloucester*'s lieutenant to do more than register each broadside as a rippling shock through the timbers under his feet.

The *Hollandia* was no easily taken prize. For some hours the battle raged back and forth, but finally Van Nes's crew were forced to strike their colours and their ship was taken into the ranks of the little English fleet. (Van Nes was wounded twice and finally killed by a round shot before his ship was boarded.)

Charles Skelton had borne his fair share of the fighting. In fact he and the first lieutenant had done more than that. Captain Holmes had, at the height of the action, staggered back with a lead ball from some Dutch musket or carronade in his chest. The wound was serious, but not critical, but it did mean that Holmes was out of the later stages of the action.

The *Hollandia* was badly damaged, but was no empty prize. She had eighty bales of fine silk on board, as well as 'much plate'. And Skelton knew that he would get his share. Looking at the *Hollandia* from the damaged decks of the *Gloucester*, it seemed a miracle that the Dutch ship still floated. There seems some evidence that the English who had boarded her and now remained as a prize crew felt the same way and spent some time in transferring the loot to the English ships. They were right to do so. After some hours the *Hollandia* gave a warning lurch from side to side and then sank.

Sir Robert saw her sink from the deck of the *Cambridge*, and knew that *Resolution* and his former flagship the *St Michael* were not in a much better shape. So as soon as night fell he ordered these two damaged ships to the Downs and then continued the chase of the Dutch with what ships he had left.

So the running fight continued up the Channel until finally the next night the Dutch drew away as the wind increased and headed for home. Sir Robert came ashore at Sandwich, and brought with him five Dutch merchantmen that he had taken as prizes.

Gloucester's second lieutenant, Charles Skelton, was now to reap the reward for his coolness in the action against the *Hollandia*. His captain, John Holmes, was knighted for his bravery, and as soon as he was sufficiently recovered from his wound was given command of the *Rupert*. Sir John noted Skelton's conduct in the Smyrna Fleet action as 'highly approved', and when he took command of the *Rupert* took young Skelton with him as 'a person in whose tried courage and conduct I can place the highest confidence'.

Skelton was on his way up. And his luck held once again when he found himself serving under Lieutenant Edward Russell in the 64-gun *Rupert*.

Here his luck lay in serving with a man who bore such a famous name. Edward Russell was only nineteen, but he was the son of Edward Russell, younger brother of William Russell, first Duke of Bedford. And as such was a useful young man to know.

We have no record of how Russell got on with Charles Skelton, but the opportunity to make friends with such a young man would not be one to miss, and there is some evidence in the continuing career of Skelton that they were certainly not enemies. In fact Russell and Skelton fought side by side in the *Rupert* with Sir John Holmes as their captain in the battle of Sole Bay on 28th May 1672, only a few months after Skelton had distinguished himself in the *Gloucester*.

The little-known battle of Sole Bay gave some sort of revenge to the Dutch for the unprovoked attack on their Smyrna Fleet. The English and French fleets, about one hundred ships in all, had sailed from Portsmouth into the North Sea, and put into Sole Bay, Southwold, to water and refit. It was there that the Dutch admiral De Ruyter[1] found them, and, attacking from

the north east with seventy ships, managed to concentrate all his force on the English Blue squadron under the Earl of Sandwich, whose flagship was blown up. At nightfall the Dutch withdrew.

Charles Skelton seems once again to have acquitted himself well, for on 5th February 1673 he was given his first command, the *Speedwell*. Not much of a command, a sixth-rate, but at least it was a ship of his own. From then on he worked his way steadily up until on 12th April 1678 he was given his first big command—the *Staveereen*, a ship which had been taken from the Dutch at the battle in which he himself had taken part several years earlier, the battle of Sole Bay.

Command now followed command. Charles Skelton obviously was a good commander, and had powerful friends—Sir Robert Holmes, Sir John Holmes (from 1677 to 1679 Admiral and Commander-in-Chief in the Downs), and Edward Russell, now captain successively of such great ships as the *Newcastle*, the *Swiftsure*, the *Tiger*. A good captain with friends in high places was a winning combination in any navy, and the Royal Navy of those times was no exception.

The summer of 1680 brought Skelton the command of the *Young Spragge*, and in 1686 the captaincy of the *Constant Warwick*. On 26th November that same year by order of the Commander of the Fleet, Lord Dartmouth, Skelton was upgraded once again to be captain of the *Lyon*.

Charles Skelton was riding high, but although his next appointment meant the command of 660 men and a 90-gun ship, and was yet another glory to add to his distinguished career, it was to end in his death and that of half of those who served with him. This appointment, which was to end in disaster, came early in 1690 when Captain Charles Skelton was given command of H.M.S. *Coronation*. The appointment led Skelton quickly into his last sea battle.

In the year that Skelton took command of the *Coronation* the affairs of England were in a sorry state. William III had taken almost all the troops there were in the country to fight in Ireland against King James's army. This seemed to Louis XIV of France, who supported James, too much of an opportunity to miss. So he started preparing a great fleet to threaten London and invade England. This invasion would, he felt sure, foment a Jacobite uprising in support of James.

The great French fleet was to be made up of two smaller fleets. One under Tourville was at Brest. The other was to be brought round by Chateaurenault from Toulon. The only thing opposing such an invasion force was the Royal Navy, but it was a navy that had been weakened by neglect.

Admiral Killigrew was sent to Cadiz to intercept the Toulon fleet, but missed it. Sir Cloudesley Shovell (to become famous

---

[1] Divers are finding traces of some of De Ruyter's earlier attacks on English ships. Former Royal Navy diver Alan Doick, now a member of Medway Branch of the British Sub-Aqua Club, decided to spend his winter diving time by exploring under the Medway. He hoped to find many relics of ancient days, as the Medway has been associated with the Navy for hundreds of years. After several unsuccessful dives in atrocious conditions—nil visibility, fast tides and the continual hazards of passing ships, not to mention tankers— he and his diving partner, Albert Gates, narrowed their search down to one small area. This was the spot where De Ruyter's ships, in June 1667, broke the boom chain across the Medway after sacking the fort at Sheerness and sank the *Royal Oak*, *Royal James*, *Loyal London*, *Mathias*, and others, before towing away the *Royal Charles*, the flagship of the English fleet. So far Alan Doick and Albert Gates have recovered a variety of cannon-balls and pieces of iron and oak. Most interesting of all, though, is their discovery of a large mud mound under water which they believe may cover the hulk of the *Mathias*.

once again in 1968 as a result of divers' discoveries in the wreckage of his flagship *Association*) was away with six ships escorting some of William's forces to Ireland. The absence of these two commanders and their ships left the English fleet in a weak state, and certainly in no shape to fight the eighty ships of the line and thirty fireships under Tourville.

The English fleet under the Earl of Torrington had, together with some Dutch ships, fifty-five warships and twenty-five fire-ships. Despite this inferiority Torrington took his fleet out to meet the French to the west of the Isle of Wight. The French declined to fight, for which small mercy Torrington thanked God.

Meanwhile Edward Russell had been appointed Treasurer of the Navy in 1689 and Admiral of the Blue squadron in the fleet under Torrington. And in 1690, when Torrington was trying to hold off the French, Edward Russell was playing a rather unsavoury role in politics in London. Because of his political services he felt he should be in command and not Torrington, and it is said that it was his intrigues that resulted in Torrington being ordered, despite his small force, to fight the French fleet.

The order came from Queen Mary and her Council and Torrington had no choice but to seek battle. *Coronation* was one of the ships on which he now had to rely, and it is some measure of the worth in which Skelton was held that Sir Ralph Delavall, Vice-Admiral of the Blue (or rear squadron) chose Skelton and *Coronation* as the ship which would carry his flag, and from which he would command that squadron. Russell, as Admiral of the Blue, should have been in command of that squadron, but was still in London watching the course of events.

Coronation was a fine ship, and, as Delavall obviously felt, a fitting one for a flagship. Launched at Portsmouth in 1685, she was listed as a second-rate man-of-war of 1366 tons with a crew of 660 men. One hundred and forty feet long and with a beam of 44 feet 9 inches, she carried twenty-six demy cannon (32-pounders), twenty-six whole culverins (18-pounders), twenty-six saker (9-pounders), ten light saker (about 6-pounders) and 2 other six-pounders—a total of ninety guns in all. Fully laden she drew some eighteen feet of water.

On 30th June 1690 the battle of Beachy Head began. The result was never really in doubt. Torrington was under orders to fight, but it seems his heart was never in it. The French won, Torrington lost eight or nine ships and withdrew into the Thames, leaving the French masters of the whole Channel.

After the battle Torrington was court-martialled, but no such charge could have been brought against Delavall, who in *Coronation* fought his Blue squadron for five hours against a much stronger force of the enemy. Oddly enough Delavall presided over Torrington's court-martial—Torrington was acquitted, but was superseded and never again employed as a commander.

Edward Russell was made Commander-in-Chief of the Fleet on 23rd December 1690, and naturally enough Charles Skelton remained in command of *Coronation* under him. But Skelton had fought his last sea battle.

During the spring and summer of the following year, Russell tried hard to bring the French fleet to battle. The Fleet, of which *Coronation* was now part, consisted of fifty-seven English ships and seventeen Dutch, but the French were not to be

drawn. Plans were made to attack the French in their ports, but they came to nothing, and not one of the attacks was made.

A bad spring was followed by a worse summer. It was windy and rough, and to these difficulties of the Fleet were added the endless, actionless patrolling of the Channel.

The log of the *Royal Oak* (now in the Public Record Office) shows that the Fleet was anchored in Torbay on 23rd August 1691. The Fleet is almost certain to have included the *Coronation*; the *Harwich* and the *Northumberland* were there for sure.

On Sunday 30th August the *Royal Oak*'s log showed them out on another Channel patrol. Great swirling copperplate writing —to fill up the big space left for the first entry on a page under 'Remarkable Observation and Accidents'—says: 'All Continuing faire and Pleasant Weather. At 8 of ye Clock this morning the West End of ye Lizard Bore NWBW 6 Leagues'.

And it is here, as we examine the last hours of both Captain Skelton and the *Coronation*, that a most extraordinary incident seems to have taken place. Before *Coronation* reached the Lizard she must have come into Falmouth Bay, hove-to and lowered one of her longboats.

On board that longboat was Mr William Passinger, first lieutenant of the *Coronation*. And Mr Passinger's orders from Captain Skelton were quite specific. He was to collect fresh water and provisions in Falmouth.

Why the *Coronation* needed fresh water and provisions within less than a week of sailing from the Torbay anchorage is difficult to understand. Perhaps the provisions were especially for the Captain's table; certainly it was unlikely that such an old hand as Skelton would have failed to refill all his water-barrels while at anchor in Torbay between patrols. But we know that the incident did take place, and what was more extraordinary, that the mission was never completed, because while Lieutenant Passinger was on shore H.M.S. *Coronation* sailed without him.

The attempts to lure the French fleet into action were still going on. At noon on Monday 31st August the log-keeper of the *Royal Oak* noted: 'Still continuing faire weather and Easy Gailes. At Noon Ushant SSE 10 Leagues'. But on the next day, Tuesday 1st September, the *Royal Oak* was only five leagues off Ushant and the weather had changed to 'squally weather blowing verry fresh'. On the 2nd 'still continuing squally freshening weather' with Ushant at eight leagues.

The Fleet now turned back for Plymouth in the early hours of the morning. The weather was obviously going from bad to worse and the log of the *Royal Oak* records 'verry Squally Stormy weather' as the great ships of the Channel Fleet raced for Plymouth and shelter.

The wind that drove them on their way from Ushant to Plymouth was first of all coming from the south, then it swung to the south-west and rushed them on their way, but finally settled in the south-south-east and freshened even more, until it was blowing a full gale.

This was the Fleet's undoing. A friendly wind blowing them home had now turned into a killer. A south-south-east gale was blowing almost at right angles across the entrance to Plymouth Harbour.

The *Northumberland* made it—only to go aground in the

The site of the loss of H.M.S. *Coronation* in 1961.
Above, the site from the shore. *Below*, the site as the diver
sees it – and records what he sees. He's sitting on an overgrown
cannon!

Photo by Jim Gill

Hamoaze, that four-mile-long part of the estuary of the Tamar which has been the principal ship anchorage of Plymouth Harbour for generations of Royal Navy ships.

The *Northumberland* was lucky. The *Harwich* was next in, and she didn't even make the Hamoaze. Captain Robinson of the *Harwich* realized his danger as the full strength of the wind hit him inside the Sound itself. He let go his anchors, but the strength of the wind and the ebb tide setting on shore made his wrecking certain. He was not helped in his attempts to keep off shore by the ships all around him which were doing their best to avoid the same fate.

Despite all Captain Robinson's efforts, he was soon in only ten feet of water at his stern and thirty feet at the bow. Pumping and bailing had little effect, and she was quickly a wreck on the rocky shore. A wreck, but not a total loss. In that position a great deal of the ship, if not the whole ship, could be salvaged.

If the *Harwich* was lost going into the Hamoaze, the *Royal Oak* at first seemed in even greater trouble. She would, it seemed, not get as far in as the *Harwich* and looked like being a total loss. But luck was on her captain's side, and he finally ran fairly gently aground 'under Mount Edgecumbe House' (and after being aground until 9th September was able to lift out her guns and be taken into the Hamoaze for repairs).

The greatest tragedy was reserved for last. Skelton brought his *Coronation* in towards the entrance to Plymouth Sound, but as he did so it seems likely that the wind increased and a gust caught her. She looked as though she was going to capsize, and the battering that she took from the huge seas that were now running had started a leak below sea-level. The *Coronation* was seen to take on a savage list. Skelton realized his danger— later they were to say that his gun-ports were not properly caulked or lined to keep out rough seas—and acted swiftly.

With the amount of water that he had below, his masts were now the danger, accentuating the list until *Coronation* felt as though she was about to turn over under his feet. His orders were trumpeted into the teeth of a full gale, and the ship's carpenters sprang to their task. Within moments the great masts toppled down; they did not need cutting right through before they snapped under their own weight.

Skelton may not yet have realized that he was lost. He was taking in water below decks. His masts had gone, and probably his anchors had been dropped. But nothing it seemed could hold him off the savage rocks of Penlee Point, the most easterly point of Cornwall. The gale now whipped the white spume off the wave-tops and *Coronation* was going even before she grounded on the sea-bed below Penlee Point. When she hit she rolled, for a moment she was seen with her only ensign staff standing, and then she was gone. And gone with her was Skelton and a great part of his crew.

The loss of *Coronation* and over three hundred men ranks as one of the greatest losses of life in any one shipwreck in the history of the Royal Navy of those times. It shocked the town of Plymouth, and, when it became known, it shocked the country too.

It even shocked Henry Greenhill, the Port Agent of Plymouth for the Commissioners of the Admiralty. But Henry Greenhill, being a pompous, miserable, mean man, did not start off with the loss of the *Coronation* in the letter he wrote to the Commissioners on 4th September 1691:

May it Please Your Honours, I have received yours of the 1st instant and shall furnish Captain Evans with what Stores shall be needful for his Ship, if they are in Stores or can be procured and am glad that you are satisfied of the injustice of his late complaints. I have written Mss. Lowes of Bideford whom I employed to hire the vessel for Kinsale to send me a Certificate of the Agreement, which shall be transmitted to you in Order to you making out a Bill for the same.

Yesterday our Fleete was forced into this Harbour by a Violent Storme of wind att S:S:East, the Coronation was unfortunately lost between the Rame Head and Pen Lee Point having first cut all her Masts by ye Board, most of the third rate made for the Hammoze where about Three or Four of them went ashore and the Harwich oversett, but the rest are or will all gett off Shore with little damage.

The Admiral hath directed me to supply such Ships as have received Damage with what is of absolute necessity for enabling them to go up this River, which we are now about and shall use the best husbandry possible and be as spareing as we can, though I fear this unhappy disaster will draw from Us a considerable quantity of Stores.

It is now reported that the Sovereign and the Dutchesse are come into the Sound, who before were missing, and several other English and most of the Dutch Ships have as yett no notice of, and suppose they did not beare away with the Fleete, but there is a rumour of their being in Torbay, God grant itt may prove true.

I beg your pardon for not giving you this Account by Express sent Last night to the Admiralty, having been on board the Elizabeth and other Ships all ye afternoone in wind and raine till late att night and greatly fatigued.

Your honoured and most humble Servant

Henry Greenhill

Plymouth ye 4th September
1691

There was about 22 of ye Seamen belonging to ye Coronation saved in their longboat and drove ashore upon some of ye Wreck, the Capn and Coll. Laston both drownd.

P.S. Since writeing the foregoing I understand that ye James Gally and Portsmouth are come in and have brought with them a Privateer of 14 Gunns they afterwards fell with 4 French Greenland men, Very Strong who engaged them in which engagement Captain Bridges lost his right Arme. I have not yet spoken with the Commanders and therefore cannot give you a more particular Account.

Greenhill is one of the few sources for investigating the last moments of the *Coronation*. The loss of the crew is generally accepted in later years to have been in the region of three hundred men, but there seems no evidence to support this figure. If, in fact, there was a full complement aboard *Coronation*, the loss would seem to have been much higher than three hundred. Greenhill himself seems only to know of twenty-two men saved in one longboat.

And the court-martial into the wreck seems to throw little more light on these losses. It was held on board the *Dutchess* in the river Medway on Thursday 22nd October 1691.

President of the court-martial was Sir John Ashby, Vice-Admiral of the Red. His fellow-judges in the great stern cabin of the *Dutchess* were Captains Jones, Nevill, Lestock, Bokenham, Gother, Hoskins, Edwards, Waters and Baker. And in careful copperplate the clerk recorded that 'all duly sworn persuant to a Late Act of Parliament instituted an Act concerning the Commissioners of ye Admiralty'.

First matter to be dealt with was the loss of the *Harwich* and after hearing the facts the court 'did discharge and acquit Captain Henry Robinson and all the rest of ye Officers belonging to ye same'.

Then came the case of Skelton and the *Coronation*. The clerk's pen squeaked steadily on:

Also enquiry was made concerning the losse of their Majesties late ship ye Coronation, which was oversett off ye Ram-head on ye Coast of Cornwall. Resolved, that the opinion of ye Court is, that by a Butt-head starting, or some Planke giving way Shee sprung a Leake, and thereby was lost. And doe not find that there was any Neglect or failure of Duty in Captain Skelton, Late Commander of ye sd Ship ye Coronation, or any of the officers belonging to ye same.

Allso itt appears to ye Court that Mr. William Passinger Lately 1st Lieutenant of ye Coronation, was absent from ye sd Ship by his Captain's Order, being sent to Falmouth for water and fresh provisions, and therfore the Court does discharge and acquit the sd Mr. Passinger, as to what relates to ye losse of ye Ship Coronation.

There, it seems, the court finished with the *Coronation* and went on to another pressing subject:

James Delgarn Gunner of their Majesties Fireship ye Vultur, was accus'd of Imbezling and taking away some their Majesties Stores belonging to ye sd Ship, viz. two Barrels of Gun-powder, one coyle of Rope, and three bundles of Marline, which matter plainly appearing to ye Court by evidence upon Oath, and allso by his own Confession, Resolved that he is Guilty of ye Charge Laid against him, and that he falls under the Eigth Article, and accordingly does passe sentence that the sd James Delgarn shall bee hang'd by the neck till he is Dead; on Board such ship as the Right Honorable Commissioners of Ye Admiralty shall direct.

Under this sentence of death all the captains have appended their signatures, and though one wonders how long Delgarn had to wait for death, there seems no way of finding out. Nor does there seem to be any other contemporary written record of the loss of *Coronation*. Certainly, even with the help of the vast knowledge of Mr A. J. Norris at the Public Record Office, I was unable to find anything more.

Perhaps there was nothing more written. The Commissioners of the Admiralty soon had other things to occupy their minds—on 12th September H.M.S. *Exeter* of 70 guns was accidently blown up in Plymouth Harbour, and the French had still to be beaten at sea (at the battle of La Hogue).

So the *Coronation* rested, or what was left of her rested, on the sea-bed off Penlee Point. She was not to be found again—though some salvage may have been done shortly after the wreck—for another 275 years.

In 1967 some Plymouth aqualung divers were working over the sea-bed in the region of Penlee Point. The divers, Terry Harrison, Alan Down and George Sandford, suddenly spotted some cannon-balls, and then some more. Few wreck detectives are lucky enough to find such an obvious trail, but it led them close in to the rocky coast until they were about half a mile from Rame Head, and there, in twenty to thirty feet of water, were cannon.

The Plymouth divers kept the position of the cannon a closely guarded secret until they made contact with Lieutenant-Commander Alan Bax, RN, and showed him where the cannon were.

Alan Bax was then still in the Royal Navy, but was already showing signs of becoming one of Britain's leading underwater archaeologists—a position that he occupies with merit today. If you think it is surprising that the Plymouth divers should suddenly reveal their secret to another diver, then it is unlikely that you have met Alan Bax. He is without doubt the essence of honesty and integrity. When others abandoned British waters for the easier kudos of underwater archaeology in the Mediterranean Alan Bax, now retired from the Navy, travelled all over Britain encouraging amateur divers to record their finds in a proper scientific manner.

A leading member of the Committee for Nautical Archaeology, he now runs the School for Nautical Archaeology at Plymouth. SNAP is part of a larger project, the formation of Britain's leading underwater centre at Fort Bovisand, Plymouth. Fort Bovisand is one of twenty-three forts built in the 1860s to defend Plymouth against possible invasion by Napoleon III, and many of the casemates which housed ten-ton muzzle-loaders have now been converted into diving stores, accommodation and classrooms.

From this centre are run courses in all aspects of diving, navigation, underwater photography, seamanship—it caters, in fact, for everyone, from complete novice to experienced diver—and, of course, is heavily occupied with underwater archaeology.

Underwater archaeology in the West Country means the School for Nautical Archaeology, which was first put on its feet by a grant from the British Sub-Aqua Club of £100. At week-end courses at the school throughout the year hundreds of amateur diver students have learned their first lessons in the underwater arts of recording and mapping the sites of the lost ships of long ago.

And so by telling Alan Bax of their find of cannon on the sea-bed off Penlee Point the Plymouth divers had found exactly the right man. Bax had the knowledge, and among the students who attended his SNAP courses he had the manpower, to map the site. He realized almost at once that the only ship of any size—big enough to carry the sort of cannon that lay there on the sea-bed—to have been lost in the area was the *Coronation*. But first he had to satisfy himself by diving exactly what had in fact been found.

On 10th April 1968 Terry Harrison led Alan Bax to the site, and Bax was amazed by what he saw. Conditions were not ideal. The log of the dive reads:

Date: 10th April, 1968.
Divers: Harrison, Bax, Clarke, Swinfield, Fletcher, Mitchell.
Time: 0950–1200
Low water: 1030
Wind: East Force 3
Sea: 3 to 4 ft. swell from S.E.
Air temp: 48 deg. F.
Water temp: 47 deg. F.
Sea-bed: Granite rocks and gullies covered with kelp two to three feet long. Sandy patches in the small clear spaces between boulders offshore. Pebbles and larger stones inshore.
Depth over cannon: 40 to 50 feet.
Current: Nil.
Underwater visibility: 15 to 20 feet.
Weather: Hazy overall.
Diving vessel: 60 ft. steel Admiralty M.F.V.

With his rough sketch-map of the area, Alan Bax included this conclusion: From the above and the Plymouth divers' reports that there are other cannon in the area, I would suggest that this is the wreck of an ancient Man of War/Merchant ship well worthy of investigation and protection.

With this report Alan Bax included a rough measurement of one of the cannon:

11 ft 9 in long and 21½ inches wide at the breech and 19 inches wide at the trunnion. The top of the cannon was flush with the area of 'crazy paving' stones in the area. The top side was weathered flat. It was difficult to tell that it was a cannon as opposed to a long stone. There are, however, signs of rust and indications of the trunnion are just visible.

On 12th May Bax went back with another diving team including his partner, Jim Gill, and got some better measurements. One cannon measured 9 ft 5 in long with a bore of 5½ in, another 12 feet long with a bore of 2 inches.

These measurements in themselves set a puzzle. Alan Bax consulted one of Britain's real experts on ancient guns. In reply to Alan Bax's request for information, Mr Austin C. Carpenter (see Appendix 2) wrote from his home in Milehouse, Plymouth:

Cannon No. 1 appears to be a 24-pounder and I would guess not of English manufacture as the trunnions normally bear some relation to the diameter of the bore. I see by your letter that the trunnions are somewhat enormous, 6 inches in length and nine inches in diameter.

No. 2 I find rather intriguing being as you state 12 foot long with a 2-inch bore. Taking that this is not a mid-nineteenth century breech-loader, it could very well be an early seventeenth century gun, as cannon of long length and small bore were produced in great quantities in the late sixteenth and early seventeenth centuries. However, this is very much conjecture. I am afraid this is a case for either extremely good underwater photography, or raising the pieces for certain identification.

Bax's troubles over his cannon had hardly begun, but he

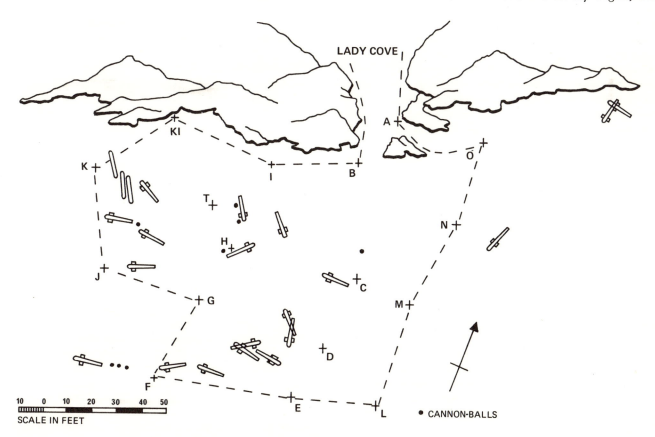

FIG 5 The *Coronation* wreck site at Penlee Point, Cornwall

was not to know that at the time. Nor was he to know that the site of the *Coronation* was to be the test-bed for many new underwater archaeology techniques—though he might have had some suspicions, for many of those techniques were to be introduced by Bax himself!

Throughout the rest of 1968 Bax and his diving teams explored the site as thoroughly as they could, taking measurements of any artifacts they found (see Fig. 5). And this provided another puzzle. The cannon were there—not enough of them to account for all the *Coronation*'s 90 guns—but where were the rest of the items that one could reasonably expect to find on such a shipwreck site? Had they indeed found the *Coronation*? If so, where was the usual sort of shipwreck material? Was there anything else to be found? If so, could they find it?

These were the sort of questions that Alan Bax set out to answer with the help of the divers who were already visiting the School of Nautical Archaeology at Plymouth. Diving on the *Coronation* became part of the course, whenever weather conditions permitted.

So in 1969 Bax hoped that he had two or three years of work ahead of him on the site of the *Coronation*, provided the remains could be left undisturbed. He could rely on the divers who came on his underwater archaeology courses—they had already proved their interest was not in looting by joining the courses—but would the rest observe such high ideals?

Because of his knowledge of the way the Committee for Nautical Archaeology had protected the *Mary Rose* site, Alan Bax decided to do the same, if he could, with the site of the *Coronation*.

So, through SNAP, the sea-bed surrounding the site was leased from the Crown Estate Commissioners. Bax went further. The local Receiver of Wreck was notified, together with other local authorities, of the divers' intentions—and the local Press was encouraged to run articles about the wreck. Bax's idea was not secrecy but to ensure that as many people as possible knew about the site—and its protection.

But Bax was still not sure that he had indeed found the *Coronation*. True, that was the only ship of her size reported lost in the area, but the true archaeologist would need more proof than that.

Bax searched through archives and records of sizes of cannon. He found that at the time of her sinking the *Coronation* probably carried the following armoury: twenty-six 32-pounders, 9½ feet long, on the lower deck; twenty-six 18-pounders 9½ feet long on the middle deck; twenty-six 9-pounders, 9 ft long, on her upper deck; ten 6-pounders, 9 ft long, on the quarterdeck, and two 6-pounders, 9 ft long on the forecastle. If, therefore, the right number of cannon could be found, of the right size and the right date, an archaeologist would be reasonably satisfied that the *Coronation* had been found.

In April 1970 Alan Bax reported on the result of his search so far:

Between April and December last year (1969) some 60 divers have put in an average of two hours each on the site, including a week and a fortnight when members of Hampstead Branch of the B.S.A.C. worked continuously. We seldom had the same divers for more than two dives running, but this still works.

The simple plan we evolved in order to search the area thoroughly, and to survey and plot the position of artifacts found was as follows:

We first laid two marks 'A' and 'B', which were mountain climbing pitons hammered into cracks in the rock, and from 'A' we laid a line South. From this, new marks were triangulated to give search areas about 100 by 50 feet. All marks were tagged with letters providing us with 'signposts' and all finds were given numbers.

The tags themselves were a problem. Many types were tried and the most effective were composed of low density polythene. This material was first suggested and used by Martin Dean of Slough Sub-Aqua Club [see Chapter 8]. The polythene is buoyant and is supplied in sheets so it could be cut to any size. The buoyancy is important, other materials need buoys for support.

Even so marine growth is a problem. It is so fierce in the Spring that numbers are often obliterated in four to six weeks. So we found that markings were best painted on with antifouling just before being taken into the water.

Having laid out the search squares in the sea-bed, which, at the site, is a jumbled mass of large and small boulders covered with a layer of kelp four feet high, the actual search was relatively easy. A light line was laid between two of the North/South lines and divers searched each side before moving sideways in 10 to 12 feet jumps. Finds were then triangulated from the marks.

The method wasn't a complete success. It was cumbersome and not too accurate among the kelp, so we replaced the light line with a tape, held straight and taut by luggage elastic—the stuff used to hold down luggage on a car roof rack—fixed to the tape with a crocodile clip and then looped around a suitably placed piece of kelp. A find could then be fixed quickly and easily by short measurements at right angles to the tape.

Why not cut the kelp? Well, it's easy enough to do with anything from a diver's knife to garden shears, but it takes time and also unless it is all taken out of the water you get great piles of cut kelp drifting backwards and forwards over the site covering up just what you want to see.

We just didn't have the time, so we cut no more kelp than was necessary to clear cannon or triangulation marks. Throughout the year, in visibility that varied from eight to 30 feet, we searched, tagged and measured and gradually our site plan grew and the cannon statistics built up steadily.

We tried out all sorts of things. Underwater paint for marking proved useless. Concrete was successful as a simple means of fixing and identifying marks provided it is jammed in a crevice so that when set it can't be pulled out. It won't bond to rock.

Mosaic and stereo photography didn't give us the results we would have liked, but we learnt enough to be confident of success later on.

That year twenty-two cannon were plotted, and Alan Bax knew there were some outside the area which had been thoroughly searched. The measurements of the cannon set another puzzle. Though Bax admits that they might be slightly out, they did come in three sizes—roughly 9 ft 3 in, 10 ft 3 in and 11 ft 3 in. These sizes do not apparently tie in with the sizes of the guns the *Coronation* should have been carrying. And Alan Bax began to worry—had he found the *Coronation* or some other ship?

The cannon were puzzling for another reason too. The majority of them appeared to have thin 'fins' or 'ears' of iron (see Appendix 2). These 'fins' varied in size from nine to eighteen inches long, three to four inches high, and were about a quarter of an inch wide. Some cannon had as many as three. To the divers they certainly seemed to be part of the casting of the cannon, and were not consistently positioned from one cannon to another. And cannon experts could not explain such things. Were they a sort of eruption of material from the metal of the cannon themselves due to long immersion in sea-water? Or did the ancient cannon-founders put these fins on to cannon for some particular reason? At the time of Bax's discoveries no one seemed to know. So at the end of 1969 Bax was left with more discoveries and more mysteries. In *Triton*, the magazine of the British Sub-Aqua Club, he asked for divers for help in further investigation of the site.

In that year too the first British undersea archaeological work to be directed by television on a ship to divers on the sea-bed was carried out on the *Coronation* site.

This is far from being the first time that television has been used underwater from a ship—the finding of the submarine *Affray* in 1951 was confirmed by a television camera being lowered from the surface—but it was the first time that such a television camera had been used in British waters to direct an archaeological survey of a wreck site.

Alan Bax recalled that 'not only could I see the measurements on the divers' tapes, but the television picture was so clear that I could read the measurements they were recording on their underwater slates'.

The system being used was the 'Hydro-eye', a £3000 TV system with a 17 lb camera. The London firm of Techmation, who took part in the experiment, claim that the camera could see up to two and a half times farther than the human eye underwater because the camera was more sensitive to light at the low levels found under water.

And if the experiment proved nothing else, it showed that the low visibility of British waters would be no bar to having the underwater work directed from the surface, and identification of artifacts carried out by specialists in such fields as ancient armaments, sitting comfortably dry in the cabin of the ship moored over the site.

Then, for a while, both Alan Bax and Jim Gill had to devote their energies elsewhere. Elsewhere didn't mean very far away from the *Coronation* site. The two men were busy turning Fort Bovisand just across the Sound into what it is today—one of the finest places for divers in Britain.

The old gun casemates have now been turned into comfortable dormitories, classrooms and even photographic darkrooms for divers who visit the underwater centre. When the weather

permitted Bax and Gill led teams of 'students' down to the underwater classroom of the *Coronation* site. Four 'scuppers'—those lead pipes set in the ship's side at regular intervals to drain away excess water (see Fig. 6)—were found. As these scuppers are an integral part of the ship's construction, they could hardly have been jettisoned to lighten the ship, as might have been the case with cannon.

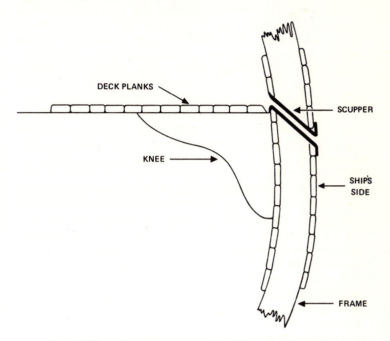

FIG. 6. How the scuppers were fitted into the *Coronation* when she was built

These discoveries meant that the ship had broken up on the site. The 'fins' of the cannon were also beginning to reveal some of their secrets. On one of the dives on the site the famous American marine archaeologist Peter Throckmorton joined the 'attack' on the positive identification of the site (see Appendix 2).

The extent of the site and the whereabouts of the full number of *Coronation*'s cannon have yet to be determined. Over one hundred divers have visited the site out of interest and with great sense of responsibility have left all the material completely undisturbed. But they do tend to say tantalizing things to Alan Bax when they meet him later. . . . 'Of course you know about the anchor . . . the cannon ball heap . . . the funny-shaped piece of iron . . . .' Alan Bax hopes he does, but often suspects these divers have seen something that he has yet to plot on the site map. But the surveying is methodically spreading outward, and only when all visible material is accurately plotted will the loose sand and shingle be carefully removed from the gullies and crevices among the rocks.

Then perhaps a fuller picture of Captain Skelton and his ship's company will emerge. Small personal items may tell us about the people on board and the larger ship pieces will tell more about the ship—perhaps even why such an experienced captain as Skelton came to grief all those years ago.

CHAPTER 6

The Case of the Scilly Shambles

including the loss of H.M.S. Association, Eagle,
Romney, Firebrand, Phoenix, to name but a few.

THE storm which sank the *Coronation* was nothing compared to the one that howled in from the Atlantic twelve years later.

On 13th November 1703 came the first of the bad weather and as storm followed storm, and gale followed gale, few ships ventured out to sea, and those that had done so ran for shelter. This wild weather lasted for nearly a fortnight. Then came a lull. The winds dropped and, though there was still a big swell running, it looked as though the storms had blown themselves out. Shipping began to move again, despite the warning of some old hands that this was indeed the lull before the storm, and that there was worse to come.

Henry Winstanley, who had designed and built the first Eddystone Lighthouse earlier that year, was one of those who ignored the warnings. He wanted to go out to his lighthouse to make any repairs necessary after the two-week battering the structure had already survived. So out he went fourteen miles to the lighthouse, which had a stone base supporting a timber superstructure.

Winstanley and his workmen reached Eddystone Rock without having too much trouble with the swell, and entered the lighthouse safely. The Eddystone light was seen shining out at midnight, but some time after that, in the early hours of 27th November 1703, a full-strength hurricane hit England. There is nothing to equal the severity of that storm in recorded history right up to the present day.

Winstanley and his lighthouse and all the workmen just disappeared. One report of the Great Storm says that it reached its climax just after 1.30 a.m. and continued at full intensity until 4.45 a.m. In those three hours and fifteen minutes the wind swung wildly from south-west to west, from west to north-west and from north-west back to west.

So great was the damage that Daniel Defoe wrote a book called *The Storm* about it, a sort of companion volume to the other disasters he had chronicled in his books about the Plague, and the Great Fire of London in 1666. London had most of its roofs ripped off, and Defoe tried to count the number of trees blown down in Kent, but gave up at seventeen thousand.

Chimneys crashed down, killing sleeping men, women and children. The Bishop of Bath and Wells was one killed in this way. Queen Anne was taken to a cellar under St James's Palace for safety. The lead was ripped off the roof of Westminster Abbey. A hundred elms in St James's Park came crashing down.

In Oxfordshire tornadoes and waterspouts ripped through the countryside. Four hundred windmills were smashed to pieces. The Severn Valley was flooded and fifteen thousand sheep were drowned. Salt covered the grass with a white coating for miles inland where the great winds had carried the spume from the sea. At Cranbrook in Kent the water was too salt to drink for weeks.

But though the death roll on land was surprisingly something under two hundred, despite the huge damage to property, it was at sea that the greatest loss of life took place—more than eight thousand men were lost in ships of every kind.

Such a death roll is not to be wondered at when you know that, amid huge flashes of lightning, the wind reached such a force that most people thought that they were experiencing an earthquake, so much did the houses move—and in some places church steeples rocked so much that the bells rang.

To be afloat in that sort of wind meant you had little or no chance of survival. Daniel Defoe reported on the sight he saw on the Thames—crumpled together in one section of the river were seven hundred craft. They had been ripped from their moorings in other places and all piled together in one heap of matchwood. Scores of men were drowned when they had thought themselves safe at anchor in the river. More than five hundred barges were lost. And nearly one hundred of those were lost between London Bridge and Hammersmith. Cellars right up and down the river banks were flooded. And that was inland. The damage at the great ports—Plymouth was particularly badly hit—was tremendous. Out at sea it was worse.

Eight great men-of-war, the Fleet now under the command of Admiral Sir Cloudesley Shovell, were at anchor about fifteen miles off Harwich at Long Sand Head, when the wind—already blowing a gale—began to gust even harder and to swing from south-west to west. Fifteen miles away, waiting for any unwary ship, lay the Galloper sandbank.

All the ships' topmasts had been struck, but this was not enough. Four anchor cables parted and four ships spun away into the night and the open sea. Shovell could do nothing, he was concerned enough with making sure that his own ship could stay in place against the wall of wind that was now tearing at the rigging. For a while the *Association*, the 90-gun flagship of Vice-Admiral Sir Stafford Fairborne, managed to hold her station, but then she too lost her anchors, and was driven straight on to the Galloper.

Fortunately for Fairborne and his crew, she did not hit on the main part of the dangerous sandbank, but slid over the tail end. This was bad enough. The shallow water was being forced up by the wind into gigantic waves. In the turmoil in those shallows, the *Association* was almost battered to pieces. Seas smashed in her upper gun ports and the tons of water that surged back and forth seemed likely to make her founder. Fairborne ordered holes cut in the deck so that the water could be channelled into the hold, where the pumps could deal with it. So the *Association* survived that mad ride over Galloper sands into easier seas where the crew could make repairs.

But the *Association*'s troubles were not over. The hurricane drove her on through the dark, and as Fairborne and his lookouts strove desperately to see what was ahead there was nothing but the storm-crests hanging as though suspended beside them, before being torn away by the howling wind.

For hours the *Association* crashed on through the night, but as dawn first started to lighten the sky the wind eased a little. At the same time the lookouts saw land ahead and Fairborne was able to anchor off the coast of Holland. The relief was short-lived. Within hours another torrent of wind made their position impossible and *Association* had to run once more—this time to Scandinavia. It was two months before she got back home again!

Even so, the *Association* was lucky. In the northern part of the Downs anchorage off Deal at the time the hurricane struck were nearly two hundred ships, most of them merchantmen. The Great Storm burst upon them and as the wind strengthened from the south-west and then veered to west ship after ship was ripped away. The North and South Goodwins were waiting, and those that missed these deadly sands found themselves on the Brake sands instead.

The men o'war in the anchorage fared no better, perhaps even worse. Two hours after the storm had reached its height, at somewhere around three in the morning, Vice-Admiral Leake on board the *Prince George* was alerted by a cry of alarm from one of the bow watch. Out of the darkness came the huge bulk of the 70-gun *Restoration*. The storm had proved too much for her anchors, and she was dragging at a great rate. For minutes on end both crews strained to hold the great ships apart, and to stop the next shuddering bump from being their last, but then suddenly the *Restoration* swung away—her anchors had, it seemed, finally snapped—and she was gone into the dark.

At dawn the *Prince George* was still there, and so were just a few others. Most had cut away their rigging. Some had even cut away their masts. But the view astern told them just how lucky they had been.

When it was day [wrote Admiral Leake], we saw 12 sail ashore upon the Goodwins, Bunt Head and Brake Sand, amongst whom was Admiral Beaumont in the *Mary*, the *Stirling Castle*, *Northumberland* and *Restoration*, who were all to pieces by ten o'clock, and all the men perished except one from the *Mary* and about 80 from the *Stirling Castle*. It was a melancholy prospect to see between two and three thousand

perish in this manner without a possibility of helping them.

These were big ships: the *Mary* carried 70 guns, as did the *Stirling Castle* and the other two, and each would carry a crew of more than six hundred men.

There are many stories of the shipwrecks on the Goodwins over the centuries, and many tales of the daring of the men of Deal in rescuing such unfortunates. It is sad to say that there are well-documented reports of quite the reverse behaviour during the Great Storm and the lesser winds that followed it. Some of the survivors of the ships driven on to the Goodwins escaped on to the sands at low tide after their ships had broken up. Though the survivors could walk on the sands they could not get to shore because of the deep water channels that cut them off.

The people of Deal did nothing to help, though they had boats out as soon as possible collecting anything of value floating on the waves. They ignored the seamen on the sands, though they knew full well what would happen. When the tide rose great waves poured over the sands, and every single survivor was drowned.

The same thing would have happened on the second day if the Mayor of Deal, Thomas Powell, had not acted. He seized boats by force and saved scores of men from sharing the same fate as those who had reached the sands the day before.

The tragedies on the Goodwins were bad enough, but the same sort of sinkings took place all round the British coasts during the storm.

At Yarmouth, a man-of-war, the *Reserve*, had come in two days before after convoy duty with a fleet of ships from Russia. The captain and the ship's surgeon had gone ashore to buy provisions. At eleven o'clock they stood on shore watching the 60-gun ship sink at anchor with the loss of her entire crew in the huge waves which overwhelmed her. And two more great ships at anchor in Yarmouth Roads were driven on to sandbanks, and broke up without survivors.

At Grimsby almost all the vessels were driven out to sea, and twenty were lost.

At Plymouth three merchant ships were sunk. At Portsmouth several vessels just disappeared. The *Resolution* of 60 guns was driven ashore on the coast of Sussex and lost. The *Newcastle*, 60 guns, was lost at Spithead.

It was the same sorry tale all around the coast. Families of thousands of lost seamen looked as though they would starve, until Queen Anne suggested that the sailors should be considered to have lost their lives in action, and so their families could be granted public funds.

The Queen had been so shocked by the reports of damage and loss brought to her that she decreed that 19th January 1704 was to be a Public Fast Day in memory of those who had died during the Great Storm.

The crew of the *Association* missed that day in England. They might not have taken very kindly to it, as they had suffered enough already on their voyage back home. In fact it was not until the end of January, 1704, that the *Association* anchored in the Medway at last.

The *Association*, despite this, was considered a lucky ship—

The fact that real people died in wrecks is often forgotten in the glamour of the treasures recovered. A stark reminder of those long-lost sailors was this skeleton of a young man in his twenties found under concretion on the site of H.M.S. *Association* Here it is arranged on the bench together with some other recoveries from the wreck.

Photo Mike Ross

lucky to have survived as she did—but it was not to prove so lucky for Admiral Sir Cloudesley Shovell. It may have been his memory of the way the *Association* had coped with that hurricane of 1703 that made Sir Cloudesley choose her as his flagship when he was at Lisbon in March 1707.

In April Sir Cloudesley and the *Association* were off Toulon, laying siege to this great port of France. By 10th April Sir Cloudesley's work was done—the French Mediterranean Fleet was destroyed, and he was free to return home to the triumph that Queen Anne would undoubtedly accord him.

Sir Cloudesley was a great man of his time—rich, famous and, most important of all, much favoured by his Queen. And the great cabin of the *Association* reflected his glory. So sumptuous were its furnishings that the Duke of Savoy had remarked when dining aboard during the siege of Toulon: 'If your Excellency had paid me a visit at Turin, I could scarce have treated you so well'.

But England was calling, and Sir Cloudesley was anxious to get home. On 29th September 1707 the *Association* led the way out of Gibraltar and through the Straits. As she did so a lone vessel joined them from the south. This was the 54-gun *Panther* from Tangiers, and now the fleet was complete and ready for the long voyage to Portsmouth. Fifteen ships of the line, five frigates and a yacht called *Isabella* made up the convoy. At first all went well and they made good progress. On 14th October they had reached latitude 47° North and began to swing to the east to enter the English Channel. But then the storms began. First a gale from the east, then one from the north, then one from the north-west and as navigation in those days was not a very strong part of seamanship, Sir Cloudesley and his ships were soon hopelessly lost. Or if not lost, at best not sure exactly where they were.

On Wednesday, 22nd October, signal flags streamed from the flagship's rigging, well displayed by the south-west wind. And in response to those signals, from all the ships of the fleet came small boats butting through the chop and converging on

70

the *Association*. A meeting of the sailing masters was to be held on board to decide their present latitude. To be fair to Admiral Shovell, as he did not know his position, he was prepared to take the advice of all the navigators at his disposal.

In the great cabin of the *Association*, Sir Cloudesley, large and lusty, whose zeal for the good things of life had in recent years made him run much to fat, listened carefully to all that was said. But even as he listened some of those present got the feeling that he was not entirely with them, but far ahead at his triumphant arrival in Portsmouth. When all had spoken Sir Cloudesley took no decision of his own, but took the majority view as being the right one. And that majority were of the opinion that the fleet was in the latitude of Ushant, and was right in the mouth of the English Channel. Only one voice was raised in strong protest at this assumption. This was Sir William Jumper of the *Lennox*.

Sir William insisted that in three hours' sailing they would reach Scilly, but Sir Cloudesley brushed that view aside and instructed that they were to proceed as though in the mouth of the Channel.

Apparently no one else supported Sir William's views—certainly Sir George Byng, Vice-Admiral of the Blue from the *Royal Anne* and Sir John Norris, Rear-Admiral of the Blue from the *Torbay* would have carried weight if they had agreed with him. But Sir Cloudesley had made up his mind. The majority verdict was the one for him. To underline this decision, and no doubt to impress this contrary sailing master with the error of his ways, Sir Cloudesley dispatched the *Lennox*, with another frigate, *La Valeur*, and the fireship *Phoenix*, ahead of the fleet to announce their imminent arrival to the authorities in Falmouth. By the time the meeting had finished it was after 4 p.m. and getting dark.

The *Lennox* and her sister ships set off, steering on the prescribed north-easterly course. Within a short time the Scillies loomed out of the dark and the *Lennox* was nearly wrecked, but managed to anchor just in time. *La Valeur* also came safely to anchor, but the *Phoenix* was badly damaged crossing a hidden reef, and ended up full of water beached in an inlet between Tresco and St Martins.

After the first glow of self-congratulation had faded from the *Lennox* sailing master's mind, he realized that the other ships of the fleet were sailing in his wake—sailing to certain destruction. There was little he could do. The wind was now blowing hard from the south-west, it was dark, and he was at anchor in a position that meant disaster for his own ship if he moved. There is no record of the *Lennox*'s actions from then on. It may be that she fired guns to warn the following ships, but if she did they were not heard.

Sir Cloudesley was on collision course with the Scillies, and leading his fleet into one of the biggest maritime disasters that England has ever known. And at almost exactly 8 p.m. the *Association* struck. Within moments she was gone, and only a few heads bobbed on the dark waters to mark her passing. The *St George* following was luckier. She struck the same rocks, but managed to get off. The 70-gun *Eagle* was not so fortunate. She went down like a stone with all hands. The *Romney*, 50 guns, sank, and only one man reached the shore. The *Firebrand*, a frigate under the command of Captain Percy, sank too, but five of her crew came ashore clinging to some wreckage, and

Captain Percy and seventeen of his men managed to get to land in a boat.

In a matter of moments it was all over. The ships had gone, and Sir Cloudesley with them. Sir George Byng in the *Royal Anne* had a narrow escape, and but for the presence of mind of his officers and crew would have joined Sir Cloudesley, drowning in the sea. The handling of the *Royal Anne* was superb. She went about, and the rocks slid by less than a ship's length away.

From the four wrecks there were twenty-three survivors—in other words, about two thousand men died in the space of a few minutes. The swiftness of the destruction was obvious to the crews of the Welsh Fleet, who, the next day, had the wretched task of collecting wreckage and bodies. There were seven men-of-war from the Welsh Fleet in the Scillies at the time, and it was boats from the *Southampton*, the *Arundel*, the *Lizard*, the *Salisbury*, *Antelope*, *Hampshire* and the *Charles* which were ordered about this task. Though the sole survivor of the *Romney*, Quartermaster Lawrence, had been badly battered on the rocks before coming ashore, he was still entered on the books of the *Salisbury* that same morning. The *Salisbury* was the ship chosen to carry the exhumed body of Sir Cloudesley Shovell from the Scillies to Plymouth. From Plymouth the body was taken to London for decent burial.

By the orders of Queen Anne there was an elaborate funeral, and a fulsome memorial is still there in Westminster Abbey to mark his last resting-place. You will find it in the South Aisle near the Choir. It depicts Sir Cloudesley reclining, dressed as a Roman. And the inscription reads:

Sir Cloudesley Shovell Knt. Rear Admirall of Great Britain and Admirall and Commander in Chief of the Fleet. The just rewards of his long and faithful Services. He was deservedly beloved of his Country and Esteem'd tho' dreaded by the Enemy, who had often experienced his Conduct and Courage. Being shipwreckt on the Rocks of Scylly in his voyage from Thoulon. The 22nd of October 1707 at Night in the 57th year of his Age. His fate was lamented by all, But especially the Sea faring part of the Nation to whom he was a Generous Patron and a worthy example.

His body was flung on the shoar and buried with others in the sands, but being soon after taken up was plac'd under this Monument which his Royall Mistress has caus'd to be Erected to commemorate His Steady Loyalty and Extraordinary Vertues.

So Sir Cloudesley rests in the Abbey, and this seems to be the right moment to investigate all the legends that concern his death.

Sir Cloudesley was washed ashore at Porth Hellick, a sandy bay south of St Mary's, nearly seven miles from the scene of the wrecks. Legend Number One says that he was still alive when washed ashore and was murdered by two women for the great emerald ring that glittered among others on his fingers. This story is embroidered to include the cutting off of the fingers to get at the rings. This possible fact is followed by the story of one Harry Pennick, who, searching the cove later, found the body and ordered it to be buried in the sand near the spot on which it came ashore.

Legend Number Two says that because Sir Cloudesley had

had a sailor hanged from the yardarm for daring to say that the ships were near the Scillies, grass would never grow on his grave, and never has done so to this day. And Legend Number Three says that the woman who actually had the emerald ring could get no benefit from it—she dare not sell it, because it would have been recognized at once. On her death-bed she made a confession of her crime, and the ring was returned to Sir Cloudseley's family.[1]

Now the facts. We do know that Sir Cloudesley's body was washed ashore and that it was buried on the beach. We know that it was exhumed for the State burial. A letter of the time states that after his body was exhumed it was noticed that 'his ring was lost from his finger, which last however left the impression on his finger as also a second. His head was not at all swelled with the water, neither had he any bruises nor scars upon him, save for a small scratch over one eye as if by a pin'. And Dr James Yonge of Plymouth, who embalmed him, thought it worth while recording that he was paid £50 for the task, but made no mention of severed fingers or wounds. And a letter written by Addison, the Under Secretary of State, dated 31st October 1707, says:

Yesterday we had news that the body of Sir Cloudesley Shovell was found on the coast of Cornwall. The fishermen, who were searching among the rocks, took a tin box out of the pocket of one of the carcasses that was floating and found in it the commission of an Admirall: upon which, examining the body more closely, they found it was poor Sir Cloudesley.

At this moment it is important that we should swing forward in time to 1967 and chart the beginning of what can only be called the 'Scilly Shambles'. Let me stress at once that the blame for this description of what was to happen next lies not with the two civilian and one Royal Navy team who were granted contracts to search for the wreck of the *Association*, but is due to some strange lack of foresight in high places.

Be that as it may, no one would, I think, argue that the credit for the relocation of the wreck of the *Association* must go to Dick Larn, who was at that time a serving Petty Officer in the Royal Navy. As Diving Officer of the Naval Air Command Sub-Aqua Club, a special branch of the British Sub-Aqua Club, he was the instigator of the Navy's search for the remains of H.M.S. *Association*. He was ideally placed for such a search, as he was stationed at H.M.S. *Culdrose*, the Fleet Air Arm's base near Helston. But he was not to know that two other civilian teams had had the same idea. The civilians concerned were Roland Morris, a former 'hard-hat' diver of great experience, and Bob

[1] Mr Roland Morris, who figures prominently in this chapter, says that the emerald ring was made into a locket and is now in possession of Sir Cloudesley's family. He told me that he has seen the smaller ring—a gold band with a crest—after being sworn to secrecy about its present ownership. All he will say is that the ring's hiding-place is 'under a stone in a Cornish kitchen floor'. He believes that sooner or later it will come on to the open market, and finds it ridiculous that after all these years it has to be kept in secret for fear of confiscation.

Rogers and Mike Ross, who had little experience, but matched it with a great deal of youthful enthusiasm.

Claims and counter-claims about who was first on the trail will go on until the end of time, but certainly it was the Naval Air Command Sub-Aqua Club (BSAC Special Branch No. 66) who relocated the wreck in 1967.

As far as the naval divers are concerned, the story starts in 1964. Then NACSAC planned an exploratory expedition to the Isles of Scilly. Dick Larn felt there had been no serious underwater exploration of the area, and part of his preparatory work was to do a survey of all the wreck information around the islands.

Dick Larn, a tall, open-faced diver of great experience, had earlier felt the thrill of research that makes a good wreck detective out of a good diver (he is now the author of several best-selling books about wrecks; see Bibliography) and his investigations into the Scilly Islands surpassed his expectations. When he left for that first diving expedition to the Scillies he took with him a list of over five hundred ships, and on that list were the names of *Association*, *Eagle*, *Romney* and *Firebrand*. There was no secret about them—the wrecking was well documented—and for a time the naval divers concentrated on more modern sinkings.

Then on 27th June 1964 the team found a single iron cannon in ninety feet of water south-east of the Old Town Gilstone, off St Mary's. From this poor eroded specimen the whole *Association* treasure hunt began.

The naval divers thought that the cannon came from the wreck of Sir Cloudesley Shovell's *Association*. (It is now pretty certain that it was in fact from a transport sunk in the 1680s.) The divers knew that the *Association* was sunk on 'the Gilstone', and assumed that they had found the lost ship. Further dives in the area produced an old anchor, nine foot long in the shank. This was it! But it wasn't, and soon the divers realized there were two Gilstones, one where they had found the cannon and the other six miles away to the west, close to the Bishop Rock. Which was the right one?

The period of naval time allocated for the expedition had come to an end, and the rest of the following winter was spent on more research. The divers had scattered to the four winds and their various naval positions, but Dick Larn didn't give up. Early on he realized that he was dealing with a story of a great naval disaster, but he was still finding it impossible to sort out one Gilstone from the other.

Finally to his great surprise he found that the log-books of the surviving ships of the fleet were still in existence in the National Maritime and Science Museums and in the Public Record Office in Chancery Lane, London—and that there were forty-four of them!

Observations in the log-books proved that all the ships that escaped had seen the St Agnes lighthouse beacon, and though their estimates of distance varied widely there was enough evidence to show that the ships had not passed south of St Agnes, and so could not have gone as far as the Inner Gilstone. So the Outer Gilstone it was.

In the summer of 1965 the Naval Air Command divers were once again in the Scillies, and they explored outward from the Gilstone Ledges. We know now that they missed the actual

Bob Rogers (*right*) helps haul aboard a beautiful bronze gun
from the wreck of H.M.S. *Association*. The cannon was inscribed
in Latin, to the effect that it was made by Thomas Pit in 1604

wreck site by just the width of two of the rock gullies which are a feature of the sea-bed there. In fact the reef under water is a mass of enormous boulders and ravines cut in among them. And it may even be that one of the divers passed over the actual wreck site, but failed to spot the outline of cannon or any other man-made object.

But the expedition returned empty-handed, and that autumn applied to the Ministry of Defence (Navy) for permission for 'search and salvage' of the *Association*. There was a great deal of newspaper publicity about the search by now, and still more when the agreement was duly completed—for such a contract was unique. Navy men wanted to use a Navy ship to look for a naval wreck.

What Dick Larn did not know at this time was that the Naval Air Command divers were not the only ones with designs on the *Association* . . . .

By an extraordinary coincidence, Roland Morris, the former hard-hat (helmet) diver and now the proprietor of the famous Admiral Benbow Restaurant in Penzance, had instructed his solicitor to get him the rights in the *Association*, the *Eagle*, the *Romney*, the *Phoenix*, the *Firebrand* and the *Colossus* (this last ship was not one of Sir Cloudesley's ships, but was sunk in 1798 on the Scillies)—at almost exactly the same time as the Naval Air Command divers applied for their salvage permission.

Morris had stopped being a salvage diver in 1959, and had hung up his copper helmet for good. But he was going to carry on with marine archaeology as a hobby. To do this—he had already lost the hearing in one ear from diving, and felt disinclined to risk the other—he formed a team of keen young divers.

With the help of this team he planned to carry out serious archaeological surveys of sunken ships—and he hoped as a bonus to satisfy his long-time desire to own a great gleaming bronze gun from some ancient wreck. The *Association*, he felt, might provide him with just such a prize.

In 1966 Roland Morris got his contract. But as he says in his book about it all (see Bibliography), the contract was not exclusive. It said so quite clearly: 'The salvor is not given any exclusive right to dive and carry out underwater salvage operations on the aforesaid vessels, and the Secretary of State for Defence hereby reserves the right to grant similar rights to any other salvor and salvors'.

It stipulated that the Secretary of State for Defence was entitled to one-half, or one-half of the market value of, anything made of gold, silver, jewellery, precious stones and any 'other objects of unusual intrinsic value'. So in fact Roland Morris, if he found his dream gun made of bronze, would it seemed be entitled to keep it. Any gold or silver coins found would be sold, and the proceeds shared. But Roland Morris did not intend to go to the Scillies with his team until summer 1967.

However, there were other divers in on the hunt too. Bob Rogers and Mike Ross of Blue Seas Divers got their contract for the *Association* in early 1966. The Ministry of Defence had now issued three contracts for the same ship. And the result could have been disastrous. The fact that nothing more than a silly shambles developed is due entirely to the good sense of all concerned.

In the summer of 1966 the naval divers made another trip

Three men and a counting. Douglas Rowe (*left*), Geoffrey Upton and Roland Morris looking at some of the coins recovered from their diving on H.M.S. *Association*

74

Photo "Daily Telegraph"

to the Scillies, but foul weather made most diving impossible. True, the Naval Air Command men got one dive in on the Outer Gilstone, but it was really nothing more than a demonstration that a dive in appalling weather could be carried out if the divers were determined enough. In any case, they found nothing.

For Dick Larn that winter meant research in every spare moment that he could snatch after work at H.M.S. *Culdrose*. And in the archives of the Hydrographic Department of the Navy he made a most significant find. This was a massive chart, hand-drawn on linen, all of six feet square, by Graham Spence of the Isles of Scilly. It is dated 1792.

Its significance lay in the fact that the rock now known as the Gilstone Ledge was then called the Shovel Rock. So Dick Larn had his map—and what looked like a vital clue.

But Roland Morris had his map too. He dived in the Scillies in the 1940s on war work, and had dreamed even then of finding Sir Cloudesley's treasure ship. But it was not until some years later that he saw in an old Cornish manor a copy of a chart drawn by Edmund Gostelo between 1707 and 1711. And that chart, which is in the Public Record Office, has written on it 'On this Gilston Sir Cloudesley was lost'.

Two men with two maps—and another group diving around the Scillies. It had all the makings of a Hollywood film. But no director of any film about sunken treasure would allow the plot to go on very much longer without something dramatic happening. And in 1967 the action really began.

The NACSAC divers timed their expedition to the Scillies perfectly. The sun shone steadily day after day, and the sea around the western rocks was mirror-smooth. Diving started on 2nd July.

That day the divers searched in the deep water to the west of the reef. They found nothing. The next day was the same. But Tuesday, 4th July, was the day. The divers rolled over from the Gemini inflatables that they were using as tenders and they landed on the sea-bed right on top of not one cannon, but dozens! They seemed to be almost in rows. Some were at a crazy angle tipped over in holes, others were clustered together in groups, as though they had rolled overboard in a heap. The area was, as the divers excitedly reported, covered in cannon—and at least three of them were bronze.

The Navy divers, as you might expect, treat this as a team affair, but to be strictly accurate the first diver to see the cannon was Lieutenant-Commander Jack Gayton, the chairman of the Naval Air Command Sub-Aqua Club.

By the end of that week—the divers and the Navy crewmen worked flat out, as they knew their time was limited—they had recovered in conditions of complete secrecy a bronze signal cannon, two breach-loaders, huge bronze rigging wheels, silver coins and the first gold coin to be found, a Portuguese 4000-reis piece dated 1704.

They had tried to raise two huge bronze cannon, but failed. The lifting equipment at their disposal would not take the strain. The Navy now gave the men an extension to continue their work. Bad weather at first held them up, but then with the aid of aircraft lifting bags with a capacity of ten tons each (air-lifted from the Royal Naval Air Station at Culdrose) the first of these magnificent guns glowed its way to the surface.

When H.M.S. *Puttenham* put into St Mary's on the evening of Monday 10th July the cannon was there for all to see hanging from her stern—and the secret was out.

The cannon that the Navy divers had raised weighed over two and a half tons and was richly decorated. The official description from the Navy at the time was as follows:

This piece of ordinance is 9 feet 7 inches from breech base ring to muzzle. It is a sixteen-pounder culverin of French origin, decorated with the crests of Old France and the House of Beaufort. It bears the inscription 'Le Duc de Beaufort' surmounted by the collars of the order of St Michael and St Espirit.

It also bears an eight-pointed cross, which is the badge of St Espirit, the Holy Ghost. The lifting rings have been cast as ornamental dolphins and the barrel forward of the trunnions is decorated with numerous fleur-de-lis and the letter 'L' surmounted by a crown. Top centre and aft of the muzzle ring is a salamander, the touch hole being in the shape of a scallop shell. The remains of an iron ball were found in the breech. (The Duke de Beaufort was the last holder of the Office of Grand Master of Navigation in France and commanded the fleet for Louis XIV until he died in 1699. The cannon was captured by the Navy at the battle of Vigo Bay in 1702.)

The news of the naval diver's find spread swiftly and the newspapers gave it some splendid headlines. Sir Cloudesley Shovell was news again—260 years after his death. Both the other contract-holders have recorded the way the news affected them.

Roland Morris in his book wrote: 'This news sent our blood pressure soaring, our anxiety complex became almost unmanageable, for this was exactly. the area where we were intending to dive on our arrival in the Islands planned for the last week of July 1967'.

And Mike Ross of Blue Seas Divers in an article in *Triton*, the magazine of the British Sub-Aqua Club, wrote:

No sooner had we set out on our plan than the news 'Navy Sub-Aqua Club Locate Association' appeared. More reports followed: 'Cannon, Gold and Coins found on wreck', '9 foot 6 inch Bronze Cannon Raised'. We were stunned. We had a contract, but it was useless without money to support us. There was no other course but to get another partner with financial backing to join us . . . .

There is no doubt that at that moment the Scillies was the centre of attention of the European diving world. Everyone wanted to get in on the act. And many did.

Though the contract-holders hurried to the scene and got down to the wreck site of the *Association* as soon as they could, the fact that they had contracts was not of great importance. The shambles had begun. The invasion of the Gilstone by divers of all sorts was not illegal. Anyone can dive on the wreck of the *Association* and bring up what they like, provided they hand what they recover to the Receiver of Wreck. In these circumstances the non-exclusive contracts handed out by the Ministry

Discoveries from H.M.S. *Association*, sunk on the Scillies in 1707
These silver coins – the odd shapes are the
Spanish pieces of eight – were found in their thousands by
divers under the rough waters over the wreck site

Photo Mike Ross

of Defence afforded no protection.

But Roland Morris was not cheated of his dream of possessing a bronze cannon—in fact he and his team raised three beauties. But the best of all was the first to come up after he had blasted two rotten old iron cannon out of the way.

It is difficult to describe the thrill that looking at one of these ancient cannon recovered from the sea gives to you. I know that when Roland Morris showed me that first prize of his in the Admiral Benbow in Penzance, my instinctive reaction was to reach out and stroke it. For these are no battered old guns, these are highly decorated works of art. This first culverin of Roland Morris is without doubt the best of them all. The lifting eyes are two dolphins. And instead of the name 'Le Duc de Beaufort' on the NACSAC gun, this one has 'Le Comte de Vermandois' on it. The decorations gleam and wink in the light, and the sight for aiming this fine piece is a delicately worked lizard or salamander. If you are in Penzance go and see it at Roland Morris's museum.

If there was any doubt about the origin of these bronze guns it was all cleared up during the cleaning of them. Roland Morris would go down each night into the cellar where his men were working on the long task of removing the encrustation and verdigris of centuries under water to see how they were getting on. One night he could hardly believe his eyes, for there, in crude letters two and a half inches high and cut three-eighths of an inch deep into the bronze of one of the guns, was the word VIGO.

'Good Lord!' exclaimed Morris, 'Why wasn't I told about this?' When the significance of the marking was explained, one of the men said: 'If it had been WIGAN we still wouldn't have known!'

The importance of the marking is obvious, but the reason for it was probably to make sure that the gun was identifiable as loot from the battle of Vigo when put among all the other prize pieces on board the fleet or else to help with the division of the spoils.

But back now to the stormy waters around the Gilstone. There was an attempt to stir up a storm over Morris's use of explosives, but such protests only show that the protesters have no idea of the *Association* site.

There is no wreck. And such artifacts as there are there have been moved many times by the sea. A careful survey and plan of the site would be of some use if you could guarantee a proper excavation, but when you know that the sea there in a storm moves around boulders weighing several tons, it does seem that archaeologically this is a site more suitable for the recovery of objects than surveying them. This, of course, goes against all archaeological practice, but there have to be exceptions to every rule.

The Ministry of Defence (Navy) did issue a statement saying that they would revoke the agreement of any contract-holder if explosives were used. But as such a ruling could not apply to the non-contract-holders it seems pointless.

Dick Larn, writing about the 'to blast or not to blast' argument in *The Second Underwater Book* (see Bibliography) puts it bluntly:

Had explosives not been used where necessary, then half the artifacts recovered would still be on the sea-bed . . . . One thing is now very obvious, if Mr Morris hadn't worked the wreck as he did, in all fairness, no one else would have taken the gamble and for that reason he deserves every praise.

The divers who worked the wreck commercially were very conscious of the value of the items they were recovering. On several occasions they worked for hours to recover the intact sole of a leather shoe or a riding spur, or just a mangled 'something' because it looked interesting. It would have been all too easy to have ploughed through everything with hammer and chisel to get at the specie.

Some idea of the care taken by these men can be seen if you visit the Isles of Scilly Museum. On display are a matching pair of spurs, a silver ladle, a sand box and seal and many other small items all carefully dug out from the marine growth of 260 years.

Dug out? What, then, is the site like? One thing is certain— it is no place for beginners. When the sea is calm everywhere else, it is still working on the Gilstone. Great waves have been known to erupt without warning from the 'calm' of the sea, and the divers—at one time there were five rival groups working the wreck—accepted them in the end as a normal hazard. As they all seemed to follow the same course, these waves were fairly simple to avoid with experience.

Mike Ross describes the site under water as a canyon—a maze of gulleys, jumbled boulders and caves under these boulders. Tons of granite from rock falls have completely obliterated parts of the site. These are Ross's words:

> There is no wreck as such to be seen, just the cannon and the anchors scattered over an area as big as two football pitches. Some cannon are 30 feet down in fissures in the rock. All manner of tools besides the usual hammers and chisels were needed. Coins and artifacts were usually covered with 'crud', hard layers of conglomerated iron oxide and pitch, and had to be dug out with hoes, shovels and even pickaxes. Explosives were essential fairly often in the search to clear the rock-falls and crumbling iron cannon. But these were used with great care.

Dick Larn says: 'The most successful diver on the Association was the one prepared to work the hardest. Coins on the Gilstone are hard won, but the rewards are high'. And rewards were high. One gold coin fetched £170 when sold at the July 1969 London auction.

With such rewards it is not surprising that archaeology came off in many instances second best. But it is also worth noting that at no time did the anticipated 'punch-up' take place between the divers who were working the site. Rival boats tied up to one another, and there is no doubt in the minds of all those involved that had any emergency arisen every man would have gone to the rescue of the other, no matter to which group he belonged. Divers are often accused of being mad or ruthless or both, but there is a bond between them which no surface-bound avarice can break.

Places on the wreck site acquired names recognized by each and every *Association* diver—'Cannon Gully', 'Death Gulch' or 'Aladdin's Cave' were just a few of the names that could be instantly identified by any diver working the site.

'Aladdin's Cave' was the one which rated the most wordage in newspaper reports. It was in fact a hole under a boulder, from which Mr Morris's divers raised some 1400 silver coins in six hard days' diving.

Coins, cannon, cannon-balls, gold wedding rings—inscribed 'God above increase our love', 'True love is endless'—bronze pulley wheels marked with the broad arrow symbol of the British Government, dividers for navigation, silver spoons,

thimbles, a chamber pot, a dagger hilt—the divers found them all.

Removing a huge iron cannon led Mike Ross and Bob Rogers to the strangest find of all. Preserved in pitch and iron oxide was a skeleton. Pieces of eight were stuck to the skull—pieces of eight that had come from a mint in South America.

But the divers were still tormented by the same question that worries archaeologists everywhere. All right, the coins were all the right date (there was not one later than 1707), the cannon and pulley wheels conformed to the theory that this was Sir Cloudesley Shovell's ship. . . . But was it? There was no single item that was absolute confirmation that this was H.M.S. *Association* among all the treasures that the divers had brought up from the Gilstone.

And for the contract-holders this was vital. Their agreements depended on this being the *Association*. It was up to them to prove that it was.

In October 1969 Bob Rogers was diving with Terry Hiron, who now runs diving holidays in the Scillies, when they made a discovery that might be the clincher.

Says Bob Rogers:

> We saw it first buried 12 feet under a huge boulder. Only the breech showed when a torch was shone on it. We managed to lasso it with the help of a noose and a ten-foot rod. Once we had the rope firmly around the breech we tied the other end to our chartered diving boat Nemo—then opened the engine full out.
>
> The cannon came out with a rush, but it took the combined efforts of the skipper, Peter Thompson, and eight of us to get the cannon off the bottom and up to the surface.

The boulder that had trapped that cannon weighed at least 100 tons, and the team could never have lifted it off, but the cannon came free fortunately—because it was unique.

Most of the other bronze cannon finds had been French, presumably the spoils of war, but this one was English. It was ornately decorated from breech to muzzle with such embellishments as the Prince of Wales's insignia and *Ich Dien*, but it bore a Latin inscription on a plaque near the breech. In free translation the Latin read: 'Charles, Earl of Devonshire and Master of Ordnance, commissioned Thomas Pit to make it in the year 1604'.

Perhaps this cannon was one of the Admiral's favourite pieces. Who can tell? But one thing was certain: instead of confirming that the ship was the *Association*, it left it even more open to doubt.

What was really needed was the discovery of some piece of evidence that was absolutely impossible to deny, and in the winter of 1969 Roland Morris and his team of divers found it. To them goes the honour of the final identification of the wreck —a justifiable honour, because of all the teams they had been the most persistent. Identification came in the form of a solid silver plate. When it was cleaned the arms of Sir Cloudesley Shovell gleamed out clearly. Diver Mark Horobin with his find had made identification certain.

After eighteen months of consideration the Ministry of Defence (Navy) announced that any items salvaged which were once the property of H.M. Government—that is, cannon, ship's fittings, other than personal property and coin, became the property of the finder—provided that the finders held MOD (Navy) contracts.

This meant that the NACSAC team, Roland Morris and Blue Seas Divers could keep many of the items they had found. Objects found by non-contract holders would receive consideration according to their value. But all specie, coins, rings and other personal items were to come under the usual Board of Trade regulations and would be auctioned—the finder to receive one-third of the sale value. So that was that. Roland Morris by his discovery of the silver plate had clinched matters.

At the auction at Sotheby's on 15th July 1969 two bronze cannon were sold for £3000 each. A Portuguese reis of 1707 made £160 and a French Louis of 1694 fetched £150. And the sale of coins and other items together brought a total of £12,354.

Now the divers had a breathing space—and we can take time to consider just how much of value there really was on H.M.S. *Association*. There were many fanciful stories about ships wallowing along heavily weighed down with treasure, but the true picture is more difficult to assess.

The Scilly Islanders were no fools, and it is doubtful if they would have allowed a fortune to remain undisturbed right on their front doorstep. Dick Larn says that it is not generally known that the wreck of the *Association* survived almost intact for a considerable time. And his researches have shown him that part of the ship showed at low water. Roland Morris's research shows that the main mast stood above water for some time.

Several bronze guns as well as iron ones and anchors were reported recovered. The amount of coin and plate also recovered is curiously enough not noted.

The trouble is that it is extremely difficult to find out exactly what was in the *Association* at the time of her sinking. Since the day she was lost she has been described as a treasure ship carrying at least a million pounds in coin, but there is no evidence of anything like that at all.

Was she carrying loot from the battle of Vigo Bay, some five years before? Did Sir Cloudesley have some private loot from the destruction of the Mediterranean Fleet, only months before? That is very possible. So is the idea that she had large sums aboard from British merchants who had been trading in Portugal, and wished a proper protection for their money on the voyage home. In addition to this she would of course had carried the fleet's money, and a deal of the Admiral's own. If he entertained on the scale that appears to be documented it seems likely that Sir Cloudesley would have had need of quite a supply of something more than small change. And we know from items recovered that he carried at least some of his own plate about with him.

One thing is certain. There were thousands of coins aboard—for the 1968 divers were late on the salvage scene, and they recovered quite a number.

The Navy's Deputy Paymaster Herbert was first on the salvage scene in 1709. He ordered a base camp for such salvage set up on Rosevear, and in July 1710 *The London Letter*, a Scottish newspaper, stated:

We hear from Scilly that the gentlemen concerned in the wreck where Sir Cloudesley Shovell was cast away, have taken several iron guns and seven brass guns with a cable,

and have found the Association in four fathom at low water, the hull of the ship being whole, wherein there is a vast treasure—the Queen's Plate, several chests of money, besides ten chests of Sir Cloudesley's own, with great riches of the Grandees of Spain.

The Divers go down in a copper engine, and continue two hours under water, of 30 fathoms deep, where they have also met with the fireship (cast away at the same time as the Association, I don't know her name). Had not the winds been westerly, which occasioned the seas to be very high and boisterous, all the Treasure before this, had been fished out.

But this was not the end of the salvage work which continued until about 1740. The site was visited again in 1852 by men working on the Bishop lighthouse, and again by divers recovering gold from the *Schiller*, which sank in May 1875 east of the Bishop with the loss of 311 lives. (The *Schiller* was carrying £60,000 in gold American 20-dollar pieces. By 6th May 1876 the divers recovered some £57,712 of this amount.)

There seems to have been no more salvage after that until the Naval Air Command divers relocated the wreck, but all those divers of the past must have taken their share of the *Association*'s treasure. What was left?

At the Sotheby's auction on 28th January 1970, the second sale of items from the *Association*, £310 was paid for a Peter II 4000 reis of 1705 and a John V 4000 reis of 1707, the year of the wreck, went for £190. Roland Morris bought back the plate which had identified the wreck for £2100 and it can be seen today at his Museum of Nautical Art in Penzance. A pewter chamber-pot of about 1700, which had also been recovered, sold amid laughter for £270—as it seemed likely that this was the Admiral's own. The laugh was on the spectators, for Roland Morris bought back the pot—only to find two gold coins encrusted under the rim!

The total for the sale was £10,175, making the amount raised by objects from the wreck up to that date to £22,529. This amount was in reality quite small—but then so was the number of coins that finally found their way to the Receiver of Wreck and the saleroom.

Roland Morris, who has been on the site for most of the time since the discovery of the wreck, has no doubts at all about what has happened. He believes that unauthorized diving has robbed the wreck of hundreds, possibly thousands of coins, which will never change hands in any official transaction. And he rightly points to this as another example of the ridiculous state of our laws about salvage—and in particular the issue of non-exclusive contracts. He believes too that we have only just 'scratched the surface of what there is to be found on the site—in ten or 20 years time there will still be pieces of gold coming up!'

The truth, of course, about the Scilly Shambles is that our maritime law is not adequate to protect the individuals whose efforts and daring make such historic finds possible. Britain needs a law which protects archaeological discoveries of historic value. And such a change in the law in long overdue.

No-one would be surprised if such men washed their hands of the whole affair and went diving on a strictly commercial basis—but it is pleasant to be able to record that Roland Morris and Dick Larn are continuing to dive and survey such ancient wrecks. When the *Association* affair died down Roland

Morris turned his attention to the other ships of Sir Cloudesley's fleet that were lost on that disastrous night.

Late in 1969 the site of the *Romney* was found on the Crebinicks Rocks and a large bronze bell and navigational slate were raised and then on 29th May 1970 a diver working for Roland Morris found the *Eagle*.

The *Eagle* was one of the ships named in Roland Morris's contract, and so it was only right and proper that one of his divers, 32-year-old Peter Grosch, found her in 135 feet of water, due west of Zantmans Rock on the Crims Reef. He found twelve small cannon and two larger guns.

Following this discovery the Naval Air Command Sub-Aqua Club, who had been the team to find the *Association*, dived there to survey the site, led by Lieutenant B. Miners. In the NACSAC team again was Chief Petty Officer Dick Larn. The report of their survey was submitted to the Committee for Nautical Archaeology.

The Crims Reef is more than half a mile long, and has deep water on both sides (see Fig. 7). It is very remote, and is exposed to winds from all directions, except the east. Atlantic rollers smash on the reef almost all the time, and even in the height of summer huge ground seas can build up very swiftly. Only six rocks break the surface, and at high tide only two of these still show.

Some idea of the diving conditions are given in the naval divers' survey report:

The average depth of water over the reef itself is between 25/30 feet, when it then falls sheer on the Western side to 130/150 feet and somewhat less on the inshore or Eastern side. Underwater visibility is usually in excess of 60 feet, and with huge towering peaks and almost frightening 'drop-offs' the Crims make spectacular, deep and often 'hairy' diving.

While surveying the site (see Fig. 8) the Navy divers moved down to the southern end of the Crim Reef, and, in the vicinity of Crim Rock and Tearing Ledge, they found the remains of two previously unknown wrecks, both iron sailing-ships of about 1875.

Back on the *Eagle* site, the divers found at the bottom of a steep underwater cliff face in 135 feet of water that there were eighteen cannon scattered on rock ledges and along a boulder-strewn gully with a sandy bottom. There was no apparent order in the lie of the cannon, and the divers' immediate impression was that they may have tumbled or slid down the face from shallower water. Apart from the cannon the most obvious wreck signs were two large iron anchors, both stockless,

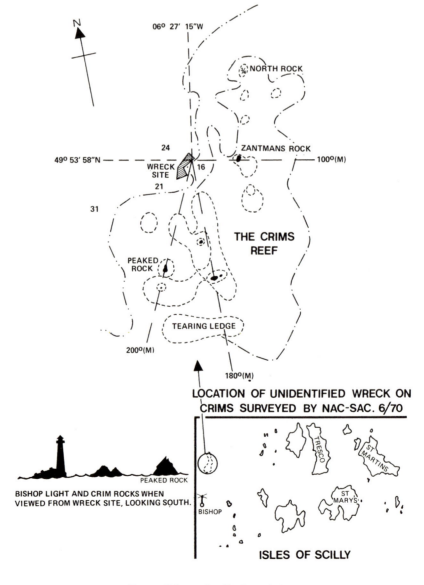

FIG. 7. Where the *Eagle* sank in 1707
Based on a drawing by Richard Larn

measuring nine and ten feet in the shank. One has a ring missing.

There were, of course, other wreck items, such as small brass guns, sheet lead, scupper pipes, and earthenware pottery. But the naval divers, well aware that Mr Morris has a contract for the wreck, merely raised two clay pipes for dating purposes and a badly damaged ship's bell about nine inches in diameter and twelve inches tall. The bell, which was very fragile, was devoid of any markings—it could be from a Dutch East Indiaman sunk in 1743—and has been handed over to Mr Morris and can be seen in his museum in Penzance.

Mr Morris's diver, Peter Grosch, had earlier brought up a pair of brass ship-navigator's dividers and five silver coins. Roland Morris believes from his researches into the loss of the *Eagle* that her master may have seen the sea breaking on an exposed pinnacle of the reef and tried to get clear by altering course to starboard. He had turned the wrong way. The open

sea lay to port, and to starboard was another submerged pinnacle waiting for the ship's bottom.

The guns on the site seem very few. But there is some evidence that all the ships in Sir Cloudesley's little fleet had reduced the number of cannon normally carried before sailing from Gibraltar in 1707. The *Association*, for example, was usually either a 90- or 96-gun vessel, but Dick Larn believes that in all the number of guns on the *Association* site (including those recorded as salvaged at the time of the wreck) is only fifty-six. But those old records are suspect, and no one can say for sure just how many cannon there should be left on the sea-bed at any particular site.

The *Eagle* site also presents other problems. Both Dick Larn and Roland Morris believe there may be more than one wreck on the site, and that an even older ship's remains may lie mingled with those of Sir Cloudesley's ship.

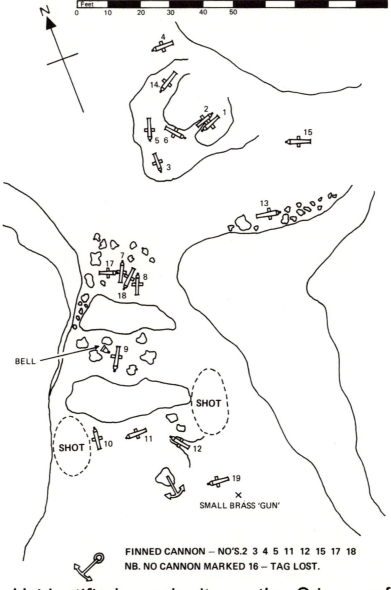

Unidentified wreck site on the Crims reef

FINNED CANNON — NO'S.2 3 4 5 11 12 15 17 18
NB. NO CANNON MARKED 16 — TAG LOST.

FIG. 8. Site plan of the Navy divers' survey of Crims reef

CHAPTER 7

The Case of the Love that was Lost

including the Kennermerlandt, 1664, and other Dutch East Indiamen, such as the De Liefde (1711) and the Amsterdam (1749). Here too is the sad story of the going down of H.M.S. Assurance, 1753.

SALVAGE work was still going on in the Scillies on the wreck of H.M.S. *Association* when another rich ship went down at the other end of Britain. Thousands of silver coins have been recovered from this ship, yet the diving work on her never captured the public imagination in the same way as the recoveries from the *Association*. Why, it is difficult to say—particularly as this is the only wreck I know of in British waters from which a treasure chest complete with silver coins was raised to the surface!

De Liefde ('The Love') was built in October 1701 for the Dutch East India Company, and the 150-foot-long ship was designed for voyages of two years to Batavia and back. She made three successful voyages to the East, but never completed the fourth.

Her master, 39-year-old Barent Muijkens, was caught in a gale on the night of 7th November 1711 and decided—there was nothing much else he could do—to run before it. In the early hours of Sunday 8th November, the *Liefde* stopped running. She crashed into the sheer cliffs of the Out Skerries, about fifteen miles north-east of Lerwick, in the Shetlands.

The impact must have been tremendous, for only one man survived it. He was found wandering by the islanders after they came out of church, but all the rest had drowned in the foam at the foot of those steep rocks.

As the crew of *Liefde* consisted of at least two hundred seamen and one hundred soldiers, that meant that some three hundred people had drowned in the wreck. Gone with them were trading goods and supplies for the company's staff at the Cape and in Batavia. Gone were all the foodstuffs that were to keep the men alive on the long voyage. And gone too were some chests of very important cargo.

The minutes of the meetings of the 'Gentlemen Seventeen' (as the directors of the Dutch East India Company were called) show that they intended to ship some 1,850,000 guilders from Amsterdam in ten ships that autumn. This means that *Liefde*—if she carried her share—would be laden with nearly 200,000 of the silver coins. Records after her sinking say that 227,000 guilders were needed to replace the loss.

The Shetland Islanders undoubtedly recovered from the wreck all they could reach, and two Dutch divers in 1712 said

that they couldn't raise anything (well, that is what they reported!). Then in between 1729 and 1735 a 'London Diver' is recorded as having recovered some 2000 ducatoons and 160 ducats (and we have only his word for that!).

So there what was left of the *Liefde*'s treasure remained for 229 years until in 1964 H.M.S. *Shoulton* with naval divers on board visited the site and found two silver coins, which were presented to Lerwick Museum.

The naval divers also found a cannon, but had no time left to raise it. But another diver did the job—Mr Eric Giles—and presented the cannon to the museum too.

In the spring of 1965 John and Peter Bannon, together with a friend, Michael Harrison, became interested in the wrecks around the Shetlands. They formed a small expedition to search for another Dutch East Indiaman, the *Kennermerlandt*, sunk in 1664. This ship was also reputed to be a treasure ship, and the Bannons added to their expedition two Service divers of experience—Lieutenant-Commander Alan Bax, RN, and a Royal Marines Officer, Malcolm Cavan.

Once in the Shetlands they heard the story of the cannon raised by Eric Giles, and decided to search that same area. Bax dived first, and found only a carpet of kelp covering a rocky sea-bed. Despite underwater visibility in excess of fifty feet, he could see nothing remotely resembling a wreck site. Then Malcolm Cavan dived in another spot. Within two minutes he surfaced, waving frantically. First thought was that he was in trouble, but as the others brought the boat closer they could hear what he was saying—'I've found it, I've found it!' And the proof was in his hand—two silver coins! So they had found an ancient wreck with coins in her cargo. But it wasn't the *Kennermerlandt*. It was the *Liefde*, wrecked some fifty years later in the same area.

After that first discovery expedition was to follow expedition to the site. Alan Bax has told the story of some of those expeditions in a chapter in *The Second Underwater Book* (see Bibliography), which I edited for the British Sub-Aqua Club. In his report on the diving site he says that that the granite cliffs, which *Liefde* struck, rise from fifty feet under the sea to nearly one hundred feet above water. The divers nicknamed the main work area 'Silver Gulley', and it is a jumble of boulders large and small in among a thick layer of kelp standing some three feet above the bottom. Visibility is seldom less that thirty feet, and the water temperature was an average 52 degrees Fahrenheit.

The divers found that all the artifacts including most of the coins were buried in a hard black substance, and this matrix was largely composed of sulphides. It seems almost as though it had been poured all over the site and the coins came out cemented together in lumps. How and why this matrix was formed no one quite knows, especially as in places it is nearly eighteen inches thick. It was this thickness that saved the treasure chest from destruction for some 258 years. The protection given meant that some of the wood of the chest was in almost the same condition as it was when the ship sank centuries ago.

Once all the measurements possible had been taken explosives were used to break up the rocks covering the site. Then everything possible was raised by hand and by air-lift to be sifted through in the boat. This use of the explosives was justified on the same grounds that Roland Morris gave for his use of them on the *Association* site. There was no other way of prising out the larger rocks which were solidly jammed in position over vital parts of the site. Every single find was listed day by day, and each item was plotted in properly on site plans. Here, for example, are the finds for two days taken from the lists of August 1968.

August 12th: 8 Ducatoons, 1 small piece of gold coin, 16 Knife handles, 1 Small piece of bell, 1 Lead stopper, 1 Wrought iron nail (3 inches long), 2 Fruit stones, various pieces pipe stem, glass, pottery, canvas, metal, and brass lock.

August 13th: 19 Ducatoons, half a cannon ball, 1 Piece of string, 1 Musket ball, 1 Small pewter spoon (in half), 2 Small wrought iron nails, 1 Piece of knife handle, 4 Small brass pieces, 1 Small piece of lead, various pieces pottery, wood, metal and bar shot.

Day by day, expedition by expedition, the divers—including such well-known names in the diving world as Jim Gill, Owen Gander, Stephen Halliday and Ian Morrison—worked on.

They found more and more evidence of the way the sailors had lived all that time ago, and more and more evidence of the kind of materials carried in a Dutch East Indiaman, but there was one major group of items missing despite all their searching.

Where were the cannon of the *Liefde*? It is true that one cannon had been found on the site—a 12-pounder raised by Eric Giles and the Shetland Islanders in 1964. But search as they might, the later divers could find no more. And there should have been another thirty-nine of them. The 150-foot-long ship with a beam of 40 feet had displaced about 500 tons, and her armament was listed as: ten iron 12-pounders, two bronze 8-pounders, eighteen iron 8-pounders and ten smaller guns.

Missing too were the eight anchors the ship would have carried—and some would have weighed more than a ton each. The divers found plenty of signs that guns had been there once. There were plenty of cannon-balls for all the weights of guns, including bar shot. The divers even found four breeches of her

four-pounders consecutively numbered and stamped 'VOC'—the initials of the company (Vereenigde Oostindische Compagnie), but still no cannon.

The only answer, of course, must be that some of those early salvors had been very good at their job, and very silent about just how much of her treasure they had recovered.

The work still goes on in the Shetlands. The vast majority of the coins discovered have been silver ducatoons dated between 1632 and 1711. Most have been in good condition, having been protected by that black matrix. The coins in the chest numbered 4000, and all were dated 1711, presumably newly minted the year that the *Liefde* sank. Some of the coins recovered have been auctioned in London, and the Dutch Government bought some lots at the sale, which realized over £14,000. John Bannon, as managing director of Scientific Survey and Location, the firm formed to deal with the exploration of the ship, has been co-operating directly with the Dutch Government as official owners of the ship.

The divers on the *Liefde* may have also located the *Kennermerlandt* site—the ship which sank in 1664 and which they originally set out to find in 1965—for on another dive in a different place they found a very badly corroded cannon in such a poor state that the barrel has disintegrated on one side, revealing the bore.

* * * * *

In 1743 a Dutch East Indiaman, under the command of Captain Jan Kelden, reportedly carrying 250,000 silver coins, was lost on her first voyage with all on board—276 passengers, soldiers and crew—off St Agnes, in the Scilly Islands.

For over three years a former Hampstead solicitor, Rex Cowan, searched for the *Hollandia*, covering both the sea-bed with his team of divers and the records of the East India Company in Holland.

At the time of writing his researches have born fruit—clumps of silver coin, more than 10,000 of them, mostly ducatoons, have been brought to the surface, and his divers have also located some 'fine bronze cannon'. To find the lost ship divers covered an area of some ten square miles! The site is exposed, so recovery of what is left of her cargo has been a long job.

A sale at Sotheby's of some of the coin and cannon raised £36,887.

* * * * *

The Dutch East India Company has provided a great number of the wrecks that are found around the coasts of Britain. The reason for this is simply the huge scale on which the Company carried out their operations.

The Vereenigde Oostindische Compagnie is described by Hugh Edwards in his excellent book about a Dutch East Indiaman *The Wreck on the Half-Moon Reef* (see Bibliography) as the most powerful single commercial concern that the world has even known. 'General Motors, British Tobacco, Ford, the Shell Company, Mitsubishi, Standard Oil—any of the other giant holdings of today are on the level of village bootmakers compared with the might and power and influence once wielded by the VOC', he writes.

Certainly the VOC was richer and stronger than many nations of its time. Its trading empire stretched from the Cape of Good Hope to India, Ceylon, Sumatra, Java, the Celebes and Spice Islands, and the ports of Malaya, China and Japan. It was authorized by the Dutch Government to make war if necessary, build forts, villages, towns, cities; it had its own law, even its own ministers of religion.

Of course, other nations didn't like it. The English complained that the Netherlanders were stubborn and complacent—'pig-headed Hollanders'. But pig-headed or not, the red, white and blue flag of Holland at one time carried the bulk of cargoes in European waters and most of the trade in spice and exotic goods from the East. The biggest herring and whaling fleets were Dutch. Amsterdam was the banking centre of the world—and the reason for all this prosperity was the Dutch East India Company.

The only thing that the VOC could not control was the weather. And the weather of the North Sea and English Channel was waiting for their ships at the beginning and end of the vast voyages they made to Batavia and beyond.

The records of the 'Gentlemen Seventeen' are well kept, and in them you can read of their successes as well as their failures. For example, Captain Willem Klump was commander of the 700-ton, 54-gun *Amsterdam* shortly after she was completed in 1748. This big merchantman was 150 feet long, had a beam of 35 feet and was intended for the Cape Town–Batavia run. In fact she was originally part of the 'Autumn' fleet, which set sail from Amsterdam in November 1748. On board there were 329 men, one-third of them soldiers en route for duty in Batavia, and three women. In her holds, apart from the usual stores for the colony in East Indies, were 'a great many thousand dozen' bottles of French wine and twenty-eight chests of silver bars.

The *Amsterdam* set sail with the rest of the fleet, and immediately ran into appalling weather. It was too much for this comparatively untried ship, and she had to turn back for repairs and alterations to her rigging which such tests by storm soon showed to be necessary. Then she tried again, only to limp back in after another battering from the high seas.

Finally Captain Klump got the *Amsterdam* out of the Zuider Zee for the third and last time on 8th January 1749—and straight into a south-westerly gale. Twelve days later—twelve days of endless tacking and battering by that same wind—she had still not passed Beachy Head and sought shelter in Pevensey Bay, which in those days was called Pevensey Haven, a well-known spot in which to shelter from south-west winds.

Klump must have thought his ship was cursed for already he had lost fifty of his crew. Some fatal disease was aboard—some said it was yellow fever brought into the ship by some crewman fresh back from the tropics—and in addition to the fifty dead he had another forty seriously ill below decks.

Those of his crew who were not down with the sickness were completely exhausted—nothing was dry in the crew's quarters, and each new storm added more water to the sodden bedding. The endless pitching did little good to the sick, whose conditions were even worse for they were lying in water most of the time.

As Klump fought his ship to shelter he might have been forgiven for thinking that nothing worse was likely to happen. But it did. Before he was properly into shelter, the ship struck a shoal and her rudder was ripped off. It was too much, and many of those aboard panicked. The ship could not now be steered, and so she drifted with the wind until her anchors finally held off Bexhill.

Some people from Hastings came aboard to assist the crew in getting the ship to Portsmouth as soon as the winds became more favourable. There is no written record of what they thought of conditions on board, but they may well have been shocked at what they saw. There, then, the *Amsterdam* stayed in apparent safety, if not comfort, until the early hours of Sunday 26th January, when fate struck a last blow at Captain Klump. Either the anchor cables couldn't stand the strain any longer, and they parted—or someone cut them. And *Amsterdam* was adrift again.

What happened then as Klump struggled to control his crew is not clear. It is known, however, that some of the crew thought that they were doomed and broke into the ship's cargo of wine. Some others must have kept their heads and fired the ship's guns to announce their distress to the shore.

Local records at Hastings say that at three in the afternoon when people were at church they heard the guns. As they rushed out of church and as most of the town gathered on the seashore, the *Amsterdam* drifted in from the sea. Came on and on, until she finally stopped, well and truly beached.

Among the first of the townspeople on the spot was Sir Charles Eversfield. A letter describing his disgust that 'all the crew were drunk' exists to this day. Very soon a large crowd had gathered on the beach opposite the stranded ship, and when the tide was low enough the crew and soldiers, who could still walk, got ashore in safety.

Then the looting began. Within a few hours hundreds of local people were plundering the wreck. A company of foot soldiers were rushed to the spot and some sort of order was restored. It is not known whether at this moment the people realized that *Amsterdam* was stuck into an area of yielding clay.

The soldiers guarded the silver and got twenty-seven chests ashore—the twenty-eighth had been broken into and only thirty of the fifty bars that should have been inside were recovered. The Mayor of Hastings was glad when the silver left under escort for London, for it meant that most of the soldiers left the town with it. The Mayor didn't like soldiers. He called them 'the greatest thieves I ever knew. They not only robbed the ship, but their quarters also'.

The Mayor may have had another reason for disliking the soldiers. Once they had gone the town was completely out of control, and even the Mayor was selling French wine from the ship at a shilling a bottle.

By February 1749 the ship had sunk into the sand as high as her upper deck, and no matter how the salvors tried to get at her main cargo the tides and water and sand beat them. And there reluctantly they had to leave it.

You could hardly call the *Amsterdam* a wreck suitable for divers, and though locally it has always been known that the wreck was there—her sides and some beams can be seen at very low spring tides about three miles west of Hastings town—there

Coins galore. Bob Earl studies some of the coins raised from the 1711 wreck of the Dutch East Indiaman, *De Liefde*, in the Shetlands

were no large-scale salvage attempts during the years that followed.

In fact it wasn't until July 1969 that modern man had a go. In this case modern man took the form of Mr Kenneth Young, the site agent for William Press and Son, Ltd. Mr Young was in charge of the building of a sewer outfall only about two hundred yards from the wreck site.

Mr Young had always been interested in wrecks, and reading about the *Amsterdam* spurred him on to have a look for her—with a mechanical excavator! He dug several deep holes into the wreck position (when the tide would let him) and out came a slice of eighteenth-century life—a pewter tankard, fine horn combs, a lady's ivory fan, wine-glasses, bottles, brass candlesticks, bronze cartridge-cases, leather shoes, bronze smoothing irons, forty green glass bottles still containing red wine, stoneware jugs. . . .

And then the most fantastic find of all—five bronze cannon, still wrapped in the sacking which had covered them when they were stored with the rest of the cargo. Each cannon was dated 1748 and bore the insignia 'VOC' entwined, with a capital 'A' above it for the Amsterdam branch of the East India Company.

At this moment Mr Young realized the importance of his find and the firm agreed that the discovery must be reported to the Committee for Nautical Archaeology. Alan Bax of the Committee went to the site, and at his request Mr Young dug a deep hole beside the ship. The photographs of that hole astounded the Committee. There, in a hole on a British holiday beach, was evidence of a major marine archaeological discovery. Not only was the main mast found to be lying alongside the ship with some of its rigging still intact, but six feet down from the upper deck were a row of gun ports, still closed by their lids!

The Committee, with the help of William Press and Son's equipment—and experts like historian and diver Bill St. John Wilkes—carried out a hurried survey at the end of September 1969, and that survey established that the ship and her contents are of the greatest importance. Peter Marsden, who did such a brilliant job of excavation on the Blackfriars ship (see Chapter 1), is now in charge of the site.

Peter Marsden feels that the ship and her contents are worthy of preservation in a special museum, perhaps built at Hastings. But building a coffer dam around the ship to excavate her and keep the sea out will cost a great deal of money. So will the actual raising of the ship which could become Britain's *Wasa*. So will the building of a special museum for her. But if only the money can be raised it will be well spent. Peter Marsden and the Committee for Nautical Archaeology will see to that.

* * * * *

His Excellency Governor Trelawney and his lady had good reason to be pleased with their voyage home from Jamaica. The Governor had acquitted himself well in his post, and now he was within sight of England—in fact, the white cliffs of the Needles were clear on the starboard bow as they started to enter the Needles Channel.

The Governor considered himself fortunate, not only in the fair weather that they had enjoyed on their voyage, but also in the ship, captain and crew which were bringing him home.

It was now well into April 1753, and the Governor thought comfortably of the bags of pieces of eight stowed carefully below—the result of careful, but in his opinion fair, administration and allocation of contracts. Those bags were going to ensure his comfort through many an English winter, which he knew would be in sharp contrast to the sunny days he had enjoyed in Jamaica.

Captain Carr Scrope was having similar thoughts as he too saw in the dawn light the thin line of white turn into the cliffs of the Isle of Wight. He too had enjoyed his days in Jamaica—for it was while he was there commanding a sloop on the Jamaica station that his promotion to captain had come through on 14th November 1752, and he had been given command of the fifth-rate 44-gun H.M.S. *Assurance*, on the deck of which he now stood.

Captain Scrope had no such rich financial baggage as the Governor, but at least his promotion had meant that all was forgiven. Until then Scrope's career in the Navy had seemed to him to be 'one damned thing after another'. His family had long been respected and rich gentry in Lincolnshire, and Carr, who was the youngest of three sons, had entered the Navy at an early age. He was appointed lieutenant aboard H.M.S. *Neptune* in 1742. And then his troubles had started.

The *Neptune* had sailed to join the Mediterranean Fleet, and Lieutenant Scrope had found himself in February 1744 off Toulon with the fleet of over twenty ships under Admiral Mathews. For a while the British Fleet merely kept a watchful eye on a combined Franco-Spanish fleet of about a similar size in harbour at Toulon.

England and Spain had been at war since 1739, but England and France, though undoubtedly on opposite sides, had not yet actually declared war on each other. It was an extremely confused situation. Spain was sending troops to Northern Italy ready for an attack on Austria's Italian possessions, and France was helping Spain to do so by placing the port of Toulon at the Spaniards' disposal. The French also seemed inclined to provide ships to help the Spaniards convoy the troops to Italy.

In the circumstances Admiral Mathews had decided that he would be justified in attacking the French ships if they formed a joint fleet with the Spaniards and sailed from Toulon. So he kept his fleet just off Toulon, and waited to see what would happen.

On 9th February the joint fleet came out of harbour—but not the troop transports. This put Mathews in a fix. If he attacked the Franco-Spanish fleet the transports would be able to slip out and away, and he might never find them again. On the other hand if he stayed and waited for the transports he would lose his chance of engaging the enemy fleet.

He had to decide quickly—and he tried to have the best of both worlds. His plan was to go after the fleet, engage it, then double back and take the transports. But it didn't work out like that. The trouble was that the rigid rules for fighting, as laid down by the Admiralty, didn't allow for such quick tactics. According to the book, Mathews should have first of all ensured that he held the windward position and then before he bore down on the enemy so arranged his line of ships that each ship was opposed to the corresponding ship in the enemy's line. Mathews got to windward all right, but couldn't wait for his

Derek Williams after
a dive on the site
of the wreck of
H.M.S. *Assurance*,
lost off the Isle of
Wight, 1753

line to be exactly covering the enemy ships—or he would miss the transports.

So he signalled the attack as soon as he could, and everyone got into a great muddle. They had expected to wait, as the rules said, until they were all nicely lined up. After a very short engagement, Mathews had to break off the battle.

Courts-martial galore followed this fiasco, and Mathews was, unfairly, dismissed from the Service—not because he had not fought hard—for he had—but because he had trespassed against the fighting instructions, fleet commanders for the use of!

Young Lieutenant Scrope must have wondered what sort of Navy he had joined, for he was called as a witness at the courts-martial of captains, vice-admirals and indeed, Admiral Mathews himself.

The sort of charges that were brought gives some idea of the confusion of the battle. Captain John Ambrose of the *Rupert* of 60 guns, was, for example, charged with:

Having neglected his duty; with firing and continuing to fire on the enemy whilst altogether out of range; with not having assisted the *Marlborough* when in extreme danger; with not having covered and protected the fireship when he might and should have done so; and with disobedience to His Majesty's instructions and the signals and commands of the Admiral, neglect of naval discipline, and being one of the principal causes of the miscarriage of His Majesty's fleet.

It was quite clear to Scrope and anyone else involved that there was a lot of needle between the various captains and admirals, and part of this dislike had been woven into the courts-martial in an attempt to wipe off old scores. If Ambrose had been found guilty of those charges he would, in normal circumstances, have been executed, but though the court held the charges to be proved 'in the principal part', in consideration of the fact that he had always 'borne the character of a vigilant and diligent officer and that his failure in the action was apparently due to a mistake in judgement' they merely ordered him cashiered during His Majesty's pleasure and fined one year's pay. Four years later he was restored to his rank, and in April 1750 was made a rear-admiral on the retired list.

What effect all this intrigue and inquiry had on Scrope we shall never know. What we do know is that he stayed in the Navy, and was promoted to commander on 11th August 1746 and appointed to H.M.S. *Whitehaven*, which seems to be described in records only as an 'armed ship'. She was probably quite small, but she didn't last long under Scrope's command, for in September one year later she was burned, and sank off the coast of Ireland. Seventeen of the crew were lost, but the rest took to the boats and were saved.

Once again Scrope found himself at a court-martial. But this time it was his own. The court was convened on 15th October the same year, and, much to his relief, Scrope was honourably acquitted of the charge of having lost his ship through neglect.

He had feared for a long time afterwards that even though he was acquitted, the stigma of having lost a ship would stick to him, but his promotion to captain had cleared such thoughts from his mind.

So Scrope in the dawn of 24th April 1753 was content. He had had nothing but fair winds from Jamaica, and even good weather after their stop at Lisbon. The crew had behaved well; so had his officers. In particular he was, he felt, blessed with his master, David Patterson, a sober, diligent and careful fellow. Such a master was indeed a blessing to any commander, judging by the tales his fellow-captains had told him of their troubles with less able men.

With the Isle of Wight coming closer and closer every moment, Captain Scrope felt that he would now leave the decision about their course to David Patterson. If they could get through the Needles Channel they would avoid the long haul around the Island to their destination at Spithead. But he would abide by Patterson's decision, despite his anxiety to be home.

'Will you take her through?' Scrope addressed this question to Patterson, who stood by his side. Patterson nodded, but Scrope wanted to make sure that his question was understood. 'She's in your charge, then?' 'She is', said Patterson.

The westerly wind looked ideal. Later Patterson was to say that the wind was west by north or west-north-west, but it made no difference to his decision to take the ship through the narrows.

David Patterson looked out over the bow, scenting the wind, and noting carefully that he had Alum Bay open with the Needle Rock. A glance at the compass—north-east ½ east. Then aloft. He noted 'All sails out, but the studding sails and the shore tack at the cathead'. The sails filled and the *Assurance* moved confidently ahead.

But for all his confidence, David Patterson had never taken a ship through that channel before. True, he had been part of the crew of many ships that had passed through, but he had never actually been in command himself.

Still, Patterson didn't worry. In fact when Governor Trelawney approached him, anxious in the early hours for a first sight of home, and asked how close to the Needles they would go, he answered a little boastfully that 'they would pass so close that the fly of the ensign might actually touch the rock'. Allowing for the boast, the truth is that David Patterson was more afraid of the Shingles on the port side. These great sandbanks appeared to Patterson to be unusually high out of the water. He feared, too, that they had shifted from their usual position. Not such a ridiculous fear either, for any Isle of Wight sailor will tell you today that the sands do shift this way and that a certain amount.

So Patterson, then, set his course closer to the Needles than he would normally have done, and relied on the tide 'horsing' the ship to the west. Not that he was afraid to take the ship through. When the captain had asked him if he would take the ship he could have decided, with St Catherine's Point seven leagues away, to go the long way round. But David Patterson felt in good spirits, and quite confident.

They were now almost up to the Needles themselves, and the 133-foot-long ship was still going well. Patterson's course took them very close to the Needles, but he had no inkling of the disaster that was about to overtake him—until the leadsman suddenly called, 'A quarter less five'.

Patterson realized his danger. 'Cast again—quick!' he

shouted. But, before the lead line even left the man's hand the ship struck with a grinding crash that stopped her as though she had run into a stone quay.

The dismay that raced through Patterson's brain was tempered with complete and utter disbelief. There was no rock charted where they had struck. According to all the charts, there was nothing but deep water at the point where *Assurance* had jerked to a standstill in helpless chaos.

Amid the pandemonium that broke loose above and below decks, David Patterson had only one thought—it ought not . . . could not . . . have happened. A year and a half he had been master of *Assurance*, and never in all his service had he done the slightest damage to the ship. Now here she was on an uncharted rock near the Needles.

At the moment of striking H.M.S. *Assurance* had stopped dead. Her only movement after the crunch of collision was for her head to fall around towards the north. Patterson had no idea of how long she stayed poised on the rock. He felt that it was a century before the damage reports started to come in, but in fact within the hour the water was gaining fast on their attempts to pump her out. Captain Scrope knew his ship was lost. He spared only a glance of pity for the frozen figure of David Patterson before organizing the safe evacuation of his passengers and crew.

The *Assurance* did not go down like a stone. In fact there was plenty of time and Governor Trelawney had sufficient to supervise the loading of his fortune into the boats before there was any urgency about leaving the stricken vessel. In the end it was several hours before the water flooded in sufficiently for the *Assurance* (the fourth to bear the name in navy records; she was built at the Heather Yard, Bursledon, and launched on 29th September 1747) to sink most of the way beneath the surface.

After that it was only a matter of time before Captain Scrope found himself before another court-martial. By an Admiralty Order dated 1st May 1753 'the Honorable Edward Boscawen, Rear-Admiral of the White Squadron of His Majesty's Fleet and Commander in Chief of His Majesty's ships at Portsmouth Harbour' was directed to 'assemble a court-martial for enquiring into the cause of the loss of His Majesty's late ship the Assurance the 24th April last, when, endeavouring to go through the Needles, the said ship struck in the Narrows and was lost, and into the Conduct of the Officers and Men on that Occasion'.

The court-martial took place on board H.M.S. *Tyger* in Portsmouth Harbour on 11th May 1753 with Boscawen as President and the other judges Captains Robert Pett, George Bridges Rodney, Jonathan Montagu, the Hon. Sam Barrington, Roger Martin, Charles Catford, Julian Legg and Sam Marshall.

Admiral Boscawen was a stern but not unkindly man, an odd mixture of sea-dog and scholar, who could write letters to his wife before setting off on some voyage which contained such poetic phrases as 'To be sure I lose the fruits of the earth, but then I am gathering the flowers of the sea'. With him as President there would be no hanky-panky of the kind that Scrope had seen years before.

Scrope felt this as he stood before the row of Navy big-wigs. Boscawen was the first to speak: 'Captain Scrope, have you any complaint to make against any of your officers or company for neglect of duty, disobedience to command, or being anyway instrumental or contributing towards the loss of the *Assurance*?'

'No, sir', said Scrope, 'they all did their duty and behaved as they ought.'

'Then how came the ship to be lost?'

'I imagine it must be by the course in which the master was mistaken.'

Boscawen looked directly at Scrope. 'Did the master willingly take charge of the ship or was it forced upon him?'

'He undertook it willingly', replied Scrope.

Boscawen now turned his attention to David Patterson.

'Master, you hear what the captain says as to your willingly taking charge of the ship?'

'I did, sir.'

'How had you the wind?'

'West by north or west-north-west'.

'And how came you then to lose the ship?'

David Patterson had rehearsed again and again in his mind what he would reply to that question. . . . 'I can but ill account for it, I thought we were in a fair way, having Alum Bay open with the Needle Rock. . . . When the man at the lead called out just before the ship struck 'a quarter less five', I called to the man to heave another cast quick . . . before he could do so, the ship struck . . .'

'Do you remember what course you steered?'

'North-east a half east by the compass.'

'What sail had you aboard?'

'All out but studding sails.'

Question followed question in quick succession.

'Did the ship go ashore with all sails full?'

'Yes, sir.'

'Had you ever charge of a ship through the Needles before?'

'No. I have been in and out often, but never had charge of a ship.'

'How came you to keep so near the Needle Rock where the Channel is so wide and you had the wind so large?'

'At the latter end of the ebb, I was afraid of the Shingles, which the tide set us directly upon. They appeared so high out of the water I concluded they had shifted nearer the Island as they will do sometimes.'

Boscawen now launched into a series of questions about courses and bearings and called Captain Scrope to confirm what Patterson had said. The reason for the questions became clear when Boscawen asked: 'Master, you say at 4 a.m. when the captain asked you if you would carry the ship through, St Katherine's Point bearing at that time north-east by north at a distance of six or seven leagues, and the Needle Point north by east, what course did you shape?'

'Directly for the Needle Point, the tide horseing us to the westward.'

And then came the punch question: 'As you was abreast of the Needles and the wind large why did you not go, why did you not go round the Island?'

Patterson could see immediately what the Admiral was getting at—had he hazarded the ship just to save a little time? There was only one answer he could give. 'I thought we should come sooner to Spithead', he said firmly.

89

Some of the finds made by Derek Williams when he located
the wreck of H.M.S. *Assurance* off the Isle of Wight.
The portion of bell at the back nearly made him think
he had found some other ship. On the left of the bell is
the 'crooked' weight

Boscawen now changed the tack of his questions. 'Did you know there was a rock so near the Needles as that you struck upon?'

'I did not know anything of a rock so far off and few people did.'

'Would you have any of the officers called in your justification?'

Patterson declined, but he did request that three pilots aboard who knew the area well should be examined. All gave evidence that they too had no idea of any rock in the place where the *Assurance* struck.

After further evidence that Patterson was a 'sober, careful, diligent officer', the President turned to his fellow judges:

'Is it your opinion that Captain Scrope was at all accessory to the loss of the *Assurance*?' 'No'. They were unanimous. 'Is it your opinion that the lieutenants were at all accessory to the loss of the said ship?' 'No'. 'Is it your opinion that the rest of the officers and crew were at all accessory?' 'No'. 'Is it your opinion that the loss of the ship was owing to the unskilfulness, negligence or carelessness of the master?'

Finally they sorted out a suitable form of words for the clerk to pen.

'No, we don't attribute the loss to the negligence or carelessness of the master, but we attribute it to his ignorance of the rock the ship run upon, which is generally said to be little known'. 'What article does the master fall under?'

'Under part of the 26th Article by running the ship unskilfully upon the rock'.

'What punishment do you award him?'

'In regard to the general good character of the master, the court are unanimously of opinion that he be imprisoned three months in the Marshalsea'.

So poor David Patterson went to prison. And no one would envy him his three months, for the Marshalsea in London was a diabolical place. It stood opposite Maypole Alley, in Borough High Street, Southwark, where there had been a prison since the fourteenth century. In the eighteenth century it became the county jail for felons, an Admiralty jail for pirates (and the likes of David Patterson) and a debtors prison. The conditions there were so bad that in the same year that David Patterson was committed John Wesley described the building as 'a picture of Hell upon Earth'. It was the prison made famous by Charles Dickens in *Little Dorrit*.

We know nothing more of what happened to David Patterson, but Captain Scrope comes back into the records when he commanded the 24-gun H.M.S. *Dolphin*, a frigate of the Mediterranean Fleet, in April 1756. He served with great gallantry during the siege of Minorca.

In 1757 Scrope was appointed captain of the *Coventry*, a frigate of 28 guns, and was in action against Rochfort. Then in 1761 he became captain of the *Hampton Court*—and ran into more trouble. That May when he was being taken ashore on his return from convoy duty, his boat capsized in a squall, and all the seamen in it were drowned. Scrope managed to survive for two hours by clinging to an oar until picked up by another boat from his ship. He seems to have suffered nothing more than exposure, for he sailed again at the end of the same month. However, he died the next year while still captain of the *Hampton Court*.

For over two hundred years the remains of the *Assurance* lay on the bottom undisturbed by anything but the fierce tides and storm surges which are a feature of the Needles area. But in 1956 one man started on the road that was to lead to her rediscovery.

Derek Williams is a draughtsman with an Isle of Wight hovercraft firm and lives in Wooton, on the Island. In 1956 he was introduced to the Aqualung by Brian Howlett of Shanklin, who owned one of the first Aqualungs on the Isle of Wight. That first Aqualung dive started him on the way to being the keen and experienced diver he is today.

But though Derek Williams and his fellow Isle of Wight divers had a great deal of pleasure from straightforward diving, he wanted something more. He wanted to find a wreck. A wreck of his own. For years he searched old records and old books for some ship that had been wrecked on the coast of the Island, and which he could be the first to find. Such dreams are rarely fulfilled, but one day he found a reference to an H.M.S. *Insurance* wrecked off the Needles in 1753.

At first he drew a blank. No one, not even the Navy, knew of an H.M.S. *Insurance*, and it wasn't until he noticed that a Prudential brochure carried the words 'Prudential Assurance Company' that he realized he had probably been slightly off course.

H.M.S. *Assurance*. Now, that was different. Lots of people in charge of records could find him information about that ship. But all they could tell him about the position was that it was 'off the Needles', and that is a mighty big area. Then he learned about the mystery rock that the ship was supposed to have struck, and he would go up on the cliffs and look down on the sea and out over the lighthouse and wonder just where she was.

It was while he was returning from just such a expedition to the cliffs overlooking the Needles that he first met Dave Cotton. Dave Cotton proved to the diver's ideal boatman. He had complete local knowledge of the tides, seas and currents of the western coastline of the island. As a lobster-pot fisherman, he had to know where the rocks were too. Dave and Derek Williams became firm friends, but Derek still didn't know where to start looking for H.M.S. *Assurance*, which had now become a complete obsession with him. His wife will vouch for that! Every spare moment was spent searching through old records, until at last Derek thought he knew—roughly—where the old ship lay.

For weeks after that [said Derek Williams], the weather wouldn't come right. But then it did—have you ever noticed how the weather and sea are perfect for diving all week and just when you're free at weekends the weather breaks up?—and off we went. We anchored close to the rock where I thought the ship was, and over the side I went. Within moments of hitting the sea-bed I suddenly realized I was over a big heap of cannon. I was so excited I just surfaced straight away. And I remember shouting 'She's there, she's there!' The wife and family were all in the big boat we were using at the time and back down I went again. I began scrabbling around picking up things like copper nails. The feeling was really quite something. It was unbelievable really—my dream had come true.

Copper nails shone bright green all around him, and he had thoughts immediately about lifting the cannon. Once back in the boat, however, with his trophies—some of the first turned out to be cheap standard-issue marlin spikes all clearly marked with the Navy's broad arrow—he had second thoughts. If he arrived back on shore with a cannon swinging from under the boat his discovery would immediately be common knowledge—and Derek wanted to keep this one to himself for the time being.

Subsequent dives proved that all the cannon were iron—there were twelve in all, and Derek has them assessed as 9-pounders. The cannon were all jumbled together in a pile and cannon-balls made up part of the same heavily concreted heap. He had seen enough to know that he wanted the wreck for himself, and there now started a long correspondence with the authorities.

He wanted to buy the wreck, but nobody was in any hurry to sell it to him. One of the letters was typical. It read:

DEAR MR WILLIAMS,

I have to inform you that if you locate a wreck and believe it to be that of a Royal Navy vessel application to purchase the wreck or to carry out salvage operations may be made to

this office by letter no special form being required for this purpose.

The name and/or navigational position of the wreck will be required. On receipt of your application the matter will be given consideration, but it is stressed that extensive enquiries may háve to be made to establish the ownership etc of the wreck before a decision can be given.

(Signed) L. V. BUTLER

for Director General Defence Contracts.

The cautious tone was quite clear. And it is obvious that the Ministry of Defence (Navy) were not going to let themselves in for the same sort of Scillies shambles that they produced by

their issue of three non-exclusive contracts for H.M.S. *Association*.

Derek Williams wanted the wreck for himself, but he knew enough not to try and keep any pieces of the wreck. All the items he found were handed in to the local Receiver at Cowes. At the time he was under the mistaken impression that this would establish some sort of right to the wreck. But, of course, after twelve months the Receiver of Wreck handed him back his pieces, saying in effect: 'Here you are. We've kept them for twelve months and nobody's claimed them, so they're yours!'

In fact Derek had not proved to everyone's satisfaction that he *had* found H.M.S. *Assurance*. The broad arrows on the material proved it was a Royal Navy wreck, but was it the *Assurance*?

On almost the very next dive Derek thought he had found

was an extremely exposed and shallow area, and though he could expect thirty to forty feet visibility, on neap tides he had only twenty minutes of slack water before the Solent tides bore down on him.

And 'bore down' is the right description of what happened under water when the tide turned. First of all the visibility would disappear as all the gunk and muck from the Hampshire coast was swept through the Narrows. The force of the tidal waters was impossible to resist. It was just possible to cling on to some object on the bottom when it started, but Derek described that sort of position as most uncomfortable, and even says that the waters give you a physical battering.

The wreck site itself measures about two hundred feet long by fifty feet wide, and is pretty well concentrated. Derek Williams has searched around the site, and there seems to be nothing further out. Near the cannon is a mortar, and it looks as though the bomb is still in position in the muzzle. He recognized the mortar immediately, as it is very similar to the one which is outside the museum at Southsea. The mortar is quite short, about four feet long and eighteen inches in diameter, in comparison with the cannon, which are all about eight feet long. All the cannon seem to be the same size and are heavily encrusted, and rather worn round the muzzles. All are iron.

Conditions on the site are often completely impossible, and once the tide starts there is no question of doing anything except to be swept to the surface.

Two hours before low slack water seems to be the best time to dive. But it is not just the diving which creates problems. Often the sea in the area has been so rough (though calm inside the bay where the diving boat is kept), that Derek and Dave have had to turn back and abandon the site for several days. The Needles have a tough reputation even for the bigger boats.

The Shingles of which David Patterson was so afraid all those years ago, create nasty overflows, and modern sailors would agree with his decision to keep clear of them. His comments about the shingle banks moving is true, and you will find a reference to this in modern sailing information.

Where are the rest of the *Assurance*'s guns? It seems quite clear that we shall have to award those to salvage efforts at the time. A fifth-rate like the *Assurance* might well have had the following guns: twenty 18-pounders, twenty 9-pounders and four 6-pounders. Yet all Derek Williams' guns appear to be 9-pounders. This is extraordinary in a way, because you would have thought that the 9-pounders would have been higher in the ship and more accessible to salvors than the heavier guns, which were usually sited as low in the ship as possible for the sake of stability.

It is, of course, just possible that Derek William had overlooked some cannon on the site, which is cut through by rock gullies, and all objects there are heavily concreted.

So he worked on. And all the time keeping a watchful eye on lines and surface conditions was Dave Cotton, the man who Derek insists is invaluable—'you couldn't wish for a better man up top'.

Was he really diving on H.M.S. *Assurance*?

To be honest, says Derek, I can't prove absolutely that I

The wreck of the *Amsterdam* near Hastings one low spring tide as the Committee for Nautical Archaeology carried out a survey in March 1970

the final proof. On the site he found three pieces of a ship's bell. Some quite clearly had lettering on them, but it wasn't until he cleaned them up and put them together that he found to his horror that the wording on the bell read 'DREAM 1838'. For a time he was shattered.

Back he went to his wreck detection. Was there such a ship as H.M.S. *Dream*? He couldn't find one. But there was a schooner called *Dream* of 162 tons built in Yarmouth, Isle of Wight in 1837 and lost somewhere around the Island. So the broad arrow marks of the Navy clearly disposed of that one. What had more than likely happened was that *Dream* had been wrecked near the same spot, and her pieces had joined those of H.M.S. *Assurance*.

So Derek went on with his underwater work. The wreck site

am diving on her. It is all circumstantial evidence. I've found the rock and at the base of it lie the cannon and all the accoutrements of an eighteenth-century Naval ship. I thought I had it when I saw that bell with the name Dream on it, but I'm not looking at the wreckage of a piffling little schooner . . . cannon, broad arrows . . . it can be nothing but a Navy ship, and there's no other Navy ship lost in the area. I'm sure, but the evidence is circumstantial.

What else has he found? Clay pipe bowls, which fit the date, and a thin gold wedding ring with some marking inside, but when I talked to Derek Williams it was impossible for us to decipher the meaning of the marks.

Down the starboard side of the probable line of the wreck are masses of big copper pins that were used to hold the timbers together, and then, close to the jumbled pile of cannon he found a sounding lead. The base of this—normally a hole filled with wax to pick up traces of the bottom and tell the leadsman what sort of sea-bed the ship was travelling over—has been rounded and battered by the sea so that the hole is gone. It is interesting to think that this is the lead whose last cast told Master David Patterson that he was in dead trouble. It is close to the probable position of the bow, and it is tempting to say that this was the very one, but such surmise is too romantic for the cold facts demanded by marine archaeologists.

Right beside the sounding lead Derek found a beautiful brass weight. Polished now, it gleams beautifully in the light, and beside the avoirdupois sign is the figure '8'. Yet oddly enough the weight weighs exactly 6 lb.

A close study of the actual figure '8' may well expose a cheating eighteenth-century ship's officer. The top loop of the '8' does look as though someone has scratched it in, thus turning a '6' into an '8'. The 'fiddling' applications in the issue of rations are obvious. The weight stands six and a quarter inches high, and is almost completely undamaged.

Close to the weight Derek Williams found marlin spikes, musket balls, copper sheathing and sheathing tacks, brass pulley block fittings and pieces of blue Delft china. Most of the finds seemed to be where the starboard side of the ship should have been. And where the stern would be if this was so, Derek found some very thick pieces of glass that might have come from the stern windows. They now look greenish-yellow tinted, but this could be due to exposure to the sea. The glass is exactly half an inch thick.

Many of the gullies in the rock sea-bed are filled with shingle which could have been the ship's ballast (builders to this day refer to shingle as ballast from that practice), and many wreck sites have this shingle deposit in places where there is no other shingle at all. The *Assurance* site is such a place. Suddenly on the site there is shingle and there is none in the immediate area, the big shingle banks being about a mile away.

Derek Williams has kept his secret well, but he knows that it is only a matter of time before other divers find out her location and join him in the investigation of the watery grave of Captain Scrope's ship. Until then he works alone on the bottom for twenty minutes at a time, chipping away patiently at the concretion of centuries under the sea, and hoping to discover the one unarguable piece of evidence (like the plate bearing Sir Cloudesley Shovell's coat of arms which proved the wreck of the *Association*) which will enable him to say 'Here lies *Assurance*'.

CHAPTER 8

The Case of the Nameless Ones

including an unknown seventeenth-century ship lost on the Farne Islands, and another ship without a name on the Mewstone, near Plymouth.

FOR eight hundred years the grey seals have come to the Farne Islands to breed. So it seems certain that only the grey seals were witnesses to a shipwreck of long ago—a shipwreck which took place in such wild weather that no one has any record of any survivor, nor is there any record of the death of the ship herself.

'Sunk without trace' would have been fair enough description of the loss in the days when only traces that existed above water could be counted, but the great ship that struck the Farne Islands left underwater clues to her disappearance which today's modern divers were able to find.

The Farne Islands lie three miles due east of Bamburgh in Northumberland, on Britain's east coast. The nearest port is Seahouses, near North Sunderland town, four miles south-west of the Islands.

Not all the islands can strictly qualify as more than rocks. They cover an area of eighty acres, and rejoice in names like Swedman, Oxcar, Glororum Shad, Knox, Crumstone, Hoppen, and Whirl. Or threaten with the Wamses, Callers, Wideopen, Hares, Harcar (Big and Little), Brownsman, Longstone, Knivestone and Fang.

They are at low tide twenty-six islets, and at high tide there are many less. To a ship working up or down the coast, they are a menace to be skirted wide. The local fishermen say that in fog only the seals' cries are warning of the waiting rocks.

In recent years there has been a great deal of controversy over the culling of the seals on the Farnes, where the colony of greys are now suffering from their own overcrowding.

Though the furore over the seals of the Farnes interested him, one man was busy thinking about the Islands for reasons which had nothing to do with seals.

W. R. Smith, better known as Bill, the Diving Officer of Tyneside Branch of the British Sub-Aqua Club was that man. In 1968 he read G. Matingley's *Defeat of the Spanish Armada* (see Bibliography) and applied parts of it to his own local knowledge. He knew that nearly one hundred years ago the fishermen of the village of Seahouses had found during their fishing a cast-iron cannon lying on top of some rocks among the Farne Islands. Those rocks were known as Gun Rocks. But were they known as that before the discovery of the cannon, or were they named after it?

At any rate, the rocks were obviously worth investigating.

Captains of ships rarely ordered cannons to be thrown overboard. If they did they were in real trouble—unlashing a cannon in the middle of a storm was far more likely to result in an uncontrollable internal battering ram than the desired lightening of the ship and escape from some underwater rocks.

So Bill Smith had good reason to think that somewhere near Gun Rocks there was a wreck. And he had a theory about what kind of ship it was. In his report of the Gun Rocks project he put it like this:

My interest was first aroused when I read Matingley's book on the Spanish Armada. The book gives an interesting account of the battles and also the epic voyage by the defeated fleet around England, Scotland and Ireland before their return to Spain. More to the point, the book tells of ships which went missing in North-Eastern waters, that is to say somewhere North of Lat. 56 degrees.

At about the time my interest started to gather momentum, I also read about the cannon found some years ago on the Farne Islands and from that date I started to ask questions and look for the answers. I was told that the cannon from Gun Rocks was supposed to be Spanish. More reading then became the order of the day, and to this end I read books by historians, naturalists, and arms experts. All I read lent strength to what was now my pet theory—one of the Spanish Armada ships had run on to what is now called Gun Rocks some time in August, 1588. It was of course only my own idea. . . .

Bill Smith began to ask himself questions and supply possible answers.

Question: Why was there never any trace of the eleven ships which went missing in the North Sea at approximately Lat. 58 degrees?

Possible answer: The ships could have gone down at sea, but it could be that if any had reached the Northumberland coast it was then so sparsely populated, particularly the area around the Farne Islands, that a shipwreck would never have been seen.

Question: Could any of the missing ships have been blown back so far south?

Answer: Yes, it would have been possible. When the Duke of Medina Sidonia turned the Armada towards the west even he wasn't sure what latitude they were in. There had been a storm most of the night and most of the day. Only after that did he find some of his ships were missing.

Question: Even so, surely they couldn't have been blown that far back?

Answer: Look at the case of the wreck of the *Forfarshire*, which sank in 1838 and made Grace Darling and her father famous for their daring rescue of the survivors. The *Forfarshire* battled through the night against a north-north-east gale up to St Abbs Head. In the early hours her engines stopped when the boilers failed. The *Forfarshire* drifted some 40 miles in a few hours and struck the Harcar Rocks. Imagine then what would happen to a damaged wooden sailing-ship in such a gale.

Question: But why Gun Rocks? Why would a ship hit Gun Rocks and not any of the others?

Answer: If a ship on a south-east drift missed the Goldstones up near Holy Island she could well hit the Gun. (Note: There are two rocks with the name Goldstone, the North and South. On 6th July 1970 Bill Smith dived and searched the sea-bed around the South Goldstone. He found pieces of copper tubing, which appeared to be from a modern wreck.)

Question: How did the cannon which is now in Bamburgh Castle come to be on top of Gun Rocks?

Answer: It could be that the ship ran on to the rock at high water, when the rock is just under water, ripped out her bottom or side and then crashed on to sink in deeper water, leaving the cannon behind on the rock.

So Bill Smith had his pet theory. The presence of a Spanish Armada wreck on the Farne Islands depended on what happened before the Duke of Medina Sidonia, on board the flagship *San Martin de Portugal*, found he had four hulks and seven of the squadron missing as he turned west to go around Britain.

Having a theory, however, is one thing. The next is to prove it. A visit to Bamburgh Castle to look at the actual cannon recovered from Gun Rocks did little to help. The gun was in a bad condition from its exposure first to the sea and then to the air. Big pieces are missing, and there are no marks to be seen. Its general dimensions—8 ft 6 in long with a bore of three and a half inches—were, however, close enough to Armada gun sizes not to do any damage to Bill Smith's theory. Now he had done the research as best he could. Only diving could add anything more.

So on 17th May 1970 the Tyneside Branch of the British Sub-Aqua Club started diving. Eight members of the team hired a drifter, *John Wesley*, from Seahouses and with a Dell Quay Dory, with five more divers in it, as close escort set out on the three and a half-mile run north-east to Gun Rocks.

They arrived on site—750 feet from the west side of Staple Island—and were slightly disconcerted to find that Gun Rocks was a little white spot that showed itself every now and then in the middle of an otherwise blank stretch of sea. This was Gun Rocks at high water.

In the *John Wesley* were divers S. Saul, R. Brown, E. Tysick, E. Dobbie, D. Russell, G. Anderson, A. Harris and the Diving Officer of the Branch, Bill Smith. In the dory—Bill Sherwin's

Zokko—there were, in addition to Sherwin, S. Inglis, R. Edmundson, M. Pratt and D. Blythe. The weather was fine, with a light wind from the south-east, and, after a briefing by Bill Smith, the divers split into two teams. The first team was to explore the south side of the Rocks, and the second team was to take the north-east area.

They dived. Within minutes the second team had found a bronze pulley wheel lying by itself. They brought the wheel back to the boat, and then continued their dive, but found nothing more. The first team were gone for about thirty minutes. On their return to the boat they said they had come across eight or nine cannon!

Bill Smith's first reaction was one of complete disbelief. Then when they persisted that it was true—there were cannon down there—he felt that his two-year-old dream was about to come true. Extracts from some of his diving reports now tell the story best:

FIRST DIVE, Sunday 17th May, 1970

13 divers in two boats:

Bill Sherwin's Dory *Zokko*—5 Divers

8 Divers in the *John Wesley*, which is owned by Jim Trotter of Seahouses.

R. Brown and S. Saul were told to dive on South side of rock—found what appeared to be 9 cast iron cannon of varying sizes and shapes. They estimated lengths to be about eight feet. No other checks were done at this time.

D. Russell and myself were swimming on N.E. side of rock when I found a bronze wheel well eroded in approx. 30–35 ft of water, no other items lying around at this spot.

Conditions on this day were fairly good—underwater visibility 30 feet plus, in places. Tide started to move fast towards the end of diving operations. Tide pushing North and not South on the ebb, this is peculiar to the Farnes and is mentioned elsewere in my report.

Work done so far:

> Reported finds to Receiver—meeting in Newcastle on Monday 1st June at 3.00 p.m.
>
> Public Library—I have gone through a very complex catalogue of maps, dates 1300 AD to 1890's to try and pin-point when the name of the rocks was given. They make no reference to this name, only old Germanic names. More checking required.

NOTES:

> Met Receiver—he is very interested and has taken copies of sketches (see Fig. 9) and he informs me that I have to fill all salvor forms in, etc., through the Area Receiver, who is at Berwick. I have written to Mr Murray to this end, awaiting his reply.

WEATHER—Fine	*AIR TEMP.* 12°C
	DATE—Sunday, 17th May 1970
WIND—South East	*WATER TEMP.* 12°C
	VISIBILITY—15/20 ft
	LOCATION—GUN ROCKS

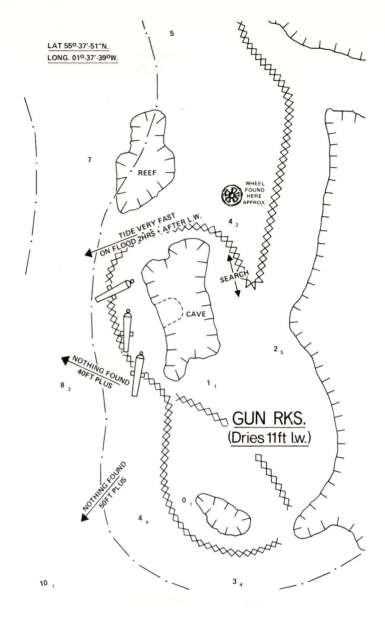

FIG. 9. First site plan of the discovery at Gun Rocks

BOATS—'John Wesley'/Dell Quay Dory 'Zokko'

	Bottle Capacity	ATS In	Out	Duration	Depth
John Wesley					
S. Saul	65 cu ft	120	20	45 min	50 ft
R. Brown	65 cu ft	145	20	45 min	50 ft
E. Tysick	75 cu ft	120	60	30 min	50 ft
E. Dobbie	65 cu ft	150	25	30 min	50 ft
W. Smith	65 cu ft	150	25	25 min	40 ft
D. Russell	65 cu ft	155	65	25 min	40 ft
G. Anderson	65 cu ft	145	130	40 min	45 ft
A. Harris	75 cu ft	160	145	40 min	45 ft
(Snorkelled after 10 min Lung Dive)					
Zokko					
S. Inglis	65 cu ft	150	10	30 min	50 ft
W. Sherwin	65 cu ft	150	10	30 min	50 ft
R. Edmundson	75 cu ft	160	95	30 min	50 ft
M. Pratt	Snorkel			30 min	25 ft
D. Blythe	Snorkel			30 min	25 ft

Metal Pulley Wheel found and brought aboard by W. R. Smith/D. Russell.

8 to 10 cannon located 40 ft deep West side of Gun Rocks by R. Brown/S. Saul.

(Bill Smith kept this sort of correct diving log for each dive. I have omitted these details from his other reports.)

THIRD DIVE, Sunday 7th June, 1970

Dive conditions foggy but went out in *John Wesley* accompanied by N. Ashmore's boat *Ran*. Slow trip out to site, good navigation by boat crew. Fog was a blessing, as it kept tourists at a safe distance (the local fishing boats run trips out to the Islands because of the bird-life and seals and also the fact that St Cuthbert spent most of his life there).

Conditions could not have been better—water was flat and we got to site before the start of slack water. Time 11.20–11.45 a.m.

We anchored on the south side of the rock (11 ft dries). Total No. of Divers on board both boats—12. I sent Snorkel divers over the site and they re-located the cannon immediately. I then sent a diver down to attach a rope to the cannon for reference.

Photographs and measuring then became the order of the morning. Refreshments were followed by searches and some objects were recovered from the bottom. The places were noted. Objects were sword handles (see Fig. 10), parts of blades and scabbards, lead shot weights from a cave entrance 10 ft down (not explored inside yet). Three assorted cannon-balls were also recovered and kept in water.

Approximate positions of all objects noted. Total amount of slack water today 2½ hours; tide starting to move fast south around site at the end of this period, which signalled end of operations for the day. Perishable items put in water for future preservation, i.e., cannon balls and ironised sword blade pieces and scabbard parts.

NOTES: 12 cannon now noted and a few more points which may be of interest later on as we start to dig. The bottom up against the rock face was glowing in the sunlight and my heart missed a beat, but on closer inspection (sharp knock with a wrecking bar) brought off a cloud of iron dust—the bottom of this point has objects buried under the crust. There appears, also, to be boxes of swords under one of the cannon, well cemented in.

SIXTH DIVE, Sunday 5th July 1970

Today's operations started at approximately 0930 hours when we went aboard, bound for Gun Rocks once again. 10 divers plus 2 TV crew were on board *John Wesley*. Nick Ashmore left at same time in his boat *Ran* with three divers on board.

We started by re-doing work that was done a few weeks ago—reason—piton 'C' pulled out. New measurement 59 ft taken and put on master sheet. Some items removed for dating, these places noted (M. Pratt being the main finder).

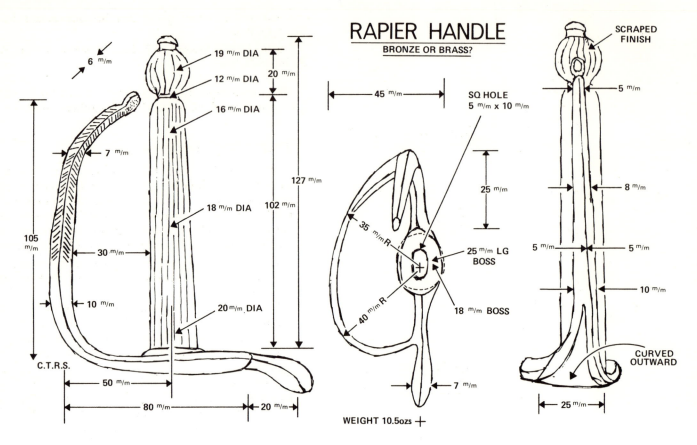

FIG. 10. One of the sword-handles found at Gun Rocks
Based on a drawing by W. R. Smith

Artifacts, cannon ball 7 in dia., very small balls 1⅞ in dia., one very small knuckle guard from a sword handle. A full list to be made for Receiver.

Other items for site plan. Cannon No. 2 has three sword handles underneath and alongside. Around No. 12 cannon which is not tagged yet, but buoyed and measured from 'Piton' (A) 54 ft from cascabel is a large mound of material. From this mound, pieces of pottery and glass. One piece of pottery has a coat of arms or a design on it. Needs verifying. Most of material brought up is for dating only. Careful note of areas taken.

Also found was a piece of metal, the shape of a tube, it has a small bore at end 'A' 11/16 in and gets larger at end 'B' 1 5/16 in. Material—Brass? Some small balls 2 in dia. also brought up which were hollow type, not yet certain. Weight 3¾ lb.

Film and sound recording done at all stages of operations today.

Cannon No. 1 not tagged yet, but marked on site plan. No. 1 cannon was re-measured and sizes are as follows: Muzzle end 10 in, cascabel end 20 in dia., and it's approximately 9 ft long. She is lying on a 10° magnetic bearing. Triangulation is necessary.

Approximate lay-out showing new pitons and work done today. Still photos required of new finds. We moved No. 5

cannon with the boat today to make sure it will lift. After moving it, I checked for damage—none to cannon or site. I searched around the site where it had been—no artifacts present, rocky bottom.

ELEVENTH DIVE, Saturday 11th July, 1970

We started fairly early on Saturday morning after a frustrating week of waiting for the buoyancy bag to arrive from Alan Bax in Plymouth. Reason for non-delivery—lost in a station somewhere in England. It arrived in Seahouses at 0930 hours by taxi laid on to bring it from Newcastle where it was found. Also a load of rope came from British Ropes which was on order—half a ton—but they sent the wrong rope, 1½ in dia. rope was delivered instead of 1¾ in circ. (we were not amused).

The weather was getting worse, winds of force 5–6 increasing and blowing W.N.W. I thought that if anything else goes wrong then we have no chance of raising the cannon this weekend. Anyway, we started to prepare the new equipment —the buoyancy bag is the type which goes inside a nylon net and has nylon lifting eyes along each side, six in number. It also has rubber grommets around the bag for securing the net. Air capacity 40 cu ft of free air at a test pressure 10 p.s.i. All equipment was loaded on boat by 1100 hours.

The mystery ship at Gun Rocks. A diver fits slings to the
cannon on the sea-bed ready for the 'Big Lift'.

Photo Nic Ashmore

(*Below*) the end of a successful operation—the same cannon
is hauled ashore on a landing trolley

Photo Beverly Christopher

Tide today well back L.W. is at 1300 hours approx. at site so speed was not that important. We arrived on site too soon, making it necessary to lie off in calmer waters for an hour or so as it is very uncomfortable lying at anchor in the tide race which is quite a spectacle on its own.

Conditions at this stage were getting worse, swell 4–5 ft, wind gusting up to 6–7. We could not get the anchor to hold. In fact, just before the end of the day's diving our 2 in anchor rope parted, leaving our No. 1 anchor on the bottom (must recover it on Monday or Tuesday).

The following is an account of our first lift attempt on Cannon No. 5. We started by putting down two 56 lb shot weights next to cannon. Next, ropes were run from the boat through the eyes on the blocks back to the boat where the buoyancy bag was made ready for hauling down to the cannon. Bag hauled down with the help of four divers who then started the job of attaching the bag to the cannon with ropes. This job completed, they then signalled to the diver in charge of the filling cylinder to go to the bottom to start his job which was slowly to fill the bag. At this stage, the TV camera was going strong, getting every operation on film for the record. The bag was at this stage OK, then, just as the cannon was getting ready to lift, the pressure of air in the bag appeared to move, throwing all the weight to the wrong end, making the bag unstable. (The reason was that the bag moved in the net.) We tried putting a small trimming bag on the muzzle end, but this failed because perhaps one or two divers were too enthusiastic putting air into bag.

It suddenly went critical and the cannon took off up to the surface the wrong way. The cannon at this stage was in a vertical position with the cascabel end about 5 ft from the sea-bed swinging about not in control by divers who, at this stage, went in all directions, leaving a very surprised diver-cum-cameraman looking for his extras—all he was left with was a swinging menace which sounded like some very large bell. What a sight, 2500 lb of cast-iron swinging around. Speed was needed to put this potential hazard back on the sea-bed. The area was cleared and two divers released the bag and allowed cannon to sink back to sea-bed. Cannon checked for damage and also the surrounding area where it lies—found to be OK.

Then came our enquiries. How did it happen? What did we do wrong? First, we had the bag too far forward over the cannon—we should have had all slings aft of trunnions, we also should have ensured that all fixing grommets were well tied to stop the bag moving inside the net and make sure that only four or six divers controlled the whole lift.

Well, we all learn by our mistakes, so we packed up all the gear and returned to Seahouses—by this time through monstrous seas.

A few last words—I think even if the lift had been successful we would not have got it back in these conditions. TV observers thought we had no chance from the very start. Divers involved in the operation today are as follows: E. Dobbie, R. Brown, M. Pratt, H. Harvey on the lifting bag. Underwater—A. Harris, myself and later C. Malvern on the air filling. G. Anderson assisted. I was overall marshal

of operations. Tomorrow a different approach will be made.

We arrived back at Seahouses at 1730 hours approx. very cold and hungry but not defeated.

TWELFTH DIVE, Sunday 12th July, 1970

THE BIG LIFT—After a good breakfast at our shore base, Beadnell Hall, we proceeded to Seahouses harbour for 0930 hours to make arrangements for today's attempt at lifting cannon from the sea-bed. After our unsuccessful attempt yesterday (Saturday) we did some re-thinking late last night. Suggestions for today's lift were as follows:

First, the bag must be fully tested and blown up (before transporting to site, and also all parts of netting and fixing grommets to be fastened *in situ* on shore. The whole bag was deflated prior to shipping out to site—this ensured that nothing could move when it is hauled down to the cannon.

Second, some other method of blowing up the bag other than a diver taking down an Aqualung bottle as this does not give sufficient control of the venting operations. One of the boat crew came up with a good suggestion in conjunction with Equipments Officer, Colin Malvern—that we leave bottles aboard and pass a hose down to a diver on the bag who will in turn take notice of signals via hose. The diver then in fact can have perfect control on air and it would make it easier to change over for more cylinders.

The diving team was then picked to do all work connected with the lift and I told all other divers to stay out of the water.

The site today was not much better than Saturday for conditions although the wind had dropped a little. We were still having difficulty in getting anchors to hold in the fast tide—remember we lost our No. 1 anchor yesterday.

I sent Harry Harvey over first, to check the conditions of the cannon and the slings after having had to drop it back to sea-bed on Saturday. He reported everything OK and proceeded to put a sling on the muzzle and complete with ring so that the buoyancy bag could be hauled down to the cannon. (Note: we did away with the blocks by using cannon as anchor point.) A rope was passed through the ring and returned to the boat where the bag was fastened on prior to hauling down. We were now ready for the attempt.

The four-man team now went into the water together to start operations—others on deck stood by at their posts, air control, ropes, haulers, divers, etc. Some difficulty was had hauling down until all air had been squeezed out of the bag. The divers promptly attached the bag by its appropriate eyes and then returned to base craft for air hose. Air was slowly let in and after a total of 17 minutes had elapsed since the start of the sea-bed operation, the gun came to the surface under reasonable control. The divers on the bottom experienced something which must be a very rare feeling of doing something really spectacular. One diver said: 'If I dive for another 100 years, I will never get the same thrill again'.

Once on the surface, speed was the order of the day—the towing rope was attached complete with a safety tow rope. I signalled to the TV crew boat that we were washing out the rest of diving as the cannon was now under tow and all haste

CAPTIVA MEMORIAL LIBRARY

was needed to get it out of the dangerous fast rip tide which was still just off our port hand. Waves in this trip were still 6–8 ft in places and very agitated. The air hose was left attached to compensate for loss due to pounding through the heavy seas. We left our No. 2 anchor buoyed for picking up by our No. 2 boat as we could only go ahead with no degree of latitude to manoeuvre.

A very precise exercise in boat handling followed by Jim Trotter, the skipper of the *John Wesley*, when he took the boat through the bad rip tide which the wind was once again whipping into a frenzy. The boat was just making way and the bag, complete with cannon and umbilical cord, looked like some big grey whale following in our wake.

Anxious moments were experienced as we started on the first leg of the four mile trip back to Seahouses through very choppy water. Our first stop, we decided, would be Longcarr Hole, which is in the Inner Farne Group, where checks on equipment, etc, would take place. The TV boat, *Clan Gillean* was on our starboard side all the way across the Staple Sound, filming progress as it happened and another Seahouses boat came out to note progress (*Silver Dawn*). It was a very heart thrilling experience (personal thought). We arrived in Longcarr Hole very relieved.

The last leg of the crossing was now in the offing after Harry Harvey reported to me that everything was OK with the bag and towing rope. All the time we were underway, the crew were standing by with sharp knife and marker line in the event of having to cut the load free, 150 ft of line and marker are also attached—the biggest danger of losing our load is that the water is 120 ft plus in places in the 'sounds'. We made steady progress across the Inner Farne Sound and approached harbour at approximately 1600 hours where we had to cast off our load as water was still only half tide. Nick's boat *Ran* came alongside and took tow rope and air cylinder for manoeuvring in shallow water of harbour. We manoeuvred the load against the harbour wall where a large crowd looked on and the film crew were doing their stuff. The cannon was then anchored in the clear waters of the harbour and we relaxed and waited for high water and the last leg of this operation which was removing it from the water.

REMOVAL—Approximately 2000 hours, I sent a diver down to check how far the muzzle of the cannon was hanging down and to swim across harbour and check depth of water. What a shock! The muzzle had dropped to 16 ft and the harbour check showed 12 ft. We then put a trimming bag on and drew the bag up to almost level and started the shifting operation.

We towed the load over with Nick's boat and divers helped by pushing towards harbour slipway some 500 yards away. Yard by yard she went towards the waiting boat trailer which we had borrowed and had taken underwater to meet the load. The trailer was attached by 200 ft of rope to shore where a Land Rover was going to pull it out of the water. By this time, a few hundred people had turned up to see the cannon brought out of the water. Once on the trailer and roped, etc, we started to haul—at this point many of the watching crowd got on the line and it flew up the slipway,

to the delight of the spectators. Well after 200 years plus, it's out of the water and waiting for the transport which will take it down to Tyne Tees Television Studio in Newcastle where it will get a very close inspection by the experts.

NOTES: The cannon will be used on the programme, then moved to Laing Art Gallery Museum to be preserved, and then it will be put on display at Science Museum, Newcastle. Awaiting technical Report and P. Napp's measurements.

THIRTEENTH DIVE, Saturday 18th July, 1970

We had to arrive very early this morning as the tides were very dodgy for getting the boat out of the harbour. The reason for this is that the tides were spring tides and very low, L.W. being 07.45 hr. We had to ferry all equipment out to the *John Wesley* in Nick Ashmore's boat *Ran* which made life that little bit more difficult. The tide was the lowest I have seen for a long time.

Eight divers turned up this morning. Including Alan Bax of the Committee for Nautical Archaeology. He came along to make personal observations of the site following his appearance on 'Today At Six', the TV programme which is helping us with the project.

Alan Bax gave us some very good pointers for future work, explaining what must be done to make this site a worthwhile attempt at underwater archaeology. A summary of his suggestions are added at the end of this report.

Work today was done mainly by six divers as two of the team were full of cold. The main jobs were to cut and harvest kelp from the site and visually observe any other relevant material such as new cannon.

Nick's job was to assist Alan Bax with photographs and notes so that he could give a more detailed opinion later this month. T. Rae and A. Harris found another cannon which they noted and cleared of kelp. Next to the cannon he found a very large lead sounding weight and a couple of pieces of pottery which have no markings on them. What was obvious today was the lack of a grid pattern. This came into Alan Bax's discussion after the dive.

One other useful job completed today was the recovery of the *John Wesley* No. 1 anchor which we lost last Saturday afternoon. I am still trying to impress the importance of not bringing artifacts to the surface. The best thing to do would be to sketch any items found and then to surface to ascertain the position, but when the grid is laid, the grid number only will be necessary. The cannon we raised last weekend and had on the TV programme was found to have a letter 'G' on the trunnion. A fuller understanding of cannon design is being undertaken by Peter Napp (Report his findings to me as soon as possible).

Suggestions put forward by A. Bax are as follows:

1. He suggested that we get our grid down as soon as possible.

2. That we put our interim report forward to the Committee for Nautical Archaeology in the hope that we can obtain a 'Sea-Bed Lease'.

The mystery ships and the clues to their identity.

Top, this underwater picture shows clearly the 'F' mark of
the maker on the trunnion of a cannon at Gun Rocks.

Photo B. G. Sheppard

(*Bottom*) these artifacts were found near the cannon on the
Mewstone site – a storage-jar neck and lid, half a bar shot and
half a tampion from one of the cannon. A 50-pence piece
is shown for size comparison

3. That we write to various people for information about the possible origin of the wreck from their respective countries. An interim report to be sent to each person.

4. He also suggests that we check out the possibility of any other wrecks in the Gun Rocks area which could also be covered by the 'Sea-Bed Lease'.

5. That we take rock samples and have them tested. If material is different to the local rock then it could be ballast.

6. He suggested only laying the grid on one side of the rock for a start.

FOURTEENTH DIVE, Sunday 19th July, 1970

Diving out on the site cancelled because of tide.

It took so long to load all equipment and get all the divers on board the *John Wesley* that by the time we got underway we had lost the benefit of the low tide.

Note: Changed the dive venue to the Crumbstone Rocks where the team relaxed diving on a modern wreck. Believed to be the *Britannia* of 4–6000 tons. Underwater vis. 15/20 feet. Conditions in the lee of the Island—good.

SIXTEENTH DIVE, Sunday 26th July, 1970

Fifteenth abandoned owing to North winds and poor underwater visibility.

Tides this week are good for loading as they are reasonably late, L.W. not until 1400 hr.. We got all gear on board by 11.45 hr and we were under way by 12.30 hr approx.

Conditions: Not too good. Wind still in North, but light. Swell quite heavy but long and slow in the Farne Sound.

Boat used—*John Wesley* as usual. Purpose was to lay out the start of our survey grid as discussed last week. Owing to the fact that some equipment is not available which meant using buoyancy bag to man-handle 56-pound weights around the site. We place the first weight with much difficulty, approx. 15 feet from Piton C which is marked on master plan. Then we proceeded to put weight No. 2 down in the same manner. A rope was passed between the two and pulled tight—we cleared all kelp along the line so that it would lie flat and straight. A couple of faults became apparent:

1. The sea-bed is not flat as we first thought and the line is 4 feet in places from the bed.

2. Our second weight is down the cliff making the rope bent—we will have to put it at the top of the cliff later. The idea of putting the rope down was to give us a base line for the next step which requires putting down our wire using Rawbolts and rigging wire as the base lines. This was not an easy operation.

The rest of the team continued cutting kelp and removing rock samples from the rock and sea-bed to ascertain whether it is ballast or not. Miss B. Christopher will get a report from Hancocks Museum about the rock.

A lot of work will be required to fix this grid but it was obvious just from that simple base line just how valuable the grid will be. Operations ceased today at 17.00 hr approx.

So the diving went on whenever possible. And Bill Smith continued to fill in his notes after each dive. He learnt a little more each time about the ship and about the difficulties of underwater archaeology on such an exposed site.

By the time they had made their last dive of the season on the Gun Rocks site, the Tyneside divers knew that their hopes of finding a Spanish Armada ship were over. As they collected information about their finds from museums and the experts in each field, it became almost certain that their lost ship dated from about 1650 to 1700.

The pottery, for example, was identified as being of the late seventeenth century—salt-glazed stoneware jugs called 'Bellarmine' manufactured in Frenchen, on the Rhine. These fat-bellied drinking jugs with a face in relief on the neck opposite the handle were nicknamed 'Bellarmine' by the Protestants of Holland to ridicule Cardinal Robert Bellarmine (1542–1621), who was well known for his influence on the Catholic theology of the time.

The brass sword-handles may be of Dutch manufacture. Their similarity and number suggests that they were made for a large concern—and this in turn points to the Dutch East-India Company, but this too is not certain.

Work went on in the attempts to trace the letters 'G', 'S' and 'F' on the cannon trunnions. But by the time the season ended only the 'F' had led to any clue.

In Copenhagen there is a similar 'F' on the left trunnion of an 18-pound 'finbanker', which has been identified as Dutch or Swedish of the late seventeenth century. Cannon No. 13 on the Gun Rocks site bears its 'F' on . . . the left trunnion! But it would be wrong at this stage even to do more than draw attention to the similarity. Maybe one of the other cannon will carry a date somewhere on its length, for it was common practice to mark the date of manufacture.

It is odd that no other ship parts or fittings apart from the sounding weights and bronze wheel have so far been found. The anchors would provide a good clue as to date, but so far there is no sign of them on the site. It is, of course, early days yet, and it may be that the anchors lie far away where they were dropped in a desperate attempt to hold the ship off the rocks that the crew could see only too well from the line of foam ahead. If all were dropped in such an attempt to stave off disaster, they will be some distance away, and may never be found.

This, then, is as far as it is possible to take the story of Gun Rocks at present. The dream of the Tyneside divers, the dream of Bill Smith—that of finding a new Armada wreck—has faded and gone. But a new dream has taken its place—to find out the name and nationality of the ship that died on Gun Rocks one wild night long ago.

It may be, of course, that those determined North-East divers will never know. That only the ancestors of the grey seals crowding the near-by rocks knew, and Time has culled them too.

But it may be—and it may be happening as you read this book—that one day a diver will pick up a tiny piece of evidence from the sea-bed at the foot of Staple Island and then these Tyneside diving detectives will have solved the mystery of yet another long-lost ship.

While the Tyneside divers puzzled over their cannon in the

stormy waters of the Farnes, another group of divers were swimming around exactly the same problem among the Devon kelp.

The divers of Croydon Branch of the British Sub-Aqua Club had based much of their diving on Newton Ferrers, probably the most beautiful inlet in the whole of the South Devon coastline.

From this estuary of the Yealm the diving boats had often taken them to dive around the Great Mewstone Rock, a sort of mini-desert-island complete with abandoned house. The Croydon divers claimed no sort of exclusivness about this site— it has been explored by many divers over the years, but until Whitsun 1968 all that those divers, both from Croydon and from other clubs all over the country, had seen were fish and kelp. Not that it isn't a marvellous spot to dive—the great kelp forests and varied marine life are worth anyone's compressed air.

But the dive that was to change all that as far as Croydon Branch were concerned was made by Dick Middlewood, and what happened is best told in his own words:

On that particular week-end we were looking for a very impressive gully that we had found on a previous occasion. We had a neon-type echo sounder which located the spot for us and we dropped anchor. We began our dive and soon I was following a gully, as we usually do in this area, when I came across some peculiarly shaped rocks. They struck me as being a bit too straight for rocks, perhaps they were logs, but then again there are no trees

on the Mewstone and very few on the mainland and small ones at that.

No, not logs! Suddenly I realised they were cannon—two 6-foot cannon. I must have consumed some 30 atmospheres of air within as many seconds. It was a rare moment. I felt I was almost certainly the first to see these pieces since they sank years ago.

Fortunately I was in seeing distance of my co-diver. I could see his bubbles on the other side of a hill. I swam over, but he was so absorbed in an attempt to catch a fish in a net shopping bag that I had to grab hold of him and signal frantically for him to follow me. Then I had an attack of mild panic—I couldn't find the cannon, they blended so well into the background.

Just before my companion turned nasty, I saw them again. This was lucky because no one would ever have believed me once I had returned to the surface claiming to have seen cannon. In fact on the way back to the boat I found a third cannon. Was I glad to have a witness!

Dick Middlewood admits that they really didn't know what to do about his discovery then. There were some ideas—ideas which would make a marine archaeologist nearly faint—one of which was to tow one of the cannon to shore under an inflatable boat and present it to a local fisherman for use as a mooring until they could think of something better to do with it. Fortunately, this idea never came to anything as Dick Middlewood and Dennis Hinchcliffe, also from Croydon BSAC, went in March 1969 on one of the many courses run by Alan Bax at the School for Nautical Archaeology at Plymouth. There they learnt

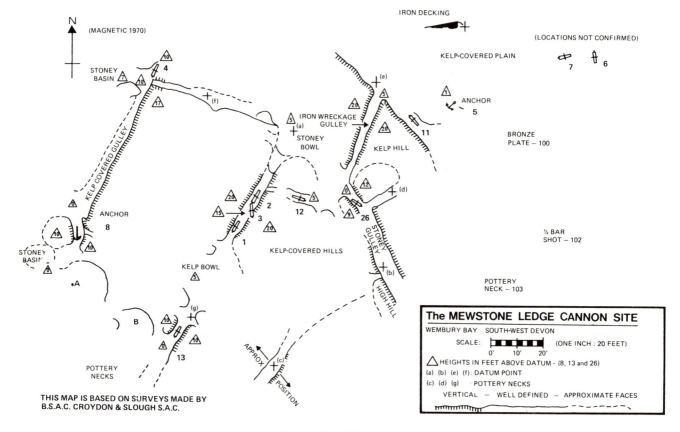

FIG. 11. The Mewstone site
Based on a drawing by R. Middlewood

that this was not exactly the thing to do with cannon found on the sea-bed! During the course the Croydon divers became completely converted to the cause of underwater archaeology, and decided to set up a small project to relocate the cannon, plot them as they lay, and then try and discover their age.

On that same course at Plymouth were two divers from Slough Sub-Aqua Club, who were keen to join in on this project. A meeting was arranged for June at Newton Ferrers, and then the two groups of divers parted to develop marker buoys, reels, bottom lines and so on that would be used in the project. Collection and manufacture of this equipment really presented no problems, but when the boat finally cleared the Yealm estuary and headed for the Mewstone the most worried man aboard was Dick Middlewood. All he had to relocate the cannon were three lines of sight. He had noted them down on the day of the discovery, but this had been passed on to someone else and lost. He thought what a fool he was going to look if they couldn't find the cannon again. And he felt an even bigger fool when he looked at the unfamiliar faces on board and realized it was he who had invited the other diving club to come along.

But there was no going back, and on arrival at the approximate position the search procedure was started. This entailed dropping a buoy and then motoring along the most reliable of the three lines of sight, paying out line for one hundred yards, before dropping another buoy. The divers would then search in pairs on both sides of the line by going down to the central line and then out at right angles to it along shorter lines, reeling them in and out and moving along the centre

line stage by stage. Well, that was the plan, but the sea had other ideas.

The only way that they found they could lay the line in practice was with the current, and Dick Middlewood feared the worst. The first two pairs went down, each equipped with a small marker buoy to release to the surface if anything was found. To his amazement and delight, the buoys soon started popping up all over the place. His delight was tempered when he found out, however, that most had been released by accident. But not all.

The first pair of divers had found a four-hundredweight anchor almost by the anchor of the diving boat. And near by was a six-foot cannon. Another pair had found another anchor, of about nine hundredweight, and a 4 ft 6 in cannon. They had relocated the site at the first attempt.

The second day's diving started differently. The divers arrived to find the site occupied—by two big black dorsal fins. They were sharks all right, but basking sharks, and usually considered harmless by divers. The divers below making measurements of the cannon and anchors didn't see the sharks under water at all, but those in the boat watched fascinated as the black triangles weaved in and out between the buoys marking the beginning and end of the central search line.

That was the real beginning of it all. The divers involved in most of the work were Dick Middlewood, Dennis Hinchcliffe and Nick Parrott of Croydon Branch of the British Sub-Aqua Club, Martin Dean and Dick Johnstone of Slough Sub-Aqua Club and John Smart of Gwynedd Branch, BSAC. But they,

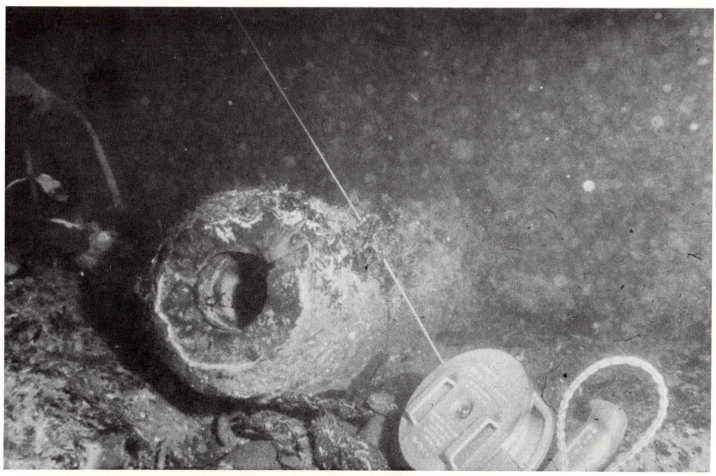

One of the cannon on the Mewstone site after the tampion had been removed. Nearby is a reel used in measuring the area of wreckage.

of course, did not do all the work alone. Many members of their clubs joined in to help. After the first few weekends of diving, the pattern changed. The teams from the two main clubs worked separately and pooled information from time to time.

The next important stage of Project Mewstone was carried out by a group from Slough SAC led by Martin Dean, together with John Smart, a professional land surveyor, who also had underwater archaeology survey experience. During two weeks in August 1969 they surveyed the area round the cannon (see Fig. 11). The method used was to attach lines to the sea-bed in a 'U' shape made up of lines of 300 feet, 100 feet and another 300 feet, A central 200-foot line was laid in the centre of the 'U' to make triangulation possible with 100-foot tapes.

This was a mammoth task, as the lines had to be held down to the sea-bed at suitable points either by skewers set in underwater cement or by pitons hammered into the rocks.

The survey was highly successful, bringing to light more cannon and now pottery. It also made possible the production of a proper site map with the items discovered marked in at their proper positions. The survey would have been even more successful if, during the last days of plotting, the whole layout had not been ripped up—Martin Dean lays this at the door (or rather hook) of an early-morning shark-fisherman, who must have wondered what on earth he had caught!

Both groups continued to search the area. The pottery was intriguing. It appeared to be pieces of red earthenware storage jars. The pieces are fairly widely scattered, and many of the fragments are under large boulders on the site, which lies off the south-western tip of the Great Mewstone Rock in Wembury Bay.

The underwater terrain is very rugged, and consists of steep-sided gullies and mounds. At low water the maximum depth is thirty-five feet, and the minimum ten to fifteen feet. Strong ebb and flow currents are present. Visibility generally exceeds thirty feet.

The Mewstone divers still had no idea of what sort of ship had been wrecked there, but some idea of the date came from the cannon and the pottery.

That date would appear to be some time in the late eighteenth century. 'Appear' is the right word to use in this context, for in all forms of archaeology things often do not turn out quite as simply as they do at first appear.

The Mewstone divers stress this in their excellent report for the Committee for Nautical Archaeology. They say that there is 'no evidence that cannon and pottery all come from a single wreck, apart from dates being approximately contemporary'.

First the pottery. This was first noticed, writes Martin Dean, the Diving Officer of Slough SAC, on the dives following the initial location and exploration of the site. He goes on to say: 'The coarse red pottery is now known to be thinly spread over at least 3000 sq ft, but appears to be concentrated in gulleys south of one of the anchors. In some places massive boulders weighing many tons sit on layers of broken pots. Two of the pieces recovered have applied plaques with monograms on them (see Fig. 12). Pieces of pottery, particularly the necks which are scattered about, are unfortunately subject to undisciplined removal by souvenir-hunters, and a total tally will therefore be impossible.

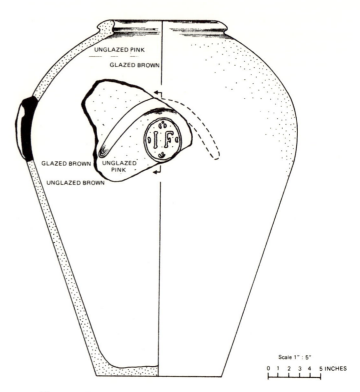

FIG. 12. Reconstruction from two fragments recovered
from the Mewstone site
Based on a full-size drawing by J. H. Ashdown

'Another complication', adds Dean, 'on this site is the wreck of the steamer *Ajax*, which overlaps the cannon area, mixing its glazed white earthenware and glass with the older coarse pottery. This at first confused us about the date of the earlier wreck'.

The *Ajax*, whose sinking is recorded, was lost on the Mewstone on 13th October 1854.

Taking great care to record the positions of any items they brought to the surface, the divers sent the pottery fragments to Mr J. H. Ashdown, the treasurer of the Society for Post-Medieval Archaeology. His first report reads as follows:

The first fragment is from a large lead-glazed earthenware storage vessel with vestigial lug handle—pink fabric with dark brown glaze to interior only, must have been nearly three feet high. Applied plaque below handle with letters 'IF' and crowns is of the same fabric. These vessels are often described as Iberian, i.e. Spanish. Source not known exactly. Date range 1750 to 1900(?) with bias, for the Mewstone jars, to the late 18th century. Examination of further fragments recovered in 1970 allowed the rim of the jar to be drawn and produced a second plaque—with the letters 'IN'.

Parallels. One is shown in painting of 'Old Custom House Quay, London' by S. Scott (in the Victoria and Albert Museum). Examples found in wrecks at Yorktown, Virginia, sunk in 1781 and in other archaeological contexts in Virginia, USA. I have found one excavated in Brentford, Middlesex, which is either late 18th or early 19th century. Half stucco or complete pots of this type existed over many 'oil' or ironmongers' shops of the mid or late 19th century.

Applied plaques. I have found another plaque, with 'IF' on it, in the Netherlands. . . . A further 'IF' plaque, just like the one shown, has been located in material from the River Thames at Wapping, London. Finally, Mr J. G. Hurst has also drawn my attention to a specimen in one of the Edinburgh museums, bearing the letters 'CB'.

Comment and conclusions. When looked for, Oil Jars are common in English archaeological material—as they are in Virginia and the West Indies. Whatever their original use (why not oil jars?), they had a valuable secondary function as fresh water containers on ships and on land. They could also be used as rubbish containers.

The question of origin is still complex, but it is likely that they were produced in many places in Spain, Portugal and Italy rather than at one spot. The 19th and 20th century examples that I have located in a garden recently, sometimes have makers' impressed marks, which are all Italian.

In conclusion, I see the importance of the Mewstone pottery in that it suggests a cargo of oil jars. All the other examples that I have located are single finds. The origin of the monogrammed plaques is obviously of interest, but is not of importance in the context of the Mewstone site. There are likely to be a great number of different monograms found in the future.

The cannon and anchors were the next to come in for detailed examination. All the cannon that the divers had found and measured—ten in all—seemed to be upside-down, that is with their offset trunnions uppermost. There were six that appeared to be 6-pounders, and four that could qualify as 3-pounders.

All were in an advanced state of decay, and extremely difficult to spot. When in position they seem to have 'grown' into the sea-bed. Striking evidence of this camouflage is the fact that Dick Middlewood is convinced that the three original cannon which he found, and which started the whole exploration of the area, have so far escaped relocation—despite the large number of dives put in on the site.

This lack of sharpness in outline created difficulty for the divers measuring the cannon. Cascabels are not visible, and mouldings or reinforcements can only be seen on two. Muzzle flare was only visible on one. Was this the design of the guns or just part of the general decay and corrosion of the cannon on the site?

Here the Mewstone divers turned to the experts of the National Maritime Museum at Greenwich for help. On their advice the trunnion positions were carefully checked, and all were found to be well off the centre line of the guns. The trunnions were searched for markings, but so far, unlike the Tyneside divers and their cannon on Gun Rocks, no markings have been found.

The Maritime Museum experts—Messrs Preston, Annis,

Some of the Mewstone diving team. *From left* Martin Dean, Dennis Hinchcliffe, Richard Middlewood, and Nicholas Parrot. In the background is the 194 feet high Mewstone

Tucker and Lyon—also told them that the only reliable evidence for dating their guns would seem to be in the positions of the trunnions and their actual size.

In the report on the cannon Dennis Hinchcliffe writes:

A Minion Ordinary of 1692 (according to *The Wooden Fighting Ships in the Royal Navy: A.D. 897–1860*, by E. H. H. Archibald) had a 3-inch bore, a length of 7 feet and projected a 3¼ lb shot. A Service 3-pounder of 1743 was 4 ft 6 in long with a calibre of 2.91 in (according to *A Practical Sea-Gunner's Companion* by William Mountaine, published in London in 1747), while by 1780, new 3-pounders of the same bore were again reduced in length to 3 ft 6 in (according to *A Treatise of Artillery*, by John Muller, 1780).

Thus our small cannon, being 4 ft 6 in long with a bore of three inches, can be dated 1743 to 1780 from the foregoing. There is, of course, no evidence to indicate that the guns are British and, since the technology of other nations possibly lagged behind ours in those days, the guns could have been made later.

Nevertheless both the Maritime Museum and Mr. B. W. Bathe, Assistant Keeper at the Science Museum London and an authority on wooden ships, have indicated similar dates from an examination of early rough drawings. Mr Bathe wrote: '. . . the dimensions you state correspond closely with those of a normal 3-pounder gun of about 1800. The larger gun is probably a 6-pounder of the same period.'

Quite late on in the investigation of the site one of the Croydon branch divers made a surprising discovery. On 26th September 1970 Paul Bernini had joined Mike Jones by the cannon which had been labelled '26' for reference. They examined it carefully, and Paul Bernini saw something blocking the mouth. He dug around it and discovered bits of wood coming out. To his amazement a cloud of gas escaped from the muzzle, and he was left holding half a tampion complete with piece of tarred string for tampions, the pulling out of!

The tampion was a piece of greasy wood, and it was tapered very slightly. The fact that the tampion was still in place after years of immersion was surprising, but the 'bung' had done its job very well. Behind the tampion the bore, which measured exactly three inches, was greasy and very smooth. The next day the divers had high hopes of being able to tip the cannon, and out would roll the cannon-ball, which they could feel with rods was still in place.

But the cannon-ball would not come free. It seemed to be rusted solidly in place, and the divers can only assume that water had entered through the touch-hole and compressed the air, driving it up the barrel until it met a stoutly rammed home tampion. The fact that the cannon was resting with the muzzle elevated slightly would have helped to bring this effect about.

What else did the divers find that has some bearing on the armament of the ship? Well, they found half a bar shot and some patches that could be the remains of cannon-balls, but so far no positive identification of these patches has been made.

Are there more cannon to be found? There may well be. But we mustn't forget the divers of long ago. Parts of the site are extremely shallow, and any cannon left on the top of 'hills' could have been easily spotted and salvaged at low tides on calm days without even diving.

Some of the cannon have 'fins' on them—something that is being reported from cannon site after cannon site (in the appendix on cannons you will find the result of some practical research made by the Croydon divers that throws some light on these mysterious projections).

So far the pottery fits in well with the cannon dating. And so we have a ship that hit the Mewstone some time in the latter half of the eighteenth century. What else is left to give a clue to the ship? The anchors.

Only two anchors have so far been found. One is nearly ten feet long; the other just over six feet. Once again acting on the advice of the Maritime Museum, the divers examined them closely, taking all possible measurements. Both appear to have pointed crowns and straight arms. The cross-section of the blade of the larger anchor—almost ten feet long—shows it to

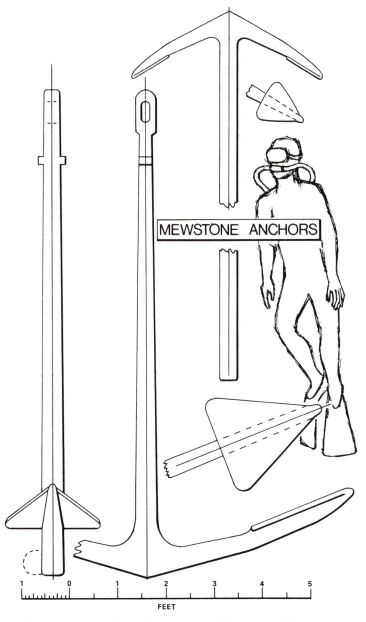

FIG. 13. The anchors of the mystery ship on the Mewstone
Based on a drawing by D. Hinchcliffe

be rectangular rather than round. The shank of the large anchor is horizontal, one arm is buried, the other standing almost vertical (see Fig. 13).

Once again the advice of Mr Bathe was sought. He wrote to the divers—'the anchors are probably late 18th century and are close to the sizes laid down for that date for anchors of nine hundredweight and four hundredweight respectively'.

So all the evidence points to a ship of the late eighteenth century striking the Mewstone at some time around that date. But like the ship that the Tyneside divers have found, her identity will have to remain a mystery until either a diver makes a lucky strike by bringing up some object which establishes her name without doubt—an unlikely but not impossible piece of good fortune—or some more research turns up some forgotten record of a ship that died before she could reach the shelter of the port of Plymouth over two hundred years ago.

Croydon Branch were awarded the Duke of Edinburgh's Prize for 1970 for their Mewstone Ledge archaeological survey of the wreck site.

Note: A point of interest from some later research which concerns the wrecks in this chapter.

First of all, the cannon. Just eighty feet from a modern break-water in Millbay, Plymouth, nine cannon were found. One of them has an 'F' on the trunnion to match that of the cannon on Gun Rocks. The Royal Arsenal, Copenhagen, claims that these markings indicate that they were made in Denmark in the eighteenth century.

CHAPTER 9

The Case of the Thirty Chinamen

who were on board the Earl of Abergavenny, lost in 1805, and including the Caroline and the Admiralty Barge (1806), H.M.S. Boreas (1807) and the Queen (1814).

IN the early days of 1805 Napoleon's plan for the invasion of England began to take shape. But before his assault troops could be ferried across the Channel from Boulogne, he had to have command of the Channel. And so began the complicated moves that were to lead Nelson to the battle of Trafalgar later in the year.

In the meantime, war or no war, England's merchantmen had to go about their business. On 1st February 1805 a convoy set sail from Portsmouth for the East Indies and trade with Bengal and China.

Five East Indiamen made up the convoy—the *Earl of Abergavenny*, the *Royal George*, the *Henry Addington*, the *Wexford* and the *Bombay Castle*. In command of the convoy, and acting as escort, was the frigate H.M.S. *Weymouth*—though many of her charges were capable of producing more firepower than she could herself. East Indiamen were no easy prey for any roving pirate.

Despite the poor weather, which started almost as soon as the ships had left port and rounded the Wight, they ploughed on into heavy seas driven on by strong south-west winds. When conditions got even worse, the *Weymouth* signalled that they should make for Portland Roads. On the Friday night a gale made it impossible for the ships to keep station, and the convoy broke up.

It was Tuesday before the convoy gathered together again in the entrance to the Portland Roads. And there was no sign of H.M.S. *Weymouth*. The weather was appalling, and about noon the *Wexford*, which had become convoy commander in the *Weymouth*'s absence, signalled that all ships which had pilots on board should run for port.

This left the *Earl of Abergavenny* alone, for she had not yet been able to pick up a pilot, nor had she one on board who knew the coast thereabouts. So she waited, and no doubt Captain Robert Wordsworth, her captain, was upset by the delay. Upset, too, were all the rest of the people on board, for the *Abergavenny* was packed. Her crew accounted for 160 men. There were 60 passengers on board, 150 recruits for the Army and the English East India Company, and 30 Chinese, who were described in the ship's documents as 'Chinamen'. In all, 400 people had to endure the rolling and heaving of the ship as they waited for the pilot boat to come out.

It was 3 p.m. before the pilot came aboard—it was surprising that he came at all in the condition the sea was now in, though the weather was moderating—and then the ship bore up for Portland and shelter inside the Roads. At this time no one could have had the slightest idea that they were standing straight into danger. Certainly Captain Wordsworth thought some of his troubles were over, and assumed that the pilot knew the coast well. He was soon to find out differently—within a few minutes a grinding crash and shock told him that the pilot had put the *Abergavenny* straight on to a rock.

They decided that they had struck the Shambles, which are about two miles off Portland Bill. The pilot is thought to have blamed this on a particular strong ebb tide, but there is no doubt that the Shambles were no place to be stuck. It is an apt name, the Shambles—for shambles they are, jagged and well-spaced rocks, some just breaking the surface, others just under it at all stages of the tide.

Even so, Captain Wordsworth thought—and so did his senior officers—that the situation was not too bad, and with any luck they should be able to get the ship off the rocks without much more damage. For an hour and a half they tried every trick of seamanship they knew, and so confident did they seem to be that there was no panic on board at all. Everyone seemed to assume that there was no cause for alarm. But after nearly two hours had passed, and the ship was just as firmly on as before, even the captain had his doubts, for he ordered twenty guns to be fired as a distress signal to the shore.

At 5 p.m. the ship's carpenter brought really alarming news. There was a big leak near the bottom of the chain pumps, and he could do nothing to stop the water gushing in. Pumping started at once, but the water gained on them.

A bailing chain was then started, with men down in the hold passing up buckets out of the forehatch, but even these efforts seemed to have no effect on the amount of water she was taking in.

By 6 p.m. it was obvious the ship was lost. Other leaks were found, and the gale-force wind increased the beating on the rocks, which the ship was now taking all the time. As the night drew on, something like panic started to break out among the passengers. Two spinsters, the Misses Evans, and other passengers began to implore the captain to set them ashore. How he was meant to do this no one could be quite sure, for the seas around the ship were mountainous. It looked as though any of the ship's boats—had they been launched—would not have lasted long. Indeed, it was as much as the Captain and crew could do to keep the *Abergavenny* afloat, so the passengers got short shrift.

The crew were now near complete exhaustion, and to keep them at work the officers issued tots of rum. More signal guns were fired. As no boats came from the shore, the captain ordered one of the ship's boats lowered, and sent into it Mr Mortimer, the purser, with the ship's papers, dispatches and an urgent request for assistance. Six seamen and the third mate, Mr Wordsworth, a cousin of the captain, were ordered to join the purser and make for the shore.

No sooner had the ship's boat been whisked away into the dark than a shout was heard from the port side, and out of the dark came a rescue boat from the land. She had a hard job coming alongisde, and the sight of the boat rising and falling in the waves was not one to give much confidence. In fact the Misses Evans had now completely changed their minds, as had other passengers. Now they wanted to stay on board. But the captain ignored their pleas and ordered them into the boats together with their companion, Mrs Blair, and three other passengers, Miss Jackson, Mr Rutledge and Mr Taylor.

Just before 9 p.m. some more boats were heard near the wreck—and the officers and crew might well have been forgiven for thinking that they were about to be saved. The boat containing the purser had reached the shore and raised the alarm, but the boats that had come out stayed away from the *Abergavenny*. Had they really come out to save lives—or were they more interested in salvaging the ship as she broke up? Despite the crew's shouts and cries for help, the boats came no nearer.

By 10 p.m. the *Abergavenny* obviously had not long to go. She was almost completely full of water, and was sinking slowly. Some of the crew gave way to despair, some prayed, others asked for more rum. When this was refused a group attacked the spirit room in an attempt to take it for themselves. The officers drove them back, and to prevent another attempt stationed a man on the door of the liquor store with a brace of pistols. He was still there as the ship started to sink. One of the crew tried pleading with him, saying: 'It will all be as one an hour hence'. The officer with the pistols is reported as replying: 'Be that as it may, let us die like men'.

It seems extraordinary that while all this was going on no more of the ship's boats were launched. But they weren't. About two minutes before the ship went under, Mr Bagget, the chief mate, went to Captain Wordsworth and said: 'We have done all we can, Sir, she will sink in a minute'. The captain looked at him in silence for a moment and then said: 'It cannot be helped—God's will be done'.

The passengers now knew that nothing more could be done for them. Some grabbed hold of anything that would float and let themselves go into the waves which were now sweeping over the deck. A Mr Forbes stripped off his clothes and dived in like the others, but he was a good swimmer and finally managed to reach one of the boats, which were still lying off the wreck, and was taken on board.

Other passengers climbed up the shrouds, and the ship sank almost gently down beneath them. She stayed quite upright—which is unusual in such circumstances—and this was later attributed to the weight of treasure she carried, some £70,000 in coin in thirty chests, together with boxes of porcelain. It is, of course, more likely that the ship was already full of water and so showed a tendency to go down without falling on her beam ends as an 'empty' wooden wreck might be expected to do.

At 11 p.m. the *Abergavenny* struck the bottom in twelve fathoms of water, and the shock of her striking tumbled some of the passengers out of the rigging to their death below. Some eighty or ninety were now left aloft, and, as the ship worked her way into the sandy bottom, the water rose up higher and higher after them. When she finally stopped sinking the tallest mast was some twenty-five feet clear of the water. Some three hundred people had now drowned.

At about 11.30 p.m. several boats were heard rowing around the wreck, and, though the people still in the rigging shouted to them they refused to pick anyone up. The excuse for this, which was given later, was that they dared not come close to the survivors and take any off because they feared that then everyone would clamber into the boats and sink them.

At midnight a sloop, which had heard the distress guns, came up, anchored close to the wreck, sent a boat across to those still clinging to the shrouds and ferried them twenty at a time back to the sloop. They were then taken to Weymouth.

Captain Wordsworth had gone down with his ship, whose cargo was then valued at some £200,000.

It was unlikely that such a valuable cargo would be left without some salvage attempts. In fact, in *The Times* of 5th May 1806 you can read under the heading of 'The Abergavenny', the following:

> The loss of this vessel in Portland Roads must still be fresh in the recollection of our readers. We have the satisfaction of stating that there is a very fair prospect of the whole of the treasure sunk in her being recovered. Twenty-seven chests of bullion have been already taken out, and the operation of the diving bell meets with no impediment. The ingenuity and perseverance of Mr Baithwaite has accomplished the proposed object beyond the most earnest expectations. He receives, we understand, as a compensation, exclusive of his expenses, 12% of the recovered property.

Mr Baithwaite had done well. He apparently did even better, for in *The Times* of 22nd August 1812 appeared this final note:

> All the money on board the Abergavenny, lost some years ago near Weymouth, to the amount of £60,000 in dollars, has been recovered by means of the diving bell. The vessel has been since blown up, underwater, so as to prevent the wreck from becoming a dangerous shoal.

Which leads us to a mystery. Did the *Abergavenny* really strike the Shambles? The original *Times* report of the wreck, written from the testimony of one of the officers who survived the disaster, and published on 8th February 1805, says quite specifically 'the ship being struck on the Shambles off the Bill of Portland, about two miles from the shore'.

Yet surely a local pilot would have known enough to avoid them? Later editions of *The Times* say the wreck was 'in Portland Roads', and then this becomes 'near Weymouth'. And where did all those boats come from to plunder or pick up survivors? Did they row all the way to the Shambles from Portland? Or did they in fact come out from Weymouth to a ship which was in fact much closer in than the survivors thought?

One man who has no doubts about where the *Abergavenny* actually lies is a well-known Weymouth diver. He is convinced that the wreck he has dived on regularly over the years is the *Earl of Abergavenny*.

Ron Parry is the 48-year-old proprietor of the diving shop 'Subaquatics' in Walpole Street, Weymouth. He is a diver with much experience in the Weymouth area and possesses great knowledge about local diving sites and wrecks.

His wreck is in Weymouth Bay and almost in Weymouth Roads, which is a long way from the Shambles. The wreck first came to his attention because fishermen kept catching their nets on the good fishing grounds in Weymouth Bay. Ron Parry went to have a look, and found himself diving on the wreck of an old wooden craft with bits of wood sticking out of the sand and big copper rivets holding portions of the wood together. This first discovery took place in 1965.

He believes that the *Abergavenny* picked up her pilot near the Shambles, and though she undoubtedly got into trouble shortly afterwards, she ran for Weymouth Bay. What makes him so sure that his wreck is the *Earl of Abergavenny*? 'Circumstantial evidence', says Ron, 'I've got some plates and saucers off her which have a crest on them bearing the letters RW—which is Robert Wordsworth, her captain. Wordsworth was washed

Puzzle picture. They are in fact the butts of muskets, still more or less in their original packing, as found by Richard Keen on the wreck of H.M.S. *Boreas*, which sank in 1807 off Guernsey

Photo Brian J. Green

112

ashore and was buried locally. Everything points that way. We've had musket flints off her—by the bucketful and there were 150 recruits on board . . . .'

On one dive Ron Parry thought he had made his fortune. He found some ingots. They looked like gold. 'But it turned out to be an alloy of copper which could have been for minting the East India Company coins.'

Ron Parry, of course, agrees that none of his evidence is cast-iron, except for the cannon they found on her. The wreck is buried in the sand under seventy feet of water, which would fit in nicely with the reports of the time. He tried air-lifting the sand in a small way, but it did not prove very successful, though on one dive they did expose her deck. They found sword-handles and scabbards, and a wine decanter.

  * * * * *

Admiral Lord Nelson died of a marksman's bullet at 4.30 p.m. on 21st October 1805 on board his flagship *Victory*, at the battle of Trafalgar. On 9th January 1806 after a State funeral, he was buried in St Paul's.

By then the Mediterranean Fleet with which he had won so great a victory had split up and gone the Navy's variously ordered ways. Most ships were still at sea, but those which had borne the brunt of the battle were under repair in British ports.

During the last days of February 1806 it was clear to the shipwrights at Milford Haven—where several Trafalgar casualties were being repaired—that supplies for those repairs were running low. So more supplies ranging from mast yards and rigging to copper washers were requisitioned from Portsmouth Dockyard—and the order was so large that it was decided to send it by sea. The vessel chosen for carrying the material was a large sailing barge. She was brought into Portsmouth and loaded to capacity.

On 5th March the barge, under escort by the 14-gun sloop *Caroline*, set sail for Milford Haven. The barge, with her small crew and large load, made slow progress down-Channel. By the evening of the 7th she was just clearing the Lizard, and the two vessels then altered course to round Land's End.

Until then the weather had been fair, but now the wind increased, and by the time they had crossed Mount's Bay it was blowing a near gale. The barge had been making slow progress anyway, but now she began wallowing in the seas and the crew fought to keep some sort of control.

Aboard the sloop, it was clear to the lieutenant in command that this was a battle that was soon to be lost, and he edged the *Caroline* closer as he anticipated the trouble that was to come. He had not long to wait. Despite everything the crew of the barge could do, she began to head straight for the Runnelstone Reef, which lies off Tol-Pedn-Penwith, near Land's End.

In rough weather the Runnelstone is a seething mass of white foam, and big breakers crash over the 'Stone', which is the main rock in the reef. The lieutenant could see quite clearly what was going to happen, and without waiting any longer he brought *Caroline* alongside and yelled to the barge's crew to jump. Despite the rise and fall of the two vessels, all made it safely across, and then the *Caroline* swung away to safety.

The barge wallowed on, one moment in the trough and the next almost broadside on at the top of a crest—and struck directly on the 'Stone'. From a safe distance the two crews on *Caroline* watched the end of the barge. Badly holed by that first impact, she was washed off the rock by the next few waves and then caught in the backwash drifted away from the rock, sinking lower and lower in the water until only a swirl on the surface marked the spot where she had sunk out of sight (see Fig. 14).

At the court-martial over her loss, the lieutenant was cleared of negligence and the file was closed. There was no record of any salvage, despite the considerable value of the barge's cargo.

Over 163 years later—in the summer of 1969—Cyril Gascoigne, a local diver of considerable experience, was diving in search of crawfish from his forty-foot former fishing trawler. In one hundred feet of water he was about to surface, having found no lobsters, when he peered over the ledge for one last look around the rocks.

At the bottom of the ledge there was a bed of sand and small rocks, and he could just see the antennae of a crawfish poking out from under a group of rocks. Swimming down, he bagged the creature, and then saw another a few yards away. Having collected this one too, he checked his depth gauge and saw that he was at 120 feet.

Glancing around to make sure that he hadn't missed any other crawfish, he was about to surface when he saw a row of small square objects sticking up from the sand a little way away. He was conscious that his air was running low, but even so he finned quickly over the spot. Just as he had thought, the row was made by the ribs of an old wooden wreck. To make sure he stuck his knife into one, and the blade sank into pulp. Around the wreck he saw several bars poking out of the sand, but by now his air was very low and he began to ascend. As he rose up more and more of the bars came into view. They had been hidden from his sight on the bottom by the surrounding rocks, and he could now see that they appeared to be lying all around the wreck.

Once on the surface he took quick landmarks and waited for the boat to pick him up. Though he thought the bars were most likely to be iron, he felt the site worth another look, and ten minutes later was finning his way down again. If the visibility had not been so good that day he felt he would never have relocated the wreck, but now, twenty feet above the bottom, he could see the shape of it clearly. But it was the bars that interested him. Swimming to the nearest one, he took out his knife and scraped it. The dark-green gave way to the green-tinted rosy hue of copper.

He looked around. Everywhere, it now seemed, he could see bars. Some were in bundles, as though they had been laid there yesterday; others looked as though a circus strong-man had been using them for practice, they were twisted, bent and scattered anyhow. By the end of his dive he had lost count of the number of bars he had seen, not to mention the thick copper washers and spikes of all sizes.

While he was decompressing under the surface he had plenty of time to think about his find. Then, when he was back in the dry, he steered the boat over to the point where he had left a small cork marker floating tied by a thin line to a copper

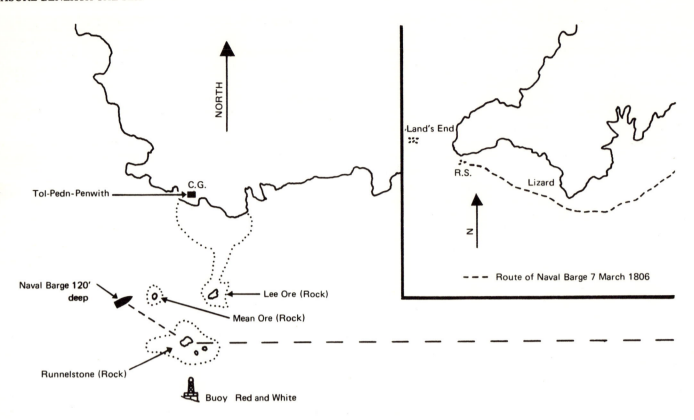

FIG. 14. Route of the barge full of copper bars, etc.,
which sank in March 1806
Based on a drawing by Dennis James

bar on the bottom. Before pulling the marker on board, he took accurate marks on the shore. With difficulty he and his boatman then pulled up the copper bar. On the way back to port he inspected the spikes and washers that he had brought up in a sack from that last dive. Scraping one of the spikes, he found the first clue to the identity of the wreck. On two sides of the spike were the same marks as were on the washers—the Royal Navy's broad arrow. The bars had no marking that he could find.

Gascoigne then set about identifying his wreck. Once he had succeeded in doing this, he obtained the salvage rights, informed the Customs and the Receiver of Wreck of his intention of working the site, and collected together a team of three other very experienced divers.

The work was not easy. Apart from the fact that the seas were rarely calm around the Stone, they were sometimes working—at high tide—in 140 feet of water. Though they usually dived in the slack water, there were times when they were caught in the 'run', which was sometimes as much as six knots. Through the summer and into the autumn the work went on until the last bar, spike and washer that they could find had been raised.

It says a great deal for the discipline and experience of this team that throughout the whole operation not one case of 'bends' developed—due entirely to their experience, and to their insistence in 'going by the book' in their decompression

stops. When the job was done the divers disbanded, having salvaged some thousands of pounds' worth of copper. All treasure, they would agree, is not gold or silver coin.

Though the shipwreck on the Runnelstone wreck took place in 1806, this was far from being the only one from that period that the divers have found recently. Take a ship which sank the very next year. . . .

* * * * *

H.M.S. *Boreas* was a new ship—built at Yarmouth in the same year as the battle of Trafalgar—when she was allocated to the task of protecting Guernsey and her shipping from the French. A frigate of 533 tons and 28 guns—though there is some reason to think that Captain Robert Scott was carrying as many as 32 guns aboard her at the time of her loss—she ranged the sea around the Guernsey station, but never had any reason to put her armament to the test of battle.

On 28th November 1807 *Boreas* set sail from St Peter Port on a mercy mission. A pilot cutter was said to be in trouble off the island, and Captain Scott found this to be true when he located the boat, took the pilots on board and the cutter in tow.

Captain Scott must have been pleased with himself at that moment. Not only had he saved the cutter and the pilots, but he now had these highly experienced men aboard to guide him in the darkness through their local waters. Before he died,

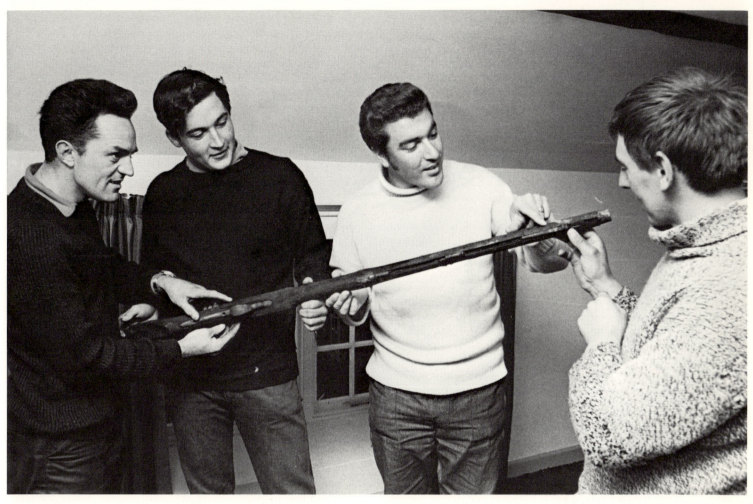

A musket from a ship
sunk in 1807. *From left,*
David Roland, Richard
Keen, David Archer and
David Froome examine
one of the muskets from
H.M.S. *Boreas*

Photo Brian J. Green

he would have reason to wonder just how good the pilots he had taken on board really were. The wind was now blowing hard from the north-east, and the *Boreas* pitched and rolled in the worsening weather.

She was now running—though the captain did not know it, and the pilots apparently didn't either—straight for the Hanois reefs. At twelve minutes to six, in the gathering darkness a sharp-eyed lookout yelled a warning of rocks ahead. At ten minutes to six, while trying to take avoiding action, the *Boreas* struck 'just aft of the mainmast'.

Captain Scott was now faced with a choice. Not much of one, but a choice. He could either lower all sail and try to anchor and hope that his ship would last until daylight. Or he could put on more sail and try to pull her away from the rocks, dealing with the damage when they got out into open water.

He seems to have chosen the second course. For exactly two minutes it seemed to work. Under the extra canvas she travelled twice her length (118 feet) and then struck again. This time no one could have any doubt about the damage. She struck hard, and she stayed stuck on some unseen rock. Unfortunately, it was high water when she hit, and as the tide ebbed the damage to her hull grew and grew. She was now taking in water fast, and the efforts of the crew at the pumps had little effect. Captain

Scott and eighty of his crew were about to die out there in the dark, but they did not give up trying to save themselves.

At this moment the pilots decided they would be better off in their own boat, and, jumping into her, they cut themselves free of the stricken frigate. It is on record that when they reached the shore they did nothing to raise a general alarm and there is certainly no indication that they behaved like heroes!

Now, on the captain's orders, the masts were cut away to try to reduce the tremendous strain on the ship as the water sank away under her. Even with the masts gone she started to lean dangerously over on her side. Waves pouring over the rocks, driven by the strong winds, did nothing to help, and each really big wave did more damage. Captain Scott must have realized that his position was hopeless. He ordered the ship's gig, launch and cutter away. The launch and cutter did manage

115

to reach the mainland of Guernsey, but most of those on board —being pressed men—disappeared into the darkness as soon as the boats touched the shore.

Some devoted men tried to return to the *Boreas* for their comrades, but heavy seas beat them in the end. On board the survivors struggled to stay alive until morning, when they felt help would surely reach them. If the ship had stayed upright they would probably have been all right, but shortly before dawn the *Boreas* could take no more pounding. She fell on her side and the seas swept in over her.

Her gunfire of distress and the blue lights and rockets that she had released earlier had not gone unnoticed on shore, but the fishermen of Guernsey said they had believed her to be French, and had not put to sea for that reason.

When the ship crashed over in her final agony those who who were still alive tried clambering on to what rocks there were showing or clinging to any piece of handy wreckage. It is said that Captain Scott managed to reach some sort of make-shift raft, but collapsed and died from exposure soon after reaching it. His body was swept away by a wave in the darkness.

The *Boreas* was a complete wreck by 2 a.m. By daylight there were only thirty seamen and marines alive on the rocks around the wreck. They and the men who had got ashore in the ship's boats were to be the only survivors. . . .

The court-martial into the loss of H.M.S. *Boreas* was held on 19th December 1807 on board H.M.S. *Gladiator* in Portsmouth Harbour. All the officers and crew were cleared of negligence— except for those who had deserted from the boats that reached shore.

It was that court-martial record that held Richard Keen's attention most as he researched into the old wreck in 1968. One phrase in the clerk's copy gave him a vital clue as to the position of the wreck today. That sentence was to the effect that the wreck was 'in the middle of the rocks'. He knew that *Boreas* drew ten to twelve feet. He knew that she was sailing towards the island from the west to round the south coast. This told him it must be one of the outside reefs.

As a good wreck detective should, he was putting the pieces together and saving himself endless hours of useless diving. The court-martial report in the Public Record Office told him too the state of the tide when she struck.

A paragraph in an old Guernsey paper, *The Comet*, added something more, though without the assistance of Mr E. W. Sharp, one of Guernsey's experts into local shipping and boat-building, he would never have found it. The item which Mr Sharp showed him was dated 5th July 1847 and it read:

On Thursday last Mr Bell, the submarine diver who has for some time been working on the barque Rose together with the crew of the Mary-Ann of Whitstable, proceeded in their boat to the locality where more than 40 years ago, the British frigate Boreas foundered near the Hanois in about three fathoms of water.

During his search, Mr Bell discovered 15 guns, a large quantity of shot in a corroded stage and some iron ballast. Not being, however, provided with the necessary apparatus, no attempts were made to recover these effects. All traces of the vessel having disappeared.

Now Richard Keen knew the depth at which he could expect to find the *Boreas* remains too. Now he could narrow down the search area to one with which he could reasonably cope. In fact on 28th October 1969 he found her.

Richard Keen, now a 21-year-old director of Sous Marine, Ltd, diving-equipment manufacturers, looks after the production side of the business in Guernsey. For a keen diver, he suffered from a strange allergy—he was allergic to neoprene, and for a time had to give up full-time diving. Now with the development of thick lined wet suits he is able to continue diving without much trouble.

The discovery of the wreck in October 1969 was made by Richard Keen and a fellow-diver Dave Archer. Dave Archer dived first and found the first trace of the wreck within twenty minutes—a small, heavily corroded iron bar. Then Richard Keen dived, and as he reached the bottom he found a piece of bronze or copper pipe almost completely buried in the shingle. In fact he only spotted it because of its bright green verdigris coloration. Kean left it where it was, and moved on. About eight feet from the first discovery he found a copper bolt, four feet long and an inch and a half in diameter.

Keen now moved up a gully in the rocks and found himself face to face with four large cannon and a great quantity of iron ballast. By the time the tide started to run heavily they had also found an anchor, but the increasing ground swell made it impossible to stay any longer.

A week later a heavy swell interrupted operations, but the divers did manage to photograph the cannon and recover the bronze pipe. In the summer of 1970, Dave Archer and Richard Keen made several trips to the wreck site. They found odd pieces of lead and some copper ship's fastenings, and two more large cannons about 7 ft 6 in long.

Despite this the divers were becoming bored. There seemed nothing of startling interest on the site, which had borne the full brunt of the Atlantic gales for over 160 years. But on the third visit of the summer, Richard Keen found, to his amaze-ment, some wood sticking out of the gravel and stones in an eight-foot-wide gully. The wood had rusty iron and small pieces of brass embedded in it.

On their next visit they started excavation at the same spot and found two rows of musket butts. Embedded in the lump of muskets were six badges. They bore the Royal Navy device of a fouled anchor, and had probably been worn on sword or musket sling.

The divers worked away until the whole lump of encrusted muskets were released from the sea-bed. Two of the divers could only just move it under water. They had no lifting bags or oil drums with them—the diving team now consisted of Richard Keen, David Archer, David Roland and David Froome —but they managed to man-handle the lump over the sea-bed until they were under the diving boat. From that position they towed their find for four hours until they reached St Peter Port. Once there they found that the lump of muskets weighed over three and a half hundredweights, and inside the lump were twenty-four muskets packed muzzle to butt in some sort of crate—together with the flints for the firing mechanisms.

Although the iron barrels of the muskets were heavily rusted, the wood preserved well after treatment. The butts were probably walnut, and the guns have survived because they were well-greased and possibly still in their original packing-case.

This is one of the best sailing-ship wrecks to have been found so far around Guernsey, and there is still a lot more of her to be uncovered.

*　　*　　*　　*　　*

Though the wrecking of practically every ship must come as a surprise to those actually involved, no-one can be surprised at the number of wrecks that took place on the seas during the early part of the nineteenth century. The days of sail had their own hazards, in particular in spots where today's engines might well haul the ship out of danger. Even so the captains and crews of those same sailing-ships might well have felt safe when in port. Take Captain Gowing of the transport *Queen*.

The *Queen* was on Government hire, and was returning from the Peninsular War. She called first at Cadiz and then at Lisbon and embarked some 325 troops, mostly sick and wounded Artillerymen, and some of their families, 63 women and 58 children, and at least ten French prisoners of war. Together with her twenty-one crew there must have been at least 477 on board her when she set out from Lisbon in convoy with seven other transports, the *Latham, Ocean Henry, Fame, Inclination, Ceres, Burton*, and *Apollo*. Escorting them was the 38-gun *Melpomene*. Destination: Portsmouth.

The voyage from Lisbon was a bad one, the Bay of Biscay living up to its reputation, but the ships battered their way on until they reached Falmouth, where it was decided to take on fresh water and more provisions. So it must have come as a great relief when in the afternoon of 10th January 1814 the ships anchored in Falmouth Roads at the mouth of the harbour.

Captain Gowing obviously felt himself to be in port, for he ordered only one anchor to be lowered, and not much cable with it. One report says thirty-five fathoms of cable were let out, which is less than half the amount usually required for a ship of her size.

Now, Falmouth is a sheltered place—except for winds from the south-east—and the ships remained happily at anchor there for three days without any trouble. At about 4 p.m. on 13th January the wind suddenly swung to the south-east, and, in no time at all, was blowing a full gale. All the ships were in some sort of trouble, but most either had more anchors out than the *Queen* or got them out quickly. The *Queen*, though, started to drag her single anchor, and did so for some while in the darkness without the captain being informed. When he was told he immediately ordered a second anchor, ready at the cat-head, to be let go.

The anchor was ready, but someone had forgotten to attach the cable to it. Though they worked desperately to bend the new cable on, they were already too late. The anchor that they had down suddenly bit and the cable could not take the sudden strain, and parted. Now the *Queen* really was in trouble. The howling wind carried her north towards Trefusis Point.

Something very close to panic then seems to have started. The troops and their families were disturbed by all the thumping and yelling above them, and came up on deck to see what was happening. They found a blizzard blowing and the ship drifting helplessly through the black night. And the sea bore

no resemblance to the sort of conditions they could expect inside a harbour. Great waves were rushing the ship along; others burst in clouds of spray on to the decks, where it froze, making the sailors' tasks even more difficult. Those who got on deck now fought to get back below for warm clothing and their belongings. Children ran through the ship searching for their parents, and added to the general uproar. Yet even so, some slept blissfully on throughout it all.

On the forecastle the crew still struggled to attach the anchor cable, but though they couldn't know it their frozen fingers had no hope of completing the work in time. They were still struggling with the cable when at 4.30 a.m. the *Queen* went ashore on Trefusis Point. Their struggle was over; the slaughter was about to begin.

As the *Queen* struck, she heeled over. She could be driven no farther by the snow-laden wind. The waves couldn't stop. Tons of water smashed on over the decks, carrying crew and rigging with them. And a great deal of that water didn't complete its run across the deck, but poured down every hatchway in such quantity that many of those below died almost at once.

Gowing ordered distress cannon to be fired, but no one could fire them. With hindsight it is possible to say that even if the cannon had been fired no one could have found the wreck even if they had heard the distress signals. Visibility was no more than a yard or two.

The list to starboard increased under the battering of the waves, and Gowing ordered the masts cut away to reduce the weight. They managed to do this—at just the wrong time. As the masts fell the ship lurched to port. And down came spars, tackle and masts on to the deck, killing and maiming scores, who had fought their way up from the water-filled hell of the holds. Then the cannon broke free and trundled back and forward into the wreckage with each lurch of the ship. Some smashed their way out through the ship's sides.

The *Queen's* hull was now pierced by rocks in many places, and the seas were going right through her. In fact in less than half an hour the once proud *Queen* was nothing more than a half-submerged hulk. And the loss of life was ghastly.

Some soldiers did manage to fight their way through the surf to the shore, and got to Flushing village to raise the alarm. Mr George Crokker Fox, who rented the manor house nearest to the Point, gathered all his servants and retainers together, added to his band all the able-bodied men of Flushing and Mylor, and started some sort of rescue operation on the shore near the wreck. They were unable, however, to drag more than a few survivors from the sea, and spent most of their time collecting the corpses. When daylight came and the storm eased there were over 350 bodies floating in the shallows, out in the Roads, or lying on the shore. Of the original complement of over 470 only eighty-five soldiers, nine women, one child and some of the French prisoners survived. The entire crew, except for the boatswain and an eleven-year-old cabin boy, were dead.

Over a mass grave of 136 bodies in Mylor churchyard there is this stone:

To the memory of the warriors, women and children, who returning from the coast of Spain, unhappily perished in the wreck of the Queen, transport, on Trefusis Point, January 14, 1814. This stone is erected as a testimony of regret by the inhabitants of this parish.

Inside the church is an even more touching memorial stone:

In memory of Catherine, wife of Lieutenant Robert Daniell, 30th Regiment, and also of his children, Margaret, Elanor, William, Robert and Edward Alexander, who unhappily perished in the wreck of the Queen, transport, on the awful morning January 14–1814, leaving an unfortunate husband and father to lament their loss to the end of his existence.

As if the tragedy itself was not enough, it is said that several troopers were caught looting the dead, and after being identified at a later date by Mr Fox and a local farmer called John Plomer, were sent for trial by court-martial. It requires little knowledge of conditions of Army service at that time to know what was the ultimate fate of those wretches.

However, some research carried out into this report by Colonel Bob Curtis in the Ministry of Defence Library in the old War Office building in Whitehall failed to substantiate the looting story. The historical records of the 30th Regiment strangely do not mention the wreck at all, but *The History of the 30th Regiment (East Lancs Regiment) 1689–1881*, by Lieutenant-Colonel Neil Bannatyne (which is also in the Ministry of Defence Library) has this to say about the wreck:

Twenty-eight (members of the 30th Regiment) were on the transport Queen which brought from the Peninsula 325 men, mostly sick and invalids of Artillery, with 63 women and 58 children; the crew numbered 21. On January 11, 1814, she anchored in Carrick Roads near Falmouth and was there caught by the great gale. Her cables parted and she went ashore on Trefusis Point, and was beaten to pieces by the sea.

One hundred men with four women got ashore, 363 perished. By some extraordinary chance the 30th men were saved except Privates Grant, Garret, Hunt, Rowden and Waters.

The gale was accompanied by snow, which buried wagons and mail coaches, and it was not until May that a route was issued for the party to march to Colchester from Exeter.

There is no mention of salvage being carried out on the *Queen* in the records of the time, but two huge brass pintles were dredged up in the harbour some years ago, and are thought to be part of the *Queen's* rudder.

Divers have tried to locate the remains of the Queen, but the area is a graveyard of many ships (including the destroyer *Torrid* which snapped her tow in 1937 and broke up almost on the same spot).

Dick Larn probably got nearest to actually touching the remains of the *Queen*. In about twenty-five feet of water, among the sand patches, amid heavy weed, he found an enormous piece of wood three and a half to four feet wide. This wood, some forty feet long, is likely to be the keelson of the *Queen*. No cannon are to be seen in the immediate area, but many foot-long copper pins have been recovered from the site. These probably held the great timbers of the *Queen* together, but nothing has been positively identified. The reason is not difficult to imagine. The ship went down in comparatively shallow water, and it was so accessible to salvage teams that they would have had little difficulty in doing major work.

CHAPTER 10

The Case of the 1875

which later turned out to be the Oregon, sunk in 1890, and including the Bremen (1881), the Norman Court (1883), and the Mohegan (1898).

PADDY Indlewick had been searching for new sites for the divers he took out from Newton Ferrers, Devon, and had been told that local fishermen had been badly damaging their nets on some obstruction in Bigbury Bay. He eventually found the obstruction on his echo-sounder, took shore marks and was confident that he could take the divers of Kingston Branch of the British Sub-Aqua Club to the spot. But for four months attempts to dive on the spot were frustrated by coastal haze. The place was several miles from shore, and it needed a very clear day to be able to pick up the marks.

But then on a summer's day in 1965, when returning from diving near Bolt Tail, Paddy Indlewick took the Kingston divers—Adrian Bradley, Bill Foley, Mick Roper, Ron Hyde, Peter Collingwood, Don Pierce and a Czech girl, Christina Grzegorzewska—on to the marks (visible at last) for the mystery obstruction.

As the men had already dived once that day, they studied the decompression tables carefully before going down again. The tables told them that, at 110 feet—the depth which showed on the echo-sounder—they could have eight minutes only.

The first pair went down. At about fifty feet the dark shape of a hull loomed up at them, and they found themselves on a wreck which stood on an even keel, but which was in a partially collapsed condition. The divers only had time for a quick examination of the wreckage—it was enough to excite them—and then they had to return to the surface.

Though their time on the wreck had been severely limited the divers could count themselves fortunate—they were on their branch diving holiday, and this was the Sunday of the first weekend. The weather held for them too, and later in the week a fuller examination was possible. The wreck was about two hundred feet long, had an iron hull and carried several large anchors. The absence of anything like machinery placed the wreck firmly into the category of sail. Large conger and lobster called the wreck home.

It was during that same week's diving that the first clue to the wreck's identity was found. 'Brad' (Adrian Bradley) was examining the remains of the wheel on the aft quarterdeck. Scraping the boss to remove some of the marine growth, he was surprised to find the date '1875' cast into the brass of the boss. From then on, to the Kingston divers the wreck was 'The

1875'. Even now, after they have known her real name for several years, they still call her that.

The Kingston divers had enough excitement out of the 1875 during those two weeks of their diving holiday to keep them talking the whole winter in the Branch's clubhouse. They talked of the mystery of the metal box. This was a large metal box riveted round with metal bands which was found among the wreckage and finally freed. It was raised to the surface by an inverted kitbag filled with air from a diver's demand valve. It reached the surface all right, but was some distance from the boat. In those days divers were still learning that lifting bags had to be lined with something like polythene or the air would escape. Before the horrified eyes of the divers in the boat the box drifted slowly away from the boat and sank—and was never found again. What was in it? The Kingston divers would love to know!

They talked too that winter of the recovery of one of the anchors of the 1875. This was raised by using a properly made lifting-bag, and when that reached the surface it was lashed to the gunwhale on one side of the boat while everyone sat on the other. Paddy Indlewick steamed slowly back to port, one hand on the wheel, the other on a diving knife, ready to cut the anchor free should the boat become unstable. The anchor weighed 5 cwt.

The divers tried raising a bigger one, with 40-gallon oil drums filled with air, but, fortunately for Paddy's peace of mind, failed. This one weighed 25 cwt!

The wreck was dived again and again by Kingston Branch, but they were still no further forward in discovering her true identity. In 1967 David Calkin of Kingston Branch came into the picture as a wreck detective on the 1875 when he and Ricky Turner decided to try to find out her real name.

They got in touch with the Hydrographic Department of the Ministry of Defence (Navy), who suggested it might be the wreck of the *Oregon*, an 800-ton sailing barque. Calkin then approached Lloyds, who confirmed the date of the loss of the *Oregon* as 18th December 1890, and Turner found more details in *The Times* of 20th December 1890. Headed 'Disasters at Sea', *The Times* report reads as follows:

Late on Thursday evening the three-masted sailing vessel

Oregon of Dundee, laden with nitrate of soda, bound from Iquique to Newcastle-on-Tyne, struck the Book Rocks, near Thurlestone Rocks, in Hope Bay on the South Devon coast.

The Oregon, which was of 800 tons register, was commanded by Captain Lowe, and she put into Falmouth on Thursday night to take a pilot on board. The Vessel appears to have got out of her course, and struck the rock during the darkness and heavy rain on Thursday night. The vessel was immediately put about, but she had sprung a leak. The captain ordered the men to save themselves in the boats. The first boat lowered was swamped, but the second boat was safely floated. The darkness was intense and the boat drifted in a tempestuous sea for 12 hours before it could make the land. About six o'clock yesterday morning guided by the light from a labourer's lantern on the shore, the sailors succeeded in reaching the fishing village of Hope, where they were treated with great kindness. The Oregon filled with water and sank soon after the crew left her. She will probably become a total wreck.

Some idea of the size and layout of the Oregon can be had by going to see the Cutty Sark at Greenwich. The Oregon was somewhat similar in size.

Was the Kingston divers' wreck really the Oregon? Further investigations brought to light a strong link. The date of her launching was August 3rd . . . 1875.

Kingston Branch have dived her often since. The wreck is a difficult one to find as she is several miles off shore, and now, since the sides of the hull have collapsed, produces only a small reading on an echo-sounder. But she's still there, complete with large anchor—but if you want to find her, you'd better take a Kingston diver who knows the marks with you!

*   *   *   *   *

The captain of the Bremen was said to be 'rather hard on the bottle', but it would be unfair to blame his indulgence on the length of time it took the three-masted sailing barque to reach the Shetlands. Certainly the 200-foot barque had taken over a month to get there since she sailed from Bremen, Germany, in early January 1881 with a cargo of salt and empty barrels, which were to be filled with petroleum products on her arrival in the United States.

Some time during that voyage, at a position that we can only say was somewhere east of the Shetlands, the captain and the first mate had a violent disagreement about where the ship actually was. Whose estimate of her position was finally accepted we do not know, but we do know that on 3rd February the Bremen was right in the middle of a fierce snow-laden north-easterly gale. Her sails were reduced, but the wind still drove her on. About midnight the lookout suddenly saw the white foam of wave against rock. The rudder was put hard over, but there wasn't time for the ship to answer. Within moments a wave had thrown her sideways on to the rocks.

The deck watch thought they saw a way of escape when the yard of the foremast almost touched the steep mountain-side at the foot of which they were wrecked. They climbed up, but the mast snapped and they were dropped into the white froth from which there could be no escape.

The watch below, who were changing to take over at the time of the wrecking came on deck and tried a similar escape route—this time up the main-mast, which was now leaning against what seemed to be the wall of a mountain. It was, in fact, the face of some steep cliffs, but once again the mast snapped before they could reach safety and a row of tiny figures plummeted down into the sea.

By now the rest of the crew had reached the deck. Most were in their underwear, and had no time to pull on their seaboots. Fortunately for them, the vessel under the pounding of the sea had now swung slightly, and one man got ashore by jumping off the poop on to a rocky ledge. The rest of the survivors followed his example. But the captain did not come. The ship's boy reported that the last he had seen of the captain was when he had been ordered to help him off with his seaboots. Presumably the captain had thought he stood a better chance without his heavy boots, but as he still did not put in an appearance, and the crew could see the ship breaking up, they decided that no one else could have escaped from the Bremen and set off to find help.

This was easier thought about than done. They scrambled up the rocks, blinded by snow which was driven on the wind, slipping and sliding and cutting their bare feet.

What those survivors did not realize was that the ship had been thrown into a V-shaped inlet in the cliffs. Originally the waves had pounded the wreck against one side of the inlet, then she had swung and the men had got ashore on the other side.

The inlet continued into the cliff in the form of a narrow ravine. As the sailors scrambled up those rocks, some of them must have fallen into the ravine and been sucked back by the sea's surge into it. When they reached the top there were only nine men left.

Then, still barefoot, they stumbled across the countryside until they saw the light of a lonely croft. It says much for these men that after leaving the ship's boy safe by the fireside they set out again, still without proper clothing, back to the wreck site to see if they could help any of their comrades. Their journey was in vain. No one else had survived, and no bodies, apart from that of the Captain,[1] were ever recovered.

On 17th July 1970 a father and son diving expedition arrived at Lerwick in the Shetlands. Gilbert Dinesen, chairman of Croydon Branch of the British Sub-Aqua Club and his sixteen-year-old son, Norman, had brought their car across to the islands, partly to be mobile, but more importantly so that they could bring their own portable compressor to supply them with air for their diving bottles.

Gilbert Dinesen and his son spent all their holiday diving and came to the Bremen wreck site as a result of a request by Mr Tom Henderson, the Curator of the Shetland Museum, who asked them if they would survey the remains for him.

---

[1] The captain's body was given a proper burial in the local graveyard. This is said to have been the first break in the Shetlands with that ancient custom of burying the bodies from shipwrecks on the shore near where they were washed up.

The famous tea
clipper *Norman Court*,
built in 1869. This is
from a painting by
Gordon Ellis, com-
missioned by
J. R. D. W. Kennan.
The *Norman Court*
remains were found
by Peter Salmon

Norman Dinesen wrote an article for the Croydon Branch
magazine about those dives:

Accompanied by a 63-year-old Shetlander, Mr Adam
Robertson, whose father had been fourteen years old at the
time of the shipwreck, we went to the actual spot to survey
the position. From the end of the road we had to walk about
three quarters of a mile over very soggy ground until we
reached the steep and mountainous shore. Close by, were the
remnants of two ancient 'Brochs', strong defence towers of
stone built by the Picts about 2000 years ago. We then
descended the fairly steep bank of the ravine, as close as we
could get to the water level.

On the large-scale map, the ravine appeared as a narrow
'V', with one arm being much longer than the other. On a
rocky ledge were two small holes made in the stone by the
Picts, presumably to contain their bait when they were fishing
from there with a line. Some distance along the long arm of
the 'V', four holes had been drilled into the rocks and rusty
remains of bolts were still to be seen. It was explained to us
that in the summer of 1881, a winch had been erected here
to enable a helmet diver to be sent down to try to recover
certain valuable parts of the wreckage, including the anchor.

However, Mr Robertson could not understand why the

winch had been erected at a place which he considered some distance away from the actual wreckage. The diving mission in 1881 was apparently a complete failure. The diver only brought up a small coal shovel, and refused to dive again 'in the open Atlantic, exposed to sharks and other sea monsters'.

We pointed out to Mr Robertson that our dive would only be possible if we could get hold of a boat. If we had ourselves to carry the heavy equipment three quarters of a mile over marshy ground and then scramble down the steep mountainside, we would be exhausted before we ever reached the water. This could be dangerous. However, Mr Robertson arranged for a number of local people to help us carry the equipment, and we were in reality given VIP treatment.

We commenced the dive by jumping off the rock as near as possible into the narrow end of the 'V' formed ravine. In the water, the mountainside went steeply down for 40 feet. At first I thought that we had reached the bottom, but then I realized that it was only a question of a ledge coming out from each side, and through a comparatively narrow gap in the middle, we descended into a rather dark underwater chamber to the depth of about 60 feet. The bottom here was covered with a 2–3 ft layer of rotting seaweed, washed in by the wave action.

Doubtless a lot of artifacts would have been washed in here from the wreck, but at this time of year the bottom could not be seen. It was most eerie to look up and see the mountain closing above us, the light only being let in through the slit in the middle. For the first time in my life I saw, in British waters, not cuttle-fish, but real octopus. They were fairly small, and, when touched, they emitted an inky cloud. The bottom now went up slightly, and the very rounded stones made it evident that during a real winter gale the fierce waves trapped in the ravine sent downwards a tremendous back-wash, which might have gouged out the chamber in the first instance.

Swimming out of the underwater cavern, we continued along the right arm of the V shaped ravine. After some time, we came across the first evidence of wreckage. What we first considered to be some twisted girders, turned out to be large brackets which had been bolted on to the underside of the deck-planks and on to the side of the ship, to give additional stability to the vessel. Another piece of metal turned up, containing two long galvanised bolts or rivets, with brass washers. Their function could not be determined. We then came across a long steel bar flattened at one end. This was the 'Dolphin-stay', which is fixed from the bowsprit and to the stem of the vessel to steady the bowsprit. Some distance further on we came across the big links of the anchor chain, between a large boulder and the mountainside. The rest of the chain, including the anchor, must have been buried by sand and stones, which had fallen down the rockside during the last 90 years.

On a sandy patch a bit further along, we came across some rectangularly shaped links of a chain. It was later explained to us that this was part of the 'messenger', an iron chain which linked one winch to another. We looked everywhere for pieces of smaller wreckage, but it was obvious that many stones had fallen down and a lot of sand had been washed

up during the last century or so. However, there is no doubt that patient digging at these spots would yield results. We swam a bit further on, but saw no more wreckage. The contour of the bottom, with its huge boulders, some of them thickly covered with brittle stars, was fantastic. However, our air was now giving up. We had to ascend to the surface, and having swum back into the ravine, willing hands helped us up onto the rocks.

Mr Robertson then explained to us that our bubbles had for some time been near the place where the winch had been erected in 1881. This was obviously the place where we found the anchor chain so there was some method in the selection of this place for the winch.

We then began the scramble up the mountain wall and the long slog across the marshy land. The following day we drew up a map showing the approximate positions of the various pieces of wreckage which we had found. We gave a detailed report to Mr Tom Henderson of the Shetland Museum, who appeared pleased with the initial survey which we had carried out. In his opinion it would be a very useful working basis for subsequent diving expeditions to this spot.

The dive was a great experience, but afterwards I could not help thinking of the poor members of the crew, who, on a cold and murky February night in 1881, and in a blinding snow storm, were washed into the seething waters of the ravine and were possibly sucked down 60 feet into the underwater chamber, which we had discovered. This might well be the reason why their bodies were never recovered.

The *Norman Court* was a fast ship—as fast as her builders expected her to be, perhaps even a little faster. She was launched as a tea clipper in 1869 at Glasgow, and took her name from the Hampshire seat of her first owner, Thomas Baring of the famous banking family.

In 1872 she put up the fastest time of the season in the run from China back to Britain in 95 days. She raced across the oceans of the world in competition with such famous tea clippers as *Cutty Sark, Thermopylae, Taeping, Black Prince* and the *Fiery Cross*. She more than held her own, but in 1878 her racing days were over—steam was ousting the clippers from their, trade—and she was converted from a clipper to a barque by the removal of one of her masts. Two years later she was sold to a Glasgow firm.

Her new owners, perhaps remembering the fast times she used to put up in her tea-clipper days, started her on the trade run to Java. On 16th December 1882 she left Java bound for Greenock with a cargo of sugar, teak and other woods. She was still a fast ship, but it wasn't until Friday, 30th March 1883, that she was off the North Wales coast—and in trouble.

A south-west gale had come howling out of the Irish Sea and her crew of twenty under the command of Captain McBride fought desperately to keep the *Norman Court* off the coast, whose rocks were coming far too close for comfort. At nightfall the battle had not been won. Before daylight it was lost—the *Norman Court* hit a rock and bottomed. She was aground in Cymyran Bay, Anglesey, and when the dawn came there was no sign of life aboard the wreck. *The Times* of Saturday, 31st March 1883, has a dramatic account of what happened then:

Lloyds agents at Holyhead telegraphed yesterday morning at 11.15 that the Norman Court, bound for Greenock from Java, got ashore on the Cymyran beach with a heavy list to port with her main mast gone and the sea making a clean breach over her.

At daylight about 20 men appeared in the fore-rigging. Rockets were fired five times, but unsuccessfully. The Rhosneigr lifeboat attempted to go to the rescue of the crew—she was filled with water twice and one man was washed out of her, but afterwards saved. One side rowlock gave way and the lifeboat was obliged to put back without saving the crew. There was a very heavy sea on. The Holyhead lifeboat, accompanied by a tug, had been ordered to go to try to save the crew . . . .

Things now looked extremely black for the crew of the Norman Court. Out there, clinging to the rigging, they could have no idea how black. The wreck could not have happened at a worse time. The Rhoscolyn lifeboat, which would have been in the best position to attempt a rescue, was out of commission. She had been severely damaged the day before in going to the aid of another vessel. The Holyhead boat tried to reach the wreck but couldn't make it, and was obliged to turn back to Holyhead.

But even though Colonel Marshall, secretary of the Rhoscolyn lifeboat branch, was unable to use his own boat, there was something he could do for the crew of the Norman Court. He telephoned Holyhead lifeboat station and persuaded Captain

Edward Jones to take his crew by special train to a point near where the Rhosneigr boat had come ashore, and take over the boat for another attempt. The men struggled across the moors in the gale, relaunched the lifeboat through heavy surf, and finally managed to rescue all the survivors. Two of the crew of the Norman Court had been lost at some time during the night. For their efforts the Holyhead men were awarded a silver medal and £3. The survivors of the Norman Court must have thought they were worth much more.

The Norman Court herself was not much use for anything after the seas had finished with her. Her cargo was destroyed and the wreck, after having been stripped of all salvageable items, was sold on 18th April 1883.

At the Board of Trade inquiry into the ship's loss on 26th April 1883 the master, Captain MacBride, was found to be in default of navigation, but was not deprived of his ticket 'owing to the hardships he had undergone'.

There for a while the story of the Norman Court ended. But in August 1965 a young Aqualung diver, Peter Salmon, heard about the wreck from some Welsh divers over a drink at Molfre, Anglesey. The idea of seeing the remains of a famous clipper ship caught his imagination, and from then on he started research into the ship and her wrecking.

Peter Salmon, now thirty, an electrical engineer and owner of Aquamatic, a firm specializing in custom-built underwater camera housings, found out a great deal about the Norman Court. Now was the time to dive on the wreck itself—if he could find it.

Salmon and his team of divers searched with masks and

The *Oregon*, which the Kingston divers always call the '1875', is now
badly broken. She sank in 1890. This underwater picture shows the
collapsed side, gunwhale and deadeyes. The fish are pouting

snorkels around what they felt was the probable area of the wreck, but found nothing. They then decided to go inshore and tow an Aqualung diver under water behind the boat. As they headed for shore they noticed an unusual patch of choppy water near some rocks called 'Starvation Island'. Were the remains of the *Norman Court* causing the disturbance? They anchored and dived. Five minutes later they surfaced, shouting to each other. There was definitely a wreck down there close to a large rock which was now just breaking the surface.

Salmon's first impressions of the wreck were very mixed. 'It was difficult at first', he says, 'to recognize any parts of a sailing ship, for after 82 years on the sea-bed most of the wood had gone. After swimming around for a while I came across a section which consisted of iron structures with large shiny brass bolts protruding about six inches. But no amount of heaving would loosen them.'

On a later dive Salmon sawed off one of those brass bolts, hoping it would bear some identifying mark. He was lucky—it bore the name 'Grenfell Inglis', and Inglis of Glasgow had built her all those years ago.

In 1967 the RAF College Special Branch of the British Sub-Aqua Club chose the survey of the *Norman Court* as their project for the year (see Fig. 15). Part of their report of that survey reads as follows:

From a previous dive it was known that there were several pieces of wreckage, so the first job was to position them in relation to a known point. Since the pontoon, which we had moored in the bay, was continually shifting with currents, we used the rock on which the *Norman Court* foundered, as our base.

The rock is exposed at low tides, so at low tide on 7th September bearings were taken on fixed points and the position of the rock was fixed at Grid SA 3018744 of sheet 106 Ord. Survey. With the observer sitting on the rock and divers in the water on the end of the various pieces of wreckage it was a fairly simple job to position the remainder of the wreck. It was found that the main portion of the wreck was only two metres from the base of the rock and from the rock there were two lines, one on a reading of 078° (M) and the second on a reading of 094° (M). There is a further large piece of wreckage on a reading of 098° (M), and almost attached to the main body. This was later found to be decking.

After siting the main parts of the wreck the divers were sent down in pairs, one with a chinagraph and perspex pad and the second with a measuring rod of two metres length divided into half metre marks painted alternately black and white. One diver measured and the second recorded until either the diver's air was exhausted or the perspex was full. This was the pattern for the diving until the wreck was completely recorded. Flight Lieutenant Howard, party leader, was the recorder and general co-ordinator of the survey divers. Eventually after a few days' work a picture of the remains of the wreck became clear.

The main body of the wreck is lying some four metres from the rock and on a bearing of 094° and is some forty metres in length. This was the main part of the hull and is lying im-bedded in the sand with a list of approx. 60° to starboard. The first four metres of wreckage is fairly intact with ribs sticking out of the sand to a height of 1.8 metres and above them are some three 'dead eyes'. (Dead eyes were the means of securing the rigging from the mast to the deck.)

After four metres of recognisable hull the wreckage deteriorates into a mass of iron sticking out of the sand in a well-defined line. Then at a further distance of 16½ metres, there is the largest recognisable piece of wreckage. This is a large piece of the hull and above the sand is a layer of the copper sheathing of the hull, extending some five metres. The copper sheathing is nailed to the wood of the hull, but above the hull the wood disappeared and only the iron framework is left. The iron framework is almost intact and it is possible to swim in and out of the frames, which are approximately one metre square. At the edge of the deck the height of the framework from the sand is three metres. Then above the level of the deck are ten dead eyes. From the middle of this framework on the deck side extended at an angle of about 60° is a section of the mast. This mast is some four metres long and one metre wide and it is possible to get a swimmer without aqualung inside. After clearing away the kelp from the mast and the area around the base, it is possible to follow the mast through what was the decking and immediately below the decking at the base of the mast is a coil of chain which is now one solid mass about one metre deep and one metre across.

Almost immediately after the mast the wreckage becomes a scattered mass of ribs and the occasional piece of decking all on a general line of 094° and then there is a section of the mast at some twelve metres from the base piece. This piece of mast is seven metres long and smaller in diameter than the main piece, being some half metre in diameter. The end of the mast disappears into the sand.

Beyond the line of general wreckage and at an angle of some 30° to the main wreckage is a section of decking some fourteen metres long and 2½ metres wide. This decking has many brass bolts in excellent condition attached to it and on many it is still possible to read the maker's name.

After this the area was searched thoroughly, particularly the many rocks to the South but nothing was found. Unfortunately it was not possible to get an aqua lift working, but it is felt that this would repay any efforts expended.

This is a good example of the sort of serious survey work which can be done by a small group of divers.

*   *   *   *   *

No chapter about 'dived' wrecks of the nineteenth century would be complete without reference to the *Mohegan*, which steamed at nearly full speed on to the Manacle Rocks in Cornwall on Friday 14th October 1898.

Her story is amazing because if she had not hit the Manacles she would have steamed straight into the Lizard itself. That suicide course had been set during her run down the Channel.

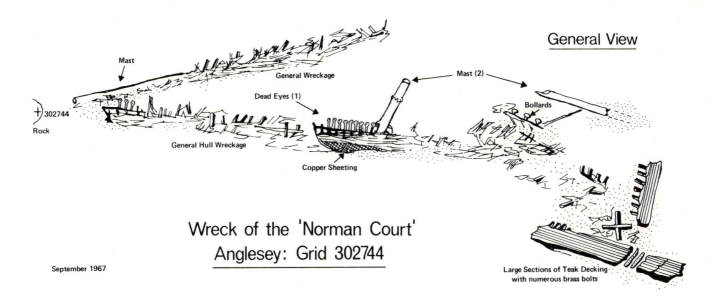

General View

Mast

General Wreckage

Mast (2)

Dead Eyes (1)

Bollards

302744

Rock

General Hull Wreckage

Copper Sheeting

Large Sections of Teak Decking
with numerous brass bolts

Wreck of the 'Norman Court'
Anglesey: Grid 302744

September 1967

FIG. 15. RAF divers' view of the wreck of the *Norman Court*

In fact as she passed the Eddystone she was heading for disaster.

The *Mohegan* was a new ship and the voyage that ended in tragedy started when she sailed from Gravesend on Thursday 13th October 1898, with fifty-three first-class passengers, a crew of ninety-seven and six cattlemen to look after the livestock. The pride of the Atlantic Transport Line, she was bound for New York with a cargo of 150 tons of jute, tin and rolls of linoleum. But when she ploughed into the Manacle Rocks 106 people died, despite the fantastic efforts of the Porhoustock lifeboat.

So 8500 tons of new liner went to the bottom—but not at once. Some salvage was done, but one day when the salvage crews went out to recover more metal from her she was gone—and nobody in the years that followed was quite sure where she had gone to.

In 1961 two experienced divers, Roy Davis (see Chapter 1) of Bromley Branch of the BSAC and Bernard Rogers, relocated the *Mohegan* by using an aquaplane—a sort of underwater sledge which is towed behind a powered boat with a diver clinging to it.

So they found the liner again. Her bow is in fifty feet of water and her stern in seventy. The boilers are there, fairly central on the line of the wreck, but masses of kelp in shallower water lead to confusion amid the tangle of steel plates. Bernard

Rogers summed up every diver's first impression of her by saying that she looked 'Like a Nissen hut that an elephant had sat on'. Readers who spent any time during the War in those curved shelters of corrugated iron will know exactly what he meant!

Since then the wreck of the *Mohegan* has become one of the favourite dives of clubs all over the country—in fact the word 'Mohegan' has become almost an indication of a kind of wreck-diving pleasure.

An article in *Snark*, the magazine of Bromley Branch, BSAC, by Barry Mason, shows just how popular the *Mohegan* wreck is to divers today:

> Soon after finding the wreck—which wasn't difficult—we came upon an almost unbelievable scene. We were attracted by a loud clanging noise. On further investigation we could see a diver trying to remove a porthole. An array of tools were littered around him, and he was bashing hell out of the piece of wreck he had found . . . one could imagine him eventually retrieving a very battered souvenir.

A sad picture, perhaps, but only to be expected when you realize that the *Mohegan* herself ushered in the age of progress and the world of noise and steam that was to follow.

The Case of the Ship that was
Made of Brass

*including the Maine and Kintuck (1917), and
the Kyarra and the Bretagne (1918).*

THE havoc created by U-boats during the First World War has left a great number of wrecks for British divers to explore. And for some divers they have provided not only the thrill of exploration, but also a source of salvage. But Britain's amateur divers have been slow to realize the possibilities in this field.

The first of the amateurs to lead the way were the divers of Torbay Branch of the British Sub-Aqua Club. The ship that was to become their very own was the *S.S. Maine*.

She came zig-zagging down the Channel on a drizzly, misty morning in March 1917. A 3600-ton cargo ship outward bound from London to Philadelphia with a crew of forty-three and five hundred tons of chalk, fifty tons of cowhair, horsehair, goatskins and fenugreek seeds in her holds. At 8 a.m. on March 23rd, when travelling at ten knots, thirteen miles south of Berry Head, she took a torpedo in her port side.

It didn't sink her, but Captain W. Johnston could feel her settling by the head. He made all speed possible for the nearest land. A torpedo-boat answered his distress call and tried towing the *Maine* in an attempt to beach her near Hope Cove or in Bigbury Bay.

It didn't work. The *Maine* was filling fast, and at 12.45 p.m. she sank—upright and almost without a struggle. Bolt Head and Bolt Tail were only a mile away. She went to the bottom the same way—upright—in seventy feet of water.

In July 1961 the Torbay divers found her. Derek Cockbill, one of the divers, who is now chairman of the British Sub-Aqua Club, described what they saw like this:

We went down the anchor rope and, approaching the 70-foot mark, a dim shape unfolded before our eyes—a complete wreck, except for the superstructure, lying upright on an even keel . . . a fabulous sight.

We had hooked into the guard-rail on the forecastle, and after checking to see that the anchor rope was not chafing we began our exploration. Going forward, we found the spare anchor in place on the forecastle and, descending over the bow, her port and starboard anchors still in the hawse-pipes. On the bottom we found various parts of the super-structure (presumably the result of wreck clearance) but apart from this the wreck was virtually intact.

This was obviously a great thrill for the Torbay divers, but more was to come. They found that the main propeller was made of bronze. And bought the wreck. After a great deal of trouble they raised the propeller—with the help of a Navy lifting ship which they hired for the day—and collected a cheque for £840 16s 9d. Not all of this was theirs. The backers had to be paid back, but there was still a handsome profit for their branch. Since then they have sold the rights in the rest of the non-ferrous metals in the ship for another £400.

The raising of the propeller was then the largest salvage operation ever carried out in this country by amateur divers. Since then others have followed in their footsteps, and it would be a very foolish diver indeed who finding a wreck today did not know enough to test the propeller with his diving knife for the tell-tale gleam of bronze! Many many divers have since dived on the *Maine*. She is one of the most shipwreck-like shipwrecks it is possible to see in this country!

*   *   *   *   *

Between Peveril Point and Anvil Point at the western end of Swanage Bay, the Admiralty Chart marks tide-rips and overfalls. Local divers and local fishermen know this only too well, and treat such information with the care that it deserves. Even so each year small boats crewed by men without local knowledge, or even the sense to look at a chart, get into trouble there. Tides reach speeds of five knots and when a tide going west meets a wind from the west then the sea gets up into a huge rolling swell and cross-currents turn the troughs into a welter of water going in all directions at once.

It is not the sort of place for novice boatmen—or for novice divers. But it is the area in which Kingston Branch of the British Sub-Aqua Club have done a great deal of their diving, though they do not allow novices along on their boat dives in the Anvil Point–Durlston Head–Peveril Point area.

Because of the strong currents much of the branch's diving there was done by drifting with the tide. Attached to the diver as he moves like a feather in the wind over the sea-bed is a large surface float.

This drift-dive technique is one used by many of us diving

around our coasts. It enables a large amount of sea-bed to be covered in the course of one dive, and at the same time means that the diver is not exhausted by swimming hard against the tide to remain in one spot. It does not mean that if something interesting is located the diver cannot hold his own for long enough to mark the spot for future exploration at slack water. All the time the divers are below the boat follows the buoy to be right on hand to give assistance if needed.

The sea in the Anvil Point area is not, of course, always rough. In fact on calm days the divers in the boat following the surface buoy could spot the position of underwater obstructions by the swirls on the surface as the tide was deflected from its normal course. One of these in particular caught their attention. They knew that the sea-bed in the area was of flat rock with an average depth of about ninety feet. They also knew that ledges rose from this bed-rock to a height of about six feet—and that under these ledges lobsters loved to hide. But the surface disturbance that they noted most of all would, they felt, have to be caused by something more than a six-foot ledge.

A run with the Branch echo-sounder over the disturbance proved them right—something rose from the sea-bed at ninety feet, to within sixty feet of the surface. There was a hump on the sea-bed. Their Admiralty charts gave the nearest wreck as about two miles SSE of Anvil Head—and as they were some way away from that position, they felt that could not be the reason for the 'hump'. The Admiralty thought it was a reef. But whatever it was, the Kingston branch divers thought it would repay investigation.

There the matter rested for some time. The conditions of tide and weather never seemed to be right for diving on the 'hump'. Not right, that is, until 15th May 1966, when two Zodiac inflatable boats belonging to the branch homed in on the site. Both trailed their anchors along the sea-bed, waiting for them to catch in the obstruction. The tide was running hard, and when the first boat's anchor caught a tremendous jerk parted the chain between the rope's end and the anchor. That will give some idea of the strength of the tides in this part of Dorset.

Ron Blake, a 44-year-old research officer with the Central Electricity Generating Board and First Class Diver of the British Sub-Aqua Club, was in the second boat with his wife, Linden, who is also a First Class Diver (no mean feat for a woman, as the First Class Diver examination of the Club is a severe test).

Within seconds of the first anchor parting, Ron felt his own boat's anchor go in with a tremendous jerk. But this time the tackle held. As the tide was still running so strongly, the divers kitted up slowly and chatted about who would dive with whom. It was decided that Ron and Linden Blake would make the first dive, taking with them another First Class diver of the Trinidad branch of the BSAC, Martin Berner, who was in this country on leave from Barclays Bank in Trinidad. Before they went in and down the anchor rope, Ron wondered to himself what Martin would make of this dive into Britain's poor-visibility waters when he compared it with the crystal clarity that Ron imagined was normal in Trinidad.

The tide was still running as Ron led the way down the anchor rope. To his surprise he found himself at the bottom—not on a reef, but on an area of teak decking. Then he looked around and found that he, Linden and Martin Berner were on the deck of a huge sunken ship stretching away to the limit of visibility. They had, it seemed to them, no time at all to explore the great hulk that was spread out around them.

The hospital ship *Kyarra*, which the Kingston divers found off Peveril
Point

Photo National Maritime Museum

The bell of the *Kyarra*
(when cleaned)
recovered by divers
from the wreck.

A mast lay at right angles to the deck, pointing out into the gloom away from the ship. Portholes, still with glass intact, seemed to lean drunkenly from every crumpled section. Many parts seemed totally collapsed, but the divers' overall impression was of teak decking everywhere, and towering up from one area a giant winch that looked as though it weighed several tons. . . . Then their air began to get low, and Ron signalled up. And up they went, back to the boat.

Recalling what happened then, Ron Blake says: 'I only had time to spit out my mouthpiece and splutter, "It's a bloody great ship!" when we were alone. All the divers had gone down to see for themselves. . . .'

And all the divers were stunned by what they saw. She was big, but what ship was she? Old wireless insulators gave a clue to the early 1900s. And the local fishermen calmly said that she was the 'old hospital ship'. And then the detective work started, and the thought of salvage with it—a scraping of one of the three blades of the huge propeller gleamed bronze-coloured in the light of a torch!

The Hydrographic Department of the Admiralty gave the nearest listed wreck to the site as that of the *Kyarra*, 6953 tons, torpedoed on 26th May 1918, but the position did not fit with the Kingston divers' wreck.

The *Kyarra* was Australian-owned, and had, it was said, at the time of her sinking, been carrying casualties of the First World War home to Australia, but even if the Admiralty's position was wrong and the Kingston wreck was the *Kyarra*, how were they to prove it?

More and more diving was the only answer. One item from the wreck might carry on it the vital clue to the ship's identity. And so it turned out. Deep down in the wreckage near the bilges a diver found a strange, curly twist of something red. It wasn't long—just six inches, in fact. But it wasn't until it came out of the sea into the boat that they were able to identify it. It was a stick of red sealing-wax. Well, you might, I suppose, find some sealing-wax in any boat of that sort and at that time. But this brittle stick of warped wax had something stamped into its surface—the name of the manufacturer and the place it was made, Sydney.

Now most of the divers felt sure that they were diving on the *Kyarra*, and that the Admiralty position for her was wrong. But they still needed something to confirm their suspicions. The diving went on, and so did the detective work on shore.

From the diving came bales of silk from the hold and some scent bottles still firmly stoppered. The scent, some of it French, still smelt quite pleasant, though the full aroma had undoubtedly faded with the years. From detective work on shore came a mass of details about the *Kyarra*. Lloyd's *Register of Shipping* was helpful. In reply to a letter from Linden Blake, Lloyd's wrote:

Dear Madam,

In reply to your letter dated 22nd May, I have to say that from information available in this Office, it would appear that the 'Kyarra' was built in 1903, by Messrs W. Denny and Brothers of Dumbarton.

She was registered at the Port of Freemantle, and was the property of the Australasia United Steam Navigation Company Ltd. Her gross tonnage was 6953 and her net 4383.

I regret we have no details regarding her loss, but she last appeared in the 1918–19 Edition of the Society's Register Book, which would appear to confirm your statement that she was lost at sea.

Yours faithfully. . . .

Another letter addressed to Mrs L. Blake at the Blakes' Weybridge home carried even more information. This time it came from Lloyd's of London:

Dear Madam,

In reply to your inquiry of May 22, the following information has been extracted from Lloyd's Records:

British steamer 'Kyarra' of Freemantle, 6953 tons gross, was sunk by a submarine 1¼ miles SSE of Anvil Point on May 26, 1918 on voyage London to Sydney with general cargo.

She was built by W. Denny and Bros., Dumbarton, in 1903, owned by Australasia United Steam Nav. Co., Ltd., and was 415·5 ft long, 52·2 ft wide and 28·6 ft deep.

Yours faithfully. . . .

The Imperial War Museum had more details in their reference library. She had two decks. The shelter deck was of steel sheathed in *teak*, and her upper steel deck was also sheathed in wood. She had electric light and wireless, and was described as a twin-screwed schooner. Her master was W. Smith, and her wartime code letters were 115755 TWSC.

She had been torpedoed without warning, and six of the crew had been lost. She had been a hospital ship, and had worked previously landing Anzac troops in the Dardenelles. The fishermen's description of her as 'the old hospital ship', the teak decking, the Australian sealing-wax, the twin-screws, it all began to fit—but there was still no positive proof.

The Kingston divers pressed on. They wrote to the Admiralty, pointing out that they had found a large wreck in a position where there was no wreck marked. The Admiralty were very interested, and waived their normal search fee in return for any information the divers could give them. They added that a survey vessel would investigate the site.

At times the Kingston divers who bought the wreck, began to think the whole ship was made of brass. Just a few of the items they found!

Photos Colin Doeg

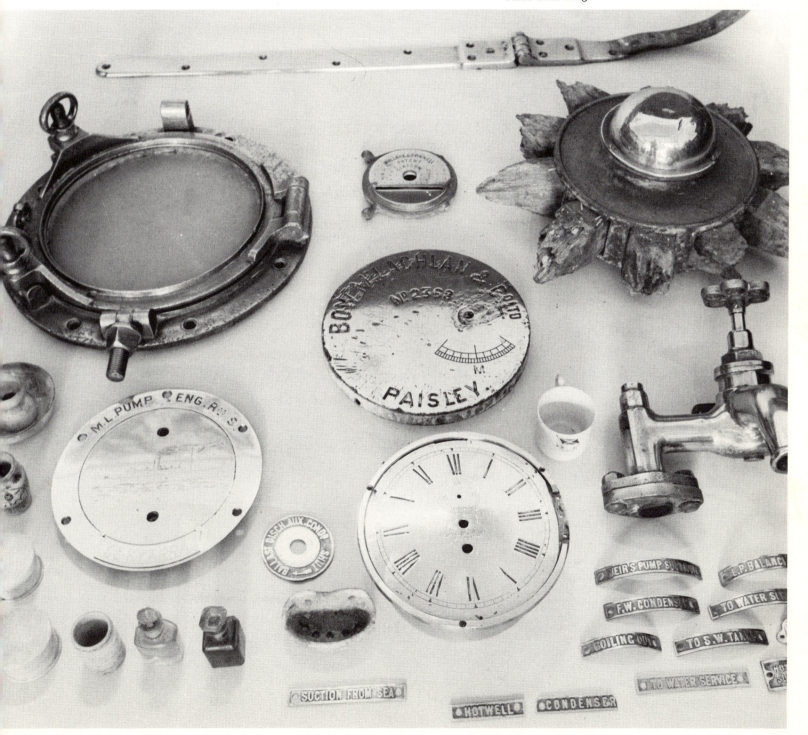

The divers wrote to William Denny and Bros. And as at the time the company was in voluntary liquidation, and the ship-yard closed, they were referred to the National Maritime Museum at Greenwich, to which the bulk of the older Denny records had been transferred. Linden Blake's file was now growing. To it she added this letter from the National Maritime Museum:

DEAR MRS BLAKE,

Thank you for your letter of the 3rd of June. The Kyarra was a twin screw passenger and cargo carrying liner.

She and her sister ship, the Kanowa, were built for the Australasia United Steam Navigation Co. Her gross tonnage was 6952·68, net tonnage 4383·1. She was powered by two triple expansion engines of 375 Nominal Horse Power each, built by Denny's.

She was launched on the 2nd of February, 1903. She was only a schooner in that she was 'schooner rigged', which means she had two pole masts, on which she could, in an emergency, set small fore and aft sails. In fact she was a steamer, and almost certainly never set any sails at all.

She had 42 first class cabins, with 3 berths each, and 20 second class cabins, with 8 berths, the lower decks were fitted out with cattle stalls.

We also hold plans of the two ships. These include a rigging plan, a lines plan, deck plans and a midships section. The best plan to show what the ship looked like would be the rigging plan. We can provide copies of all these plans . . .

Yours sincerely. . . .

There was now little doubt in the divers' minds. They had found the *Kyarra*, they were certain of that. But the one piece of undeniable evidence still eluded them.

If the Australasia United Steam Navigation Company had gone out of business, as seemed certain, who had taken over? The company, it seemed, had disposed of the fifteen vessels it once owned, one by one, until the last was sold to a small company in Honkong. After a lot of research it became clear that the rest of the company had been taken over by Inchcape and Company, who could not have been more helpful.

Their records showed that the *Kyarra* had been fitted out by the Government for the transport of invalids in the winter of 1917. On 24th May 1918 she had sailed from Tilbury bound for Devonport, where she was to embark about one thousand war-wounded and sick troops, presumably to take them home to Australia. But she never reach Devonport.

The 26th of May, 1918, was a very calm day and Mrs Geoffrey Worssam and her husband looked out to sea from their home at The View (now Durlston Cliff) and saw the *Kyarra* steam quietly round Durlston Head and out of sight.

A few minutes later, [Mrs Worssam wrote to the *Swanage Times* in 1968], we saw her drift back into view and with horror saw her sinking rapidly by the bow. She was so close in that we could see the launching of her lifeboat and after only about seven minutes the stern seemed to rear up as she plunged below the surface.

We wept as we thought of the wounded trapped in her. Later we learned that she was to have been taking wounded but her orders had been changed at the last minute and she had sailed without them. It was believed that the offending German submarine was the one which was cornered and sunk near Sandbanks shortly afterwards.

Six men died, and reports at the time suggest that some of the survivors were scalded with steam from the boilers. This confirms her torpedoing amidships, as her boilers were placed very close to the central point of the vessel. Her master tried to run for the shore to beach her, but it was hopeless.

It all fitted in with the things the divers had found. But they had not found positive proof. That discovery when it came was in a form that could not be denied.

Two Kingston divers, David Weightman and Julian Bamford found, between the giant winch which loomed menacingly over the deck and what had been part of the first-class accommodation, a giant 'brass bucket'. It was in fact the ship's bell. Nearly two feet high, it bore in great letters the word 'KYARRA', and then the initials of her company. No one can argue with that sort of evidence!

This discovery only crystallized what had been in the minds of the Kingston and Hounslow branch divers for some time. They had found the ship; now could they really call it theirs?

Further inquiries made it clear that if they wanted to buy, the Ministry of Transport, who paid out—through the War Damage Commission—£190,000 (of which £125,521 seems to be value put on the cargo) would be willing to sell.

So there came about 'an agreement made in duplicate this eighteenth day of April One thousand nine hundred and sixty seven between the Minister of Transport of St Christopher House, Southwark Street, London, S.E.1 (hereinafter referred to as "the Minister" of the one part and. . . .' the divers (hereinafter referred to as 'the Purchaser') of the other part.

WHEREAS the ship 'Kyarra' of 6953 tons gross built 1903 was lost by enemy action on the 26th May 1918 off Anvil Point in the County of Dorset: and WHEREAS the said wreck was abandoned to Her Majesty's Government on settlement for the total loss of the said ship; AND WHEREAS the rights in the said wreck are now vested in the Minister:—

NOW THEREFORE IT IS HEREBY AGREED between the parties as follows:

1. In consideration of the payment by the Purchaser to the Minister of the sum of ONE HUNDRED AND TWENTY POUNDS and the purchaser's agreement to fulfil the obligations of owner of the wreck the Minister HEREBY TRANSFERS all title in the said wreck to the Purchaser.

2. This agreement does not extend to any cargo which may remain in the said wreck.

3. The said sum of ONE HUNDRED AND TWENTY POUNDS shall be paid by the Purchaser to the Minister on the signing of this Agreement.

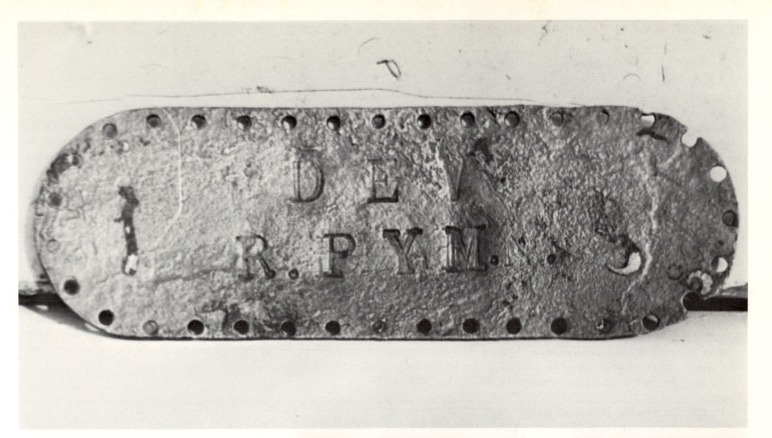

This small brass plaque found by divers in the wreckage of s.s. *Bretagne* led them to a meeting with Mr R. Pym (*below*), one of the last living survivors of her sinking

So ran the agreement. Once signed and suitably witnessed, and once the money had been handed over, the *Kyarra* was theirs. And Section 2 of the agreement did not worry the divers overmuch, for the Ministry told them that the cargo would mostly be valueless, consisting as it did of cotton goods, cigarettes, and manufactured articles, though there was some phosphor-bronze sieving and copper boiler tubes worth over £1500 at the time of loss.

Now the diving could and did begin in earnest. The new owners of *Kyarra* showed their agreement to the Receiver of Wreck in Poole, so that there should be no misunderstandings later over their ownership, and then started to explore their new kingdom.

Each dive brought some new discovery. In the bow they found the sail lockers, judging by the number of brass sail eyelets left behind, and, says Adrian Warren, who has dived the *Kyarra* many times, this area seemed to be particularly attractive for some unknown reason to really big edible crabs.

In a way it was like letting schoolboys loose in a sweet-shop —the wreck was a treasure-house of trophies. From the lamp-trimmer's room came one of the much-prized big navigation lights. . . . Portholes—there must have been nearly two hundred of them—were so common as to be almost disregarded after the first few dives. Moving back from the stern into the shambles that had once been the flying bridge and first class dining-room and accommodation, they found plates with the company insignia, bottles of beer marked with the words 'Tower Bridge Bottling Co' (it still exists, and is now part of Courages), and more luxurious items like champagne. On the surface when the cork came out the champagne fizzed, but it was hopeless to drink, the sea having filtered in through the cork.

It was about this time that the divers found the safe. Recalling this moment, Blake says his thought was: 'My God, gold . . . we're in. There'll be sovereigns in there at least!'

A study of the plans of the ship had convinced the divers that the safe which appeared to have fallen down from somewhere above and lodged in the wreckage—was that of the ship's purser. Operation Safe Recovery was launched on the very next tide. At slack water they fitted chains around the safe, to these chains they attached three large lifting bags—easily enough to lift the 500 lbs they estimated that the safe weighed— and up she went. On the surface their troubles were by no means over. Towing the safe ashore by means of a small fishing-boat became a major operation. The strain of towing the safe broke the boat's rudder, then the A-bracket, and finally they realized that the only thing moving them towards Swanage was the tide. This was all right until they had to turn. It was hopeless. They couldn't move the safe against it, and had to wait for the tide to change once again. In all it took over six hours to get the safe ashore. Then they had to get it open.

A cold chisel on the back seemed the only solution on the beach, and there were the divers, covered in rust hammering away like fiends before a goggle-eyed audience of nearly two hundred holidaymakers. Finally the safe surrendered. Papers? Fivers? No—old code papers showing the signal frequencies they were to use, and what to do in the event of being captured.

Full of hope, the divers now moved to the middle shelf. Nothing. Now for the big moment—the cash compartment. A leather bag! It was rotting and giving way, but there were undoubtedly round objects inside. Ron Blake tipped a stream of them into his hand. Round and white, they lay on his hand as he stared at them. Pearls? 'They're mothballs', said a horified voice. And a great guffaw went up from the holidaymakers. Suddenly the divers were alone with a battered safe, some fragments of papers and some over fifty-year-old mothballs. It seemed a poor return for so much effort!

The amazing thing about the *Kyarra* is the amount of brass work on her. Even the bath taps are solid brass. Some of the stanchions which surrounded the first-class section are solid brass. A clock the divers recovered from the wreckage has a face and bodywork of solid brass. This is certainly one case where those who say 'They don't build them like that any more' are undeniably right.

*   *   *   *   *

But just because a ship sank during the War years you cannot assume that the sinking, even if another ship was involved, is due to enemy action.

Take the case of a wreck that was known to be about four miles east of Berry Head near Brixham. Admiralty surveys had located the wreck, but no-one, it seemed, was prepared to put a name to her.

No-one, that is, until the Bristol Aeroplane Company Special Branch of the British Sub-Aqua Club decided to look into the matter. The fact that the BAC divers were a Special Branch means that membership was confined to staff of the company.

In September 1969 the Bristol divers slid down from their diving boat to the top of the unknown wreck some eighty-five feet below.

They found a steamer, upright on a sea-bed 120 feet down, very corroded with large holes containing conger and big pollack. The superstructure had been obliterated by explosive charges during wreck-clearing in the area, but it was still a ship-like wreck—in fact the stern gun was still there, and was used thereafter by the divers as a handy reference point.

A very large angler fish seemed to have claimed the after deck as his own, and as the visibility varied from nil to fifteen feet this was noted as another hazard. Very big angler fish are inclined to be snappy and bad-tempered, and as the species is practically all mouth, it does not do to place a limb within easy swallowing distance. This particular fish was over three feet across.

The main purpose of that September dive was of course to identify the wreck. And identify it they did.

A diver surfaced and cried: 'We've found the bell!' The diving boat, which only seconds before had been drowsing in the sun, came to life with a jerk. A rope was passed to the diver who sank down to join his companions on the wreck below.

Those left on the surface waited for the tugs on the line which would be the signal to haul away. It seemed ages before the signal was given, and after a long, steady haul a barnacle-encrusted lump which was only vaguely bell-shaped was lifted aboard.

The thick crust was carefully scraped away, and there were the words: 'BRETAGNE 1903 CHRISTIANIA'.

So now they knew. The ship was called *Bretagne*. She was built or launched in 1903. And she came from Christiania, which we now call Oslo, Norway.

The bell weighed 44 lb and put a considerable strain on a beam in the finder's home, but that was hardly the end of the matter. Once divers have found a wreck they become infected with the wreck detectives' desire to know all about the ship and her crew, and how the sinking happened. From Lloyd's *Shipping Register* they found out that the ship was classed as a schooner, the builder's name, the type of engine and the skipper's name—Johannesson. Lloyd's were most helpful with the divers' further inquiries.

The steamer *Bretagne* was, it seemed, sailing from Barry to Rouen with a cargo of coal. On that voyage she was in collision with the steamer *Renée Marthe* on 10th August 1918, about four miles north-east of Hope's Nose, Devon, and sank during salvage operations. She was in tow at the time of her sinking.

By now the wreck had aroused so much interest in the Branch that they decided to explore the possibilities of buying it. The *Bretagne* had been requisitioned by the Ministry of War Transport, and was now the responsibility of the Board of Trade.

Soon the Branch were the owners of the *Bretagne*. To them it was now 'our wreck', and they carried out many more dives on her. It was during one of these later dives that they made a discovery which was to lead to a meeting with one of the crew who was actually on board the *Bretagne* at the time of her sinking.

Says John Toller: 'While finning towards the bow on the starboard side my companion and I came across a few lumps of metal covered with the usual mud and barnacles.' One of these when cleaned up turned out to be a brass plate bearing the letters 'DEV' and 'R. PYM'.

This last must be someone's name, and so John Toller wrote to the Register and Record Office for Shipping and Seamen at Cardiff. To his delight this office not only possessed the ship's register and official log, but were able to send them to the Merchantile Marine offices at Avonmouth so that he could examine them. Such documents are usually only kept for thirty years, but if a death occurs on board the papers are retained for ever.

The ship's log was most precise. It listed three collisions in six months. The third was the important one. It read: 'This is to certify that at 10.30 a.m. yesterday (10. 8. 18) the steamer Renée Marthe, French steamer, during dense fog, collided with my steamer. Damage was so serious that she foundered shortly after. Chief Officer Mr H. Watterson losing his life.'

The Register too was interesting. It showed the signature of an R. Pym, a Royal Navy gunner from Torquay, serving at a rate of 28 shillings per week. He was twenty-six. John Toller realized that Mr Pym could still be alive, and wrote at once to the address given in the register. No reply. The Central Library at Torquay replied to another letter saying that Mr Pym left his address between 1935 and 1937. There for a while inquiries had to stop. They remained stopped until he found a man in his own company whose father was a Torquay postman. Through this contact Mr Pym's address was finally found. Another letter brought a reply from Mr Pym's daughter saying that her father was alive and well and only his eyesight had stopped him from replying himself.

On Sunday 2nd November 1969 at 2.30 in the afternoon John Toller found himself shaking hands with a man who had stepped off the *Bretagne* to safety fifty-one years before, and heard about the collision, which had led to the wreck on which he dived, at first hand.

Mr Pym had good reason to remember that day well. The collision had damaged the steering gear so badly that it was jammed solid over to starboard. Mr Pym and the first mate had stayed on board in an attempt to free it and give the trawlers, which now had the *Bretagne* in tow, a better chance of making headway.

'We called it a day when the water was lapping over the deck', said Mr Pym. The captain had ordered him and the first mate to the boats, but the mate had gone below to collect some of his belongings first. A wave had slopped over the ship and closed the outer door—moments later the ship nose-dived to the bottom with the mate still trapped on board.

The brass plate? It had been on an ammunition box, and there were five more like it down below, said Mr Pym.

Meanwhile, though the Bristol divers have not yet found another of Mr Pym's ammunition boxes, they still dive regularly on the *Bretagne*.

CHAPTER 12

The Cases of the M1 and M2

the full story of the loss of M2 in 1932, the attempts to raise, her and what she looks like today.

FRIDAY, the 13th of November, 1925, was to live up to everything that superstition forecasts for such a day and such a date —at least as far as H.M. Submarine *M1* was concerned.

For it was on that day, Friday the 13th, that the *M1* was reported missing in the Channel during exercises that had started the previous day. . . .

The 'M' Class of submarines were unique. They were 300 feet long, and had a surface speed of 15½ knots with 9½ knots submerged. The *M1* was originally laid down in 1916, when she was designated as the *K18*. The class was the brainchild of the then First Sea Lord, Lord 'Jackie' Fisher. His idea was to create a class of submarine that could not only act as counters to the successful German U-boats, but which could creep along under water and while still submerged pound German battleships with shells from a forward-mounted 12-inch gun.

This was a colossal gun to mount on a submarine—in all the fleets of the world at that time the biggest gun carried by a submarine was a 5-inch. The idea of the 'M' class was that the gun was loaded while on the surface and was then laid for high-elevation shooting. The guns for the M-boats were taken from ships of the *Dreadnought* class. Once the gun was loaded the submarine was submerged to between 12 and 20 feet, leaving the muzzle just poking out of the water. The muzzle had a bead sight on it so that the gunnery officer looking through the periscope could aim and fire while the boat itself was running submerged just under the surface. There was only one drawback to this method of surprise attack—to reload the submarine had to surface.

The *M1* and *M2* were ordered from Vickers and the *M3* and *M4* from Armstrong's. Only the first three were completed, and the contract for the *M4* was cancelled. *M1*, the first to be launched, never fired a shot in anger—the war ended before she had completed her sea trials. *M2* and *M3* were completed in 1920.

Submarine *M1*, despite days of searching and diving off Start Point, was not located, and it was assumed from damage found to a Swedish ship, *Vidar*—and from paint found on that damage and identified as similar to that of the *M1*—that the submarine had been accidentally rammed and sunk.

So finally it was no surprise when, on 2nd December 1925 the Admiralty announced: 'Diving operations in connexion

with the submarine *M1* have been discontinued as no positive results have been obtained. It is not considered necessary to prolong the search as the cause of her loss has been so fully established.' There the matter rested. And the years passed and, except for those who still mourned, submarine *M1* was almost forgotten. She stayed that way until one September day nearly forty-two years later Captain Silas Oates manœuvred his 134-ton salvage vessel, *Comrades*, off Start Point in search of sunken ships.

The *Comrades* based on Penzance, Cornwall, carried four divers using Aqualung equipment, and Captain Oates, who was not looking for sunken submarines but a torpedoed ship, stopped engines over a likely spot. The first diver down was 28-year-old Frank Charles. He reached the sea-bed at 150 feet and finned slowly forward through the mist of visibility.

A great wreck loomed out of the murk, and at first sight Frank Charles thought it was an old steamer. A closer look, and he knew what he was looking at was an enormous submarine.

> She is sitting more or less level on the bottom of sand and shale [reported Mr Charles]. She is coated with barnacle growth, but as I swam along her side I could make out the letter 'M' quite distinctly. Alongside it was a numeral which could only be '1', though it was difficult to make out. She looks enormous, a very unusual design for a submarine. There was this great tube thing up front, which I couldn't make out. But now I've seen a photograph of the *M1*, I am completely satisfied that it is her and that it was probably her gun I was looking at. Some of the plating forward appears to be missing.

Captain Oates felt sure that the *M1* was undamaged enough to be raised by pumping compressed air into her through hollow bolts fired into her hull. And naval historians thought that the *M1* should be raised as a museum-piece.

But the Royal Navy thought differently. They regard sunken naval vessels which contain bodies as being as sacrosanct as a graveyard (indeed, there are many sunken Royal Navy ships in our waters and abroad which as they were sunk during both World Wars are designated as 'war graves'). So they refused permission, saying that 'relatives are still alive and to raise here would only resurrect the whole tragedy'. And Captain Oates, of course, respected their wishes.

But the *M1* had been cold in her grave off Start Point for only a little over six years and two months when it all happened again—to her sister ship the *M2*.

The first Admiralty announcement came on the night of 26th January 1932:

> News has been received this evening that Submarine *M2* dived at about 10.30 this morning off Portland, and since then no further communication has been received from her.
>
> Destroyers and submarines from Portland are searching the area in which she was last known to be, and every endeavour is being made to establish communication with her.

M2, like *M1*, was unique. Like her sister ship, she was built to carry the huge 12-inch gun. She was laid down in 1916 and completed in 1920, but in 1927 her huge gun was removed. In the space that used to be taken up by the gun mounting, a hangar for a small seaplane, the Parnall Pixie, was installed. The Pixie's wings folded for stowage in the hangar.

In addition to the seaplane, the 296-foot-long sub—her beam was 24·5 feet—carried a 3-inch 'disappearing' gun, two Lewis guns, and four 18-inch bow torpedo tubes.

The seaplane, one of the smallest two-seaters in the world at that time, was designed to be launched by catapult off a runway on the submarine's deck. When the plane returned to the submarine it was hoisted on board and into its hangar by means of a small crane. Because of the plane, the *M2* became known as the first undersea aircraft-carrier in the world. Some holidaymakers at Gosport in 1930 had good cause to remember this when the seaplane, which had just taken off from the submarine, stalled and crashed on to the beach near them.

On 26th January, *M2* left Portland Harbour for routine exercises. There was no reason to think that this day would be any different from any other. The *M2* was considered safe and seaworthy. True, she had been badly battered in a gale in November 1929, on a voyage from Portsmouth to Portland, and her bridge and conning-tower had been damaged. But that damage had been repaired long ago, and the fact that the submarine had survived such appalling weather had given the crew even more confidence in her.

The sea off Portland on that January day in 1932 when the *M2* put out, soon after 9 a.m., for West Bay to the west of Portland Bill, was fairly calm. There was a little fog about, but nothing to cause any anxiety. The fact that she was exercising alone was nothing unusual. Combined exercises with submarines *L67* and *L71* from Portsmouth, and with other units of the Sixth Submarine Flotilla based on Portland, were to take place later, but for the time being *M2* was alone.

For a while all went well. *M2* kept in touch with her parent ship, H.M.S. *Titania*, and at 10.11 a.m. her captain, Lieutenant-Commander J. D. de M. Leathes, signalled: 'I am going to dive'. On board *Titania* the wireless operators were busy with other submarines going out. So it was not until one wireless operator reported that he could not establish contact with *M2* that any anxiety was felt. But even then it was felt that this was probably only a communications problem. When, however, the submarine failed to return to Portland Harbour (she was due at 4.15 p.m.), a full alarm was raised.

Soon the whole area knew about it. Men in theatres and cinemas were recalled and ordered to report to their ships. Cars and coaches were sent from Portland to Weymouth to round them up and hurry them back to base. Managers of cinemas interrupted performances to go on stage and make the recall announcements. Police called at private houses of naval men to tell them of the recall.

A number of officers taking part in a dress rehearsal of an amateur dramatic show at Weymouth Pavilion were recalled by police—and rushed to their ships without even bothering to change. By 9 p.m.—the full alarm had been given just before eight o'clock—some five hundred men had got back to their ships, and they sailed shortly afterwards.

But action had been taken even earlier than this. By 5.30—an hour and fifteen minutes after *M2* had failed to return to harbour—H.M.S. *Salmon*, *Torrid*, *Thruster* and *Rowena*, all destroyers, had sailed. Two submarines, *H44* and *H49*, followed at 7 p.m., and then more surface ships, carrying the men recalled from the surrounding areas, at a few minutes after 9 p.m. Even if the submarine had failed to surface there were some grounds for hope that some men could still escape.

The *M2* had enough air to remain under water for forty-eight hours. In addition to this she carried the latest life-saving equipment. In this case that meant the new Davis Escape Apparatus. The Davis equipment had already proved its worth. Only in June of the year before, H.M.S. *Poseidon* had sunk in collision off the coast of China. The total death-roll had been twenty, but for the first time in naval history men had escaped from the sunken submarine, after being trapped for a number of hours, by using the Davis equipment. (Six escaped from the sunken boat. Two, however, had died after being picked up. Five officers and thirty ratings had also been rescued after jumping from the sub before she sank.)

So there was still a chance for the men of the *M2*. And just after midnight the Admiralty announced that a contact had been made: 'An object, presumed to be submarine M2, has been located three miles west of Portland Bill, in 17 fathoms, on a sandy bottom. Salvage craft and divers have been sent from Portsmouth to this position with the utmost despatch.'

Utmost despatch was right. H.M.S. *Sabre*, a destroyer, carrying divers 'specially trained for deep-sea work in connection with submarines' set out from Portsmouth and sped at 25 knots to the scene. *Sabre* was expected to arrive at the contact point at about 2 a.m. Two submarine salvage ships left shortly after her, but with their slower speed would not be at the scene of operations before dawn.

In the meantime the newspapers had contacted Mr R. H. Davis (later to become Sir Robert), inventor of the Davis Escape Apparatus, for his views on the chances of the crew of *M2*, which the Admiralty now said consisted of seven officers and fifty-three men, including two members of the Royal Air Force. Mr Davis was hopeful.

> There is no need to abandon hope at all [he said]. The submarine might easily remain under water for forty-eight hours or even more, and then rise again to the surface. The

The *M1* leaving port on a training exercise. Note the
huge gun, which never fired a shot in anger.

officers would make every effort to remedy any defect in the vessel's machinery and would not abandon their vessel until every hope was gone. Even then the officers and men would have every chance of escape by means of my apparatus.

This would not only bring them to the surface one by one, but would also enable them to keep afloat for a considerable period. Of course, one cannot overlook the possibility of the submarine being badly damaged, although it appears from the official statement that she did not sink as a result of a collision, and therefore would only have mechanical trouble.

I think that the officers will now be doing everything in their power to put the vessel right. They will still continue their efforts to bring her to the surface for some time yet. I am quite sure they will not abandon ship till all hope of getting her up is passed. In the end if they have to take this course, the means of escape for every man on board is available.

His son, Mr R. W. G. Davis, who was a director of Siebe, Gorman and Company, the submarine engineers, was equally hopeful when told of the supposed position of the *M2*, and said:

Divers can work fairly comfortably at 17 fathoms under the surface, providing, of course, they work in short periods on the shift system. The fact that the submarine is on a sandy bottom means that their task should not be impeded by mud churning up. It is very difficult to surmise what is wrong with the craft. It may be that her gear has gone wrong, and that the crew are trying to repair it, or that they may be standing to, hoping to be found. The raising of a huge submarine is, of course, a big job, but the fact that she is only 17 fathoms down makes the men's chances brighter.

Despite these hopeful thoughts, by the afternoon of Wednesday, 27th January, Portsmouth, where fourteen of the *M2* crew had their homes, was a city of mourning again—telegrams had been sent to the relatives of all members of the crew. They read: 'Regret to inform you that your husband (or son) is missing and feared drowned in submarine *M2*, believed sunk off Portland on Tuesday'.

One of the families who got such a telegram was that of Able Seaman Thomas Morris, who was twenty-five. His wife lived with three young children in Ermine Road, Lewisham, London, and she had been looking forward to her husband leaving the submarine service in a month's time when he completed his twelve years' service with the Navy. The telegram was an even greater shock because Able Seaman Morris had been a survivor of the *Poseidon* disaster—he escaped by jumping over the side.

Some of the *M2*'s crew had been more fortunate. One, interviewed by the *Daily Mail*, was Able Seaman E. A. Evans.

On the very day that *M2* went out for her trials his discharge came through, and he did not sail. Because his father had died, he wanted to go home to South Africa and help his mother, so he bought his discharge. It arrived just in time. Another few hours and he would have been, as he said, 'with my pals on the bottom'.

He, of course, had no idea what had happened:

> I know they had everything aboard to help. The latest Davis escape apparatus was there, and also extra supplies of oxygen—a new thing in submarines. One of my pals who has gone was in the *Poseidon*—Morris. He escaped by jumping clear. His luck was good then; now . . . But no one ever talked to him about that disaster. It's strange, you may think; after one escape he went back to submarines . . . In two days I shall be in a great liner sailing for home. Luck, amazing luck; I can't get over it.

A London *Star* reporter (the *Star* was later taken over by the London *Evening News*) had a strange experience on the day after the disaster. He found himself sitting opposite a sailor in the Tube. The young man, who is never named in the interview, had 'Submarine M2' in gilt letters on his cap.

The *Star* reporter, doing his job, interviewed the man, who 'was labouring under the stress of deep emotion and when I spoke to him he broke down completely'. The interview went like this:

> I began my Christmas leave on Saturday [he told me]. By an arrangement with one of my mates I stayed on duty over Christmas while he went home to his wife and family.

> I wish I'd never consented to the change. Here I am, single, with no ties compared to him—and some people call me lucky! Lucky!—to lose my mates and know they've left behind those who will, naturally, miss them more than I should have been missed if I'd been there instead of any one of them. On a submarine you get to know each other much better than you do on a battleship or cruiser. The officers are closer to you. Not a man in *M2* but swore that Commander Leathes was the finest 'Old Man' in the Navy and the lieutenants were all close up to us, without losing discipline. It's queer when you first submerge in a submarine, but we get used to it and to the boat. Warrant-Engineer Hayes (one of the missing men) could do anything he liked with the *M2*, though no tricks or stunts were ever carried out.

> I'd come to London to make arrangements for my wedding. Two of the men on the boat were to have been at the ceremony—one of them would have been best man. There's just a chance they'll get them up alive.

But now the weather took a hand, and even that slim chance faded. The divers went down all right, but when they could go down heavy seas, wind and tides made it impossible for them to reach the contact. They had got to seventy feet down, thirty feet short of the bottom. Then with the return of the lifting lighters, which had been at sea off Portland Bill, all hope for the crew was drowned.

In the meantime the Admiralty were interested in a report that the master of a Newcastle coasting vessel had seen the *M2* shortly before she disappeared—so interested that they sent an official to talk to the captain of the coaster when he arrived at Gravelines, near Calais. The coaster had put into Portland to bunker, and while there the captain had asked in conversation if it was not unusual for a submarine to dive stern first, as that is what he had seen in West Bay, off Chesil Beach on the west of Portland Bill.

At 10.30 p.m. on 27th January the Admiralty issued another statement:

> The following information was received tonight from the Rear-Admiral of Submarines (Rear-Admiral Little) who is conducting search operations to the westward of Portland Bill for Submarine *M2*: Two objects have been located by sweep-wires, but, owing to the strong tide, divers have had difficulty in reaching the bottom to investigate. Diving is being continued when possible throughout the night . . . .

In the early hours of Thursday, 28th January the *Daily Mail* were able to feed new information to the Admiralty. Their reporter had located the captain who had seen a submarine dive stern-first near Portland Bill before the Admiralty officials could reach him. In a dramatic dispatch from Gravelines, near Calais, the *Mail*'s special correspondent reported:

> I have just had the first interview with Captain A. E. Howard of the Newcastle-on-Tyne steamer, *Tynesider*, the last vessel to see the *M2* before she disappeared. I found him asleep in his cabin just after midnight two miles off Gravelines Harbour, which the *Tynesider* will only be able to enter at 3 a.m.

> There can be no doubt, Mr Howard said to me, that the submarine I saw yesterday morning is the same which disappeared off Portland.

> I was coming from Charleston, Cornwall, with a cargo of China clay yesterday at 11.30 a.m. As I was getting near Portland I saw the submarine. I could read quite clearly her mark M. She was on top of the water, but I soon noticed that her head was getting right out of the water. Before I could approach I saw her sink rather suddenly, her stern first.

> I did not pay too much attention to it at first, since I had never seen a submarine dive. However, when I called at Portland at 2.30 p.m. I told the news to a man on the quayside and asked him if it was the right way for a submarine to go down. He said he had never seen a ship sink, so I did not trouble any more.

> When I left the harbour I met a submarine going in and I thought that it was the one I had seen earlier and that everything was all right. Of course I was sorry to learn this evening on the wireless that *M2* was lost.

> But the position the Admiralty gave is not a good one. When I saw the *M2* she was approximately 8 miles N.W. by N. from Portland Bill, two and a half miles from shore. I am afraid they are searching in the wrong place.

By 8 a.m. on 28th January the Rear-Admiral Submarines

Old newspaper
photographs of
the diving suit
used by the
German team
who helped the
Royal Navy to
try and find the
sunken *M1*

138

had been in touch with the Admiralty, who issued two state-ments. The first detailed a signal from the Rear-Admiral:

Regret no progress during night. Am concentrating our efforts on the two obstructions previously reported, and also in vicinity position, seven miles 300 degrees from Portland Bill, to which Tynesider and schooner Crown of Denmark have drawn attention.

The second Admiralty statement was an eleboration of the first:

The following information was received last night from the captain in charge, Portland: The master of the motor auxiliary schooner, Crown of Denmark, reports that while on passage to Portland he was approximately 16 miles at log S.E. of Lyme Regis, about 6.40 p.m. on Tuesday, when he saw on his port beam a very sudden bright light of about three seconds duration, which dimmed, reappearing very bright, and then disappearing altogether. The light was followed 10 minutes later by two loud explosions like guns going off. Weather was thick at the time. His craft anchored at Portland at 9.3 p.m. on Tuesday. Neither the light nor the explosions can be accounted for.

But the fact that both the Tynesider and the Crown of Denmark reported something in the same area had caused the new search there. Captain Hunt, the master of the Crown of Denmark, said later:

Immediately I saw the flash I thought something was wrong. It was a brilliant white flash and was repeated two or three times. There was then a loud report which echoed over the water, but I could not see anything on the surface to account for it. It occured to me at the time that it might be a

submarine, and as soon as I heard that the M2 was missing I put into Portland and made a statement to the authorities. The position that Captain Hunt gave was within half a mile of the place where Captain Howard of the Tynesider had seen M2 dive.

The Navy now had several positions to search and those who knew West Bay—which was now being called 'Dead Men's Bay'—had every sympathy with them in their search. For West Bay was also called 'The Bay of a Thousand Wrecks'. There was no telling whether the sweep wire from the searching vessels had caught an old wreck or the M2—until divers went down and checked the wreckage.

For example H.M.S. Sabre, the destroyer, caught something in her sweep wires. She cast her lead, and it came up covered with paint. She dumped an anchor on the spot, and oil welled to the surface. The M2, releasing oil to recognize that she had been located, or an old wreck?

H.M.S. Thruster, another destroyer, heard tappings on her listening gear. Natural, or the M2 trying to attract attention? Either way, it was another position for the divers to search. And the divers, no matter how hard they tried, could not always reach the obstruction at the end of the sweep wires. The tides swept them back at each new attempt. The whole of the submarine's possible exercise ground was swept again and again, and more and more obstructions were found.

At 8.30 p.m. that day the Admiralty put out a new statement. It gave some idea of the difficulties facing them:

The following information was received at 6.40 p.m. from the Rear-Admiral Submarines, who is in charge of the search for M2: We have temporarily abandoned operations on the obstruction first discovered on Tuesday evening as the sweep keeps slipping so that divers cannot reach it. The

The M2 launches her seaplane. Called the world's first aircraft-carrier, she was not long in following her sister boat M1 to a grave on the sea-bed where the divers found her recently

divers have not reached the other obstruction found yesterday, but may do so at next tide. Further search of the area today has revealed another obstruction, North 30 degrees West, six miles from Portland Bill. Divers have been on the bottom near it and have so far failed to reach the obstruction. The operations continue.

Operations continued all right, and everyone in the Royal Navy knew that they had no more time, but they worked on. And so did the exhausted divers. Diving went on all night by the light of underwater lamps. At 5 a.m. on 29th January Rear-Admiral Submarines:

The obstruction discovered six miles North 30 degrees West from Portland Bill is an old wreck. Shall sweep in the vicinity, as an earlier sweep which parted brought up a pair of submarine hand flags in canvas case. General search will continue as well.

No hope now of saving life.

That night from Admiralty: 'The latest information received from Rear-Admiral Submarines is to the effect that divers have examined further obstructions, which have proved to be old wrecks. The search still continues'.

And then later: 'The Secretary of the Admiralty regrets to announce that in view of a report now received from Rear-Admiral Submarines, who has been attempting to salve the sunken submarine *M2*, it is no longer possible to hope for the rescue of any of the officers and men on board'.

At the same time as this chilling statement the Admiralty issued a list of seven officers and fifty-three petty officers and ratings on board the submarine at the time, adding 'their death must therefore now be presumed'.

The King sent his deep sympathy and that of the Queen to be conveyed to the families of all those who had been lost, and also to all the officers and men serving in His Majesty's submarines on the loss of their comrades.

But still there was no sign of the position of *M2*. The submarine signalling flags bore no distinctive markings, and could have come from anywhere. Every time the divers went down they found an old wreck—and there were said to be at least two hundred in West Bay dating from the Spanish Armadas.

But the diving went on, for the Navy now considered it imperative to find out what had happened to the *M2*—'in the interests of the submarine service as a whole'.

After five days and nights of continuous searching the usual questions were being raised by those who were in a position to question authority. Was there any point in keeping submarines in peacetime? Why were the divers unable to reach the contacts? This last one was easily answered. Although the weather was calm, currents made diving very difficult. One diver, for example, went down and was laid flat on his back by the tide. He remained in this, a highly dangerous position for a man in a hard-hat diving suit, for some eighteen minutes before he could be brought back to the surface.

A more difficult question to answer was the story of the peculiar behaviour of *M2* on Wednesday of the week before her last dive. When the *M2* was in dock at Portsmouth that day

there appeared, according to dockworkers, to be considerable difficulty in handling her. First her stern went up in the air and then her bows, before she disappeared under water on an even keel. Divers went down with her next time for about five minutes before she came to the surface again, when the stern-up, bow-up procedure was repeated.

Incidentally, some indication of how tired the naval divers were by now, is the fact that Mr Charles Perry was standing by at Portsmouth Dockyard. Mr Perry, who had tried to reach the *Lusitania* and had been involved in some arduous diving on behalf of the Navy, was a civilian diver employed at the Dockyard.

On 1st February 1932 the *Dail Mail* reported a much more serious possibility in the words of Commander H. M. Daniel. Said Commander Daniel:

It seems possible, however, that the *M2* was practising a special evolution peculiar to her function as a seaplane carrier. She may have been practising getting her plane away in the minimum of time from surfacing after an unseen approach underwater and it may be that over-keen men attempted to gain access to the hangar a second or two before the submarine was right up.

The front doors of the hangar would obviously be designed to be water-tight; their existence, nevertheless, appears to be in conflict with well-established principles of submarine design. Not only are the huge flat surfaces not streamlined, but they are of a shape ill suited to withstand the great underwater pressures.

If these doors had become leaky two or three hundred tons of water may have accumulated in the hangar unknown to the crew and, on the opening of the hatch, may have poured in an overpowering deluge into the boat.

No one could dismiss Commander Daniel's theory—especially in view of Captain Howard's stern-first sight of the *M2* sinking.

This theory, thought experts at the time, would explain the lack of signals from the submarine. If the theory was right everyone on board would have been drowned almost at once.

On 2nd February newspapers reported a fisherman saying that he had picked up the body of a man in a white sweater (standard submarine wear) while fishing in West Bay. The body, unfortunately, had not been recovered, and had fallen back into the sea when the fisherman had tried to haul it into his boat.

This was the first clue. That same day, the First Lord of the Admiralty, Sir Bolton Eyres Monsell, announced in the House of Commons that the searchings had found: a cap belonging to the coxwain of the *M2* floating in a canvas bag and a collar belonging to a chief petty officer. The cap had been found floating, and the collar had been brought to the surface by a sweep wire.

The hunters were obviously getting close. And on 3rd February the Admiralty released the news that *M2* had been found, announcing shortly after 11 p.m.: 'The Rear-Admiral Submarines has reported that he has located Submarine *M2* position 50 deg 31.2 min N., 5.8 miles from Portland Bill'.

The official description of how the wreck was found was that H.M.S. *Torrid*, a destroyer equipped with powerful listening apparatus (Asdic), found the contact, and the finding was confirmed by minesweepers H.M.S. *Pangborne* and H.M.S. *Dunnon* with sweep wires. The sounds picked up by *Torrid* were 'of a nature which indicated the presence of a newly sunk submarine'. Divers were sent down, but were at first unable to reach the bottom because of the strong tides and poor visibility. Four 'diving lanterns' were sent down to the divers, and at 10.11 p.m.—over eight days since she had dived to disaster— the divers reported that it was indeed the *M2*.

The divers had gone down from H.M.S. *Albury*, and they found *M2* in eighteen fathoms of water. A wreck buoy was placed, and the Navy began to think about raising the vessel. The buoy was three miles from the point where Captain Howard of the *Tynesider* had reported seeing the *M2* dive, and not far from the position spotlighted by the report from Captain Hunt of the *Crown of Denmark*. One immediate question that this raised was: Did the *M2*, crippled by an inrush of water, still manage to crawl two miles under water, unable to rise? Or was the sighting wrong?

While the experts worried over this, Mr A. V. Alexander wrote in a letter to *The Times*:

> The disasters to the *H47*, to the *Poseidon* and the *M2* within the last two years have all contained features which must convince any right-thinking person that the Powers ought to agree to abolish the use of this type of war vessel, and I very much hope that representatives at Geneva will raise the question once more and that they will be met with better fortune in the matter than we experienced at the London Naval Conference.

There is no doubt that A. V. Alexander, Co-operative and Labour M.P. for the Hillsborough Division of Sheffield and secretary of the Parliamentary Committee of the Co-operative Congress, was expressing the view of many people in Britain at that time. It is ironic that Mr Alexander (who later became Earl Alexander of Hillsborough) should have put forward such a view. He was First Lord of the Admiralty three times— particularly during the 1939–45 War, when a great deal of his time must have been taken up by the effect of the German U-boat fleet's disastrous attacks on our supply lines.

As the hours passed, more details were disclosed of the way the submarine was found. The Portland Race, which divers reported as flowing at seven knots at times, hampered the search, and it was not until one diver saw the conning-tower letters 'M2' that the discovery was confirmed. The divers found her lying with her stern in the sand and shingle and her bow slightly raised off the sea-bed. This gave rise to theories about the possibility of some sort of stern-dive to disaster, but later teams of divers sent down to the wreck were unable to find any damage to the submarine. The bow was, however, high enough off the sea-bed for the divers to walk underneath.

The *M2* was lying close to another wreck or wrecks, and these were variously described as 'a U-boat and a Q-ship'.

One report, which it seems difficult to pin down to any authority, said that the *M2* was in fact pinned between the two wrecks. This provoked more theories about the sub creeping forward disabled over the sea-bed in a desperate attempt to reach shallower water. But, for the time being, the reason for the disaster remained a mystery. And that mystery had to be solved. Team after team of divers were used to survey the sunken boat.

On 5th February—the day that a memorial service was held over the sunken sub—the Admiralty made a late-night announcement that started to throw some light on the cause of the disaster:

> Diving operations on *M2* up to date have revealed that the hangar door and the upper conning tower hatch are open and that the forward hatch and engine-room hatch are closed. It has not yet been ascertained whether the lower conning tower hatch and the hatch inside the hangar giving access to the interior of the submarine are closed or open. It has been decided that the salvage of *M2* is to continue, weather permitting.

From that statement it seemed reasonable to assume that the *M2* was practising a rapid launch of her seaplane—surface, open hangar doors, catapult aeroplane, close doors, submerge. Some of those who had worked closely with *M2* believed this was the drill being practised and said that when the conning-tower was clear of the surface the hangar doors were still submerged. Did someone open those doors too quickly? If the inside hatch of the hangar was also open, then the water would rush through the submarine and she would go down stern first, as the captain of the *Tynesider* had described.

But is that what happened? The Admiralty desperately needed to know, and at that moment the right man to help them came forward.

Ernest Cox was a legend in the salvage world. In 1924 he bought the scuttled German Fleet in Scapa Flow from the Admiralty, who thought, together with other salvage experts, that the ships could not be raised. But Cox did it, and did it quickly in terms of the tonnage he brought to the surface (the largest single ship was the 28,000-ton battle cruiser *Hindenburg*). His methods were unorthodox but they worked. He lifted ships that were upside down, turned them upright, clamped patches over every opening in hulls and pumped compressed air into them. And they came up.

Now he offered his services to the Admiralty. And his offer was gratefully accepted. Ernest Cox was put in charge of the salvage operation and all the Navy divers and Admiralty equipment were put at his disposal. His first move was a classic one in the art of man-management. On arrival at Portland he went on board H.M.S. *Tedworth* and spoke to all the divers and the salvage crew. He told them his plan—basically the same one that had worked in Scapa Flow: to close all apertures and then pump in compressed air—and boosted their confidence in him by saying that should the weather hold, the *M2* should be up within a week. In fact some of his audience had visions of *M2* popping to the surface and being towed into Portland Harbour within hours.

But it didn't work out like that. Cox's confident chat took place on 7th February 1932. On 8th February hundreds of tons of special quick-setting sea-water cement were moved to Portland ready for the sealing of the hangar. The same day divers from H.M.S. *Tedworth* went down and fixed steel hawsers to the seaplane, still inside the hangar of the submarine. The other ends of the hawsers were attached to a powerful tug called *Kennet*. Then the *Kennet* steamed full ahead. The seaplane was torn from its undercarriage and out of the hangar, to surface in a swirl of foam.

The job was done without any diver entering the small space inside the hangar where the seaplane had fitted with folded wings. It was considered too risky, with too much chance of lifelines being entangled if the divers did go in. The weather began to break and the fifty-one divers in H.M.S. *Tedworth*, the Fleet diving ship, were unable to do as much work as Cox had hoped, but they did start work on sealing the conning-tower hatch. Cox revised his estimate to a fortnight to raise the *M2*.

The *M2*'s seaplane was landed at Portland by lighter. It was little more than a crumpled mass, but the usual stories circulated about 'a clock on the instrument panel was rewound and started straight away'.

The weather was breaking. Mooring buoys were torn away, but still the salvage work went on. It stopped, however, when snow came from the east and the wind strengthened into a gale.

The rumours strengthened with the wind. 'A party of men were evidently trapped in the forward part, and doubtless died the slow death which those in submarines know must follow the exhaustion of their oxygen supply'. This was said to explain tapping noises heard by the listening ships on the day after the accident. Such rumours concerned the Admiralty so much that they took the unusual step of issuing a statement:

There is no evidence whatever to show that any compartment of H.M. Submarine *M2* remained habitable after she sank. Nine vessels were employed with the object of detecting any tappings or other signals without result. Echo-sounding gear was used in the search, and investigations show that this was the source of some tappings reported.

The weather continued foul, and salvage operations were suspended. In the lull in activity questions were raised in the House. Sir B. Eyres Monsell, First Lord of the Admiralty, in reply to Rear-Admiral Sueter:

The weight of the seaplane structure (hangar and catapult) fitted to the *M2* is 40 tons, compared with 120 tons in the same vertical position as originally designed for a 12-in gun. Experience with the *M2* since she was fitted with the seaplane structure has proved that she was easy to control and trim under all conditions. In the early days of submarines, while they were still in the experimental stage, a surface escort was provided, but for over 20 years this precaution has been considered unnecessary except on those occasions when a submarine is carrying out trials of an experimental nature.

Replying to a further question from Rear-Admiral Sueter:

The weather conditions at the end of last week rendered it impossible to make progress with the salvage operations in connexion with *M2*, and opportunity is therefore being taken to improve the salvage equipment of H.M.S. *Tedworth* from which diving operations are conducted. Weather permitting she will then return to the position of the wreck.

On 4th March H.M.S. *Tedworth* did return to the site. She carried three heavy plates, which were to be cemented over the open hatches, but a fresh gale forced another suspension of work. On 11th March salvage operations were reported as nearly complete, and preparations for the actual raising were well advanced. On the 14th a body was found in the aeroplane hangar, but was left in position in view of the probability of the whole submarine being raised very shortly.

But on 15th March another open hatch was discovered. More sealing was necessary. Then the weather intervened again. On the 18th March the body was recovered. It was identified as Leading Seaman Albert Ernest Jacobs of Manor Road, Southsea, from papers found in the clothing and was brought ashore by drifter. The inquest was held on 21st March, at the Royal Naval Barracks at Portland, and was opened by Major G. G. H. Symes, the South Dorset Coroner. He sat without a jury.

Mrs Emily Alice Jacobs, his wife, identified the body. She said that her husband was twenty-eight, had been in the Navy for fourteen years starting as a boy, and that they had one little girl aged two.

Petty Officer Edwin Griffin, of the Royal Naval Hospital, Portland, gave further evidence of identification. He said that he was on *M2* on 26th January before she sailed, and saw Jacobs with whom he had served for twenty months on board the submarine. Jacobs was in charge of the battery and electric control instruments.

Surgeon-Commander W.W. Biddulph said that the body was brought to Portland on Friday in the drifter *Lunar Bow*. There were no definite external injuries, with the exception of those to the head, which were probably caused after death in contact with something.

The Coroner: I suppose you cannot say that death was caused by drowning? Only presumably, but of course he might have been gassed.

At this stage the Coroner told Mrs Jacobs, who was sobbing bitterly, that if the evidence was distressing her she could leave the court. Mrs Jacobs did so.

Commander E. G. Stanley, of H.M.S. *Titania*, commanding the 6th Submarine Flotilla at Portsmouth, consulted the log which he had with him to ascertain the day on which the *M2* came into Portland Harbour. She came in to perform independent tactical exercises in the West Bay, and she was using the harbour as a base. She came there on 14th January, but she was not under his control. On 26th January she passed his ship at 8.30 a.m. and proceeded into the West Bay.

The Coroner: Was she in communication with your ship during these exercises?

She could have been. She had been in previous exercises.

I mean the previous exercises and on the day in question?

On previous occasions she had been in communication with my ship, and on the day in question.

Was it her duty to do so? Oh, yes, it is always her duty, and she did communicate with me on the day in question.

What was she talking about? Ordinary routine signals, and at 10.8 a.m. she informed me by wireless that she was diving.

Was it her duty to do that? Yes.

Did she speak to you again? No.

She did not return to harbour? No.

And after some days' search she was eventually found?

After several days she was found stranded.

William W. Brown, chief shipwright of H.M.S. *Tedworth*, the diving ship, said he was doing diving work in the *M2* salvage. He first saw the body of Jacobs on Friday morning.

The Coroner: You were then engaged in diving? Yes, I had instructions to get to the hatch inside the hangar and I landed just in front of it and made my way into the hangar on the starboard side. The hangar door opens away from the hangar and it was flat. The hangar was flooded. I went inside. It was pitch black. I had reached the aeroplane trolley and had just got round the other side when I felt something soft against my leg.

Had anybody been in the hangar before? Yes, but not on this particular side. I found that it was a body, and I telephoned to the diving officer in charge for instructions. I told him I could get it clear and my instructions were to send it up. I got the body clear of the hangar and asked for a line, but I then decided, owing to the risk of fouling, to take the body up myself. The line was passed under the armpits of the body which I got in the crook of my left arm and I then brought it up.

The Coroner found that Jacobs died on 26th January, having been found drowned on 18th March in the seaplane hangar of H.M. submarine *M2*, which sank in eighteen fathoms of water in West Bay, Dorset.

On 3rd April *M2* was still on the sea-bed and Ernest Cox, who was moving back and forth between Scapa Flow and Portland, addressed the Institute of Marine Engineers about the salvage problems. He said that the submarine was on an even keel. Divers had found that the hatch inside the hangar was open, and that the conning-tower hatch was also open. The hangar hatch had been sealed with concrete, and the conning-tower had been closed with a steel hatch. It was hoped that every internal door in the sub was open, as the first attempt to raise her would be by blowing compressed air in to blow the water out. Failing this, it was planned to drill holes in the sides to get the trapped water out. He was positive that if they could get more than half-buoyancy on the submarine the nose would lift, and water would trickle out. If they could not lift the stern,

owing to water in the bulkhead, they proposed to use cables under the stern and lift that way.

He did not mention any other hatch that was open, but it soon became known that the engine-room hatch behind the conning-tower was also open. When work on sealing that began it was found that the after hatch in the crew's quarters was also open.

This discovery caused a lot of comment. It seemed to the onlooker that every hatch in the *M2* had been partially open when she dived stern-first to the bottom. Were all hatches opened too soon? Did she dive with all hatches open? Did the crew make attempts to escape? There were no answers to these questions, but they delayed all lifting attempts. The divers were being tossed about 'like corks', while each hatch had to be closed down with a steel jack, and then concrete poured over the whole hatch to stop it opening when air was forced into the hull. In addition to this, other divers were employed in cutting holes in the pressure hull under the engine-room and other compartments to allow water to escape when the air pressure was put on.

By the beginning of June this work was still going on. On 5th June Diver Helen was injured—he suffered burns which were 'not of a serious character', even though he had to go to hospital—when an underwater explosion blew two divers away from the submarine. Helen and another man were cutting a hole in the hull with an oxy-hydrogen torch. Helen's diving suit was ripped, and he narrowly escaped drowning. The accident, it seemed, was nothing to do with trapped gases in the submarine, but due entirely to the cutting apparatus.

Despite this explosion, the work went on. Now the cry—it had been the same each week since the *M2* was located—was that the sub would be raised 'by the end of the month'.

The fact that the submarine was still obstinately on the bottom after all these months was hardly the fault of the Navy's divers. For example, from 5th March to 30th May, 247 hours had been spent under water on the wreck. One diver spent a continuous period at one hundred feet of 5 hours 40 minutes. But success, it seemed, was near now. Valves to let the water out had been fitted, and so had the means to pump the air in. Over one hundred tons of loose water, they thought, could not be forced out of the *M2*, and, though it was planned to raise her bow-first, her stability would be the most pressing problem once she reached the surface. By 26th June the salvage operations had reached a cost of £10,000 and a new difficulty was found—some of the ballast tanks could not be pumped clear of water (only seven of the eighteen were suitable for the air inflation technique).

On the 1st July another body was found—in complete flying kit. Once again Major Symes held an inquest. This time the body was identified as that of Leading Aircraftman Leslie Gregory of Haslar Road, Gosport. The body was found about fifteen feet away from the submarine, near the port-side rudder. It was assumed that it had been pulled out of the hangar when the seaplane was salvaged.

And so it went on. *M2* was always going to be raised tomorrow, never today. On 13th July 1932 the First Lord of the Admiralty was asked for a statement on the progress of the work of raising the submarine. The reply was made by Lord Stanley, Parliamentary Secretary to the Admiralty, who said:

It was found on June 23 that the main tank blowing valves inside the hull were open, resulting in the interconnexion of these tanks, a state of affairs which was not previously apparent. As a result it was found necessary to suspend lifting operations until this unforeseen circumstance could be dealt with. Work continued satisfactorily until June 29, when a change to south-westerly weather made work impossible.

On July 5, weather and tide conditions were again favourable and work was recommenced and was still in progress. In addition, four lifting pontoons, or 'camels', were being placed in position, one at each side of bow and stern, for the purpose of supplying a further reserve of buoyancy now considered necessary.

During the weekend of July 9-11 an attempt to raise *M2* was made. At this attempt the bow of the vessel was raised some 15 feet without difficulty, but a serious leak from the bow torpedo tubes developed and it proved too great to allow any further attempt to be made until the leak had been located and stopped.

Work then started on sealing up the tubes. The job proved particularly difficult. Cutting torches had to be used. Then the forward hatch proved difficult despite three tons of special hardening cement and a leak developed. The cement had to be chipped away by pneumatic drills and a specially designed cover fitted.

By 25th September the big lift was ready, but bad weather forced the salvage vessels to shelter in Weymouth Bay. To do this five divers had to be hauled to the surface prematurely as the wind freshened, and all five had to be put into the recompression chamber on board H.M.S. *Tedworth* as she ran for shelter.

On 27th September all vessels were back on station and the lift began. *M2* came up steadily, and all seemed to be going well. The foremost pontoon came to the surface normally, but the port one carried away—a wire was chafed through—and the bows sank to the bottom despite the stern-lift. There was only one thing to do, and they did it—they lowered the sub down again.

On the 28th they tried again. This time the *M2* came so close to the surface that Ernest Cox said that 'men in the boats saw her black lines beginning to loom through the waves'. But at this vital moment, when *M2* was within eighteen feet of the surface, a hawser to H.M.S. *Moordale* snapped, ripping away the winch to which it was attached, and the bows of the *M2* fell back almost to the sea-bed. The salvage crews, robbed of their prize when so close to success, worked all night, but they were fighting a losing battle, and when dawn was near they had to lower the submarine to the sea-bed again.

A period of bad weather followed almost at once, and the divers and salvage crews were given seven days' shore leave with a special £10 bonus for their work. Salvage costs were now calculated to be in the region of £12,000, and the sub was still on the sea-bed.

On 4th October 1932 salvage operations were resumed, and the first fears that the whole operation might have to be abandoned were being openly voiced. The real problem seemed to be with the linkage between the submarine and the pontoons called by the salvage crews 'camels'. During the bad weather, when the crews had been on leave, yet another of the camels had broken away, and was washed ashore on Chesil Beach. The six-inch wire hawser which had attached it to *M2* had worn through in a similar way to the one that had foiled the salvage attempt of 27th September.

In the second week of October a conference was held at the Admiralty. Submarine experts as well as salvage men attended, and the whole of the work so far was reviewed. It seemed almost certain that as a result of the conference the work on *M2* would be abandoned until the following spring, if not for ever. But on the night of 17th October the Admiralty announced that work would go on. The next lifting attempt would be made, weather permitting, in November. Cost of operations so far was about £15,000.

The lifting pontoons—the cylindrical camels which were pumped full of compressed air to give the lifting power—were raised, and the next ten days were spent in sinking them in place and re-attaching them with stronger hawsers to the sub. On 27th October it was announced that H.M.S. *Tedworth* was in trouble. Wires were tangled round her propeller, and she had to be towed into Portland.

On 14th November a fresh attempt at a lift looked imminent. The divers went down to attach the air-hoses to the valves in the submarine's hull, and to the lifting pontoons. On 19th November faults were found in two of the 'camels' and the lift was delayed again. On 22nd November these faults had been put right. But the weather broke.

On 30th November the First Lord of the Admiralty, Sir Bolton Eyres Monsell, answered questions in the House of Commons about the delayed salvage. As he spoke a gale ripped over the grave of the *M2* and made diving impossible. In the warmth and silence of the House of Commons, Sir Bolton said:

> The attempt to raise *M2* at the end of September was considered sufficiently promising to justify further operations with a view to another attempt being made as soon as possible. These operations are proceeding. Work has been slow owing to adverse weather conditions, which are to be expected at this time of year, only about one-third of the period, October-November, having been suitable for any operations to be undertaken.

Mr C. Williams (Torquay, Unionist): What is the cost of operations to date?

Sir Bolton: The last time I inquired the cost was about £12,000. For that sum we have in hand a very valuable air-compressor and a great deal of valuable experience that we did not have before.

Hear, hear, said voices in the Chamber.

Lieutenant-Commander Agnew (Camborne, Unionist): What is the future policy of the Board of the Admiralty likely to be in the matter of the salvage of the vessel?

Sir Boulton: As the operations are so far in advance it is proposed to make a last attempt to raise the wreck. Should it fail or should bad weather spoil the operations already made, salvage will have to be abandoned. Members will realize that this would be a grave disappointment to those engaged in the work, which has been both arduous and difficult and has been carried on with great zeal by those concerned.

Hear, hear, said the voices.

The last attempt to raise *M2* began on the night of 6th December. Work on board the recovery ships started under a clear starry sky. By the light of a brilliant dawn the last air-hoses were being connected. With the sunrise came the wind, and the sea began to swell at the first few gusts.

By 11 a.m. when the air compressors were started the weather showed all the signs of setting into yet another gale. But the pumping went on. It was now or never. For hours nothing happened, but the experts had not expected quick results. They were not prepared, however, for the next thing that happened. At exactly 3.20 p.m. two pontoons came to the surface in a lather of foam—and with them the stern of the submarine.

Something was very wrong. According to all the salvage calculations her periscope should have been the first thing to show. This would have meant that the submarine was on an even keel. And at first *M2* had shown all the signs of behaving herself. Her bow had risen some sixteen feet off the sea-bed, but then the stern had tilted up and risen far faster than the bow pontoons. *M2* was now hanging perpendicularly in the water with her bow on the sea-bed and her stern just below the surface. The engines of the compressors on H.M.S. *Tedworth* screamed as they were accelerated in a desperate attempt to get more lift into the bow. But nothing would shift her, and at 4 p.m., as the wind increased even more and darkness crept over the sea, they lowered her stern back down again. The fight to salve *M2* was lost.

On 8th December the Admiralty issued the decision to stop work to the Rear-Admiral Submarines like this:

It has been decided to abandon finally all salvage operations on *M2*. In taking this decision their Lordships very fully appreciate the magnificent work done during the last ten months under adverse conditions by the divers and all concerned in the salvage operations.

Their Lordships desire that you will convey their appreciation to all ranks and ratings who have taken part in the salvage operations. They fully realize the great efforts that have been made to overcome the numerous difficulties which have been intensified by the varying weather conditions, the depth of water, and the strength of the tides.

Although the conclusion must be a bitter disappointment, particularly to those who have been given such skill, courageous and persistent devotion to it, the experience gained has fully justified the operations, which reflect great credit on those concerned.

'Great credit' was right. In appalling weather conditions twenty-six Royal Navy divers had made over 1500 dives during the salvage attempt, to 108 feet. The average length of time spent on the bottom during these dives was about one and a half hours.

To this bottom time you have to add the decompression ascent time of seventy-two minutes. So, in fact, the average dive took about 2 hours 42 minutes. The longest dive took 5 hours 40 minutes.

Few dives were simple. Sealing the apertures in the hull took hours—and all the time the divers were fighting the tides. These tidal races sometimes swept the divers to the wrong side of the diving ship for surfacing. No wonder that one diver, describing his feelings as he came ashore after the salvage work was abandoned, said: 'We could have cried'.

Ernest Cox, salvage expert, obviously felt the same way, but in defeat he would not surrender: 'We have been beaten by the merest fluke. It is hard lines on all the men to be defeated in this way. No-one can be blamed for the failure and I am as certain as ever I was that the wreck can be raised'. He was not to have another chance. *M2* was abandoned. For years no diver visited her, but the Navy did not forget her. She was used regularly as a fixed target for training naval sonar operators, but that was all. To the Navy she is the grave of sixty men.

Having lost *M1* and *M2*, the Admiralty took no chances with *M3*. For a while she was converted for use as some kind of minesweeper, but within a year of the loss of *M2* she was scrapped and broken up.

Quite recently the *M2* was located by amateur skin-divers, and though they knew that she was, in the Navy's opinion, the equivalent of a 'war grave', they did not feel that there was any disrespect in exploring the outside of the submarine.

The *M2* will never become a dive for any but the most experienced divers, lying as she does in over one hundred feet of water some considerable distance from the coast. For example, one highly experienced group from three BSAC branches dived on her on 6th September 1970. In a trawler from Bridport were Bob Woodmason, the expedition organizer and leader (Cotswold Branch), Ray Bishop (Bristol), George Skuse (Cotswold), Ted Mills (Cotswold), John Hunt (Cotswold), Martin Cox (Cotswold), John Gardiner (Cotswold) Andy Wheeler (Bristol), Stephen Sinclair (Cotswold), Eric Brady, Charles Clarke, Stewart Ashby, Jock Vickers, John Kennedy and Nobby Clarke (all from Gloucestershire Fire Service Special Branch).

George Skuse's account of that dive says that:

Navigation was easy. The trawler worked in these waters and in addition she carried the Decca Navigation System, which enabled the wreck to be pinpointed with uncanny accuracy.

Indeed it appeared so simple that we had an hour at anchor on the wreck waiting for the tide to slacken enough for diving. This enabled those who wished to have a little to eat and drink and for the inflatable to be made ready. As the diving boat was to remain anchored, we had taken along the inflatable and motor to provide surface cover. We also streamed a buoy astern to enable anyone adrift to catch hold of it when they surfaced.

The first three divers down were Bob Woodmason, George Skuse and Ray Bishop. They reached the bottom at 110 feet and encountered practically no tidal movement at all. But they couldn't see the submarine—and it should have been there. The anchor appeared to have dragged, and they followed the drag marks for 50 yards and then there she was. The divers had scarcely any time at all on the wreck, having used up most of their air on following the anchor marks to the site. They surfaced and the skipper of the trawler remedied the anchor position. Later divers had much more success, being able to go right round the sub in their seventeen minutes bottom time allowed by the decompression tables.

The *M2* is on an even keel, a little sunk into the sand, all in one piece and showing very little damage. The hangar door is open, and the interior two-thirds full of silt. The rear elevators are set to rise at an angle of about 40 degrees and the spare propeller is still strapped to the casing on the stern. Near the conning-tower the divers noticed several holes, but these, they believed, were part of the salvage operations. The dive was a great success, and as proper safety precautions had been taken at all times, the divers were rightly pleased with themselves.

Later that same month, however, the *M2* was to be the scene of yet another tragedy. Thirty-year-old Frank Thorne, a father of three, who lived near Taunton, dived with Toby Morris on the *M2*. During that dive they became separated, and Mr Thorne failed to surface. Nobody knows how the fatality occurred.

There have been other dives on the *M2* without incident. One was that carried out by Trevor Smith, proprietor of the London diving firm 'Subaqua Services'. Trevor Smith has formed a special branch of the British Sub-Aqua Club out of his staff—they call themselves the Aquarius Aquanauts—and is the branch diving officer. The wreck in West Bay was once again located by the use of Decca Navigation instruments, and the divers were blessed with visibility of over twenty feet.

This was a memorable dive [says Trevor Smith], she sits on an even keel as if she were still operational, just resting and waiting to go into action. Her dark grey paint has been covered by a living skin of white sponges, small starfish and other forms of marine life, so you cannot see any identification marks on her.

The diver coming over her bow at first notices her two anchors. The starboard one is still dogged tight in position, but the port one has slipped a bit and juts out of the hull. As you swim towards the stern along the foredeck you come to the launching catapult. The two raised slipways are set far enough apart for the diver to swim between and look at the complex of hydraulic pipes, valves and pulleys used to get the plane off the deck.

Behind this is the hangar, which gapes open like a large black mouth. This section of the wreck is badly silted up, the silt angled inside from floor to ceiling. The slightest touch disturbs this silt, sending the visibility down to nil. Leaving the hangar you come to the conning tower. The diver can stand behind the periscopes which are still raised and get the same view that her skipper must have had years ago.

Behind the conning tower the rear casing curves away aft forming a sharp point in line with the stern. Dropping over the diver lands on the rudder and looking forward past the one remaining propeller—the starboard prop and the gun are the only things I saw missing from the wreck—you can see the angle of the rear elevators.

They point towards the surface. Under them in the dark shadow of the hull are tangles of steel hawsers, rubber piping and other rigging used in the salvage operations. And so back to the bow where the forward elevators too thrust towards the surface. All the hatches are sealed with steel and concrete. The conning tower outer hatch is open but the second hatch is sealed in the same way as the others.

These divers, like all the others, take nothing from the wreck. They are only with her briefly, and when they have gone the steel tomb remains, a great pale outline in the gloom of the deep water.

CHAPTER 13

The Case of the Bent Beaufighter

including the loss of the Somali (1941), the Persier (1945), a landing craft in 1950, and the Torrey Canyon (1967).

THE steam was shut off, but the engine was still turning when the crew tried to abandon the s.s. *Persier*. As lifeboat No. 1 slid down towards the stormy sea the first of the horrors happened. A rope twisted round a stoker's foot, and as the boat drew away he was left hanging by his foot with his head in the sea, and each lift of the waves battered him relentlessly against the ship's side. But worse was to come—as the ship continued to move forward the great frothing propeller cut not one, but two boats in half as they were drawn in to the ship's side.

The *Persier* might have treated her crew better if she had gone down more quickly after the torpedo smashed into the port side opposite No. 2 hold, but she was not a ship that gave up easily. In fact she didn't start out on the first of her voyages as the *Persier* at all. When she slid down the launching slipway in 1918 at Newcastle all 5382 tons of her was christened *War Buffalo*. At some time later in her career she became the *Persier*, under the orders of the Belgian Maritime Company.

I can find little record of her activities between the wars, but, thanks to Paul Scarceriaux of the magazine *Wanderlaer-sur-L'Eau*, her adventures during the Second World War are fully documented.

After evacuating fifty-two soldiers and six civilians from Cherbourg to England in 1940, she became just a unit in the convoys sailing from Britain to the United States and back. On her seventy-sixth voyage the *Persier* joined a convoy from New York that was to become part of history.

The *Persier* sailed from New York at the end of October 1940 with 6833 tons of steel for the war factories of Britain. The convoy was code-numbered HX 84, and consisted of thirty-seven cargo ships and oil-tankers escorted by the auxiliary cruiser *Jervis Bay* under the command of Captain Fegen, RN. There seemed little of note about this convoy, at the start and, after eight days of sailing, all went well. The *Persier* kept her station, and so did most of the other ships of the convoy. It was going well. Too well. For twenty miles away the pocket-battleship *Admiral Scheer* was waiting.

At 4.30 p.m. on the afternoon of 5th November, the battle started. *Admiral Scheer* opened fire at extreme range, and though Captain Fegen must have known that he was signing his own death warrant, the *Jervis Bay* left the convoy and steamed at full speed straight at Germany's pocket-battleship. She was hit again and again until she was a blazing shambles before she could even get within proper range, but Captain Fegen's act of heroism did at least give the convoy time to scatter.

Even so the *Scheer* was able to attack ship after ship, including the tanker *San Demetrio*, loaded with 11,000 tons of petrol. As the crew of the tanker abandoned ship, she received a direct hit and burst into flames. After a night and most of the next day in the boats in mountainous seas, and with a full gale blowing, the crew of the *San Demetrio* were amazed to find their own ship still afloat. They reboarded her and fought the fire and managed to bring her back to Britain. Though blackened, burnt, holed and leaking, the *San Demetrio*'s crew brought 10,000 tons of precious petrol back to Britain. (It is not surprising that such a dramatic real-life story was recreated on film, under the simple title of *San Demetrio, London*.)

The *Persier* was more fortunate, and when the convoy was ordered to scatter she escaped and reached Hull in safety. Her luck seemed to hold on her next voyage when she survived attack by two German bombers with minor damage on the outward voyage to Halifax, but on the return on 13th February 1941 what luck she had seemed to drain away. Storm after storm hit her in mid-Atlantic, she lost her convoy, and finally went aground on the coast of Iceland on 28th February, and it wasn't until the 18th June 1942 that she reached Jarrow, after being refloated at the end of May.

Several voyages without incident followed her repair. In 1944 the Belgian Government offered her together with the *Belgium* as two of the ships to be scuttled on the Normandy beaches as part of the Mulberry Harbour operation. The *Persier* arrived too late. She was on voyage, from Freetown and docked at Liverpool on 23rd June 1944. Then again she was earmarked as a blockship for the Normandy beaches, but the rapid advance of the troops after D-Day made this unnecessary. *Persier* was back on normal duty, and on 8th February 1945 she left Cardiff on a mercy mission—she was to be the first ship to take food to the starving people of Belgium. She was also chosen as the ship to carry the convoy commander, Commodore Edmund Wood, RNR, and his staff of three signallers.

There were sixty-three people on board the *Persier* when she set sail—and many of them were survivors of the s.s. *Leopoldville*, which had been torpedoed and sunk off Cherbourg on Christmas night, 1944. These survivors had asked to be repatriated, and the *Persier* was the first ship to be headed in the direction of the Belgian ports.

The convoy went well at first, but a southerly gale made it difficult for the smaller ships to keep up, and Commodore Wood took his little fleet into Clovelly for shelter. They set off again on 10th February, but the weather was still too rough for the small vessels, and he sought shelter this time in the lee of Lundy Island. After eighteen hours there the Commodore set sail again (as the weather seemed to be improving) with just three of the larger ships, and joined them to another convoy heading from Barry Roads to Southampton. Seas were still heavy, and the regulation distance of half a mile between each ship soon stretched, until the convoy was covering about ten miles of sea with a corvette at the head, and the *Persier* the last ship in line. There were now ten ships in the convoy (called BTC 65), but this was increased when two small cargo boats and a landing craft tagged on.

On 11th February the members of BTC 65 might be forgiven for thinking that they were in pretty safe waters. After all, they were between the Eddystone Lighthouse and the shore. But this sense of security was abruptly shattered. Almost at the same moment that Commodore Wood received a report from one of the small escort vessels that a periscope had been seen, a column of water shot skyward on the port side of the convoy. The time was 5.20, but the explosion seemed to have no immediate explanation. There was no ship in that position, but the more experienced hands guessed immediately that it was the premature explosion of a German torpedo. They braced themselves for the worst, and within seconds the worst happened. The white wake of a second torpedo hissed by the stern of the *Persier* from port to starboard and disappeared.

On the *Persier*'s bridge eyes peered into the gathering dusk, straining to spot in time the tell-tale sign of another torpedo. Captain Mathieu, First Officer Lardinoy and Commodore Wood knew that the attack was not yet over. At 5.25 precisely the third torpedo struck the port side opposite No. 2 hold and forward of the bridge. The explosion knocked Lardinoy over and broke his nose.

As the water flooded into No. 2 hold, the boxes of powdered egg started to disintegrate and the tinned meat and crates of soap broke loose from their stacks under the pressure. The *Persier* started to list to port with the water heavy in her belly. The crew gathered on deck and the lifeboats were ready to be launched at Mathieu's order. But *Persier* was still functioning and signals flashed to the Commander-in-Chief, Devonport, told him what had happened. The reaction from Devonport was to order Force 27 to the aid of the Convoy.

H.M.S. *Rosevean* and H.M.S. *Fir* reached the scene at 7 p.m. and started to hunt for the submarine which had done the damage. H.M.S. *Ellesmere*, which had been prepared to escort convoy COC 76, starting at 6 p.m., found herself switched to go to the aid of the *Persier*. But the first of all to reach the scene was H.M.S. *Cornelian*, which was already at sea and waiting for the convoy at a prearranged rendezvous.

The abandonment of the *Persier* took only six minutes, but the fact that the engine was still turning ruined many people's

chances of safety. Lifeboat No. 1, containing Commodore Wood and ten others, was launched properly, but the heavy seas unhooked the bow and left it suspended by the stern, spilling everyone into the water. Lifeboat No. 3 was drawn into the still spinning propeller and was badly damaged. No. 1 Lifeboat was righted, and three men slid down the falls to her. One of the three, a stoker, got his foot caught and was left hanging, smashed against the ship by every wave. The two other men reached the boat, but it too was drawn in by the ship's forward motor and chopped completely in half by the huge propeller.

The *Persier* was now about four miles from the Eddystone in a wind of Force 6 or 7. The seas were colossal. But rafts were launched, and men managed to cling to them, despite the battering they received. At least they had one thing to be grateful for—the *Persier* had stopped moving at last, and her propeller was no longer spinning. But she was obviously not long for the surface. Her stern was lifted almost completely out of the water. And still on board were her captain Mathieu, First Officer Lardinoy and five others.

One of the three ships following *Persier* was s.s. *Gem*, a 640-ton cargo vessel under the command of Captain Neil Campbell. Campbell had seen it all and knew that the *Persier*—judging by the way her bow was down—would soon be gone. At this moment Captain Campbell made his decision. Strictly against orders, he decided to stay by the stricken ship and do what he could to help. Manoeuvring his little ship to windward of the *Persier* took over half an hour, but at last he was in a position to get life-lines across to Lifeboat No. 4 and start rescue operations. From this boat and rafts the *Gem* managed to pick up eighteen men and two women.

H.M.S. *Cornelian* commanded by Lieutenant-Commander Sydney Gorrell, DSC, RNVR, arrived on the scene and after dropping a depth-charge pattern without success, ordered the *Gem* to rejoin the convoy while she took over the rescue work. In the meantime, on board the *Persier* the seven men still there were in a desperate position. The ship was obviously sinking under them. But there was not a boat or raft left on board that was in a fit condition to support seven men.

It was at this moment of crisis that First Officer Lardinoy came to the fore. Despite the severe wound to his nose, Lardinoy offered to swim to the s.s. *Birker Force*, the other small cargo ship, which had been following the *Persier* in the convoy, and ask the Captain to come in and rescue them. In such a gale and the icy seas that piled up before it Lardinoy's chances—despite the fact that he was a good swimmer—seemed very small. But then Lardinoy was no ordinary man. He had survived the sinking by a mine of the s.s. *Katanga*, had behaved with great courage when in command of a lifeboat from the s.s. *Gardia*, and had survived the torpedoing of the s.s. *Leopold-ville*. This was the fourth ship that had been sunk under him!

Lardinoy checked his lifejacket and then ordered his six companions to throw him as far away from the *Persier* as they could—and away from the propeller, which though it seemed to have stopped turning for the moment, had done such terrible damage to the other men who had tried to escape.

At the time Lardinoy hit the water H.M.S. *Cornelian* was still firing depth charges, and each explosion made him feel that he was being punched by some giant boxer. The explosions had

The s.s. *Persier*, torpedoed as she was taking food supplies to liberated Belgium, has been located by divers. As she sank her propeller chopped lifeboats in half

another terrible effect too—the vibrations started the *Persier*'s engines working again. (And they went on working until one of the men left aboard went down and tightened the locking screw on the regulator.) Despite all this, Lardinoy finally reached a lifeboat which had been launched with great difficulty by the *Birker Force* and delivered his message. Now the *Birker Force* moved in to the *Persier*, and at the same time the men left aboard flung an old unseaworthy raft in the sea and jumped for it. All were finally picked up.

There were forty-four survivors from the *Persier*. But no-one actually saw the end of the ship herself. Tugs sent out from Plymouth searched for her in vain. *Persier* died in the night, and no-one knew exactly where. And no-one would know now if it had not been for the activities of Plymouth Sound Branch of the British Sub-Aqua Club.

The story of the rediscovery of the s.s. *Persier* really began in the winter of 1968 when Colin Hopkins, the branch's chairman,

was talking with a sea-angling friend whom he had not seen for some time. The friend told Colin about a spot in Bigbury Bay where he frequently lost ground tackle, and suggested that it might be a good spot to dive. The marks given to Colin Hopkins did not, however, inspire him with much confidence. It seemed to be a case of picking up two sets of marks and then turning the boat out to sea and travelling for five minutes, trailing a set of feathers until they became snagged.

So Colin Hopkins thought little more about it until one Sunday in May 1969, when with his fifteen-foot runabout he and three other club members set out for a dive from Wembury. As the sea was calm and the weather fine it occurred to Colin that this might be the day to have a look at his friend's fishing spot. Though it meant a long boat trip—the position seemed about six miles from Wembury—all were agreeable, and so they set off.

On the way they had to pass the caravan site where Colin's

149

friend lived, so they landed to see if he would come with them. When the divers arrived they found him painting his caravan, and he said that as he had been out fishing all morning his wife would not take kindly to him downing his brush and setting off again. So Colin took the opportunity to hear the marks once more . . . 'Five minutes running from the marks straight out to sea and you can't miss it. . . .'

What happened next is told in Colin Hopkin's own words:

Leaving him behind with his paint brush, we set off to find the land marks he had given from about two miles out in the bay. We arrived at the spot and, as his boat was a ten foot dinghy with a Seagull outboard and mine a high speed runabout with a 50 h.p. outboard, I had to do a quick bit of mental guesswork as to how far his boat would travel in five minutes. We arrived at a point which I guessed would be about the position, and I threw the anchor over and started dragging the bottom. After about two minutes it hooked into something and would not come free and so we decided to dive.

The other divers in the boat were Ken Miles, Peter Foster 1 and Peter Foster 2 (same name but unrelated and numbered to avoid confusion). As we were over new ground in about 100 ft of water, it was decided that I should stay in the boat with Peter 2 and Ken would dive with Peter 1. The plan was, that, since I was not at all sure we were in the right position, Ken would dive to the bottom and look around. If he found nothing of interest, he would give two pulls on the anchor line, lift the anchor out and do a normal drift dive.

Ken and Peter dived and I sat in the boat holding the anchor line and waiting for a signal. None came, Peter 2 and I waited anxiously on the surface for a full twenty minutes—which seemed like an hour, until Ken and Peter 1 surfaced up the anchor line. I looked enquiringly at Ken as his head broke the surface, but all he did was shake his head. I was about to ask him why he hadn't carried out a drift search when he burst into laughter and held up two lobsters, one in each hand. We had dropped anchor right in the middle of a large wreck. Ken and Peter 1 had spent their entire dive just swimming towards the bow and back to the anchor line. Now it was time for Peter 2 and I to dive and since the other two divers had gone forward, we decided to go towards the stern on our dive and look for the obvious.

We went down the anchor rope and found ourselves in amongst a tangled heap of metal. The only things that were recognisable were the tops of two huge boilers. We turned towards the stern, and started working our way through twisted hunks of steel plate, spars, masts and metal of all shapes and sizes until we came to the smooth plated side of the ship. Swimming became easier here and we made our way back along the line of the hull where it met the sand of the bottom. Out of the gloom ahead appeared a propellor blade. It seemed massive. I went over to it, took out my knife and had a scrape. As I scraped away the concretions it gleamed, it was bronze! Peter 2 and I went into raptures, gesticulating at one another and blowing bubbles. We finished our dive by going around the stern and swimming back along the other side of the ship.

When we surfaced and climbed back in board, the problem of finding the spot again came up. I had nothing in the boat with which to buoy the position. As I felt that we had found it originally more by luck than good management, we spent a good half hour scanning the coastline to find better marks. They were few and far between and the original ones seemed to be the only ones which came to the eye. So we stuck to those with a slight adjustment to allow for the five minutes travel bit.

We re-dived on the wreck five times using the same marks, not missing once, but since then, on subsequent dives, I have spent up to four hours in hazy visibility without finding it. I am still amazed at how we discovered it in the first place, as we have found several times since that if we missed the spot by 100 feet or so, we would end up on a large reef of rocks. They show up the same as the wreck on an echo sounder, and also catch the anchor when dragging. If we had landed on this reef in the first instance we would probably have taken that as the cause of the lost fishing tackle. Now that we had found our wreck, unknown, uncharted, never before dived upon, all we had to do was buy it, but from who and how?

We spent about two months quietly diving on the wreck trying to find a name or number or some means of identification. I made several local enquiries in the coastal area around the spot to find out whether anyone knew of a wreck in the area, but no-one could give any information. During this time, I had a chat with Alan Bax, with whom we had been doing some archaeological searches and he suggested that I should contact Alec Reynolds at the Hydrographers Department at Taunton. By this time we had discovered that the ship was a large, armed merchantman. There was a 4.7 gun on the stern and two Oerlikon guns, one on the stern and one amidships on the bridge.

The ship was of riveted construction and seemed to be an early design. It was very much broken up amidships and only the stern and bow sections were anything like recognisable. I sent a letter to Alex Reynolds giving the position of the wreck, as closely as we could get it on the chart, and all the details we had so far gained. I fully expected a name, number, owner and full details by return of post, and was very disappointed when I received a letter from Alec saying that, from the details given, the wreck could be any one of about four hundred ships lost in the area and could he please have further details.

From that time on for the next nine months I was in constant touch with Alec, giving him further information and chasing up leads as he gave them to me. The first definite piece of information we obtained from the ship was a name on the steering pedestal which we raised. The name was Robert Roger and Co. Ltd., Stockton-on-Tees. I tried to find out about this company, but no-one had ever heard of them and so that was a 'dead-end'.

A picture of the ship was gradually being built up. We measured the approximate length and breadth of the ship using a 1000 ft coil of rope. We attached the rope to the stern with one pair of divers. The next pair swam the full length of the hull on the sand line and marked a knot at the bow. We then took the coil of line back to the shore and

In the dim light 90 feet down on the Cornish sea-bed lies the wreckage of a Second World War Bristol Beaufighter. These pictures, from colour transparencies by Ray Dennis, show what the sea has done to the plane since 1941, when Flying Officer McDonald ditched her on the surface at the end of a flight from Malta

Left. the chairman of Penzance Branch of the British Sub-Aqua Club, Alan Griffiths, steadies himself by the port engine. Note the marine growth on one of the propeller blades.

Below, a belt of bullets protrudes from one of the machine-gun mountings.

Right, a closer view of the port engine cowling and spinner: the 'tennis ball' is a sea-urchin.

unreeled it and could not believe our eyes when it measured 417 ft. We also measured the 'prop' and found it to be 17 ft in diameter.

We dismantled parts of the gun and found some letters and numbers on them. These we sent to the Board of Trade but had no luck in that direction. We spent hours scraping away at the propeller boss to find some indication of the wreck's identity, but to no avail.

I had been given the names of twelve different wrecks which were 'possibles' and one of these began to make sense, a ship called the *Silver Laurel*. Everything seemed to point to this ship being the one and I went so far as to purchase a plan of the vessel from the builders and start negotiations for her purchase with the War Risks Insurance Office. When we received the plan, however, we found that the stern shape of the *Silver Laurel* and our wreck were completely different.

During this period of searchings, because we were weekend only divers, we had to be very careful not to disclose the position of our 'find' as we could, quite easily, have been left standing by one of several professional and semi-professional 'scrappers', who operate out of Plymouth. Word had got out and all sorts of divers started appearing at the Tavern where our club held its dry meetings.

For this reason, we could not leave a marker buoy over the wreck and had to search for it on each occasion. We had several abortive trips, arriving on the scene only to find that visibility was not quite good enough to enable us to pick up the distant land marks. The matter became very urgent from our point of view, when I heard from Alec Reynolds that others from the Plymouth area were making enquiries about a wreck in Bigbury Bay, position unknown. I also heard from the War Risks Insurance Office that someone else had made enquiries about the *Silver Laurel*. We were now certain that this was not the ship that we had found and so we let the idea circulate that it probably was.

Two more 'possibles' were given me by Alec, one named *Modavia* and the other *Clan Stuart* or *Clan Ross*. *Modavia* turned out to be in Lyme Bay and some cargo salvage had already been undertaken by Risden Beazley in the early '50s. This left *Clan Stuart* or *Clan Ross*, which were built by Swan Hunter in 1914. Once more I sent for the plans and waited.

Things were now becoming a bit 'hot' for us and Alec suggested that, although he had been in close contact with Lloyd's Shipping Editor, it would also be a good idea if I contacted them direct. This I did and, in a couple of days, I had a 'phone call from Alec saying that Lloyd's had come up with a 90% certainty and I would receive a letter in the next post. The letter arrived with an invoice for thirty shillings search fee in Lloyd's Records. A better thirty bob's worth I have yet to see!

The Details given were as follows:

Lloyds
April 30, 1970

DEAR SIR,

In reply to your letter of April 26th, I am of the opinion that the wreck you have found in Bigbury Bay is that of the Belgian steamer 'PERSIER', which was torpedoed by a German submarine at 4.30 p.m. on February 11th 1945 when 4 miles 360° from the Eddystone.

The tug 'RESCUE' was sent to assist the 'PERSIER' but owing to bad weather and the fact that the Persier was awash, salvage was impossible. The night of February 11–12th, the derelict was lost sight of in darkness and sank in Bigbury Bay.

There followed a list of cargo, and the ship's details: The *Persier* was built by the Northumberland Shipbuilding Co. Ltd., Newcastle-Upon-Tyne (Hull No. 248) and was completed in June 1918 as the *War Buffalo*. Three years later she was sold to Compagnie Maritime Belge (Lloyd Royal) Société Anonyme of Antwerp—her owners at the time of loss—and renamed.

Particulars of Vessel:

5382 tons gross
3293 tons net
8175 tons dead weight
11,375 tons full load displacement
Length overall—412 ft
Length between perpendiculars—400·2 ft
Breadth—52·3 ft
Depth of hold 28·5 ft
Moulded depth 31 ft
Maximum draft 25·25 ft
Length of poop 49 ft
Length of bridge deck 113 ft
Length of forecastle 39 ft
Tonnage of steel used in construction of hull 2225 Machinery
Triple expansion Steam engine, having three cylinders of 27 in × 48 in, 44 in × 48 in and 73 in × 48 in (bore and stroke)
Boilers—Three single ended boilers having a grate surface of 190 sq ft and heating surface of 7668 sq ft
Dimensions of boilers—15 ft 6 in × 11 ft 6 in
Engines and Boilers manufactured by North Eastern Marine Engineering Co. Ltd. of Newcastle-Upon-Tyne. The total weight of main and auxiliary machinery was 570 tons
Riveted construction
Single Screw
Counter Stern

The letter finished with a suggestion that I should again contact Mr Rowden at the War Risks Insurance Office in respect of acquisition of salvage rights, purchase of wreck etc.

I immediately followed this advice but having already made a false move with regard to *Silver Laurel*, Mr Rowden suggested, that as we were only 90% certain, we should continue diving until we were absolutely sure that this was the ship. Although everything seemed to fall into place from the details given with what we had seen on the bottom, there was one thing which did not tie exactly. In all our dives we had only seen two boilers and *Persier* had three.

We dived again the following weekend, armed with our letter from Lloyd's and a more definite idea of what to look for. On closer examination of the boilers we found the third. It had somehow been buried beneath the other two in the general mass of plating and wreckage. This was a lucky weekend. Ed Wills, another member of the team, came up with the best clue. As he surfaced he held up a broken piece of a mug and shouted back to the boat 'Would you believe—made in Belgium?' There, stamped on the bottom, in English for our benefit, were the words 'Made in Belgium' and the maker's name. In our own minds we were now certain that here, at last, was proof.

The following week I again contacted Mr Rowden. He felt that the proof was not yet conclusive, but if we wanted to go ahead on the evidence which we had, then 'fair enough'. We discussed the problem amongst ourselves. We knew that, although we were the only ones who knew the exact location of the wreck, others could still buy it over our heads. We decided to act on the information we had. I agreed a purchase price and a salvage contract with Mr Rowden and sent off an offer on the Thursday of that week.

As soon as I had received the letter from Lloyd's naming the *Persier* I had tried to get details from the builders, but found that they had gone out of business in the 1920's. Lloyd's, however, informed me that this 'War' Class ship was one of many that had been built at that time, and gave me names and builders of several sister ships. One of these builders was Swan Hunter and they had built five of this type of vessel. I had already sent to Swan Hunter for a copy of the plan of the *Clan Stuart* and so I contacted them to find out if they could let me have a plan of a 'War' class vessel, instead of that of the *Clan Stuart*. I was too late to save a print being made of the *Clan Stuart*, but was told that the Company was in the process of clearing out old negatives. Some were to be sent to the Maritime Museum and others to be destroyed that I could have a $7\frac{1}{2}$ in $\times$ 5 in negative of the $\frac{1}{8}$–1 ft scale general layout plan of the *War Puma*. I, of course, jumped at the opportunity and it duly arrived with the print of the *Clan Stuart* layout.

We obtained our negative plan of the *War Puma* in time for our dive on the weekend following the day when we 'burned our bridges' and made an offer for our wreck. We now knew approximately where different parts of the ship should be amongst the wreckage and this helped to make sense of some of the jumbled heap we had on the bottom. We knew too approximately where to look for the ship's bell, much coveted and searched for since the beginning.

Ken Miles found it, buried in sand with just an inch of the rim showing. We brought it up into the boat and frantically started to clean it around the side where the name would be. We were confident that the name *Persier* would appear. Letter by letter the wording appeared but it did not fit. An 'A' appeared and a 'U' and we all thought that we had made our offer for the wrong ship. A few more letters appeared and then we realized that the original name on the bell had not been changed and it still read *War Buffalo*.

Now that we were sure, Ken Miles contacted the Belgian owners at the time of sinking and they sent a photograph of the ship together with extracts from a magazine concerning the wartime activities and eventual sinking of the *Persier*. The magazine article was, of course, in French, and we had to wait until it was translated before we could know the tragic events which followed the torpedo strike and the fact that the *Persier* was the first ship to attempt to take relief supplies to Belgium at the end of the war. Her cargo was: 2200 tons soap, 6 tons electrical apparatus, one case of steel, 16 tons of leather, 5 tons woollen blankets, 9 tons baby food, 968 tons canned meat, 16 tons rationing stamps, 1186 tons dried eggs, 8 tons motor-car parts and under one ton of other cargo.

Mr Rowden had informed us when we had purchased the wreck that War Risks Insurance Office had paid out nearly £1,000,000 compensation on the cargo. Our agreement to purchase was made on the 5th June 1970, just over one year after we had found the wreck.

The hull of the *Persier* cost us £300 to buy, together with £25, as a deposit on a 70%–30% cargo salvage agreement between the War Risks Insurance Office and myself. Twelve of us put the money up to purchase the wreck and it was purchased in my name to give a definite owner.

The twelve, all long-standing members of Plymouth Sound Branch BSAC, were, the four original finders Peter Foster 1, Peter Foster 2, Ken Miles and myself, together with Carl Jensen, and Ed Wills, Oslo Barakoff, Bill Harris, Will Jenkin, Ian Skelton, Colin Hannaford and Mike Wood. Since the purchase it has been found that diving on a wreck such as this is a very tie-ing occupation and leaves very little time for other diving. We have bought a 25-ft cutter from which to dive, and the trip there and back, including diving time and finding the wreck, always works out in excess of six hours. For this reason our numbers continuing with the project have dwindled to seven.

The propeller, with which we decided to start salvage operations has proved particularly difficult. The ship is resting over on her port side, leaving us a clear working area from above, but, two blades of the four bladed propeller are buried into the sand and gravel. We managed to get the nut off quite well by splitting it with explosives and unscrewing it. We then put a charge in between the hull and the propeller, but shifted it only four inches on our first blow. We then found that it was being held by the two sunken blades. . . . We tried to clear a pit behind it to allow movement, but it refilled quicker than we could clear it.

We have now managed to get it off by shearing the collars inside the hull and blowing the shaft inwards away from the prop. We are now left with a propeller in four pieces, but at least it makes it easier to lift.

There at the time of writing the story of the *Persier* ends, but the diving goes on . . . .

*   *   *   *   *

Though submarines took a huge toll of shipping in the Second World War, aircraft added their share to the wreckage on the sea-bed.

On 25th March 1941, the 458-foot cargo ship s.s. *Somali* was making her way up the Northumberland coast to join a convoy. Her final destination was China, and in her holds she carried non-ferrous metals, medical supplies, heavy vehicle tyres, a quantity of coin and some jeeps. The *Somali* stood little chance when the German bomber dropped out of the clouds and attacked. Within moments the ship was ablaze, and when all attempts to put the fire out failed the captain ordered the crew to abandon ship.

But the *Somali* was not finished yet. For two days she drifted, still burning. The possibility of saving her was too good to miss, and after having been assured that there were no explosives in the cargo, a salvage crew boarded the vessel. A destroyer took the listing ship in tow and started to tow her towards Seahouses, where it was planned to beach her. Two local lifeboats followed just in case.

Three miles off shore—when it looked as though the *Somali* would be saved—a colossal explosion broke windows in the village of Beadnell. As the startled villagers looked out to sea they could see a great black mushroom cloud hanging over the spot where only a second before had been the s.s. *Somali*. She was gone—down to the sea-bed one hundred feet below. And the salvage crew, who had all been standing aft at the time of the explosion, were blown off the deck, right over the lifeboats and into the water beyond. Amazingly enough, they were all picked up alive.

tale gleam of brass when the first diving knife scraped the dark growth away.

Says Douglas Hamer: 'We think the other divers were misled into thinking that the prop was iron . . . because they were in fact looking at the spare screw on the deck. It was at an angle, making it look as though this was the main screw and the ship's collision with the sea-bed had pushed it through the decking'.

But no matter whether the other divers had been misled or not, Harry and Douglas Hamer decided there and then—or rather as soon as they surfaced—that they would buy the wreck and go in for salvage full time. Hemsley and Hamer are now 'Ocean Diving Services' of Leeds. They employ John Ingle and Bob Pert as professional divers, and have learnt their business the hard way—beginning with this wreck and, literally, starting from the bottom and working their way up.

Can such a venture pay off? That was the question I asked Douglas Hamer. He replied:

Harry and I put all our savings into buying the wreck and the necessary equipment. Harry had gained professional experience when working with another salvage company, including the use of explosives, before we started on our own. This knowledge he has passed on to me. We decided to have a crack on our own, because we came to the conclusion that it's no good sitting back when you're an old man and saying 'I wish I'd had a go when I was young. . . .'

The price for a good wreck is always several hundred pounds and you always have trouble buying them unless you know how. Recently we have bought another wreck in Oban, Scotland, called s.s. *Breda*, which was bombed and sank a quarter of a mile off shore. We've also got tenders out for two others. And we've bought another near the Farnes, which was carrying 10,000 tons of wheat.

The venture so far has been a little hand-to-mouth as we have ploughed all our money back into the business, but we hope to show a decent profit by the end of the year. We've bought a 50 ft fishing trawler built in Norway called the *Logresund*, which we've equipped for salvage work. . . . And we're going on from there.

* * * * *

As the pace of diving round Britain increases, divers are finding not only the wreckage of ships sent to the bottom by aircraft, but also the wreckage of aircraft that came down in the sea for one reason or another. Most aircraft wrecks date from the Second World War.

For example, while looking for scallops in a bay near Kirkwall, in the Orkneys, two divers, Eric Giles of London and Otto Klass from South Wales, found the wreckage of a British fighter in thirty-five feet of water. Scattered around the wreckage were hundreds of rounds of machine-gun ammunition. And some of the ammunition appeared to the divers to have exploded before the plane hit the sea—fire marks are quite distinct on some parts of the wreck.

While freeing a trawl for a fisherman, divers of Brighton Branch of the BSAC found the wreck of a four-engined bomber. It was so badly damaged and half buried that they could not

Return to the surface after 30 years under the sea. One engine, propeller and main wing section of the Penzance Beaufighter are swung clear of the water

Photo K. P. Clark

That, as far as most people were concerned, was that. Some of the Chinese coins had been blown on to the beaches by the explosion, but gradually the *Somali* was forgotten by all those who had not seen or heard that giant explosion out at sea.

The only visitors to her were fish and the seals from the near-by Farne Islands—until Harry Hemsley, Douglas Hamer and John Ingle of Leeds Branch of the British Sub-Aqua Club paid the wreckage a visit. At first, they say, they thought they were looking at a huge block of flats under the sea, so big did the *Somali* seem on first acquaintance. But the awe which they felt soon turned to joy. Other divers had told them that the 'screw' was iron, but it wasn't. Once again there was that tell-

155

even discover in the short time available to them whether it was British, American or German.

More fortunate from the point of view of identification were the divers of Penzance Branch of the BSAC. Ever since the branch had been formed in 1961, there had been talk of finding an aircraft which had come down in the bay during the War. Ideas for finding the aircraft were put forward regularly at meetings in the pub used by branch members. But it wasn't until August 1969 that John Chalcraft, Richard Trethowan and Alan Griffiths, the branch chairman, were exploring the area underwater to the south-east of Low Lee reef that they came upon the first real evidence of where the mystery plane lay. The evidence was a strip of metal that could have come from nothing else but an aircraft. But they still did not see the wreck. The discovery did, however, stimulate enough interest for a more serious search to be made.

The next month Bob Carswell was given some marks for an obstruction by a local fisherman, and as it seemed in the 'aircraft area', some of the branch divers decided to give it a try. The day chosen was hardly ideal, and in fact the wind was so strong that the anchor dragged when first lowered. After a short period of bumping over the bottom, the anchor finally caught.

First descent was made by Bob Carswell, Ray Dennis, Dr Morley Phillips, Peter Uterhark and Jim Wheeler. And there in 90 feet of water resting on the silty sand was an almost intact Bristol Beaufighter. From a position on the sand ahead of her, she looked for all the world as though waiting on a foggy airfield for the weather to clear.

But a closer inspection in the gloomy visibility showed that the tail was missing. The port engine looked as though it had seized, as some of the cylinder heads were hanging off. Only the blades of the propellers that were stuck in the sand were buckled, indicating to the divers that she had made a reasonably soft belly-landing on the sea. The four cannon and six machine-guns were still there fully loaded.

The Penzance divers now naturally wanted to know more about their find, which lay about one hundred yards south-east from Low Lee Buoy, between Newlyn and Mousehole. Soon they knew that it was a Beaufighter Mark I No. T3249 on a flight from Gibraltar to St Eval, and the plane was from 252 Squadron.

The Penzance branch then asked me for help. A careful search through records showed that this particular Beaufighter had crashed into the sea on 22nd May 1941. The pilot was Flying Officer Charles Seaver Henry McDonald, who had survived the War, stayed in the Service until 1948, coming out as a Squadron Leader and remaining on the RAF Reserve until 1959.

A letter forwarded to Squadron Leader McDonald via RAF Records brought no reply, but a long-shot look in the London telephone directory did produce a C. S. H. McDonald living in Barnes. Was it the same one? I dialled the number without much hope, though the similarity of the initials meant that I had to try. Within seconds I was speaking to the man who all those years ago put that Beaufighter down on the sea near Low Lee Buoy, off the Cornish coast.

Later we met, and Mr McDonald told me the story of that flight. After operations in Malta four Beaufighters were ordered to fly singly to Britain via Gibraltar to bring out fresh aircraft. The flight of T3249 was uneventful as far as Gibraltar. Mr McDonald took alternate spells of flying with his passenger, another 252 Squadron pilot, Flying Officer George Lemar, and the observer Sergeant Gibbs operated the wireless and navigated.

The weather forecast at Gibraltar told of a bad front in the Bay of Biscay, but that visibility would improve as they neared the English coast. Somewhere over the Bay the wireless packed in and they flew into the bad weather front. McDonald tried to climb above it, but at 11,000 feet it seemed to be even worse. He returned to within sight of the sea and flew all the way across the Bay of Biscay and right up to the coast of Cornwall at 150 feet above the sea with only a few hundred yards forward visibility.

When they knew the Cornish coast must be only minutes ahead this lack of visibility was positively terrifying. Suddenly McDonald saw cliffs right in front of him with waves breaking at the bottom and the tops of the cliffs in the clouds. He pulled the Beaufighter up violently over the top of the cliffs. Their situation was now critical. The wireless was still out of action and they were running out of petrol, so even if they could have been diverted they were unlikely to have made it. There was no sign of a break in the clouds.

There were now two alternatives. One, they could climb and then jump with their parachutes. This had obvious dangers—the wind could blow them away from the land into the sea. The only other thing to do was to ditch the aircraft.

The men were all of one mind—to ditch. McDonald flew south, and then turned to approach the cliffs at an angle. As he did so he saw a fishing-boat in a bay and ditched the Beaufighter with flaps down and wheels up—she was still doing about eighty knots when she hit the sea. They couldn't get the dinghy out—all were slightly injured; McDonald where his face had smashed into the gunsight—and floated in their Mae Wests. The aircraft was gone in ninety seconds.

Says McDonald, remembering the moment of impact, 'it was like hitting a brick wall. So there we were floating around in a freezing sea. And it was my birthday too!'

The crew of the Beaufighter were all picked up by the fishing-boat. McDonald soon returned to flying duties. Sergeant Gibbs was killed later off Norway flying with another squadron. And George Lemar was killed later in the War when a Liberator crashed at night.

Since our meeting Mr McDonald has been down to Penzance, where the Branch have presented him with a souvenir of his aircraft—one of the instruments by which he guided that Beaufighter back to Britain one misty day many years ago.

And the Beaufighter itself has been raised—all four and a half tons of it. Hampstead, Hatfield Polytechnic and Penzance branches of the British Sub-Aqua Club did the diving work. The project, organized by diver Peter Cornish, was undertaken on behalf of the RAF Museum and Hatfield Polytechnic Department of Aeronautical Engineering.

* * * * *

Viv Barrett first started diving at Lulworth in 1956 with a Mark I Heinke demand valve and a dry suit over thick woolly sweaters. He looks back on those times with some nostalgia—'there was never anyone else there'. A little later on he and his friends formed 60 Group, BSAC, and during the Branch's ups and downs he was five times its diving officer. In non-diving life he is a production supervisor in an electronics factory producing radio-telephones.

During his many visits to Lulworth Cove he heard stories about a big landing craft coming into the cove to let the crew of a large ship anchored out at sea ashore for the night. At some time in the early 1950s, went the story, the crew had returned to the landing craft after a happy night on shore, had motored out of the cove, hit the reef and sunk, with, fortunately, no loss of life.

Viv Barrett got the impression from these tales that the mother ship had been anchored out to the east and that the landing craft had gone out through the gap at the left of the cove, had grazed the reef and carried on to sink somewhere well out. Each year that he and his friends had visited Lulworth they had looked for the wreck, but found nothing.

They were prepared to think that the sinking of the landing craft was just a local story with no foundation in fact until at Easter 1968 they found her! Says Viv Barrett:

Jim Wardle and I went out from the entrance of Lulworth for about half-a-mile, lowered the anchor and then drifted with it. The current was running East to West at about five knots and after about five minutes of this drifting we suddenly saw the outline of a boat—or rather we saw two large propellers. We just managed to fight the current to the wreck and hooked the anchor over a propeller shaft. By getting down below the level of the wreck we escaped most of the tide and could examine it. It was a landing craft all right. Upside down and holed. We found the engine room telegraph equipment lying clear of her and surfaced with it.

Once on the surface they took some quick shore marks, and a month later returned to the wreck. To their delight they saw that the two large props were phosphor-bronze on shafts of similar metal. Inside the upside-down cabin over the engine-room were two large Chrysler engines—as the cylinders and gear-boxes were upside down too, of course, there was a good chance that these would be protected by the engine oil. The wooden parts of the boat were crumbling, but most of the metal was intact.

Whose landing craft was it? In an attempt to answer this question Viv Barrett cleaned up the telegraph system and found the markings S/N D10127/1C. The system was made by Teleflex (who supply many, many similar systems today) and when Barrett wrote to them all they could say was that the units were supplied in bulk to the Navy during the War. The local authorities could not help either. There is no record of the incident, and contact with various Service departments brought no further information. No one, it seemed, wanted to own the landing craft.

So, just in case someone's conscience should prick them, your landing craft, Sir, is lying in sixty feet of water with almost all her thirty-five feet some six feet off the sand, a half-mile out from Lulworth Cove. It's a favourite haunt of pouting, Sir, and though the engines are possibly worth salvaging no one has touched them yet. The props, I am happy to report Sir, have gone.

*   *   *   *   *

Every wreck sets up a record in some way. Sometimes, unhappily, it is the number of people lost that sets an all time high in tragedy. Other wrecks are the first or the last to be the victims of some disaster reef. All have some reason for being remembered—certainly in the lifetime of the youngest survivor.

In March 1967 one particular ship set up a new record. She was the largest ship ever to be wrecked around Britain. She was the *Torrey Canyon*—and she set alarm bells ringing all over southern England.

The *Torrey Canyon* was big, there was no doubt about that. Her exact length was 974 feet 5 inches, and she was a super-tanker. And she struck Pollard Rock in the Seven Stones Reef at 8.50 a.m. on that grey Saturday morning, 18th March 1967. The Reef is six miles north-east of the Scillies, and the moment that the *Torrey Canyon* tore her bottom open on the rocks oil started to pour out, menacing the holiday coastline of the West of England. Finally Buccaneer and Hunter aircraft were sent in to bomb open the tanks and burn the oil. Then a massive clear-up operation coped with the oil on the beaches.

Royal Navy divers went in afterwards to make sure that all the tanks had been opened and that no further massive pollution threat remained after all the bombing and rocketing. They found the main wreckage sixty-five feet down. The bow had dropped into a deep gully, but most of the ship was unrecognizable after the fierce bombing.

Dick Larn, who has figured in so many West Country diving reports, adds this:

The highest part of the wreck was less than 15 feet underwater and this was a section with handrails. The main wreckage is very broken, with the stern gone off into deep water. Her spare bronze prop, weighing something like 18 tons, is sitting in 50 feet of water, almost clear of overhanging wreckage. It looks as though it is almost waiting to be lifted! Diving on her is an eerie sensation—loose plates creak and grind all the time so that the ship appears to be alive. Great sheets of metal flap back and forth in the ground seas. It's not very nice down there, but she'll soon settle down to being a normal wreck.

It is interesting to note that a wreck diver of such experience as Dick Larn should talk of a wreck settling down—as though it were a living thing about to be tamed by the sea.

But every diver will know what he means. Soon the *Torrey Canyon* will start to merge into the sea-bed. The newness is gone from her already. In the years to come, the rust will start to bite and she will become a history book to be discovered once again by some wreck detective of the future. One can only hope that he will feel, as have all the divers in this book, the thrill of spotting some long-lost clue to our seafaring past.

Sources for Wreck Location

including a full guide to the way to identify a wreck, the places to go for information, and how to use those sources once you get there.

PART of the excitement of wreck detection comes with the research into the history of each ship and the events that led up to her sinking—putting clue together with clue until the whole picture emerges. It would be a very strange diver indeed who, once having found some wreckage, didn't want to know the whole story of that lost ship. And wreck research can work the other way round and save hours of fruitless searching under water.

Here then are the sources of information, which no wreck detective could afford to be without:

The Public Record Office,
Chancery Lane, London, WC2A 1LR

This is one of the biggest sources of information for the wreck detective. The staff are incredibly helpful, and should be treated with the respect their knowledge deserves.

The Office contains millions of documents relating to the actions of the Government of Britain and its courts of law from the eleventh century—and included in all those documents are hundreds of thousands which concern ships and their wrecking.

But it is no use just going along and expecting to be shown exactly what you want without some preliminary work on your part. First of all, just to get inside the building, you must fill in an application form for either a Reader's Ticket, which is valid for three years, or for a temporary permit, which is valid for one week only. Write to the Secretary for the form.

For the Reader's ticket you will have to get someone 'of a recognized position to whom the applicant is known personally or from a recognized institution' to sign the form. Recognized position will be covered by a barrister, solicitor, doctor or anyone in public life. And 'recognized institution' includes embassies and universities.

For the temporary permit you must call at the PRO and no recommendation is required, but the issuing officer there will want proof of identity, and has to satisfy himself that you are a responsible person. The permit is only valid for a week and if your research takes longer you'll have to get a proper Reader's ticket.

Once you've got your permission, then you can start tracking down that wreck. The Chancery Lane search rooms are open from 9.30 a.m. to 5 p.m. Monday to Friday and some records can be consulted on Saturday mornings, but only if ordered in advance.

Don't take a biro or fountain pen with you. Their use is forbidden. Pencils only, but there is some accommodation (limited) for those who want to use tape-recorders or typewriters. Ask about this at the Office.

First port of call once you have signed the book at the entrance should be the Enquiries Desk, where, so long as you have a clear idea of what you want to see, they'll direct you to the correct Search Room.

On your first visit you may well find it all a bit awe-inspiring, but don't let it put you off. The staff are there to help you, and they will.

But do have a clear idea in your mind of what you expect to find. Mr E. K. Timings, Head of the Search Department, gave all wreck researchers a first-class tip when he told me that you 'should look further than the wreck itself . . . think who would have been affected by it'. With this in mind, here are some of the sources you will find in the PRO files.

If it was a naval ship and there were survivors it is likely (though not always certain) that someone will have been court-martialled. Sometimes these courts-martial were used more as a method of getting at the cause of the loss of the ship than of apportioning blame, and so you can expect to find a deal of information from them. In one that I read, for example, the actual rock the ship hit is named and a little research would have saved at least two groups of wreck-hunters a great deal of useless diving! So your ship may be in the *Digest of Courts-Martial*, which cover the period from 1755 to 1806. The index number is 4779.

From the digest you can go to the actual report of the court-martial. These come under the Admiralty 1 series (5253 onwards) and are mostly in the beautiful copper-plate hand of some long-dead clerk, who quilled away as the court-martial was actually being held in the great cabin of some anchored man o'war. The court-martial records run from 1680 right up until the one hundred-year Rule applies. This rule means that no modern court-martial documents will be available until one hundred years have passed. (Don't despair here. In many cases the Press were present, although not at secret sessions. For these try the British Museum Newspaper Library at Colindale. See under British Museum.)

If your ship was likely to have been involved in an affair of some consequence from the time of Henry VIII onward (the Spanish Armada is a good example), then you should find something about her in the State Papers (Domestic) in the Round Room. For the Spanish ships wrecked in Ireland you'll want the State Papers (Irish). There's a printed calendar to guide you towards both of these.

Still no luck? Don't despair yet. All the 'In' letters to the Admiralty are preserved (there are gaps of course, but there are a great number left), and here you'll find the letters from the Port Admirals and the Port Agents, and even from the officers in charge of lookout points around the coasts. These were often concerned with reporting losses to the Admiralty. You'll find them under Admiralty 1, List and Indexes 18. There's an Admiralty Digest subject index there with a key to all Admiralty papers. All wrecks too are listed per year. You'll find this under Wrecks (Cut No. 31 in the Digest).

And if the log survived it may well be in the PRO. Even if it didn't (I've noted that in some cases where a ship was lost by what can only be called 'demned carelessness', even though there was plenty of time to get everything else off, the log mysteriously drowned), the logs of any ships in the area can be revealing. Captains' logs are under Admiralty 51, and the logs of Masters under Admiralty 52.

Was there any salvage done on your ship? Was there a legal squabble about her? Try the High Court of Admiralty records at the PRO or the records of the Admiralty Division of the Supreme Court (from 1873).

And don't think that if you do strike lucky you have to copy out all the details laboriously with a pencil. The PRO has a fine photocopying service at reasonable prices.

You'll find in your research that one thing leads to another. For example, if it's a treasure ship you're after there may well be a great deal of information about her in the Treasury records for that period. This is what is meant by looking 'further than the wreck itself'. If the treasure was State money its loss will not go unrecorded among papers that on the face of it have nothing to do with ships.

Did your ship carry troops? Then the military records at the PRO may well give you information. After all, if a whole troop was lost, someone was going to have to report it to someone higher up the chain of command.

So, there's a pretty good chance that the Public Records Office can find you something about your ship. But don't expect them to give you a map and mark the spot she sank with an 'X'. Though come to think of it, that's what happened to Roland Morris (see Chapter 6) during his research—he found a map that said 'Association lost here'. And that's in the Public Records Office too!

Hydrographic Dept., Ministry of Defence, Taunton, Somerset

Old charts can give vital clues. The classic example of this can be found as already mentioned in Chapter 6, in which you will see that Roland Morris found an old map which actually named the rock on which the *Association* was lost.

Remember that the names of rocks and headlands have changed a great deal over the years. So see if the Hydrographic Department can give you a copy of a chart that was in use at the time of the loss of your ship.

Write to the Curator, who will tell you what is available. Basically they have a large number of manuscript documents from which the charts were compiled. These date from the early 1800s. Earlier material than this is very limited, but there are some surveys from the late 1700s, and a few hand-drawn charts from earlier dates. Photographic copies of sections of them can be obtained at reasonable prices.

The Wrecks Section, Hydrographic Department, Ministry of Defence, Beadon Road, Taunton, Somerset

The Wrecks Section set up a card index in 1913 on which every known wreck was allotted a card. This was not to help divers with their searches, but so that a record could be kept of wrecks that were, or might become, a danger to navigation.

Their records now hold details of every known wreck—*from 1913 onward*—such as the name, tonnage, date sunk and depth of water over wreck. If it was dispersed (*i.e.*, because it was a danger to navigation) this is on record also.

They have a handy leaflet available (Wrecks Section Booklet RL/69) giving some sources of information, and which also stresses that their wreck records are of little value for:

(a) Historical wrecks and Wrecks sunk prior to 1913. In general, information on wrecks prior to the 20th Century is very scant and positions are frequently unreliable.

(b) Ownership (a very important point when intending to recover articles from a wreck).

(c) Wrecks in areas for which the Admiralty Chart is not the primary authority.

(d) The Law relating to salvage, acquisition of wrecks etc.

It should be pointed out that many wrecks exist, the names of which are not known, and many more which have never been located. It is therefore of great value if salvage concerns, Sub-Aqua Clubs and similar bodies send details of wrecks found to the Hydrographic Department, giving as much information as possible. In order to provide a better service than hitherto, it is present policy to add to the wreck records details of ownership, voyage and cargo at time of loss, and any other information which may be of general interest.

A person interested in obtaining information from the index cards is advised to use the following procedure:

(i) Buy a Catalogue of Admiralty Charts (Home Edition—price 5p. World Edition—price 67½p) from any chart agent. From this select and buy the largest scale chart available for the area concerned.

(ii) Take off the position of any wreck of interest in latitude and longitude; or decide on the area of interest (e.g. 'All wrecks within 20 fathoms between Burmouth light and Castle Head').

(iii) Write, giving these details, and a brief statement of the reason for the enquiry, to the following address:

Wrecks Section,
Hydrographic Department,
Ministry of Defence,
Beadon Road,
TAUNTON,
Somerset

(iv) A search fee is charged that is commensurate with the work . . . involved in producing the information required. Cheques and or Postal Orders should be made payable to the 'Cashier', Hydrographic Department.

(v) In the case of an enquiry of an academic nature, or where the provision of new information leads to the enlargement of the wreck records, all or part of the search fee may be waived.

It is interesting to note here that the deep-draught supertankers of today have forced the Wrecks Section to increase the danger depth of wrecks (it used to be 48 feet in 1963) to 90 ft. So many 'harmless' wrecks of the past may in future have to be dispersed as a danger to navigation, and wreck divers will have lost another chance to explore these sunken ships.

Board of Trade (War Risk Insurance Office), Parliament Square House, 34-36, Parliament Street, London, SW1A 2ND

They will help with details of Allied merchantmen lost (due to enemy action) during both the First and Second World Wars. They can also give details of ownership and cargo.

Director General of Defence Contracts (Naval) Section 85, Ensleigh, Bath, Somerset

These are the people to contact if you want to buy a Navy wreck!

Lloyd's Register of Shipping, 69-71 Fenchurch Street, London, EC3M 4BS

They have brief details of the ship and how she was lost from their Quarterly Returns since 1890. Write to the Principal Clerk in charge of the Statistics Department, giving her name and date of loss.

Trinity House, Tower Hill, London, EC3N 4DH

This can give, in return for name and general position of wrecks in home waters, details of dispersal, position, buoyage, cargo etc. But unfortunately their pre-1940 records were destroyed by fire.

The British Museum, Bloomsbury, London, WC1B 3DG

I do not propose here to try to tell you everything that is in the British Museum! But early newspapers and maps are of particular interest to the wreck detective, and this is where they are.

To use the facilities of the British Museum Reading Room and associated libraries, you must have a ticket (a long-period one lasts for a year and the short-period one for six days only). Applications for either have to follow a certain form, because the British Museum is there to provide readers with 'facilities for research and reference which are not readily available in other libraries normally accessible to them'. Write to the Director's Office (Readers' Tickets) and they'll send you a form telling you how to apply.

London newspapers printed before 1801 are kept at the British Museum itself, and there is a *Times* file from 1809 to the present day. For most of the others you will have to go to the British Museum Newspaper Library, Colindale, London, NW9 5HE (where once again you will need a Reader's Ticket). The Newspaper Library is opposite Colindale Underground Station, and there you will find all the newspapers in the National Collection, including, of course, English provincial newspapers, but the London, Edinburgh, Belfast and Dublin *Gazettes* are kept at Bloomsbury. To save time, and to find out exactly what you can see, write to the Superintendent. Lloyd's List is also kept at Colindale.

Old maps are kept at Bloomsbury, and date from the earliest maps made.

Imperial War Museum, Lambeth Road, London, SE1 6HZ

This can supply information only about the date and location of British merchantmen and Royal Navy ships lost by enemy action in the First and Second World Wars. The lists do not include ships lost during those wars due to storms or other causes. But official histories and ship histories are available in the museum's Printed Books Section, and you can get photostats of documents.

Customs House Library, Kings Beam House, 39-41 Mark Lane, London, EC3R 7HE

This has ship registers dating back to the early eighteenth century.

The National Maritime Museum, Greenwich, London, SE10 9NF

Is a mass of experts and information. They prefer you to write to them first (to the Director) and not just drop in if you have any specific query. This is not because they are trying to complicate life—they are all keen to help—but because unless you do write the expert in the field in which you require help may not be available.

Basically, then, here is how the National Maritime and its extensive collections can help you. When you write your letter will be guided to the right department, which could be:

The Navigation Department, which holds an extensive collection of charts from the sixteenth century onward, together with a fine range of nautical instruments from the same period.

The Manuscript Department. Here are the builder's plans of Admiralty ships from the eighteenth century (and if they haven't got them for your particular ship there is the chance of finding those of a sister ship, or one of her class). Commercial builder's plans date mostly from the late nineteenth century, both steam and sail, iron and wood, to the present day.

The Library. If you know the name and the approximate date of the wreck it will help, but here are just a few of the sources open to you:

They have: Lloyd's *Register of Shipping* from 1764; Lloyd's *List Reprints* 1741–1826; Lloyd's *Lists* 1869–1953; Lloyd's *Manuscript Wreck Registers* 1855–95; Lloyd's *Dictionary of Disasters at Sea* 1824–1962; Mercantile Navy List from 1857; reports of wrecks and courts of enquiry in the *Nautical Magazine* (March 1832 to date); a collection of books on individual shipwrecks, shipwrecks in general and wrecks of particular areas; articles and notes on wrecks past and present in *Sea Breezes*; and many other books and papers.

Just for a moment, let's suppose that you've found a ship fitting that you can't recognize. That unidentifiable (by you) piece of material may well be instantly recognized by one of the Museum's experts. Write first, and send a photograph if you can.

Found a cannon or any kind of armament? Send measurements, photographs and all details you can. They'll do their best.

Do you know what your ship looked like—or the captain, or the admiral? Try the Museum's Picture Library. They have an extensive collection of prints, oil paintings, water colours, engravings, portraits and photographs, and will let you have copies very reasonably.

Sea Breezes, 19 James St, Liverpool, L2 7PE

A monthly magazine published by the Journal of Commerce in Liverpool aimed at all who are interested in ships and the sea. The letter column is a mine of information, and if you get a letter asking for information published you'll get a surprising response from other readers. Write to the Editor, Craig J. M. Carter, Esq., Subscription for a year, including postage, is £2.10.

The Science Museum, South Kensington, London, SW7 2DD

Very good source for constructional details of ships and their equipment. **Mr B. W. Bathe**, Assistant Keeper of the Department of Water Transport, is very helpful.

Lloyd's, Lime Street, London, EC3M 7HA

They have brief details of the vessel at time of loss, cargo, and the way she was lost, and usually have ownership at time of loss, but not after any claims have been settled. These reports have appeared (and do appear today) in the marine casualty columns of Lloyd's *List*. The earliest copies date from 1741, and can be seen at the offices of the Shipping Editor. Records are world-wide, and if you want them to find your ship they'll charge you a search fee, depending on how much searching they have to do.

The Committee for Nautical Archaeology, Institute of Archaeology, 31–34, Gordon Square, London, WC1H 0PP

Not so much a source as a source for sources. For the CNA will help, advise and guide you to people who can assist you—if you are undertaking a serious survey or excavation of a sunken ship. Founded in 1964 to develop and guide underwater archaeology, its aims are:

To promote research in Nautical Archaeology.

To promote underwater training in this field.

To provide contact between divers, archaeologists and historians.

To safeguard the archaeological content of underwater sites.

To safeguard the rights of divers co-operating with the CNA.

The Committee publish a journal, the *International Journal of Nautical Archaeology*, which contains research articles, field reports (should it be sea reports?). Subscription is £2.50 per year from Seminar Press, 24–28 Oval Road, London, NW1.

Though the Committee is financially ill endowed, it does sponsor the School for Nautical Archaeology at Fort Bovisand, Plymouth, Devon. Known as SNAP, the school runs courses, in theory and practice, on all aspects of diving and nautical archaeology. Apply to Alan Bax at the Fort for full details.

Sources for tracing crashed RAF aircraft

If the aircraft's number is visible write to: Air Historical Branch, RAF, Queen Anne's Chambers, 3 Dean Farrar Street, London, SW1H 9JX. They have aircraft record cards showing units, squadrons, pilots' names, etc for aircraft anywhere in the world from 1937 onward.

If the only details available are the type of plane and the date of the crash, contact Flight Safety Branch FS3b, RAF, Tavistock House, 1–6 Tavistock Square, London WC1H 9NL. Note that the Flight Safety Branch can only help with aircraft down in the United Kingdom. Local papers often carry stories of plane crashes, so types and dates can often be gleaned from these sources if you are not sure about them. Wartime aircraft are more difficult, but the RAF will do their best.

Sources. General

To say that the world is wide-open and that there are sources of information everywhere is stretching things a bit far, but the real wreck detective will find himself following some strange trails and collecting vital information from surprising sources. Take the pin wreck of Dick Larn's (see Chapter 1). Now, a pin to most men is a pin and that is that, but to a woman a pin is something that she really knows about. Dick Larn gave me one of the hand-made brass pins from his wreck to illustrate what he was writing about. I showed it to a secretary, Miss Lindsey Bartlett, and she set off on the trail of that pin with a determination that only a woman could show. The *Encyclopedia Britannia, Chambers*, and any other encyclopedia she could lay her hands on, didn't, in her opinion, tell her enough about pins like the one she held in her hands. The British Museum was turned over and found wanting until she finally found the firm to whom I am grateful for the information about pins in Appendix 2!

So do not give up the slightest chance of picking up information. Try local newspaper, local museum, churchyard (many a good wreck has been found from an old tombstone), anywhere, in fact, that has the remotest chance of being able to add information to what you already know.

And don't forget your local public library. They can help you by getting a loan of such books as *Biographia Navalis*, by John Charnock. This gives lives of Royal Navy captains and officers from 1660 to 1798. It was published in the eighteenth century and was kept up to date by various additional volumes. It contains a lot of interesting tittle-tattle, and can be a good source if not taken as gospel. It can also be seen in the PRO.

Tackle old people, old fishermen, old colonels, old and present coastguards, Customs men, local historical or archaeological societies. Cultivate the local librarian (some libraries have extra material that never appears on their shelves). Call on salvage firms—never write and expect a reply. If they are any good, they'll often be too busy diving to answer letters, and my experience is that divers have a built-in thing against answering letters anyway! Visit lifeboat stations and check what old records they hold.

Alan Bax told me—I suppose I should have known it—that most trawler-skippers keep a list or chart of 'fasteners' (obstructions which damage their trawls). This list could, of course, be a guide to wrecks. Bromley BSAC found several wrecks this way. Certainly such obstructions would be good diving spots. In his list of sources of information Alan Bax also lists dredger operators, pipe-layers, and marine biologists. This is interesting, because I believe that one South Coast pipe-layer and cable-checker holds the clue to an amphora wreck. He has talked over drinks of finding pottery—and his description of it leaves no doubt in my mind that he is talking about ancient wine-jars—but is such an elusive fellow to pin down that I have so far failed to nail down the exact spot!

All the sources mentioned so far are those that can be checked out at leisure during those parts of the winter in which diving becomes, if not impossible, certainly uncomfortable.

Once afloat, however, another range of sources become available—if money to pay for them is to hand as well.

In Chapter 2, for example, you will have read of the use of side-scan sonar, and sonar itself is a source of much information if used properly. Most sonar, of course, works on the simple echo-sounder principle—bouncing sound waves off the sea-bed. In this age of technology the simplest of these sonar instruments is the cheap echo-sounder, but the wreck detective who relies on the light pattern on these instruments indicating depth to show him anything more than a large obstruction of the sea-bottom is an expert indeed. To be fair, it is said that the men who can really use these inexpensive instruments can tell when a single large fish crosses under the boat, but my experience is that you have to go one stage further to really get the benefit from an echo-sounder. I refer to the echo-sounder which traces a picture of the sea-bed on a roll of paper unravelling inside the instrument. Using this (in my case the Ferguson) I have watched yards and yards of sea-bed faithfully recorded in the boat above—and have used the instrument to return again and again to exactly the same spot.

And when a wreck appears below you there is not the slightest doubt about it. The echo-sounder pen goes into a steep climb and 'writes' a trace which only an idiot could misinterpret.

Moving on again a stage further into the range of electronic gear, we come to the proton magnetometer. Basically this instrument is a device for measuring the Earth's magnetic field. It measures the difference in behaviour of protons—tiny charged particles in two bottles of liquid (either distilled water or methylated spirit) every few seconds, and records it on a meter. The differences arise as a result of interference in the local magnetic field caused by sunken objects. One instrument produced by Wardle and Davenport Ltd, of Leek, Staffs., which cost about £100 could record as little as one and a half tons of ferrous metal at 50 feet, or 50 tons at 132 feet, which is adequate for any normal purpose.

From this point the sky's the limit as far as cost is concerned in the electronic devices for the detection of sunken ships—and few of them are within the range of the usual group of divers, though the Committee for Nautical Archaeology may be able to persuade the owners to give your wreck a run if they consider her of sufficient archaeological interest. Electronic equipment was used in a survey of the Spanish Armada ship *La Trinidad Valencera* (see Chapter 4). Simple metal-detectors can be water-proofed for underwater use, and have helped some groups a great deal with their detection work.

Anything you find in the sea near a wreck should be treated as a source of information about that ship. One of the most extraordinary pieces of source material was found by Phil Baker, Chairman of Doncaster Branch of the BSAC, during a dive at Oban near the wreckage of a then unknown drifter.

> Near the wreck [he says], I found a brass ship's candlestick with gimbal pivots, the type with the candle pushed up inside the stem by a plunger with a spring beneath it. When cleaning the candlestick I started to remove the gunge from the bottom end which had lost its screw-on cap and was picking out oderiferous seaweed when I was amazed to find the seaweed was printed with type!
>
> After that I extracted the whole thing with great care and was able to unfold a still-readable sheet of newspaper dated 1936 which had been used as a bung to replace the lost spring. It was a page of Glasgow's *The Bulletin*.

Unfortunately, this find did not identify the wreck, but it does give a date before which she is most unlikely to have sunk.

What happened next illustrates one thing you must possess—and if you don't possess it, no list of sources will be of any use to you—and that is determination. If you set out to solve the mystery of a wreck, then you must keep after it, even though clue after clue leads you to a dead end.

Phil Baker did his homework first—lists of losses showed that three small naval vessels had been lost during the 1939-45 War near Oban. The *Appletree* was lost by collision on 15th October 1940, the *Young Fisherman* was wrecked on 29th November 1940, and the *Golden Gift* was lost by collision on 6th April 1943.

Then he went back to Oban. The locals, both divers and others, had various stories to tell. 'She was lost well into the war' . . . 'She was a fishing boat engaged in fishing at the time' . . . 'She was a drifter acting as a stores carrier around the anchorage' . . . 'She was lost by fire' . . . 'She was a Puffer. . . .'

Says Baker: 'I dived and found her mostly intact, a true schoolboy adventure book wreck, with the planks beginning to open at the seams and a large tank and her funnel lying alongside. She was a typical steam drifter in form'.

More inquiries led to more confusion, but Phil Baker did find an eye-witness of the sinking, who as a youngster saw her rammed by the m.v. *Lochinvar*—'She swung round and drove right up the beach, all her crew dropped off dry foot, then she slipped off to where she lies now.' 'Was she the *Golden Gift*?' 'Never heard of her, she was the *Golden Line*', said the eye-witness firmly.

More checking—and a list of warships serving in the Second World War mentioned *Golden Line* as being returned to her owners. How can you return a wreck to her owners? But Phil Baker was now determined to sort the matter out. He wrote to *Sea Breezes* (see earlier reference in this appendix), and ten months later his letter was published.

I received a most gratifying response [says Baker], one gentleman suggested that the names were switched in wartime to confuse the enemy. Big ships, maybe, but would they do it for small fry like drifters? I wondered. But the man went on to state that both *Golden Line* and *Golden Gift* were Lowestoft-based, and gave me the address of the Lowestoft Port Research Society. They wrote back, quoting the part-owner of *Golden Gift*, that she had been lost in Oban Bay on 6th April 1943. They added that *Golden Line* had been returned to her owners, fished for several years more, and her remains were said to lie in a graveyard of steam drifters at Oulton Broad. And the Great Yarmouth and Gorleston Marine Society kindly sent Phil Baker a picture of *Golden Gift*.

So the *Golden Gift*, steam drifter, built by Richards of Lowestoft in the early 1900s, Registered Number LT706, 89 tons, which had served the Navy as a flare drifter, auxiliary patrol boat and as a stone carrier, lies there in Oban, known to divers as the 'Post Office Wreck', because her position is opposite the Esplanade Post Office. But because of one man's determination we do at least know her real name.

163

Cannon, Anchors, Pins and Bottles

including the way to identify cannon and the people who will do it for you, an investigation into those mysterious 'fins', and good advice on sources for further help.

CANNON

ONE of the features of the amazing growth in skin-diving is the extraordinary number of cannon being found on the sea-bed by divers. From Bouley Bay in Jersey, from Porth Daffach Bay in Wales, from Brighton in Sussex, and from all the other sites mentioned in this book the reports flow in. And they all have the same story to tell—cannon. Cannon lying under water, either singly or in heaps. Some are so encrusted into the sea-bed that divers almost miss spotting them. Others are piled up so obviously that the diver who finds them cannot believe he is the first on the scene.

Some are bronze, like the one found recently by Roy Davis and Brian Smith near Padstow, Cornwall. Most are iron.

This report on the Mewstone Cannon (see Chapter 8) by Dennis Hinchcliffe shows the sort of problems the divers face:

All the cannons are poor specimens in an advanced state of decay. The outlines are not sharp and measurements were therefore difficult to make with accuracy. Cascabels are not visible, but simple spherical pommellions are generally intact. Mouldings, or reinforcements, are only discernible on cannons 11 and 13 and muzzle flare is only present on 13. It is not known whether the absence of the above features is due to general decay and corrosion, or to the design of the guns.

On the advice of the National Maritime Museum, Greenwich, the trunnion positions were carefully checked. This was done by laying a straight edge across the two, and we can confirm that they all are situated well off the centre line. We have not yet been able to find evidence of markings on the trunnions, nor have any gun carriage fastenings been found.

Since the position of the trunnions and the actual size of the guns appear to be the only reliable evidence available for dating purposes, it is interesting to examine the dimensions of guns corresponding to cannons 11 and 13.

A Minnion Ordinary of 1692 had a 3 in bore, a length of 7 feet and projected a 3¼ lb shot. A Service 3 pounder of the Establishment of 1743 was 4 ft 6 in long, with a calibre of 2·91 in. By 1780, new 3 pounders of the same bore were again reduced in length to 3 ft 6 in. Although new 6 pounders

were only 4 ft 4 in long, the bore was 3·7 in. Thus our small cannon, being 4 ft 6 in long with a bore of 3 in, can be dated 1743 to 1870 from the foregoing. There is, of course, no evidence to indicate that the guns are British and the guns could have been made later. Nevertheless, both the Maritime Museum and Mr B. W. Bathe have indicated similar dates from an examination of early rough drawings. Mr Bathe writes, '. . . the dimensions you state correspond closely with those of a normal 3 pounder gun of about 1800. The larger gun is probably a 6 pounder of the same period'.

The most puzzling features of the cannon are the odd-misshapen protrusions. At first we thought that plates had been added to the guns to facilitate their use as ballast, but finding all the trunnions uppermost and the tampion intact on one seemed to indicate an original shipwreck. The wreck of the steamer *Ajax* has provided plentiful iron wreckage in the area and the accretion of some pieces of wrought iron to the cast iron cannon seems a plausible explanation.

To check this theory pieces were removed from the protrusion or 'fin' and trunnion of a cannon. The piece from the trunnion showed a typical cast-iron isotectic structure. The oxidation is not complete and bright metal iron particles still sparkle on the black surface of the polished specimen, which can still be magnetised. The surface is exceedingly porous and drops of water are rapidly absorbed. All this is, of course, typical.

A section of the fin shows a totally different structure. The material was uniformly black or brown and exhibited a distinct cleavage. This is consistent with water penetration along a joint or low impedance path. The forging caused oxides to be present at the junctions of the layers, which would provide an easy path for salt water. It is reasonably certain, therefore, that the fins are wrought iron, and it is difficult to refute the theory of accretion, particularly since there is no pattern to the fin shape or position. All the same, there are some puzzling features since the fins are parallel with the axis of the cannons and there are no other loose pieces or iron wreckage anywhere near the guns.

The 'fins' on cannon found on these old sites is causing a

great deal of controversy among divers and archaeologists. The real trouble is that our documentation of cannon is really not very good. And the men who really know about them (see the end of this appendix) are few in number.

Were the 'fins' part of the cannon or were they added by the action of the sea and corrosion later.

For example, cannon on both the *Association* site and the site of the *Eagle* have 'fins' on them. But whereas Dick Larn tended at first to the idea that these fins were added to the cannon for some reason after the cannon were cast, Roland Morris believes that the 'fins' are caused by the cannon rolling about in heavy seas and damaging themselves. The fins he thinks are some form of iron growth due to corrosion and encrustation at one of the damage points. Morris also points out that only a few of the cannon on such sites have such fins. This, he claims, gives more strength to his theory.

In the report of the Naval Air Command Sub-Aqua Club Isles of Scilly expedition in 1970 (Chapter 6), there is this paragraph about the wreck of H.M.S. *Eagle*:

The most obvious and interesting feature of the site are the 'finned' cannon, and a number of sketches were made to show the different combinations and orientation of these fins. In order to establish that these were in fact metal and not random marine growths, an already badly damaged fin was chipped away, showing clearly that it was made of iron, attached to the cannon and quite substantial . . . .

But in Alan Bax's latest report on the work on the *Coronation* (see Chapter 5) you find this:

The fins of the cannon are also beginning to reveal their secrets. On a dive with American marine archaeologist Peter Throckmorton, the fins of two cannon were carefully 'attacked' with hammer and chisel. It was found that they were as one with the concretion covering the whole of the guns, and no part of the guns themselves. Further, the iron—of a dull grey-black colour—revealed beneath the three-quarter inch layer of concretion appeared to be in good condition. There is, therefore, every hope that if the remainder of the concretion is carefully chiselled away engravings or cast figures will be revealed which may lead to positive identity. . . .'

Fins or no fins, cannon are becoming more and more important to divers. From full identification of their finds, the ship can be dated with some accuracy. Not every cannon—in fact very few—carry the sort of splendid coats-of arms that have been found on the *Association* cannon and those from the *Amsterdam* and *La Trinidad Valencera*. But every cannon, to the expert, can tell a good part of a story. Part of the fascination of cannon is undoubtedly the fact that they feature importantly in such evocative words as 'broadside', but they also hold all the interest that guns have held for mankind—unfortunately—since their invention. Those cannon lying mute on the sea-bed are also still recognizable as weapons of war. In some cases they are still almost ready to fire. It is interesting to note here that Holland and Holland, the gunsmiths, who paid about £3000 for one of the cannon from H.M.S. *Association*, had no difficulty a short time later in firing it—for the first time since the 1700s.

It would be foolish here for me to attempt to tell you all about cannon, even if I could, but I can do better. The two top experts in this country on cannon have agreed that I should give them here as sources for the identification of cannon found by divers.

But before you write to them with details of your cannon find, let me stress one or two important points. First of all, do have the courtesy to include a stamped addressed envelope for their reply. Secondly, I think it is important to quote what the experts say about what they can do—and about what you should do:

Source: Austin C. Carpenter, Esq, Department of the Environment, 1-3 Albert Road, Devonport, Plymouth, Devon, PL2 1AA.

Mr Carpenter has a wide knowledge of ancient armaments, and has already helped many divers, particularly in the West Country, with identification and dating of cannon. While agreeing to act as a source for the identification of cannon, he did say this:

I should like to point out that for many years I have on occasion been sent approximate sizes of guns lying on the sea-bed, which are encrusted with marine growth and concretion, and have been asked to identify same. This is impossible. Occasionally one may find a bronze gun which has remained clean and, with good underwater photographs and good detail of dimensions, one could give a pretty near date and provenance etc. But unless guns are raised from the sea-bed and in most cases cleaned, one cannot honestly give good and genuine identification.

Cast-iron guns are normally better left and not raised as they will, unless put through costly preservation treatment, break down in structure and disintegrate. However, I see no reason why a cast-iron gun could not be raised, cleaned, identified and then returned to its last resting place.

The basic points to note in trying to identify a gun, cast-iron, bronze, or wrought-iron, are as follows:

(1) Length of piece.
(2) Diameter at muzzle.
(3) Diameter at breech.
(4) Size of bore.
(5) Number and position of mouldings.
(6) Shape of cascabel (knob at the breech end).
(7) Length of trunnions and size, their position on the gun in relation to the bore.
(8) Markings on end faces of trunnions.
(9) Coat-of-arms, Iron founders' marks, weights and shot poundage are also in the 'first reinforce', in other

words in the region of one to two feet up the barrel from the breech end.

Source: A. N. Kennard Esq, Assistant Master of the Armouries, New Armouries, H.M. Tower of London, London, E.C.3.

Mr Kennard has a great knowledge of cannon and a great deal of experience of helping divers to identify their finds. He says:

> The help I am able to give divers in identifying cannon depends very largely on the information they provide. If the cannon or cannons are (*a*) well preserved (*b*) clear of accretions and (*c*) carefully described—then one can often provide quite a lot of information.
>
> Unfortunately these three things are very seldom present all together. Very corroded iron guns have sometimes been reduced to little more than a lump of metal, only just recognizable as a gun; others are so covered with marine deposits that the outline is lost, and some divers seem quite unable to describe what they have found in clear terms and do not realize the importance of measurements.

So take note. Take all the measurements you can and supply them to the experts. Help them and they'll help you.

Here are the terms mostly used in describing cannon (see Fig. 16):

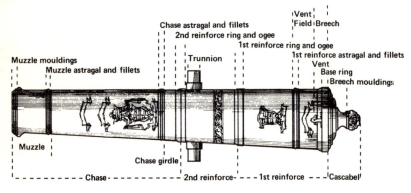

FIG. 16. The parts of a cannon
Based on a 'Gus' drawing

Bore: The inside of the barrel along which the cannon-ball is shot.

Bore diameter: The distance across the bore, and can be taken at the muzzle.

The bore length: The distance along the inside of the cannon from the muzzle to where the bore finishes just behind the touchholes.

Breech: The rear end of the cannon between the cascabel and the touchhole.

Calibre: The internal diameter of the bore. A 3-inch gun would have a bore three inches across. Also used as a ratio of bore to bore length—*i.e.*, 30-calibre cannon would be a cannon whose bore-length was thirty times its bore-diameter. So a 3-inch 30-calibre gun would have a bore-length of 90 inches (30 × 3).

Cannon: A general term to denote a muzzle-loading gun. However, a cannon was also a particular type of ordnance, as opposed to, say, a culverin, during the sixteenth century.

Cascabel: The handle-like protuberance at the back end of the cannon rather like a door-knob, occasionally pierced with a hole to enable the cannon to be fired with a hot iron, or decorated with iron loops to enable training-ropes to be fixed.

Chase: The front half or third of the gun-barrel. The part in front of the trunnions. The area between the breech and the first reinforcing ring was known as the First Reinforce, and the area between the first reinforcing ring and the second reinforcing ring was known as the Second Reinforce.

Chase diameter: The diameter of the outside of the gun-barrel measured behind the muzzle mouldings.

Dolphins: Ornamented handles styled as dolphins, placed at the point of balance to enable the cannon to be lifted.

Elevation: The angle between the horizontal and the highest point to which the muzzle can be raised.

Grommet: A rope ring placed in the bore after the cannon-ball to retain the ball when the cannon is moved.

Lay or Train: To aim a cannon.

Length: The overall distance between the front and back of the cannon, but not including the cascabel.

Muzzle: The front end of the cannon from which the ball emerges.

Point Blank: The point where the ball would first strike when fired from a horizontal bore on level ground.

Quoin: A wedge placed under the breech of the cannon to alter its elevation.

Reinforcing Rings: Really decorations dating back to the days when cannon were bound in the manner of barrels—*i.e.*, the early Lombards. Astragals and fillets are small mouldings going around the cannon in the same manner as the reinforcing rings. They served no purpose other than decoration. Reinforcing rings were cast with the cannon, and not applied after casting.

Touch-hole: Or vent. A hole into the bore of the cannon from the outside, placed at the back of the breech-end of the gun to enable the powder to be ignited.

Trajectory: The path taken by a ball from the cannon's mouth to its target. The trajectory is curved.

Trunnions: Two integral parts of the cannon, one on either side, placed about midway along the cannon to facilitate the vertical movement of the barrel. They are cast with the gun, and are usually the same diameter as the bore of the gun.

Vent-field diameter: The diameter on the outside of the gun-barrel at the touch-hole.

Windage: The difference between the diameter of the shot and the diameter of the bore.

From the 1500s, cannon improved until on land each weapon could be used and moved by two horses and three men. Cartridges appeared, and these saved loading time by allowing the charge to be rammed rather than ladled. Later fixed ammunition with ball attached to the cartridges enabled guns to be fired even more rapidly. As cannon improved, so artillery units became more important to the campaigner, and the whole style of battle changed. As the cartridges changed, so did the shot. All sorts of variation came into use, from grape-shot, which was like a little bag with a wooden core around which were clustered musket-balls—rather like grapes on a bunch—to powder-filled and fused shells that exploded in the air or at the target. For sea warfare there was chain shot, which was two round shot joined by a short length of chain, and bar-shot, which was a divided shot with a bar holding the two hemispheres apart, which were fired to break an enemy's rigging or masts. Canister-shot was similar to grape, but was contained in a can or case. Rifling of cannon-barrels, although understood long before, did not come into general use until the middle 1800s.

During the Armada campaign the cannon were of three main types. Luis Collado, Spanish mathematician and Royal Engineer to His Most Catholic Majesty, agreed with this grading, and called culverins and sakers, cannon of the first class; cannon, cannon of the second class; and periers or pedreros, cannon of the third class. First-class cannon were long pieces that could strike the enemy from long range, battering cannon of the second class were used to break down walls and smash other cannon batteries; while third-class cannon were defence cannon, for installation in shore batteries against ships or advancing troops.

From now on the technique of cannon-manufacture becomes very complicated. To illustrate this point, here is a list of the principal English guns of the sixteenth century, together with their weights:

Name	Weight (in pounds)
Rabinet	300
Serpentine	400
Falconet	500
Falcon	680
Minion	1050
Saker	1400
Culverin bastard	3000
Demi-culverin	3400
Pedrero	3800
Basilisk	4000
Demi-cannon	4000
Bastard cannon	4500
Culverin	4840
Cannon serpentine	5500
Cannon	6000
Cannon royal	8000

Even with this sort of list the diver who finds cannon must rely heavily on the expert, for a Spanish list of first-class cannon for the same period contains names like *esmeril; pasavolente; sacre; moyana; culebrina; doble culebrina* . . . and what diver would be brave enough to put a name to one cannon among so many!

Markings are, of course, important. English cannon bore the crowned Tudor rose and/or the broad arrow of the Navy. French cannon had cascabels in the shape of a tulip. Spanish cannon had markings like a pancake. But none of these markings were uniform—and can only be used as a rough guide. Study the trunnions particularly carefully. Sometimes, the maker's mark can be found there. (See Chapter 8.)

There is more confusion when you study other lists of cannon of approximately the same date. Captain John Smith (of Pocahontas fame) in his *Sea Grammar* published in 1627 (see Bibliography) lists the guns he would put into 'A Table of Proportion for the weight and shooting of great Ordnance' like this:

Rabonet, 300 pounds, Sarpentine, 400, Faulconet, 500, Faulcon, 660 (and another Faulcon of 800), Minion, 1000, Sacre, 1400, Bastard Culvering, 3000, Demy Culvering, 3400, Basilisco, 4000, Culvering, 4500, Canon Petro, 3000, Demy Canon, 4000, Bastard Canon, 4500, Canon Serpentine, 5500, Canon, 6000, Canon Royall, 8000.

Incidentally, Smith's book is a mine of information about shot, cannon and the whole art of shooting in those days.

So I have included in the Bibliography some books—your local library may have to get them for you—which can help you about cannon, but the information is spread far and wide. So far and so wide, in fact, that anyone who was to write the complete book about cannon would earn a lot of people's grateful thanks.

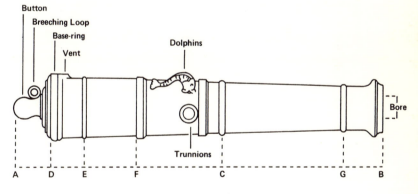

FIG. 17. The way to measure your cannon

PINS

Earlier on in Appendix 1 I mentioned the pins which Dick Larn found in his wreck in Cornwall, and the great help given by Newey Goodman, Ltd., of Robin Hood Lane, Hall Green, Birmingham 28. Newey Goodman have in fact produced a short account of 'the history, location and manufacturing problems and developments in the pin industry'. With their permission I am reproducing a short extract from that account here. It shows just how much information can be concealed by the head of a pin!

The origin of the pin can be traced back as far as 26,000 to 30,000 B.C. Quite naturally, the first tools of man were hunting implements, and very soon many uses were found for a small pointed pin made from many kinds of materials. Thorns such as agave, found in Mexico, bones from prehistoric fish and reptiles and flint have been found in furs and garments traced back as far as the Lower Palaeolithic Age.

Later, in the Upper Palaeolithic Age, the pins were often more artistically shaped and carved by hand; crude metal pins have been found by archaeologists from the Bronze and Iron Ages.

Roman pins were quite often hand-forged iron spikes with elaborate heads. These were used not only for domestic purposes, but also had a fashion and monetary value.

Catherine Howard has been credited as the first person to introduce brass pins into England from France, although in the 14th Century Edward III ordered 12,000 pins to be delivered to Princess Joan and in 1483 Richard III prohibited by statute the import of pins, i.e. bone, boxwood, ivory etc.

In 1400, the Duchess of Orleans purchased from John Breconnier '500 de la facon d'Angleterre' indicating that English pins were exported to France on this early occasion.

Henry VII's Queen, Elizabeth of York, bought 300 pins at 4d per 100 and, considering a sheep cost 20d, it indicates the value of this article in those days. In 1543 Henry VIII made the first step towards controlling the quality of pins: 'That no person shall put to sale any pinnes but only as shall be double headed and have the heads soldered fast to the shank of the pins, well smoothed, the shank well shapen, the point well and round, filed, canted and sharpened'.

In 'Hamlet' appear the words 'I do not set my life at a pin's fee' and to show just how high that fee may have been, Addison 100 years later commented 'What would a foreigner think of a lover giving up his mistress because he was unwilling to keep her in pins'—i.e. £500–600 per year.

A guild of pinners was established in London in 1356 and there are records of a similar guild in Bristol in 1497. Around the early 17th Century, there was an increasing requirement by parishes for means of employing their poor. An experiment of combining parishes to one corporate body in Bristol employing the paupers of the workhouse in the pin industry proved very successful. From 1608–1626 John Tilsley employed 1500 people in Bristol and at this time a Protection Act 'fobidding the import of pins except by the pinners themselves' was passed.

The Workhouse Method spread to Gloucestershire in 1626, an agreement being made between John Tilsley and the Mayor of Gloucester. During the 18th Century Pin Mills moved into the Gloucestershire valleys to take advantage of water power. During the 19th Century the industry moved to Birmingham because of its better economical and geographical location and the use of steam power.

The origin of the term 'pin money' has never been clearly established. Charles I renewed import restrictions, receiving £500 per year in return, this money he then gave to Henrietta Maria as part of her income, or 'pin money'.

In Henry VIII's reign pins could only be obtained in London on two days in January. The women, therefore, had to save money throughout the year to buy their pins. Their savings have been defined as 'pin money'.

In 1636, the Rylands family established a small firm in Birmingham. Charles II confirmed the Pin Charter, undertaking to provide the Pinners with £20,000 of wire on condition that they provide £70,000 worth of ordnance to the Master of Ordnance half-yearly.

Pins at this time were still very highly valued, and in fact almost headed the list amongst the goods and chattels of a certain Lettice, Countess of Leicester.

Realising their dependence upon England for manufactured goods, in 1775 the State Of Carolina in America offered prizes for native-made pins and needles.

In 1785 Samual Rylands transferred his business to his cousin, Mr Thomas Phipson & Son. About this time, Adam Smith, in his now classic book 'The Wealth of Nations' described at length the eighteen distinct operations carried out by a pin craftsman and how, by detailing one craftsman to each operation, production was increased from 20 to 4800 pins per man per day. This equals approximately 12 lb per day.

In 1797 the first record of a Patent (No. 2182) for the pin industry appears. This was brought out by Timothy Harris who headed . . . pins by placing the shank in a mould and pouring in lead. They were then dipped into sulphuric acid, rinsed, scoured in grain tin, rod argol and water, copper coated by immersion in copper sulphate solution and finally whitened by being placed in a copper vessel containing warm water argo or Cream of Tartar.

In 1812 the Howe Manufacturing Co., was established in Birmingham, Connecticut, making pins, adding another similarity to the two industrial cities bearing the same name. In 1817 Seth Hunt placed a Patent for a machine making solid headed pins, but this was not very successful. In 1824 an American, Lemuel W. Wright from Massachusetts, arrived in England and patented a solid headed pin machine, Patent No. 4955. He also established a business in Lambeth and later moved to Stroud. The first solid headed pin was sold in London in 1833. Wright sold his Patent to Daniel Foot Tayler who started a mill at Lightpool Mill near Stroud, but later went in to liquidation. The stock was purchased by John Alfred Williams, who moved the machinery to a 2½ acre of factory at Newhall Works, George Street, Birmingham, where it has since been modernised.

The industry is now established in Gloucestershire and Birmingham using machines of various types, many of which have been continually developed until today pins are made wholly by one machine from a coil of wire, leaving only the finishing and packing processes to be completed.

ANCHORS

Anchors are the other large objects besides cannon which you might expect to find on a shipwreck site. On occasions they can tell more about the ship than the cannon she carried, which might have been prizes. The expert will want to know whether the arms are straight or curved, whether the cross-section of the blade is rectangular or round, what the shank is like, what the palm is like and so on. And above all he will want dimensions.

For further information contact either the National Maritime Museum or the Science Museum.

And one last thought while on the subject of items you find on wrecks—don't throw that empty bottle aside. Old bottles are an excellent aid to dating your wreck, and collectors will give good money if your bottle turns out to be one of the rare ones.

Very briefly: Bottles earlier than the middle 18th century tend to be short, fat and flat bottomed with long necks.

Bottles with pointed bottoms were patented in 1814 by William Hamilton and are called—of course—Hamiltons.

Bottles with a glass marble in the neck were introduced in 1875 by Hiram Codd. Codds were used for aerated waters and the marble was held up by the gas pressure against a rubber ring so sealing the bottlle.

Hamiltons can have Codd necks. All bottles from wrecks tend to be exceptionally fragile. Take care.

APPENDIX 3

The Diver and the Law

including the way a diver can protect his wreck, how he stands legally about diving on other people's wrecks, the law's shortcomings and how it could be improved.

THE law, as we all know, is an ass, particularly when we come into contact with it ourselves. And in these modern times when it is legal to park your car at a meter so long as it is working, but illegal when that same meter has a bag over its head saying out of order, nothing that I can tell you about the strange workings of the law will surprise you.

But the law about parking is a classic example of legal clarity when compared with the laws about wrecks. They are a maze, through which the wreck detective must tread extremely warily. The wreck hunter bent on salvage or recovery of items from a sunken wreck should show even more care where he places his feet, for he is entering an uncharted minefield.

General guidance is all that I can offer you here. For fine legal definition you should turn to Halsbury's Laws of England (third edition, 1961), Volume 35, Shipping and Navigation. And may the Lord have mercy on your soul!

All wrecks belong to someone. That is the first point of general guidance—and you should therefore make every effort to trace who that someone is before taking anything, anything at all, from a wreck.

Second point: Anything found on a wreck or in the sea must be reported to the local Receiver of Wreck at the nearest Custom House.

You have found a wreck. For the moment let us assume that it is a fairly modern one. It is probable that the ship and her cargo were covered by insurance. When she sank claims for total loss may well have been paid. In that case it is likely that the rights in this particular ship will still belong to the underwriters concerned, and they are often willing to sell the rights in that wreck and her cargo for a purely nominal sum (around the £100–£200 mark). Lloyd's will probably be able to help you to trace the underwriters (see Appendix 1). If she was a wartime casualty try the Board of Trade, War Risk Insurance Office (see Appendix 1).

You therefore conclude an agreement with the underwriters or owners, and you decide to do some small salvage work. Now you should write to the General Lighthouse Authority concerned in case your salvage operation could be classified as a danger to navigation. The addresses are: The Secretary, Trinity House, London, E.C.3; The Secretary, Commissioners of Irish Lights, 16 Lower Pembroke Street, Box 73, Dublin 2; The General Manager and Secretary, Northern Lighthouse Board, 84 George Street, Edinburgh, Scotland.

And now the Merchant Shipping Act of 1894 comes into the picture. You must bear in mind that the Act was drawn up to cover situations of that day and age—and could take no allowance for the 1970s and the boom in skin-diving (it would have taken a legal Jules Verne to have visualized such a thing, and laws are not made by such creatures!).

Section 518 of the Act reads:

Where any person finds or takes possession of any wreck within the limits of the United Kingdom he shall—

(*a*) if he is the owner thereof, give notice to the receiver of the district stating that he has found or taken possession of the same and describing the marks by which the same may be recognized;

(*b*) if he is not the owner thereof, as soon as possible deliver the same to the receiver of the district: and if any person fails without reasonable cause to comply with this section, he shall, for each offence, be liable to a fine not exceeding one hundred pounds, and shall, in addition, if he is not the owner, forfeit any claim to salvage, and shall be liable to pay to the owner of the wreck if it is claimed, or, if it is unclaimed to the person entitled to same, double the value thereof, to be recovered in the same way as a fine or a like amount under the Act.

The Act, of course, has to define what is meant by wreck and decided that it included jetsam, flotsam, lagan and derelicts found in or on the shores of the sea or any tidal water. Which is pretty sweeping, especially as jetsam covers all objects which have been thrown overboard from a ship that later sinks, flotsam covers the objects which remain afloat after a ship has sunk, lagan means objects that have been thrown overboard attached to a buoy or marker, and a derelict is a vessel that has been abandoned without hope of return.

Section 525 of the Act provides for the disposal of unclaimed wreck and reads:

Where no owner establishes a claim to any wreck, found in the United Kingdom and in the possession of a receiver, within one year after it came into his possession, the wreck shall be dealt with as follows:

(1) If the wreck is claimed by any admiral, vice-admiral, lord of a manor, heritable proprietor, or other person who has delivered such a statement to the receiver as hereinbefore provided, and has proved to the satisfaction of the receiver his title to receive unclaimed wreck found at the place where that wreck was found, the wreck after payment of all expenses, costs, fees and salvage due in respect thereof, shall be delivered to him;

(2) If the wreck is not claimed by any admiral, vice-admiral, lord of a manor, heritable proprietor, or other person as aforesaid, the receiver shall sell the same and shall pay the proceeds of the sale (after deducting therefrom the expenses of the sale, and any other expenses incurred by him, and his fees, and paying thereout to the salvors such amounts of salvage as the Board of Trade may in each case, or by general rule, determine) for the benefit of the Crown, as follows: (that is to say),

(a) the wreck is claimed in right of Her Majesty's duchy of Lancaster, to the Receiver-General of that duchy or his deputies, as part of the revenues of the duchy;

(b) If the wreck is claimed in right of the duchy of Cornwall, to the Receiver-General of the duchy or his deputies as part of the revenues of the duchy; and

(c) If the wreck is not so claimed, the receiver shall pay the proceeds of sale after the decease of Her present Majesty to her heirs and successors.

You will see from the above that it is possible to claim the wreck after a year, or if it is not claimed you can be granted salvage. But all these legal matters are rather overwhelming to the amateur, and to avoid them it is possible to purchase a wreck on the bottom, and then, as legal owner, set about taking it apart piece by piece to your heart's content. However, you are not out of the wood yet, as the law regards wrecks with a very careful eye, and it becomes an offence to salve only part of a wreck and leave the remains behind, for as an owner you are responsible for your wreck, and should another vessel be damaged or sunk by it, then you would be liable for the damage done. A rather worrying thought if you happened to be responsible for the loss of a liner or an aircraft-carrier!

Although there are these responsibilities, it is quite pleasant to be the owner of a ship, even though that ship is at present on the bottom of the sea. From time to time the Admiralty offer ships for sale, and it is possible to tender for them. Here again rules and regulations are produced to distress the prospective buyer, but these are not quite so bad. However, the Admiralty always retain the right of inspection of the wreck, and will at all times have access to the wreck as Licensees of the Purchaser. Also no cash, or notes, or personal effects, or fittings of a confidential nature, are included in the sale. So should you discover a chest of Navy Pay in your recently acquired . . . hulk, then you are, regrettably, bound to hand it

over to their Lordships. Remember this is general advice, and there have been exceptions to this.

The Act of 1894 in fact lays down that all wreck recovered inside territorial waters (or recovered outside and brought inside) must be delivered to the nearest Receiver of Wreck as soon as possible. If all goes smoothly the salvor will collect some sort of award of between 30 and 50 per cent of the value or the same percentage of the proceeds of the sale of the material recovered.

There is nothing in the Act to prevent anyone diving on a wreck or raising material from it provided he declares all his finds as soon as possible to the local Receiver of Wreck. Indeed Alan Bax of the Committee for Nautical Archaeology feels that the Act is utterly useless from the point of view of safeguarding ancient wrecks against trespass or damage and not worth much more when it comes to protecting modern wrecks.

In his view the two main shortcomings of the Act in protecting ancient wrecks from underwater looting are firstly, that the black market sale of recovered material, like ancient coins, at an immediate 100 per cent reward is so much more attractive than the official 30 per cent after protracted negotiations; and secondly that it does not prevent underwater trespass.

In addition to this the Receiver of Wreck cannot do anything else than accept material handed to him, regardless of its ownership, historic worth or the fact that the contract for salvage of the ship may be someone else's.

Though Alan Bax did not say so, I know that the sort of thing he has in mind in the first complaint about abuse of the Act is the fact that coins from H.M.S. *Association* were openly on sale in Amsterdam within a short period of the wreck of Sir Cloudesley's ship being found and the general gold rush taking place.

And the unsatisfactory state of the law on wrecks was further highlighted recently when the Isles of Scilly magistrates accepted a defence argument that an ancient pair of ship's dividers found on the sea-bed were the personal property of an unknown mariner, could not be proved to be from a shipwreck, and were therefore outside the provision of the Merchant Shipping Act of 1894.

In a powerful article in *Sub-Aqua World*, Alan Bax wrote:

Required: (1) A means of controlling salvage, that is, man-made material found on the sea-bed and shore, be it ancient or modern. The boot should be placed on the other foot, salvor should require permission or licence to salve, rather than owners need a court injunction to protect their own property.

(2) An increase in salvage awards for the recovery of CROWN material—i.e. that which reverts after one year when no owner appears: otherwise illegal transactions will continue to be exceedingly attractive.

The law, even with the strongest parliamentary backing, can only be amended after some years. I feel I have sounded somewhat pessimistic and that it would appear that there is little that can be done to protect a find or property underwater.

This is indeed partly true, for as I have already indicated, the law is in desperate need of amendment. However, there are various steps which can be taken by the finder of ancient or potentially ancient material and they are:

(1) Obtain public support.
(2) Consult the Committee for Nautical Archaeology.
(3) Establish himself as FIRST SALVOR.
(4) Purchase the wreck.
(5) Lease the sea-bed.

I would like to go on to discuss these points in turn as they concern the safeguarding of Ancient Wreck. (As a rough guide this is wreck over 100 years old, i.e. before 1870, but this is not to say that a vessel built in 1825 and lost in 1890 is not of interest.)

One point that must be kept in mind throughout these discussions is that there is no urgency to recover wreck which has settled comfortably into the sea-bed over at least a century. Owners are seldom readily found and salvors are even more rarely asked to salve such wreck, they do so in their own interests whatever they may be! It is at this point, too, that the position of the Admiralty or Ministry of Defence (Navy)—MOD (Navy)—should be made clear. It is nothing more than that of a rather large and well established ship-owner.

I consider that public support is the major factor, when protection of historically valuable material is considered.

History concerns us all, as the modern trend to study 'People' as opposed to those awful impersonal Kings and Queens readily shows.

We are and always have been a sea-faring nation. The remains of ships and buildings round our coasts can provide historians with facts concerning maritime people and events. The interpretation of these facts can be passed on to us, the people of today, and so enable us to learn from the lessons of the past. This interpretation is only worthwhile if the people of today would like to have it, for it will cost money.

Public support is also needed for two other reasons. One, so that present day vandals are not condoned for work, which is nothing more nor less than destruction of valuable historic material. Finders of material should, I recommend, publicise their intention to investigate a site by every means at their disposal. Everyone will then know of their intention, and if it is a good one, it will almost certainly obtain public sympathy and an official smile, if not sanction. Factors which may prove vital in the event of on-site interference.

Underwater archaeologists also have a responsibility in this matter, for they must publish their interpretation of finds and show just what can be made of the clues beneath the sea. At the same time illustrating that their standard of work can be as high as that on land, and that there is no excuse for destruction by unconsidered lifting. Public outcry against ill-considered work will be one of its major deterrents.

The second reason is that before money is spent on the much-needed amendment to the law, and then on the means to implement it, the public must consider that such money is well spent. So when it comes to protecting ancient wreck, our first task is to persuade everyone that such protection matters.

The First Salvor. The finder is able to take possession of wreck and then obtain restraining injunctions against subsequent salvors.

The rules which govern this right of the 'first salvor' are established in a legal precedent which concerned the salvage of the merchant vessel *Tubania* in 1922.

The most important aspect to the amateur finder is 'taking possession'. The law is inevitably difficult and arguable, but I feel that if the following few steps are taken, they go a long way towards establishing possession.

1. Publicise your intentions—again those who are not on the side of the righteous, fight shy of publicity.

2. Specifically inform the Receiver of Wreck and Coast Guard of your intentions.

3. Keep a thorough and accurate record of your work on site.

4. Establish equipment underwater on site.

N.B.—In archaeological work, survey is required long before any excavation, and the lines and bench arcs required for this work are ideal to establish the area which is of interest to you.

There are two other comments I would make:

1. That the FIRST SALVOR has some responsibility to the owner. Thus if the method of work or competence of salvor is in doubt, the owner can again obtain an injunction to stop him working.

2. Finally the nigger in the woodpile—COSTS. Even if the FIRST SALVOR wins his case, and obtains an injunction, the chances are that he must pay his own legal costs. These can mount up and regrettably, I doubt if the finder would be given legal aid!

Here perhaps is the right place to mention 'salvage contracts'. If the owner of the wreck is known, a would-be salvor would do well to draw up a contract with him. The salvage award so agreed would hopefully be higher than the normal 30% arbitrated by the Receiver. Such a contract cannot however give exclusive rights to dive on a wreck, and so is of no value in protecting ancient material, although on any site it is obviously better to have one, because even on an archaeological site, some material will eventually be lifted, and it is wise that its disposal is agreed well ahead.

Purchase of Wreck. This is an obvious step for any finder; it gives him a right to control other salvors and to keep all material from a site and dispose of it as he will. The problem with ancient wreck is its identification and proof of ownership.

Warships back to the 17th century, and merchant vessels back to the 18th century can be traced, but before these dates the records are very sparse.

Leasing the Sea-bed. The Crown owns the sea-bed from the line of Mean Low Water Springs to the limit of territorial waters, except for some areas—which by ancient right belongs to others, e.g. the Duchy of Cornwall owns the sea-bed of Plymouth Harbour.

The sea-bed belonging to the Crown, is administered by the Crown State Commissioners, and it is they, for instance, who have controlled the allocation of drilling rights in the North and Irish Seas.

The sea-bed in the area of a valuable ancient wreck has been leased by the Commissioners to one or two responsible bodies, on the recommendation of the Committee for Nautical Archaeology, to whom application should first be made. Its worth as a protective measure for wreck or other ancient material has yet to be determined legally.

Finally, I would like to point out a couple of differences between the Law of the Land and Sea.

On land, material discovered which is of archaeological worth may be 'scheduled' by the Ancient Monuments Division of the Ministry of Public Buildings and Works, which has funds and power to purchase grounds and finds, in order to prevent their destruction. There is no equivalent law which permits the scheduling of similar underwater finds. The other land rule, which is very often misconstrued as being relevant underwater, is that of Treasure Trove. This rule states roughly that the finder of ancient material which was hidden, as opposed to lost on land, receives the full market value of the material as found, tax free! This rule makes the likely 30% salvage award for a similar underwater find look a trifle unsatisfactory.

The Law as it might be. The following notes, outline a scheme which I appreciate is by no means perfect. I hope though that it will stimulate a response from the possible Finder, Salvor, Owner, Historian or Archaeologist. The Committee for Nautical Archaeology are very much concerned with rationalising the present situation. This scheme is intended to supplement the 1894 Act, the major change being, that no material is to be recovered without the authority of the Receiver of Wreck. It then establishes a licensing and scheduling system, whereby the recovery of material may be controlled.

The scheme as shown would be administered by the Board of Trade, through the Receivers and enforced by the Coastguard. In particular the fines mentioned in the 1894 Act need to be greatly increased.

Notes:

1. 'Salvage Material' includes wreck as at present defined and any man-made article found below MLWS.

2. Ownerless material to be advertised as at present, BUT after one year it reverts to the FINDER provided he is willing to pay all Crown expenses plus a fee of 10% of the market value of the material.

3. Undated material is treated as being over 100 years old.

4. Declaration to the Receiver automatically gives the finder opportunity for either a contract with the owner or ownership (note 2). As material may not be lifted without authority from the Receiver, finders' and owners' exclusive rights are automatically recognized in law.

5. Recovery may only take place on scheduled wreck on authority of the Receiver of Wreck by persons approved by the CNA.

6. If a contract is not agreed between finder and owner within 12 months of declaration then the finder's rights cease.

7. The finder of a scheduled material will be eligible for a reward of 75% of the market value of all that which is recovered irrespective of licence.

Licences. To be of three types:

(*a*) Professional—Issued by the BOT on an annual basis, authorizing the recovery of material from up to 100 wrecks, provided contracts have been agreed with the owners. The cost of the licence being such that it establishes the professional status of the applicant—say £250.

(*b*) Special—Granted FREE to a suitable applicant, recommended by the Committee for Nautical Archaeology, for a period of three years, for the excavation of a scheduled wreck. Issued by the BOT.

(*c*) Temporary—Issued to a person making a chance find for the recovery of material from one wreck only. One person or group of persons may hold only four such licences at any one time. Cost £25 per licence, valid for one year.

Alan Bax's suggestions are worth careful study, for there is little doubt of the need for some revision of the law as it now stands. At last this seems to have penetrated into Ministerial thinking. In March 1970 Mr John Nott, M.P., tabled amendments to the Merchant Shipping Act. His amendments sought to prohibit people interfering with historic wrecks unless they had been authorized by the Board of Trade to excavate or remove such wrecks.

But the Minister thought the matter too complex to be dealt with at that time, and said that the legislation would be examined in detail, with a view to protecting historic wrecks. On this basis Mr Nott withdrew his amendments.

Later on that year the Minister of State, Board of Trade, set up a committee with these terms of reference:

To review the revisions of the Merchant Shipping Acts dealing with wreck and with the functions of Receivers of Wreck; to consider what changes are desirable in the law on wreck in the light of modern conditions and, in particular, for the purpose of protecting wreck of historical or archaeological interest; and to make recommendations.

So we may get some new laws soon to replace those that did not and could not envisage such a thing as an Aqualung diver— let alone a wreck detective!

Bibliography

including those books you ought to have read, those you should read, and those that ought to be on your bookshelf.

THIS bibliography is short. Short, because at the time of publication of this book there were very few books that were directly or indirectly concerned with underwater work on wrecks around the coasts of Britain. I have included some Mediterranean diving books, but only because they contain information about first principles of archaeological work under water. There are no how-to-dive books in this list, as any bookshop will be able to supply such titles. Anyway, you can't learn to dive from books—only by receiving proper instruction, for which you should join the British Sub-Aqua Club.

The Wreck on the Half-Moon Reef. Hugh Edwards (Robert Hale, 1971). Contains good information on the Dutch East India Company and their ships.

The Wreck Hunters. Roger Jefferis and Kendall McDonald (Harrap, 1966). Out of print, but contains a great number of British wreck stories and detail of the diving done on them.

Shipwrecks Around Britain. A diver's guide. Leo Zanelli (Kaye and Ward, 1970). Contains precise locations of four hundred wrecks around our coasts.

Nautical Archaeology. Bill St John Wilkes (David and Charles, 1971). Practical guide to underwater archaeology, particularly wreck survey. Good list of sources. Preservation etc.

The Defeat of the Spanish Armada. Garrett Mattingly (Pelican). One of the best-researched books on the Spanish Armada you can find.

Cornish Shipwrecks. Richard Larn and Clive Carter. (David and Charles, 1969-71). Three volumes covering the North Coast, the South Coast, the Isles of Scilly. Excellent reference books to Cornish wrecks.

The Underwater Book. Kendall McDonald (Pelham, 1968). Collection of reports of the work done by British divers around our coasts, includes wrecks.

The Second Underwater Book. Kendall McDonald (Pelham, 1970). More stories of British divers. More wrecks too.

The Deepest Days. Robert Stenuit (Hodder and Stoughton, 1967). Tells the story of the really deep diving in the life of the man who discovered the *Girona*.

History Under the Sea. Mendel Peterson (David and Charles, 1969). Until recently this was the only reference book available to divers on the preservation and identification of objects recovered from the sea.

The Lost Land. John Dunbar. (Collins, 1958). Tells the story of early wreck diving attempts in the Scillies, particularly the search for the *Colossus*.

Oil and Water. Edward Cowan (William Kimber, 1969). Full documentation of the loss and oil-on-the-beaches disaster of the *Torrey Canyon*.

Island Treasure. Roland Morris (Hutchinson, 1969). His own story of the *Association* and the recoveries by divers from her.

Deep-Water Archaeology. Frédéric Dumas. (Routledge and Kegan Paul, 1962.) Mediterranean-slanted, but useful for airlift and other equipment details.

A Sea Grammar. Captain John Smith (Michael Joseph, 1970). First published in London in 1627, this was a sort of handbook for young seamen. Invaluable for understanding ships and life at sea for the period, this edition is edited by Kermit Goell and is full of useful footnotes.

The British Sailor. Peter Kemp (Dent, 1970). Again a useful book for understanding the background to the Briton's life at sea. A social history of British seamen through the ages.

Samuel Pepys. Arthur Bryant (Collins). A series of books, particularly 'The Saviour of the Navy' (1967), which fill in the background to the ships of the period.

Shipbuilders of the Thames and Medway. Philip Banbury (David and Charles, 1971). Covers the period from the Tudors onwards. Valuable for the lists of ships built as well as more detailed material.

Marine Archaeology. Joan du Plat Taylor (Hutchinson, 1965). All Mediterranean underwater work, but is important because of the way it shows the form in which surveys, excavations and drawings should be presented.

Archaeology Under Water. George F. Bass (Thames and Hudson, 1966). Covers mostly Mediterranean work, but is also useful for its technical chapters on excavation and the equipment needed.

Camera Underwater. Horace Dobbs (Focal Press, 1962). How-to-do-it book on underwater photography—and you need to know how to take pictures of your finds *in situ*.

Photography on Expeditions. D. H. O. John (Focal Press, 1965). For the same reason as above. Has a special section on underwater photography.

Camera Below. Frey and Tzimoulis. (Association Press, U.S.A., 1968.) Another very good book on taking pictures underwater.

Guns. Dudley Pope. (Weidenfeld and Nicolson, 1965; Spring Books, 1969.) Wonderfully illustrated book with a great deal of useful information about cannon for the diver.

Pieces of Eight. Kip Wagner. (Longmans, 1967.) Just for dreaming—the story of the man who really did find a Spanish treasure fleet.

Finders Losers. Jack Slack. (Hutchinson, 1968.) A dreadful warning about what could happen if you did find that Spanish treasure ship on a dive.

The Ancient Mariners. Lionel Casson. (Gollancz, 1959.) Splendidly readable book about the very early seaman and his ships.

History Under the Sea. Alexander McKee. (Hutchinson, 1968.) A very good reference book, laced with the author's own experiences, about underwater archaeology, some of it around the coasts of Britain.

Vasa, The King's Ship. Bengt Ohrelius (Cassell, 1962). The story of the raising of the ship which sank in 1628.

The Lost Ships. Peter Throckmorton (Cape, 1965). Very readable story of the author's discovery of ancient shipwrecks off Turkey.

Under the Mediterranean. Honor Frost. (Routledge and Kegan Paul, 1963.) As the title says, but useful for techniques and early anchor material.

Armada Guns. Michael Lewis (Allen and Unwin, 1961). As this is sub-titled 'A Comparative study of English and Spanish Armament', there's no more to be said.

The Mortar Wreck at Mellieha Bay. Honor Frost. (Appetron Press, 1969.) Important for techniques including methods of fixing site.

The Divers' Swimline Search. Commander J. Grattan. (British Sub-Aqua Club Paper No. 2.) The full description of the search method which found the *Santa Maria de la Rosa*—and how to apply it to searching for other lost wrecks.

Wasa. Anders Franzen. (Nanstedt and Bonnier, Stockholm, 1964.) Another book about the famous ship. This time by the diver who found her.

The Ship. Bjorn Landstrom (Allen and Unwin, 1961.) A fine book which traces the evolution of the ship through the ages.

The Dutch Seaborne Empire. C. R. Boxer (Hutchinson, 1965.) You'll need this as background the day you find another lost Dutch East Indiaman.

Gunfounders of England. C. Ffoulkes (Cambridge University Press, 1969). Vital for cannon information.

Practical Sea-Gunner's Companion. William Mountaine. Published in London in 1747. Can be seen at National Maritime Museum.

A Treatise of Artillery. John Muller. Published in London in 1768. Can be seen at National Maritime Museum.

A Treatise on Ships' Anchors. George Cotsell. Published 1856. Can be seen at British Museum.

Surveying in Archaeology Underwater. P. Throckmorton, and others. (Quaritch, 1969.) Very valuable for detailed information as titled.

What to Do with Your Wreck
When You Find Her

including sound advice from Joan du Plat Taylor
of the Committee for Nautical Archaeology.

JOAN du Plat Taylor, one of the founder members of the Committee for Nautical Archaeology, has always been interested in—and a great help to—divers of all nationalities. She has listened to their tales of discovery with much patience—divers often tend to ramble when they are on their favourite subject (diving)—and has advised them with great skill about those same discoveries. It has often been largely due to her *sympatique* that divers have shown items from the sea-bed that would otherwise have been lost for ever on some 'trophy' shelf.

So I am especially grateful to her for the time she has taken in preparing this article on the recording of underwater discoveries:

In recent years many ancient wrecks have been noted by divers and more are being rapidly discovered. Further, isolated finds such as stone anchors, pottery items and other objects which may indicate the existence of an anchorage are of interest to archaeologists, not only in themselves, but particularly for the places in which they are found; as these may indicate stopping places on ancient trade routes.

The Committee for Nautical Archaeology has, from the first, advocated the proper recording of these discoveries and sites, in order that no scrap of information of archaeological interest should be lost. A questionnaire was originally designed for preliminary reports, but since the inception of SNAP, divers have been able to learn how to make a preliminary survey of a wreck, or other site with underwater remains.

Though this type of survey may warrant the raising of one or two objects for identification, it does *not* constitute training in excavation. This should only be undertaken with a thorough knowledge of archaeological procedures, in the first instance preferably gained on a land. But before excavation, a suitable wreck, worthy of the outlay, must be selected and this can only be done from the results of a preliminary survey to identify such a wreck and assess its merits.

Any diving group, which will take the trouble to learn some elementary underwater archaeological surveying can do this; a number of books (see Bibliography, Appendix 4), have been written on this subject. Here it is proposed to outline the essentials required for such a preliminary survey to ensure that the maximum of information is economically obtained.

A wreck site can usually be recognized from a fairly closely grouped series of objects; but the importance of the position of an isolated find must not be minimized. A pot or anchor may indicate the position of a roadstead, a fishing ground or a route along the coast. So this apparently insignificant find may well be an extremely important archaeological clue.

Therefore, before touching any object, be it on a wreck site, or an isolated find, its position should be noted and a thorough search of the neighbourhood be made for other finds; and it may well be that more than one visit to an area will be required before other objects turn up.

Having identified a wreck, or other underwater site, the first requirement is to mark its position so that it can be found again. Good note should be taken of the neighbouring underwater features and a search made to get an idea of the extent of the site. The position of these features on the sea-bed must then be fixed on the chart of the coast by sextant or compass bearing, from small buoys set up on significant features of the site. Where shore features are sufficiently close, a new method of fixing the site can be done by means of photographs (Frost. *Mellieha Bay*. See Appendix 4). Thus, the finding of the site again is ensured.

Next, notes should be made on the environment of that piece of sea-bed: orientation with regard to the coast, depth, type of bottom, weed, slope, currents, prevailing winds, exposure, water temperatures, visibility, etc. Relative features of the coast, cliffs, sand, habitations, ancient and modern, means of access. Remember that as the information will be used by non-diving archaeologists, and others who may not visit the site, care should be taken in making the descriptions very clear.

Photographs of the site are the next requirement. As these will be used by archaeologists and historians, who are not familiar with the sea-bed, pictures should be oriented so as to include, if possible, some recognizable feature on the plan, on which the position from which it is taken should be marked. Further, a scale or rod, graduated in centimetres or decimetres, should be included to give proportion to the viewer. A knife or fin is not very scientific and any diver who wishes to take archaeological photos should provide himself with a rod, as described in *Surveying in Archaeology Underwater*. (Appendix 4.) If an arrowhead is added at one end, it is useful for future identification to lay it on the sea-bed pointing north in the vicinity of the object. Such photographs, taken in the form of a mosaic, can be of great help in preparing the plan.

The Plan. Having assessed the site, appropriate methods for making the plan should be selected and the work organized; all the principal features and objects should be tagged with a suitable numbering system for reference on the plan. The size of the plan, which should bear both a metric and feet scale, will to some extent be governed by the size of the site; but, as it may well be required for subsequent publication in comparison with other plans, it should be drawn to a known scale, i.e. 1:100, 1:50, 1:20, etc, which can be easily reduced. Add also the north point. As the lettering on a plan will also be reduced on reproduction, the size of the letters should be sufficiently large, but thick lines should be avoided as these tend to blur and be hard to read.

A profile or vertical section along the main axis of the site will show the slope, rock peaks etc, and give an impression of how the wreck or objects are disposed on an irregular sea-bed. Some areas may contain a large number of small objects and it will be necessary to draw this part of the plan at a larger scale. The area may be defined by a rectangle on the larger plan and the details of the area drawn on a separate sheet at 1:10, 1:20, etc. The grid frame can be used for this purpose.

Having completed the plan and taken the photographs, the tagged and numbered objects should be carefully checked and their numbers transferred to the plan. Certain large objects like guns, anchors etc, will be measured and drawn on the sea-bed individually. The essentials for this record are quite easily done with a little practice and patience on the sea-bed; and render the raising of such objects unnecessary, particularly if further work is intended on the site when the pattern of objects might be spoiled.

The requirements for the identification of guns are set out in Fig. 17.

In addition to the names of parts given on the diagram, A–D is Cascabel; A–E, Breech; E–F, First Reinforce; F–C, Second Reinforce; C–G, Chase. The following information should be given: Length A–B . . . . .; Bore diam . . . . .; Bronze . . . . .; Iron . . . . .; Dolphins present? . . . .; Breeching-loop present? . . . .; Markings on breech, reinforce or trunnions . . . . .; Founder's name . . . . .

It should be noted that the gun shown is composite, but covers all the essential particulars which should be recorded. 'Dolphins' —i.e. lifting loops, will be rarely found on iron guns, while breech-loops will rarely appear on bronze guns. Bronze guns frequently bear the founder's name on the base-ring, and sometimes on the first reinforce. Iron guns rarely bear a founder's name, though initials may occur, often at the ends of the trunnions. The weight of the piece is often incised on the cascabel, or on a trunnion end. With this information it is possible to identify the type of gun, which can give a useful clue to date of a wreck. (See Appendix 2.)

Iron anchors should also be measured on the sea-bed and drawn to a known scale, say 1:10. A simple plan is required, with, if visible, a side view of the flukes and ring. Sections through different parts should be added where they are not circular.

Stone anchors and fishing weights should be recorded as on the finds sheet which follows and drawn to a known scale as in Fig. 18. Roman lead anchor stocks should be treated in the same way, showing top and side view.

Major objects should not be raised without due consideration; to raise anchors does not add to our knowledge if they have been measured and drawn on the sea-bed, and the same applies to guns. If, subsequently, it is found that an object is of particular interest, then due provision can be made in advance for its conservation. Iron and wood are the most vulnerable of materials from underwater and both are difficult and costly to conserve, needing laboratory conditions. A useful note on the difficulties of conserving iron from the sea is to be found in *CNA Newsletter No. 4, 1970*. Wood must be sent to museums or laboratories having suitable tanks, and these are usually too fully occupied with existing material to deal with casual finds.

ANCHORS
SPECIMEN FINDS-SHEET

Finder's name:

Description of Site:

Sightings   Chart or map reference
Depth in metres   Approx. distance from shore
Offshore shallows? Harbour?
Type of bottom (sand, rock etc)
On or near a wreck?
Was the anchor alone? or have the surroundings been searched for others?

Description of Anchor:
Stone or metal?
If metal, what kind? and what state of preservation?
If stone, what stone (take sample chip)?
If lime or sandstone, describe colour (when stone is dry)
Also, identifiable components (cemented shells, flint etc)

Weight in kg

Inscriptions

Dressing and tool marks:
Hammer-dressed? chisel or gouge (give gauge)?

Piercings:
How many?
By bow-drill? or drill mounted with stone bit? or chisel-cut?
If so, tubular or squared?

Reports of anchors should be sent to: Miss Honor Frost,
                                          c/o The Institute of
                                             Archaeology,
                                          31 Gordon Square,
                                          LONDON W.C.1.

If one or two objects must be raised, this should be done in consultation with the CNA representative for the area, or with the local museum curator, and the most important items for dating or other identification selected. Divers are reminded that they are under obligation to declare finds to the Receiver of Wreck; this is now an advantage, for, through the good relations of the CNA with the Board of Trade, it is possible for a declared object to be relinquished by the Receiver to a responsible person for conservation and study.

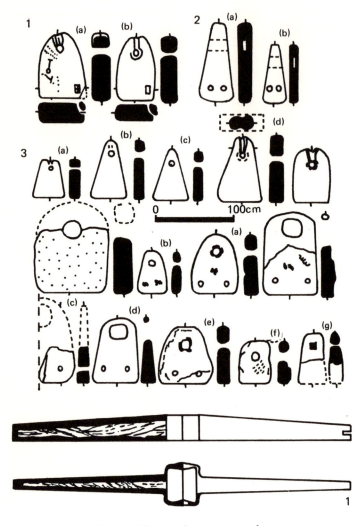

FIG. 18. How to draw your anchor

it is important that all can be reduced to a similar size. Objects grouped on one sheet should all be to the same scale, so that no measurements need be written on the drawing. Examples of methods of drawing objects are to be found in C. Brodribb, *Drawing Archaeological Finds for Publication* (Baker, 1970).

Photographs. Similarly these should be taken in profile, or from above, and should contain a black-and-white scale of centimetres and inches. A ruler, or a piece of measuring tape, is not acceptable, as the divisions are often illegible in the photos. It is very easy to make a scale with a piece of card, drawing the scale in black ink, and to inclue it in every photo.

The background for objects should be white. A sheet hung well behind the object will obviate much shadow. With small objects taken from above, difficult heavy shadows may be avoided by placing them on a sheet of glass covered with tracing paper and supported by the edges on two chairs, or crates. In photos taken from above the shadows will almost be eliminated, but if they are still too strong, the sheet may be lighted from below with a hand lamp or torch.

To recap briefly on the requirements for recording underwater discoveries. Having chosen a site:

(*a*) Explore the area thoroughly and fix its position in relation to the coast.

(*b*) Describe the environment and add any local information about the site which is obtainable.

(*c*) Take photographs of the site.

Finally, it is necessary to write a report to put on record the results of the investigation, so that archaeologists may evaluate the site for future study.

First, the objects raised must be recorded according to archaeological conventions, preparatory to submitting them for identification. A glance at a report on a land site will give an idea how this is done.

The main points to consider are:

Description. State the type of object and give some indication of its shape, condition, missing parts etc, name the material of which it is made; visible details regarding manufacture, finish and decoration; size, two greatest dimensions in cm.

Drawing. Objects should be drawn full size, in profile with section cut away to show thickness of material (see Fig. 19). Very small objects may be drawn 2:1; while very large ones like amphorae are conventionally drawn at 1:5, so that they can be reduced to a uniform scale of 1:10. Most objects like pottery are published at a ½ or ⅓, and for the sake of comparison

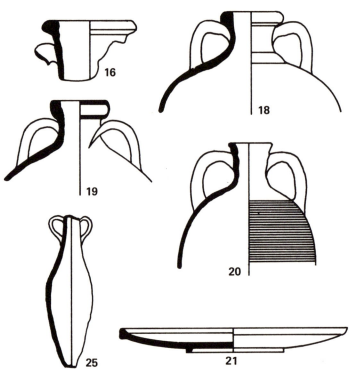

FIG. 19. How to draw the objects you find under the sea

178

(*d*) Make the survey plan.

(*e*) Note the principal objects and record them on the sea-bed.

(*f*) Before raising any object, consult with the CNA representative or the local museum, and inform the Receiver of Wreck.

(*g*) Consider what conservation the objects may need and prepare in advance.

(*h*) Record the objects for reference and further identification.

(*i*) Prepare a report for CNA on above lines.

(*j*) In consultation with the CNA, begin research to identify the wreck or object.

The CNA will be glad to receive such reports, to help with research and publish suitable items in the *International Journal of Nautical Archaeology and Underwater Exploration.*

Wrecks Around the Coasts of Britain

including a sensible wreck list of the ships you can hope to find if you dive for them, but not including any stupid treasure stories of ships which don't exist!

100	ROMAN barge in the Thames. Site located (see Chapter 1).
851	DRAKKAR (the Serpent). Viking ship lost in Thames.
1439	GRACE DIEU, warship built by Henry V in 1418. Accidentally burnt in 1439. Timbers still to be seen in river Hamble (see Chapter 2).
1509	The ships of a fleet taking Joan of Castile back to Spain were caught in a storm in the Channel, and though Joan of Castile landed safely at Weymouth, two ships were lost off the mouth of the Erme. Alan Bax has been searching for these wrecks.
20 July 1545	MARY ROSE, lost in full view of King Henry VIII. Located by Alexander McKee (see Chapter 2).
18 August 1588	EL GRAN GRIFON. Wrecked on Fair Isle, Shetlands. Some salvage done in 1970 (see Chapter 3).
16 September 1588	LA TRINIDAD VALENCERA foundered at anchor. Site discovered by City of Derry divers (see Chapter 4).
16 October 1588	GIRONA, Spanish Armada casualty. Wrecked Giants Causeway. Almost totally salved by Robert Stenuit (see Chapter 4).
21 October 1588	SANTA MARIA DE LA ROSA. Wrecked in Blasket Sound. Located by Sydney Wignall (see Chapter 3).
1 November 1588	SAN PEDRO EL MAYOR. Spanish Armada Hospital Ship, wrecked in Hope Cove, Devon (see Chapter 4).
1590	SANTA CATARINA, galleon lost near Colliestow, Aberdeenshire. Searches have been made without success.
1656	PRIMROSE, 22-gun vessel. Wrecked at Seven Stones.
1664	KENNERMERLANDT, Dutch East Indiaman sunk in Shetlands (see Chapter 7).
25 March 1675	MARY, 8-gun Royal Yacht, wrecked off the Skerries (see Chapter 4).
11 January 1679	SANTA CRUZ, lost galleon off Pembroke, Wales. Said to be a treasure ship. Local searches made without success.
1 September 1691	CORONATION. Caught in storm while trying to enter Plymouth Harbour. Great loss of life. Located by Plymouth divers (see Chapter 5).
1 September 1691	HARWICH, 70 guns (see Chapter 5).
7 January 1701	MICHAEL, Merchantman, wrecked off the Casquetts, Alderney.
26 November 1703	STIRLING CASTLE, 70 guns. MARY, 70 guns. NORTHUMBERLAND, 70 guns, all three lost on the Goodwins. VANGUARD, 70 guns, sunk at Chatham. YORK, 70 guns, lost near Harwich; all lost but four men. RESOLUTION, 60 guns, coast of Sussex. NEWCASTLE, 60 guns, at Spithead, 193 drowned. RESERVE, 60 guns, at Yarmouth, 173 perished. (Great storm caused loss of all above. See Chapter 6.)
30 October 1706	NASSAU, third rate, 80 guns. Wrecked off the Kent coast.
22 October 1707	ASSOCIATION, 70 guns, wrecked with other vessels below off the Scilly Isles. Scene of Britain's first real underwater treasure discovery. Located by Navy divers (see Chapter 6). EAGLE, 70 guns. ROMNEY, 50 guns. FIREBRAND, fireship. Hundreds of men died in minutes (see Chapter 6).
15 October 1711	EDGAR, 70 guns, blew up at Spithead, all on board dead (see Chapter 2).
1711	DE LIEFDE, East Indiaman, sunk Shetlands (see Chapter 7).

7 December 1721	HIND, 20-gun, wrecked off the Channel Isles.
21 September 1744	COLCHESTER, 50 guns, wrecked on Kentish Knock, 50 men lost.
5 October 1744	VICTORY, 100 guns, near the Isle of Alderney; all drowned.
26 January 1749	AMSTERDAM, Dutch East Indiaman near Hastings (see Chapter 7).
24 April 1753	ASSURANCE on the Isle of Wight. Site located and dived (see Chapter 7).
14 February 1760	RAMILLIES, 90 guns, second-rate. 26 ratings only survived her storm wrecking on Bolt Tail, Devon. Property now of Mike Borrow and David Langfield. Debris on bottom — cannon, cannonballs etc — is theirs. Divers have been warned!
15 February 1760	CONQUEROR, lost on St Nicholas's Island, Plymouth.
3 November 1760	ANN, Frigate, wrecked off Caernarvon Bay, Wales.
	PEARL, Merchantman, wrecked Caernarvon Bay.
1772	CHANTILOUPE, vessel returning from West Indies wrecked close to Bantham. All lost except one man. On board was a woman, who put on her richest gems and clothes, hoping that if she was washed on shore her appearance would help. Locals, however, waiting for loot, seized her, stripped her of clothes and gems. Even cut off fingers for rings, mangled her ears for earrings, and left her to die. Proved at inquiry that she was alive when she reached shore and was deliberately murdered.
1774	DRIAD, Schooner, wrecked near Raven Rock, Bantham, in the great storm of 1774.
2 March 1782	BRITANNIA, Storeship, 20 gun. Wrecked Kentish Knock.
29 August 1782	ROYAL GEORGE, about 900 drowned (see Chapter 2).
1785	I. A. JUNO, merchantman disappeared until found recently by Steve Burrows in the Scillies.
6 January 1786	HALSEWELL, East Indiaman wrecked Seacombe, Isle of Purbeck. Sometimes known as the 'ship in the Cave', as some people escaped into cave when ship sank. 182 died. Bob Campbell has dived in search of her. Found very few traces.
18 December 1795	CATHARINE, trading vessel wrecked near Fleet, Weymouth.
	PIEDMONT, Merchantman wrecked near Fleet, Weymouth.
	THOMAS, Merchantman, wrecked near Fleet.
	VENUS, Merchantman wrecked near Fleet.
4 May 1795	BOYNE, by fire at Spithead. Man-of-war of 98 guns, destroyed by fire at Portsmouth by the explosion of the magazine; 14 killed. Portions were recovered in June 1838 when she was blown up as a danger to navigation. Alexander McKee discovered shingle mound covering wreck in May 1965.
29 December 1795	AMETHYST, 38 guns, wrecked near Alderney, C.I.'s.
26 January 1796	DUTTON, East Indiaman, wrecked Plymouth Hoe, Devon.
15 July 1796	TROMPEUSE, Brig sloop, 16 guns, wrecked Kinsale Head, S. Ireland.
1798	L'AMITIÉ or AMITÉ, French ship intended to aid Irish rebellion in Londonderry, wrecked near Belfast. The site known as 'Cannon's Hole' was investigated by Robert and Maureen Trouton of Belfast Branch of BSAC, who found eight cast-iron cannon there. One raised identified as a demi-culverin.
10 December 1798	H.M.S. COLOSSUS wrecked on Scillies with precious cargo of antiques. Roland Morris searching for her.
9–10 October 1799	H.M.S. LUTINE, 32 guns, was wrecked off Vlieland, coast of Holland; only one saved, who died before reaching England. The Lutine was a former French ship captained by Admiral Duncan. She contained much bullion and money, belonging to merchants; a great loss to the underwriters at Lloyds.
10 February 1799	H.M.S. WEAZLE, being lost with all hands on Baggy Point, N. Devon, Ilfracombe divers have located her cannon.
19 October 1799	H.M.S. IMPREGNABLE, Captain Jonathan Faulknor, struck near entrance to Langstone Harbour after convoy duty from Lisbon. Salved. Cannon found by Southsea diver John Eberhard. More by Alex McKee and Maurice Harknett.
2 November 1799	GUERNSEY LILY, lost at entrance to Solent in Yarmouth Roads. Described as an ordance transport; all saved.
16 November 1799	ESPION, 36 guns, wrecked off Goodwin Sands.
14 January 1800	QUEEN, transport, on Trefusis Point; 369 dead (see Chapter 8).
16 March 1801	INVINCIBLE, 74 guns, wrecked Harborough Sands, Yarmouth. Captain J. Rennie and crew drowned, 126 saved.
10 January 1803	ACTIVE, 350-ton West Indiaman from Greenock. Carried £67,000 in gold. Sunk in storm at Margate. Most of gold salvaged.

12 January 1803	HINDOSTAN, East Indiaman, off Westgate, Kent. Silver bullion on board in 13 chests. 11 recovered.
16 November 1803	CIRCE, frigate, 32 guns, off Yarmouth.
13 October 1804	FIREBRAND, fireship, wrecked nr. Dover.
24 November 1804	VENERABLE, 74 guns, at Torbay; lost 8 men.
6 February 1805	EARL OF ABERGAVENNY, East Indiaman foundered Weymouth. Has been provisionally located by Ron Parry (see Chapter 9).
20 October 1806	ATHENIENNE, 64 guns, wrecked off Scillies.
17 November 1807	GLASGOW, mail packet vessel. Wrecked Farne Islands.
28 November 1807	BOREAS, 28 guns, wrecked on Hanois Rocks, Guernsey (see Chapter 9).
29 December 1807	H.M.S. ANSON, 44 guns, wrecked on Loe Bar, near Pothleven; many lives lost. Located. Some cannon raised recently.
21 January 1809	DISPATCH, transport carrying men and horses of the 7th Dragoons from Corunna, on Lowland Point, The Manacles, Cornwall. 7 men survived.
	PRIMROSE, brig on Manacles, one boy saved out of 126 on board.
14 October 1811	POMONE, 38 guns, wrecked off Needles, I.O.W.
14 January 1814	QUEEN, transport, on Trefusis Point, Falmouth, over 350 dead (see Chapter 9).
17 December 1814	BRITISH QUEEN, packet, wrecked on the Goodwin Sands, and all on board lost.
21 January 1817	TELEGRAPH, Schooner, 14 guns, wrecked Mount Batten, Plymouth.
23 October 1817	WILLIAM AND MARY, packet, struck on the Willeys rocks, near the Holmes lighthouse, Bristol Channel, nearly 60 persons perished.
8 August 1821	EARL OF MOIRA, on the Burbo Bank, near Liverpool; 40 drowned.
26 December 1821	JULIANA, East Indiaman, on the Kentish Knock; 40 drowned.
3 February 1822	THAMES, Indiaman, off Beachy Head.
14 December 1822	RACEHORSE, Brig Sloop, 18 guns, wrecked off Isle of Man. Located.
17 August 1831	ROTHSAY CASTLE, wooden steamer, wrecked in Dutchmans Bank, Menai Strait.
15 October 1833	UNITED KINGDOM, West Indiaman, with rich cargo; run down by the QUEEN OF SCOTLAND steamer off Northfleet, near Gravesend.
6 September 1838	FORFARSHIRE, steamer, on its passage from Hull to Dundee, was wrecked in a violent gale, and 38 persons out of 53 were drowned. Lighthouse-keeper, James Darling, and his heroic daughter Grace, ventured out in a tremendous sea in a coble, and rescued several of the passengers (see Chapter 8).
4 January 1841	THAMES, steamer, Captain Gray, from Dublin to Liverpool, wrecked off St. Ives, Captain and 55 persons lost.
30 March 1850	ROYAL ADELAIDE, steamer, wrecked on the Tongue Sands, off Margate, 400 lost.
24 December 1852	LILY, stranded and blown up by gunpowder on the Calf-of-Man, 30 lost.
29 September 1853	ANNIE JANE, of Liverpool, and emigrant vessel driven on shore on the Barra Islands, on the west coast of Scotland; about 348 lives lost.
19 October 1853	DALHOUSIE, foundered off Beachy Head; the Captain (Butterworth) the passengers, and all the crew (excepting one), about 60 persons in all, drowned.
30 November 1853	MARSHALL, steamer, foundered off mouth of Humber.
1 December 1854	NILE, screw-steamer, struck on the Godevry Rock, St Ives Bay; and all drowned.
3 May 1855	JOHN, immigrant ship bound for Quebec, on the Manacle, Cornwall. 196 men, women and children drowned.
2 June 1857	NORTHERN BELLE, a large American vessel, was wrecked near Broadstairs. The American Government sent 21 silver medals and £270 to be distributed among the heroic boatmen of the place, who saved the crew.
25–26 October 1859	ROYAL CHARTER, screw-steamer, Captain Taylor, totally wrecked off Moelfre, on the Anglesey coast; 446 lives lost. The vessel contained gold amounting in value to between £700,00 and £800,00; much of this has been recovered. Some diving has taken place without much success.
19 February 1860	ONDINE, steamer; lost through collision with the HERIONE of Bideford, abreast of Beachy Head; the captain and about 50 lost.
28 February 1860	NIMROD, steamer, wrecked on rocks near St David's Head; 40 lives lost.
April 1862	MARS, Waterford steamer, struck on a rock near Milford Haven, about 50 lost.
20 December 1862	LIFEGUARD, steamer, left Newcastle, with about 41 passengers, never since heard of, supposed to have foundered off Flamborough Head.
14 January 1865	LELIA, steamer; foundered near Great Orme Head, Mersey.
23 March 1866	SPIRIT OF THE OCEAN, steamer; wrecked on Start Point, all lost except 4.

10 July 1866 — AMAZON, screw sloop, and screw steamer OSPREY, sunk by collision near Plymouth. Several passengers and sailors drowned.

19 August 1866 — BRUISER, steamer, sunk by collision with the HASWELL, off Aldbrough, about 15 lives lost.

5 January 1867 — JAMES CROSFIELD, iron ship; wrecked off Langness, Isle of Man; all on board lost.

25 March 1867 — JONKHEER MEESTER VAN DE WALL PUTTERSHOCK, East Indiaman, wrecked Poldhu Cove, Cornwall.

23 May 1868 — GARRONE on Buck Rocks, near Lamorna Cove. Many lost. Dennis James has located some wreckage.

28 January 1869 — PADARN, brigantine, wrecked Mothercombe, Devon.

1 February 1869 — AMALIE, brig; wrecked Chesil Cove, Portland Bill.

13 February 1869 — JANE AND MARGARET, sloop, foundered Ramsey Bay, Isle of Man.

28 August 1869 — ANNE LONGTON, full-rigged ship, foundered Goodwin Sands.

12 September 1869 — ONEIDI, brigantine; wrecked 300 yards west of Langley Point, Sussex.

13 September 1869 — CARAVAN, barque; wrecked Walton Bay, Somerset.

13 February 1870 — SEA QUEEN, steamer; wrecked North Scroby Sand, Norfolk.

7 March 1870 — NORMANDY, steamer, by collision with the steamer MARY off the Isle of Wight; the captain and 33 others lost.

27 October 1870 — GENEVA, full-rigged ship; wrecked Stones Reef, Cornwall.

31 January 1872 — MANITOBAH, barque; wrecked Buck Rocks, Cornwall.

26 November 1872 — DALMATION, steamer; wrecked Hells Mouth, Cardigan Bay.

17 November 1872 — MADRE, brig, wrecked Sow-and-Pigs Rocks, Blyth.

1 March 1873 — BOYNE, barque; wrecked off Mohilo Bay, Cornwall; about 20 lost.

March 1873 — LALLA ROOKH, from Shanghai, bound London. Wrecked March 1873 on Prawle Point. Cargo 1300 tons of tea and 60 tons tobacco. All crew except Chief Mate saved by rocket apparatus. Tea washed in and left in ten-foot-high wall at high-tide mark.

21 October 1874 — CHUSAN, trading vessel; wrecked Crinan Rocks, Ardrossan, W. Scotland.

1 September 1875 — VANGUARD, battleship; collision off Wicklow.

6 December 1875 — DEUTSCHLAND, Atlantic steamer, from Bremen to New York, went on sandbank, the Kentish Knock, at the mouth of the Thames during a gale; about 70 lost (many emigrants).

17 February 1875 — STRATHCLYDE, Glasgow steamer, sunk by collision with the Hamburg ship FRANCONIA, in Dover Bay in daylight; about 17 lost. (Verdict of manslaughter against Kuhn, captain of Franconia, quashed on appeal; 7 judges against 6 decided against British jurisdiction, 13 November 1876.)

5 January 1877 — OSCAR, steamer; wrecked Whitby Rocks, Yorks.

18 August 1877 — COMMODORE, brigantine, wrecked Encombe Ledges, Kimmeridge.

14 September 1877 — IRISHMAN, steamer; wrecked Burial Is., Ballyhalbert, Co. Down.

19 September 1877 — BLACKWATCH, full-rigged ship; wrecked West Point, Fair Isle.

15 October 1877 — PAULINE, schooner, wrecked Rickham Pt., Devon.

31 October 1877 — PAULINE, brigantine, wrecked Rickham Cove, Devon.

10 November 1877 — ANGER H. CURTIS, brigantine; wrecked W. side Walney Lighthouse, Irish Sea.

28 December 1877 — FAIRY QUEEN, steamer; wrecked North Carr Rocks, Fifeness.

4 January 1878 — BALMORAL, steamer; wrecked on rocks 1 mile NW of Hartlepool, Heugh Light, Durham.

23 January 1878 — PIONEER, steamer; wrecked Puffin Islands, Menai Strait.

26 January 1878 — MYRTLE, steamer; wrecked Ballycastle, Co. Antrim.

22 February 1878 — MOLDAVIA, steamer; wrecked Nash Rock, Glamorgan.

3 September 1878 — PRINCESS ALICE, by collision with the screw steamer BYWELL CASTLE in the Thames near Woolwich; between 600 and 700 lost.

25 November 1878 — POMERANIA, Hamburg-American mail steamer sunk off Folkestone by Moel Elian, iron barque, of Caernarvon a little after midnight, 162 saved by boats; about 48 missing.

11 January 1879 — LOCH SUNART; full-rigged ship, wrecked Skull-martin Reef, Ballywalter Bay, Co. Down.

13 January 1879 — SCHIEHALLION, iron barque, wrecked ¾ mile E. of Blackgang Chine, I.O.W.

DON QUIXOTE, brigantine, wrecked N. Arran, Galway Bay.

27 January 1879 — EDITH OWEN, steamer, wrecked Coal Rock, Anglesey.

26 June 1879 — GLEANEN, brig; stranded Gunfleet Sands, Thames.

13 August 1879	CITY OF LONDON, Aberdeen steamer; run down and sunk by the VESTA, in the Thames.	2 April 1885	QUEEN VICTORIA, barque; wrecked Swallow Bank, New Romney.
17 July 1880	HYDASPES, sailing-ship, sank in collision with CENTURION, screw steamer, off Dungeness in a fog, both blamed; no lives lost.	15 October 1885	NORDSTJERNEN, brig; wrecked the Binks, Spurn Point, Yorks.
		1 November 1885	ELEANOR DODSON, barque; wrecked near Orford Haven, CG Station, Suffolk.
16 January 1881	EDITH MORGAN, schooner; wrecked Black Rocks, Sound of Islay.	25 November 1885	AURORA, steamer; wrecked off Hartlepool, Durham.
18 January 1881	SAINTE ANN, schooner wrecked Penarth Head, Bristol Channel.	1 March 1886	MISSOURI, screw barque; lost off Anglesey, found by divers 1963.
27 January 1881	CLAREMONT, steamer, wrecked Atherfield, Isle of Wight.	15 May 1886	PALA, steamer; wrecked Kimmeridge Ledge, I.O.W.
	RUPERRA, steamer; wrecked near Bolt Head, Devon.	30 August 1886	BELFORT, steamer; wrecked Selle Rock, Guernsey, C.I.
4 February 1881	BREMEN, full-rigged ship; Levenwick, Shetland Isles (see Chapter 10).	15 October 1886	MALLENY, Liverpool iron steamer; foundered on the Tuskar reef, Bristol Channel, all 20 hands lost in the gale.
19 February 1881	CALEDONIA, steamer; wrecked Oyster Rock, Jersey, C.I.		TEVIOTDALE, steamer; of Glasgow, lost on the Carmarthen coast; 18 lives lost.
6 March 1881	ESSEN, steamer; wrecked ½ mile west of St Catherine's Light, I.O.W.		BEN-Y-GLOE, iron ship; stranded near Nash Pt., Glamorganshire.
29 April 1882	ALEXANDROVNA, Liverpool ship, wrecked off Swanage; all crew lost.	25 November 1886	STRATHPEFFER, steamer; stranded near Workington, Cumberland.
16 October 1882	CONSTANTIA and CITY OF ANTWERP, steamers; sunk by collision off the Eddystone, about 14 lost.	10 December 1886	BALNACRAIG, steamer; foundered off North Foreland, Kent.
26 November 1882	CAMBRONNE, steamer; sunk by collision with MARION, near Lundy.	2 September 1887	AVENIR, brig; wrecked Maplin Sand, Essex.
27 January 1883	JAMES GRAY, steamer; wrecked Tuskar Rock, near Porthcawl.	27 October 1887	FLYING HAWK, steam tug, wrecked Maiden Rocks, Dalkey Is., Co. Dublin.
7 February 1883	SILKSWORTH, steamer; wrecked river Weir entrance.	30 October 1887	ST LUKAS, brigantine, wrecked Portlet Bay, Guernsey, C.I.
30 March 1883	NORMAN COURT lost off Anglesey (see Chapter 10).	1 November 1887	MAYO, steamer; wrecked St Albans Head, Dorset.
24 April, 1883	BRITISH COMMERCE, sunk by collison with COUNTY OF ABERDEEN off Selsey Bill; 25 lost.	2 December 1887	CAPRI, steamer; wrecked Kentish Knock, Essex.
9 May 1883	STRATHENERICK, steamer; wrecked off Linney Head, Pembrokeshire.	8 March 1888	LANOMA, iron barque, wrecked near Weymouth; 12 lives lost.
10 May 1883	MERCURY, steamer; wrecked Blackpool, Lancashire.	9 March 1888	CITY OF CORINTH, sunk by collision with TASMANIA, near Dungeness.
7 June 1883	LIVELY, steamer; wooden. Wrecked Chicken Rocks, Stornoway Harbour.	7 October 1889	ST GEORGE, full-rigged ship, wrecked near Peel, I.O.M.
21 July 1883	PRISCILLA, barquentine; wrecked Redcar Rocks, Yorkshire.		HEROS, barque; wrecked Hare Island, Co. Galway.
1 September 1883	CHRISTIANE, barque wrecked Chesil Cove, Portland.	5 November 1889	GOTEBORG, wooden steamer; wrecked Salt Scar Rocks, Redcar.
2 January 1884	BENTUTHER, barque; wrecked Grassholm Is., Pembrokeshire.	29 December 1889	CLEDDY, steamer; sunk after collision with ISLE OF CYPRUS steamer, off St Catherine's. About 13 lives lost.
12 January 1884	HILDA, schooner, wrecked 5 miles south of Bridlington, Yorkshire.	17 January 1890	ARBUTUS, steamer; wrecked Goldstone Rock, Holy Is., Durham.
2–3 August 1884	DIONE, steamer; sunk by collision with CAMDEN, steamer, near Gravesend; about 17 persons drowned (captain of the DIONE punished for reckless navigation).	19 January 1890	PENTHESILEA, iron full-rigged ship; wrecked Baggy Point, Devon.
		25 January 1890	IREX, full-rigged ship; wrecked Scratchells Bay, Isle of Wight.

	THORNE, iron barque; wrecked Douglas Bay, Isle of Man.
19 February 1890	HIGHGATE, steamer, and SOVEREIGN, ship, both sunk by collision off Lundy Island; 12 lost.
21 April 1890	BRANKELOW, steamer, wrecked Loe Bar, Porthleven, Cornwall.
16 June 1890	HERMINE, lost Anglesey; very broken up, says Bill Butland who has dived on her.
23 November 1890	UPPINGHAM, Cardiff steamer, bound for China, struck on a Rock below Hartland Quay, Cornwall; about 7 drowned.
18 December 1890	OREGON, 800-ton barque, lost near Thurlestone. Located by Kingston Branch divers (see Chapter 10).
1891	MARANA in snowstorm struck the Blackstone Rocks off Start Lighthouse. Went to pieces in minutes. Some 30 crew took to boats, but only 4 reached shore; they were Swedes. Located by George Tessyman. Very broken up.
	DRYAD, barque, possibly Blackstone Rocks, a few hours after MARANA.
26 October 1891	CHARLWOOD, barque, sunk by collision with the BOSTON, near the Eddystone lighthouse; 15 lost.
11 November 1891	BENVENUE, full-rigged ship, bound for Sydney and wrecked off Sandgate; 27 persons suspended in the rigging for 16 hours; were saved with great difficulty by the Sandgate lifeboat and taken to Folkestone; Captain James Moddrel and 4 men drowned.
1 July 1892	CITY OF CHICAGO, Inman Atlantic liner, run ashore near Old Head of Kinsale, during a fog; passengers landed 1 July; totally wrecked 7 July. Ship broke in two. Divers have located badly broken up wreckage.
21 February 1892	FRATELLI F., barque; lost near Lands End. Found by divers recently.
24 February 1892	FOREST QUEEN, steamer; sunk by collision with the LOUGHBOROUGH, steamer, near Flamborough Head; about 14 lives lost
14 August 1892	THRACIA, barque, capsized near Port Erin, Isle of Man, 17 lives lost.
18 November 1893	HAMPSHIRE, steamer, of London, owners Messrs MacBeth and Grey of Glasgow (Captain Weir and 22 men) sunk off St Ives, Cornwall, all lost except Mr James Swanson, Chief Officer.
1894	THEODORA, brigantine from Hamburg, ashore on Thurlestone Sands during gale in February 1894. Cargo of cotton seed

	and dye woods. Captain and 2 hands lost. Mate and lads saved.
15 April 1896	ELBE, North German Lloyd steamer, from Bremen to New York, sunk in collision with the CRATHIE of Aberdeen, off Lowestoft, about 6 a.m. 334 lives lost, including Captain von Gössel.
16 June 1897	SUSANNAH KELLY, steamer, sunk in a gale in Belfast Lough; captain and 9 men lost.
	FOUDROYANT, H.M.S., 80 guns, wrecked Nr. Blackpool.
1 February 1898	CHANNEL QUEEN, steamer; from Plymouth, wrecked on the Black Rock off Guernsey; 12 passengers and some of the crew drowned.
14 October 1898	MOHEGAN, Atlantic Transport Company steamer, wrecked on the Manacles, off Cornwall by error of navigation; Captain R. Griffiths and 106 drowned (see Chapter 10).
11 February 1899	ARNO, steam collier, wrecked near Selsey Bill, 13 deaths.
30 March 1899	STELLA, excursion steamer from Southampton to Guernsey (S.W.R.), wrecked at 4 p.m. while going at full speed in a fog on the Black Rock near the Casquets, 8 miles off Alderney. Out of the 140 passengers and the 40 members of the crew, 105 persons were drowned, including Captain Reeks. Great heroism was shown, and there was no panic; the ship sank in eight minutes.
16 September 1900	GORDON CASTLE, Glasgow steamer, and the Hamburg steamer STORMAN sunk by collision during a fog in Cardigan Bay; Captain Casey and 19 others from the GORDON CASTLE lost.
28 December 1900	PRIMROSE HILL. Iron Barque; lost near Holyhead. Dived by Bill Butland. Very broken up.
14–15 January 1903	MANCHESTER MERCHANT, steamer; with 7000 bales of cotton on fire, scuttled in Dingle Bay, Kerry.
18 March 1904	Submarine A.1 off Spithead; 11 lost.
18 August 1904	H.M.S. destroyer ZEPHYR, rammed in Portsmouth Harbour.
23 January 1905	A.7 submarine; foundered Whitesand Bay, Cornwall.
4 April 1905	Destroyer SPITEFUL, in collision off Yarmouth (I.O.W.); 2 drowned.
8 June 1905	Submarine A.8 off Plymouth; 15 drowned.
16 October 1905	Submarine A.4 sunk in Portsmouth Harbour after explosion.
1906	BLESK, Russian oil-tanker, came on shore in a cove a little above the Greystone in thick fog. As she broke up oil floated up to Kingsbridge, South Devon. Many lobster, crab and fish killed.

185

18 March 1907 — DJEBBA, 4000-ton West Africa mail-boat, ran aground Bolt Tail. Boilers and plates still remain.

2 October 1907 — ALFRED ERLANDSEN, of Copenhagen. St Abbs. No survivors despite search by Eyemouth lifeboat. Located by Edinburgh Branch of the BSAC.

7 November 1910 — PREUSSEN, at Dover, the largest steel sailing-ship—five-masted—of her time. 4768 tons, she was in collision with the cross-Channel steamer BRIGHTON. Preussen badly damaged, finally sank despite salvage attempts in Crab (or Fan) Bay. Has been visited by many BSAC branches, including a Bromley Branch team under Malcolm Todd and Reg Dunton. Very broken up.

13 November 1911 — ANGELE, brigantine; wrecked Doom Bar, Padstow, Cornwall.

HANSEY; full-rigged ship, wrecked Housel Bay, Lizard.

11 February 1912 — PINDOS, barque, wrecked near Coverack, S. Cornwall.

28 December 1912 — CECIL RHODES, spritsail barge; foundered ½ mile off Margate.

1 January 1915 — H.M.S. FORMIDABLE, battleship torpedoed by U-24. Has been found by Silas Oates salvage team. Is a war grave.

7 May 1915 — LUSITANIA, Cunard liner; torpedoed by U-20. Has been dived by John Light.

28 October 1915 — ARGYLL, H.M. Cruiser; wrecked Bell Rock, Arbroath. Has been located and dived by Scottish divers.

27 March 1916 — EMPRESS OF MIDLAND, steamer; mined North Foreland, Kent.

11 July 1916 — KARA, steamer; mined Gorton, Norfolk.

23 January 1917 — LAURENTIC, 14,892 tons, sank 3 miles north-west of Dunaff Head, N.I. after hitting a mine. 100 ft to wreck, which shows only 20 feet above seabed now. Was carrying £6 million in gold. Almost all recovered now in epic salvage operation. Boilers there, proud in the middle of what diver Leo Zanelli describes as a scrapyard.

23 March 1917 — s.s. MAINE, torpedoed, sank Bolt Head, Devon; all saved. Heavily dived. Property of Torbay Branch BSAC (see Chapter 11).

2 October 1917 — H.M.S. DRAKE, cruiser of 14,100 tons. Abandoned safely after torpedoing off Rathlin Island, Northern Ireland. Capsized and sank. Belfast Branch BSAC have dived on her frequently. Drake rises from sea-bed at 50 feet to within few feet of surface.

4 December 1917 — RIVERSDALE, 2085 tons. Upright in 150 feet of water. Is the property of Torbay Branch, BSAC, who dive her often.

24 May 1917 — GRELTORIA, steamer; torpedoed; Flamborough Head.

30 December 1917 — EL TORO, Admiralty Oiler, wrecked Blasket Is., S. Ireland.

25 January 1918 — FOLMINA, steamer; torpedoed, near Sunderland.

25 March 1918 — HERCULES, steamer; torpedoed Filey Bay.

18 August 1918 — CLAN MACVEY, armed British merchant ship, 3710 tons. Torpedoed off Poole, Dorset. Cargo coal. 45 feet, very broken up.

26 May 1918 — KYARRA, hospital ship; torpedoed off Durleston Head (see Chapter 11).

24 July 1918 — PINCHER, destroyer; wrecked Seven Stones reef.

28 July 1918 — JOHN RETTIG, steamer; torpedoed Bridlington Bay, Yorks.

10 August 1918 — BRETAGNE, steamer; sunk after collision with French ship (see Chapter 11).

17 August 1918 — EROS, steamer; torpedoed near Filey.

8 October 1923 — CITY OF WESTMINSTER, steamer; wrecked Runnelstone, Cornwall.

12 November 1925 — M.1 H.M. Submarine, lost off Start Point (see Chapter 12).

19 September 1931 — LYMINGE, steamer; wrecked Gunnards Head, N. Cornwall.

26 January 1932 — M.2, H.M. submarine, off Portland (see Chapter 12).

25 March 1936 — HERZOGIN CECILIE, famous grain-race four-masted clipper, struck Hamstone, finally sank in Salcombe Estuary. Much dived; very broken up.

13 April 1937 — ISLAND, 2000-ton steamer ran aground off the Isle of May in the Firth of Forth. Bought for Perth Branch of the BSAC by diving officer Phil Rodgers. 163 passengers and 39 crew saved, but ship later slipped off rocks and sank in 60 feet of water. Had been royal yacht of King Christian X of Denmark.

17 September 1939 — H.M.S. COURAGEOUS, aircraft carrier; torpedoed.

14 October 1939 — H.M.S. ROYAL OAK, battleship; torpedoed. Has been dived.

13 November 1939 — BLANCHE, steamer, mined and sunk, Thames Estuary.

8 December 1939 — LOUIS SHIED, 5945-ton Belgian cargo vessel ran aground 100 yards from Links Hotel, Thurlestone, S. Devon. Very broken up, but still a dive for beginners.

3 May 1940 — KYLE FIRTH went ashore, Anglesey. Located by Bill Butland.

1 November 1940 — PLACIDAS FARROULT, gate vessel to Salcombe Estuary boom. Hit Blackstone Rocks in gale. Much dived. On even keel. Still ship-shaped.

1 December 1940 EMPIRE POLITICIAN, sank after going aground in the Sound of Eriskay, South Uist, Scotland. This ship was the inspiration for Sir Compton Mackenzie's novel and the film *Whisky Galore*. Lieutenant George Wookey, the record helmet diver, was one of a team who relocated her. The whisky was just drinkable, even if it had a tendency to turn green after opening!

25 March 1941 SOMALI, cargo ship; set on fire by German bomber near Seahouses (see Chapter 13).

23 June 1942 LENY, Dutch motor vessel of 343 tons sunk by mine off Poole, Dorset. Very broken up and scattered 45 feet deep.

17 March 1942 ADEPT, H.M. Tug, wrecked Hebrides, W. Scotland.

31 March 1943 CAULONIA, Admiralty trawler; foundered Rye Bay, Sussex.

6 April 1943 GOLDEN GIFT, Admiralty trawler, collision, Oban Bay, W. Scotland (see Appendix 1).

1 February 1945 PERSIER, torpedoed; near Eddystone (see Chapter 14).

21 March 1945 JAMES EAGAN LAYNE, 7000-ton Liberty ship. Torpedoed and sank in Whitesand Bay, Devon. Mast shows above water, and keel is at 75 feet on sandy bottom. Much dived, but is now dangerous owing to salvage work. Cargo: trucks, tractors and agricultural machinery.

20 March 1944 P.715, submarine; wrecked west side of Islay.

18 June 1944 ALBERT C. FIELD, steamer; aerial torpedo, St Catherine's Point.

19 September 1945 MINERVE, submarine; wrecked Portland Bill.

3 November 1962 JEANNE GOUGY, trawler; wrecked Lands End, Cornwall.

17 November 1962 GREEN RANGER, Admiralty tanker; wrecked Hartland Point, Devon.

24 October 1963 JUAN FERRER, motor vessel, Carn Boscawen, near Lands End.

2 January 1969 CETA, motor vessel sunk by tanker off Rye. Found by Malcolm Inch and Bromley branch divers.

26 April 1970 GLEN STRATHALLEN, 330 tons, steam yacht, scuttled outside Plymouth Sound to carry out dying wish of her former owner. 50 feet deep, she is used as a training wreck for the School of Nautical Archaeology and also for study of marine growth. So don't touch!

18 March 1967 TORREY CANYON, supertanker struck the Seven Stones Reef. Later bombed to stop oil pollution (see Chapter 13).

WARNING: **in 1944 the** *Richard Montgomery,* **a United States Liberty ship, sank in the Thames Estuary after running aground less than 4000 yards off Sheerness. She was carrying some 3000 tons of high explosives and bombs. These explosives are still dangerous, and experts say that the damage she could do if disturbed in any way is colossal.**

DO NOT ATTEMPT TO DIVE ON HER.

Index